NEW ZEALAND'S LONDON

NEW ZEALAND'S LONDON

A Colony and its Metropolis

FELICITY BARNES

AUCKLAND
UNIVERSITY
PRESS

First published 2012

Auckland University Press
University of Auckland
Private Bag 92019
Auckland 1142
New Zealand
www.press.auckland.ac.nz

© Felicity Barnes, 2012

ISBN 978 1 86940 585 4

Publication is kindly assisted by creative nz

National Library of New Zealand Cataloguing-in-Publication Data
Barnes, Felicity.
New Zealand's London : a colony and its metropolis /
Felicity Barnes.
Includes bibliographical references and index.
ISBN 978-1-86940-585-4
1. New Zealand—Civilization—British influences.
2. New Zealand—Relations—England—London—History.
I. Title.
306.0993—dc 23

This book is copyright. Apart from fair dealing for the purpose of private study, research, criticism or review, as permitted under the Copyright Act, no part may be reproduced by any process without prior permission of the publisher.

Cover design: Carolyn Lewis

Printed in China by Everbest Printing Co. Ltd

CONTENTS

Acknowledgements *vi*

Introduction 1

One New Zealand's London 14

Two At Home in London 41

Three A 'New' New Zealand 70

Four London Literate:
New Zealand Writers in London 96

Five London's Farm 123

Six 'Produced by Britons for British Homes' 154

Seven London's Imaginative Hinterland:
Mass Media and Identity 189

Eight Home Movies: London on Film 221

Nine London's Legacy:
New Zealand on Television, 1960–1989 247

Epilogue London Revisited 273

Notes 279

Select Bibliography 310

Index 327

ACKNOWLEDGEMENTS

It is a great pleasure to begin this book by thanking those who made it possible. There are plenty of them – proof that while writing might be a solitary pastime, creating a book never is. *New Zealand's London* first came to life as a doctoral thesis in the History Department at the University of Auckland, so my first thanks are to the staff there who guided and encouraged the project, then and now, in various ways: Barry Reay, Caroline Daley, Deborah Montgomerie and Malcolm Campbell. James Belich deserves special thanks for supervising the thesis and for his continued interest and input as it evolved into a book. I am also grateful for the support provided by a University of Auckland Doctoral Scholarship, and the Eric and Myra McCormick Scholarship in History. Research overseas was made possible by the University of Auckland Research Grants Committee and by the History Department's use of PRBF funding to support graduate research.

Research in general was made easier through the expert assistance of staff at the Alexander Turnbull Library, Archives New Zealand, the Auckland Museum Library, the British Film Institute, the British Library, the National Archives (UK), the New Zealand Film Archive, the Sir George Grey Special Collections at Auckland City Libraries and Special Collections at the University of Auckland. The university's history librarian, Philip Abela, happily provided early research assistance, and sorted out some of my more unusual lending requests. My thanks to the interloan staff who chased down obscure collections and persuaded other libraries to make them available. I must also thank Anne Elder and the Feist family for making personal papers available, and Des Monaghan and John McCready for sharing their histories of television in New Zealand. Tom Finlayson and Marcia Russell were also invaluable, not only as sources of information, but also as generous listeners, readers of drafts and kind critics. Lydia Wevers and others at the Stout Research Centre for New Zealand Studies, Roger Blackley, Leah and Nick Lambert, Vaughan Bradley and Kay Lyes, and an array of friends and family also supported the project in different ways and I am grateful for their help.

Some of the material in this book has appeared in other forms. Material in Chapter One began as ' "Familiar London": New Zealand Travel Writing and the Imagined Metropolis, 1890–1940', *Studies in Travel Writing*, Vol. 14, No. 4, 2010 and appears here with the permission of Taylor and Francis Ltd. Parts of Chapter Seven and the epilogue were developed in 'War Zones: The Metropolis and New Zealand, 1940 and 2005', *History Compass*, Vol. 1, Issue 3, 2005, and are reproduced here courtesy of John Wiley and Sons Inc.

The images in this book really require their own special set of acknowledgements. A number of archivists and librarians went to great trouble to find and then allow reproduction of the images in this book. I would like to thank Paul Johnston, at the National Archives (UK), for tracking down the Empire Marketing material, then turning those vast posters into images we could squeeze into a book; Shaun Higgins at the Auckland Museum Library, for sifting through the *Auckland Star* negatives to find previously unpublished images of Howard Morrison and other stars of television's opening night, and Anna Cable for making these and a number of other images available; staff at Archives New Zealand, the National Library of New Zealand and the University of Canterbury; Owen Manning and Shara Hudson at the New Zealand Film Archive for allowing me to fossick through their files; Lissa Mitchell at Te Papa for giving me access to the wonderful photo albums of Harry Moult; Jo Birks at Special Collections, University of Auckland; Alison Clarke at the Hocken Library; and especially the staff of Sir George Grey Special Collections, Auckland City Libraries. Elspeth Orwin, Keith Giles and others made complicated image requests easy. I also need to thank Lesley Mensah at Television New Zealand, James Branthwaite at Fairfax Media Group, APN Ltd, Fonterra Brands NZ Ltd and Dover Publishing for giving their permission for some of these pictures to be reproduced. I am glad they could be, because these pictures are more than just illustrations. Travellers' photographs, newspaper images, marketing posters and picture postcards construct and convey the relationship between New Zealand and London. They are part of the story.

That story was finally brought together with the expert (and patient) guidance of the team at Auckland University Press – Sam Elworthy, Anna Hodge, Katrina Duncan, Poppy Haynes and their reviewer – and skilfully edited by Ginny Sullivan. I am very grateful to all of them. Of course, I owe my greatest thanks to my family: Michael, Hope and Piper Whitehead. But this book is dedicated to Paul and Judy Barnes: in their own ways, I think they might have enjoyed it.

INTRODUCTION

IN 1840, THE SAME YEAR that New Zealand was formally incorporated into the British Empire, a mysterious New Zealander appeared in London's metaphorical landscape. In a review of a history of Catholicism, Thomas Macaulay invoked the image of 'some traveller from New Zealand' (in 1840, this meant a Maori traveller) who, at some undetermined time in the future, might 'in the midst of a vast solitude, take his stand upon a broken arch of London Bridge to sketch the ruins of St Paul's'.¹ Unwittingly, he spawned a small industry. The New Zealander on the bridge took on a life of its own as literary cliché, with a variety of uses: as a prophet of future doom, as a reminder of London's dystopian aspects, as a symbol of the inevitable decline of empire and as a disquieting premonition of who might really inherit the earth.² Whenever the metropole needed a symbol of the primitive periphery to contrast with its own civilised state, the New Zealander could be set upon the bridge. In 1872, Gustave Doré turned the by then well-worn words into an iconic illustration for the publication *London: A Pilgrimage*, and thus granted it a further lease of life. By this time 'the New Zealander on the bridge' had already made it to the top of *Punch* magazine's list of 'used up, exhausted, threadbare, stale and hackneyed' expressions. This was no small achievement given the competition, which included 'the bull that is always being taken by the horns... the British Lion... the Black Sheep... the Dodo... the Thin End of the Wedge'.³

The fictive New Zealander on London Bridge was one more expression worn through in the process of creating the metropole as civilised centre. Colonial peripheries and their peoples commonly served as

The New Zealander by Gustave Doré. Gustave Doré and Blanchard Jerrold, *London: A Pilgrimage*, reprinted New York, 1970, n.p.

1

symbols of humankind's primitive past. Indeed, they could be trapped within that past: London, and the civilisation it symbolised, might rise and fall, but the New Zealander viewing the ruins remained a marker of the past. New Zealand, part of the colonial periphery, was summoned up as London's 'other', just as 'one might cite Timbuktu or Furthest Tartary or the Back of Beyond'.[4] When he reached across 12,000 miles[5] to antipodean time and space to forge his metaphor, Macaulay created and reflected the cultural meanings of both places, fixing them in space and time: London as the present centre, and New Zealand as distant place and time. Over the next twenty-five years, the constant presence of the traveller on the bridge led *Punch* to plead that 'the retirement of this veteran is indispensable. He can no longer be suffered to impede the traffic over London Bridge. Much wanted at the present time in his own country. May return when London is in ruins.'[6]

And there, fixed as a phantom form of otherness, the New Zealander might have stayed. Yet by the turn of the century, a strange shift in this convention was occurring. New Zealanders could still be found on London Bridge, but they were not symbols of 'otherness' anymore. Instead, they took physical, not phantom, form as 'Britons' 'at home' in their imperial metropolis. Furthermore, they had left New Zealand, former symbol par excellence of a distant time, so that they might discover their heritage by returning to London and England. 'New Zealand' took on a new shape in the metropolis. It was no longer part of the past: old, colonial New Zealand, with its Maori, myths and pioneering migrants, was metamorphosing into a dominion, a new and modern member of empire. Space was changing too: London, 'home city of empire', became a joint New Zealand possession and, by way of exchange, New Zealand considered itself to be a farming hinterland of the metropolis, and a distant colony no longer.

London, then the biggest city in the world, had become New Zealand's cultural capital. But this was no cringing colonialism. It was cultural co-ownership. The 'Britons on the bridge' claimed London's streets as their streets, and its history as their heritage too. New Zealand's literature was published there, and its news was collected in Fleet Street. New Zealand's butter, meat and cheese filled the windows of London chain stores, and New Zealand's school children were quizzed on the best routes to send these products there. Visitors from New Zealand did not beg for invitations to royal garden parties; they went to New Zealand House to demand them. They used London as if it really were part of New Zealand. In some respects they still do. London is no longer the biggest city in the world, but it remains home to an estimated 100,000 New Zealanders, making it second only to Australia as the choice for expatriates.[7] Many of them are there on that particular antipodean rite of passage, the long working holiday known as the Big OE (overseas experience). This has become so much a feature of New Zealand's culture that whenever Britain attempts to tighten its migration laws, New Zealanders feel they have a special right to object. In February 2008, for example, when the British government proposed changes to an ancestry visa permitting some New Zealanders special access to Britain, New Zealand's Prime Minister claimed the government 'would make a very strong submission in response. Many New Zealanders greatly value their connection with the UK especially those whose grandparents were born there.'[8] Much is made of New Zealanders' ancestral links with England. But you do not need to have a British grandparent to want to live and work in London. In 2008, less than two thousand ancestry visas were issued. Five times that number of New Zealanders enter annually on working-holiday visas.[9] Even in the twenty-first century, New Zealanders can still use London as if it were an extension of New Zealand.

This long attachment to London has become a familiar part of New Zealand culture, so natural that it has never been examined. If asked to explain it, we might see the relationship as an outcome of New Zealand's settler past, as a quaintly sentimental colonial habit or as a faintly embarrassing echo of empire. However, as reasonable as these explanations appear, none of them is entirely accurate. The cultural relationship between London and New Zealand was, of course, a product of the colonial past. But as the statistics for visas suggest, ties of kinship only partially explain London's attractiveness to New Zealanders. Having a direct connection with London was less important than imagining such a connection, and, from around the end of the nineteenth century, that was easy to do. From that time, new communication technologies began working to draw the former colony and metropolis closer together. In books and in newspapers, in films and eventually on television, London was a constant presence. When children got out their Monopoly sets, they fought over who owned London's Park Lane and Mayfair, not Atlantic City's Park Place and the Boardwalk. Imagined as a familiar New Zealand city, London came to be used that way. Visitors toured London's iconic geography, finding their heritage in its monumental architecture. New Zealand writers 'haunted' Fleet Street, arriving broke but expecting to use London as a natural extension of their working world. Soldiers on leave during two world wars went broke there, spending their pay in a city that was their 'home away from home'. Histories have missed it, but for the best part of a century, New Zealand's most important city was 12,000 miles away. It was New Zealand's London, and it shaped our culture. This book is about that relationship. London's role was much more significant than our histories have allowed. By overlooking it, we have misunderstood a key part of our past.

LOCATING LONDON

London may have been a constant presence in New Zealand's cultural life, but it has had only a marginal presence in our histories. Like other white settler societies, New Zealand has a strong vein of nationalist historiography. The formative era of New Zealand history writing, ushered in by Keith Sinclair and W. H. Oliver, inaugurated a continuing interest in examining and identifying New Zealand's distinctive nationalism. These histories emphasised the steady, if gradual, emergence of an independent New Zealand identity – even if they did not agree on when exactly it emerged – rather than the continuing effect of England's metropolis on New Zealand's culture. Indeed, those effects were considered obstacles to the development of an authentic, local identity, and lingering ties with Home were treated as vaguely embarrassing examples of cultural immaturity. Sinclair described colonial New Zealand as having grown up 'in an English dream', one that had 'profound – and pathetic – consequences'.[10] Newer cultural nationalist histories perpetuate the idea that metropolitan relationships were impediments to cultural progress, their 'pathetic consequences' often taking the form of 'colonial', or 'cultural', cringe.[11] Such perspectives had a contemporary parallel in metropolitan imperial studies, where British historians, too, 'could see little that was lasting and less that was positive in the history of the British Empire'.[12] Here the nationalist focus of the former white dominions dovetailed neatly with the development of a 'highly introverted view of the British past' after World War II.[13] Early nationhood suited an unravelling interest in empire's broad effects, and New Zealand historian J. G. A. Pocock's lone 'plea for a new subject' that would reintegrate these nationally bound histories seemed to go unheard.[14]

Recently, though, historians in New Zealand, Canada and Australia have begun to reassess the nature and extent of their imperial relationship. New studies have described more complex and subtle processes of disengagement.[15] The 'Britishness' they have recovered can now be considered a component of these dominion identities rather than a competitor to them. However, whilst the persistence of Britishness has been convincingly demonstrated through a wide variety of research, it still tends to be explained as a legacy of settlement. This is, in one sense, quite reasonable: migrants to Australia, Canada and New Zealand in particular were overwhelmingly of 'British' stock, even if the mix of Scots, English, Welsh and Irish might have differed. In the case of New Zealand's links with London, it is significant that the 'London hinterland counties of Surrey, Essex, and Kent' were important sources of migrants.[16] However, studies in Britain itself suggest the importance of culture, not simply demography, in forming Britishness and Englishness. Numerous works consider these descriptors of identity as contingent cultural constructions, not curious cultural relics.[17]

Despite growing interest in the roles of Britain and its former colonies in the construction of 'British' identities, New Zealand historians have only slowly begun to revisit this aspect of our past. In a postcolonial version of that older, nationalist reluctance, the re-examination of Britishness in the New Zealand context is considered 'awkward', 'uncomfortable' and even 'irrelevant' on the basis that 'reveal[ing] a British past is assumed to reassert it in the present'.[18] However, the opposite effect is more likely. For example, reluctance to revisit empire for fear of reinscribing it has perpetuated the idea that ties Home are 'natural' legacies of settler origins. But Britishness was invented as much as it was inherited, constructed by settlers at the same time as they themselves were embodiments of it. This matters because, as Peter Gibbons has argued, colonisation is not simply the process of land appropriation but a cultural process as well. The construction of 'Britishness' in New Zealand was a colonising act.[19] It is most easy to identify this conjunction in the ways New Zealand was created as a settler colony during the nineteenth century. In this period, Britishness was constantly invoked and reiterated – New Zealand was a 'Greater Britain', 'Britain under the Southern Cross', 'The Britain of the South' – so that a former frontier colony was recast as suitable, and suitably familiar, home for settlers. But, as this book argues, the construction of New Zealand as 'British', in different form, continued well into the twentieth century, with London at the heart of that process. In New Zealand, Britishness was not simply a 'natural' consequence of settler demography, Home was not just a nostalgic habit and London as cultural capital was more than a symbol of colonial immaturity. They were instead elements of a complex cultural relationship that played a crucial role in recreating old colonial New Zealand as a modern, first-world member of empire.

If London's cultural role has been neglected in New Zealand's histories, then new histories of empire have returned the favour. Increasingly, if not unanimously, British historians have come to see the imperial experience as an integral part of domestic life. As historians such as John MacKenzie have argued, empire is intricately woven into metropolitan culture both high and low, found in cups of tea and in popular fiction, in music halls as well as in museums, in the definition of masculinity and in the development of women's suffrage.[20] As a result, imperialism has become deeply implicated in the cultural construction of 'Britishness'. Yet in this metropolitan context, empire and it effects have been limited to the dependent empire, to colonies such as India or those in the Caribbean.[21] By contrast, the impact of the white settler colonies, once empire's most committed adherents, remains relatively unexplored.[22] Although Macaulay could remark upon a New Zealander on London Bridge in 1840, when New Zealand itself was barely a colony, the later arrival of New Zealand's 'Britons on the bridge' has hardly raised a metropolitan eyebrow. But the impact of the other colonies suggests it should. Newer research like Antoinette Burton's study of Indians in the heart of London has shown how those particular 'colonials' negotiated Englishness and their place within empire.[23] Their presence did more than simply breach the old barriers separating the imperial centre from its colonies. As they toured London's streets, travelling Indians demonstrated that 'London could be possessed by its colonial subjects'.[24] This new possession was part of redefining what metropolis and colony were. White colonials at the heart of empire also participated in the definition process, using the metropolis to construct Britishness and secure their place in empire's hierarchy. Yet there is a critical difference. Imperial power over subject colonies was predicated on the construction of fundamental differences between the civilised centre and those colonies. The spectacle of Indian subjects laying claim to Britishness upset this imperial order. But when visitors from white settler colonies such as New Zealand followed the same tourist trails, they were not merely returning Home, but helping reinforce London's identity as that home. As appropriate inheritors of the civilised centre, their enthusiastic acquisition of the metropolis helped strengthen rather than destabilise the hierarchy of empire.

Home was neither a natural legacy of colonial settlement, destined to decay, nor an imperial category imposed upon a colony. Instead, the appearance of Britons on London Bridge symbolised a productive interdependence between colony and metropolis. The timing of this relationship suggests that development of national identities is rather more complicated than a steady, gradual trajectory, and that what passes as cultural relic might be instead an active construction. The nature of the relationship suggests London's role was different in New Zealand than in the dependent empire, and that in London, New Zealand gave 'colony' a different set of meanings. But for all that, New Zealand's relationship with London is only partly explained by empire. In fact, empire may well obscure the workings of a quite different relationship.

COLONIES AND HINTERLANDS

Around the end of the nineteenth century, the heart of empire also became the heart of a new economic system. From this time, New Zealand's struggling colonial economy, based largely on extractive industries and imported money and migrants, began to be replaced by a pastoral economy, which specialised in sending large quantities of just a few products – meat, butter and cheese, along with an older staple, wool – to London. There, in the reciprocal fashion that marks this relationship, these products helped create an expanding market. London's population had almost tripled in the years between 1850 and 1900, from 2.3 million to 6.6 million.[25] Its size was compounded by a growing demand for foods previously confined to the upper classes.[26] One solution to the unmet urban demand for butter, for example, was a competition for substitutes at the Paris Exhibition of 1866.[27] (The winner, margarine, was to become farming New Zealand's *bête noire*.) But the most common response was to import rather than invent food. London's rapid growth had exhausted the potential of its own hinterlands, and it turned, over the century, to Ireland, Europe and America for grain, meat and dairy products.

It was another creative invention, refrigeration, that enabled New Zealand's entry into this expanding market place. In 1882, the first successful shipment of frozen New Zealand sheep meat arrived in Britain, significant enough to be heralded in a *Times* editorial as a 'prodigious' fact.[28] Dairy exports followed and, by 1933, New Zealand supplied 'roughly half of Britain's imports of lamb, mutton, cheese and butter combined'.[29] This economic shift was the impetus for a broader social, political and cultural transformation. New Zealand's emphasis on pastoral exports to Britain concentrated and tightened the links between the two countries, creating a different relationship between the formerly distant periphery and its metropolis. James Belich has termed this phenomenon 'recolonisation': 'in some respects, New Zealand and the relevant bits of Britain made up a single entity. Essentially, New Zealand became a town supply district of London. London became the cultural capital of New Zealand.'[30]

Rethinking New Zealand's relationship with London as one between a city and its hinterland gives us a new vantage point from which to view London's role in New Zealand's culture. Empire remains important, but it was not the only factor in the creation of London as a 'natural' part of New Zealand's culture. Recolonisation worked between a city and its hinterland: it did not require an imperial relationship to do so. For New Zealand, London performed the same function as New York and Chicago did for the American west. As William Cronon has noted, 'the central story of the nineteenth-century West is that of an expanding metropolitan economy creating ever more elaborate and intimate linkages between city and country'. The prairies may have been in Chicago's thrall, but the city's role was as metropolis, not as centre of empire. Similarly, beneath the trappings of New Zealand's imperial relationship with London lay a more prosaic one. New Zealand acted as farming hinterland of London, and cities can exert a powerful cultural influence on their hinterlands.[31]

Chicago and its hinterland are, of course, contiguous. New Zealand and London, on the other hand, are separated by 12,000 miles of ocean. However, a hinterland relationship was made possible by a suite of new technologies that developed during the latter part of the nineteenth century and changed the nature of distance. Some of these technologies were incredibly effective as agents of economic transformation: by 1924, the cost of shipping butter to London from its New Zealand hinterland was 'only marginally greater than shipping it by rail from Wisconsin to New York'.[32] They were also effective agents of cultural change. Benedict Anderson argues that modern communication, in his case the power of the press, gave rise to those 'imagined communities' called nations.[33] The role of modernity in nation-making lies at the heart of Keith Sinclair's work *A Destiny Apart*, conceived as an exploration of New Zealand's progress towards a national identity. He reveals that 'there was, in the late nineteenth and early twentieth centuries, a perceptible strengthening and extension of both the foundations and the structure of nationalism. This was largely a result of the creation of networks of communications which had been lacking in the earlier, provincial period of the country's history.'[34] These were impressive networks indeed: 2000 telephones by 1904; 1700 post offices by 1900, handling 70 million post articles; 3.5 million telegraphs; and 250,000 telephone toll calls. Rail connected Auckland and Wellington in 1908.[35]

Although these new technologies are usually implicated in the construction of nations, they were also very effective at connecting cities with their virtual hinterlands. The compression of space and time, so often noted as a feature of the late Victorian age, meant that the same processes that were enabling New Zealanders to think of themselves as a unified nation were also connecting them more closely with their old home.[36] And these technologies were not limited to faster steamships, more railways or frozen sheep. As later chapters will show, the innovations underwriting economic change were joined by another set of powerful cultural channels that specialised in distorting space and time – film, radio, sound recording, cabled news – and these, too, would intensify the old connections with London.

Colonial peripheries are often conceived of as the cultural antithesis of the modern, civilising centre, existing simultaneously with that centre, although separated by time and space. They are the home of Macaulay's New Zealander on the bridge. Hinterlands are different: they are by their very nature part of the city system, functionally different yet contiguous in time and, usually, space. New Zealand at the turn of the twentieth century no longer needed to see itself as separated from the centre by time and space, nor did it want to be defined by colonial characteristics. Instead, it used London to pull off a complex manoeuvre in self-imaging. New Zealand had become technologically and socially modern, without becoming 'industrialised'. Nor was it urban: despite the rapid rise in urban dwellers from the close of the nineteenth century, the country preferred to imagine itself as rural. But New Zealand did not entirely lack metropolitan sophistication or culture as a result. Like any other hinterland, New Zealand accessed these through its metropolis. For New Zealand, real urban life was located in London.

However, London's cultural impact upon New Zealand is not simply an old story of colonial domination in a city/hinterland guise. Instead, it was a complex and at times reciprocal relationship, although it was not necessarily equal: London was always more important to New Zealand than the other way around. But New Zealand's impact on London is part of the story, and this has implications for metropolitan history. Some of the cultural roles assigned to London and England, and considered part of British history, were also partly created by white settler colonials reconstructing Home. The myths of rural England are a product of immigration as well as of industrialisation and urbanisation. Visitors returning Home also created London as the centre of 'British' history and heritage. Its role as high cultural centre was also something of a colonial collaboration. Most obvious, yet least visible of all, London's sheer size was supported by imports of familiar commodities. Yet studies of London's role as the heart of empire have yet to take this into account. The massive trade in, and dependence on, meat, butter, cheese, apples and wheat is routinely eclipsed by the (paradoxically) more familiar renderings of empire as home of exotica such as spices.[37] The economic, social and cultural impacts of exotic colonial foods on British life are the subject of a growing literature,[38] but Australian wheat, Canadian cheese and New Zealand lamb and butter, also shaped metropolitan culture, again by reinforcing constructions of Britishness. Cheap and plentiful imported meat, butter, wheat and cheese were familiar 'British' food, and cheap and plentiful supplies from the white settler colonies made greater consumption of this 'British' food possible.

A GUIDE TO NEW ZEALAND'S LONDON

Like New Zealanders in London, this book roams widely. There is no cohesive archive, no definitive guide to London's cultural influence. Instead, I have selected a variety of locales where the relationship becomes visible. In some cases, these are literary, although textual analysis here is a means to an end rather than an end in itself. Further, I define literature very broadly, as literary sources can sometimes be unreliable guides to general public opinion. So published travel writing about Home, potentially an elite and unrepresentative source, has been leavened with the unpublished letters and diaries of 'Bill Massey's tourists' in London, more familiar as the soldiers of World War I. Similarly, butter sculptures, short films for schools and meat posters share space and significance with more conventional items from the New Zealand cultural canon. The less privileged cultural sources have attracted less study or left fewer traces. For example, New Zealand's commodity marketing and advertising have rich sources, but no critical literature, whereas short films have some historical context, but little evidence remains of viewing practices. Most of the material considered here is new, which reflects my choices amongst these locales, and the fact that the relationship with London generally has provoked little study.

The subject matter is organised in two ways. First, the material follows a rough chronology, from beginnings of the hinterland phenomenon, around the end of the nineteenth century, to its eventual dismantling in the last quarter of the twentieth. Emphasis is greatest on the period from 1890 to 1940, when the phenomenon was most powerful. Second, although the book as a whole considers London's role in transforming New Zealand from a distant colony to modern, neighbouring hinterland, each chapter focuses on just one aspect of that change: space or time. The book opens with the imaginative expansion of New Zealand's borders to incorporate London. New Zealanders felt 'at home' in London in part because they believed they were co-owners of it. The second chapter considers the physical appropriation of the metropolis. These opening chapters differentiate between the imaginative creation and expression of London and the rather more concrete co-option of London space as New Zealand place. New Zealand House, as the New Zealand High Commission in London is called, is one example of this, while the experiences of World War I soldiers on leave in the 'Big Smoke' are another.

Having co-opted metropolitan space, New Zealand also co-opted metropolitan time. Colonies usually existed in what Anne McClintock has described as 'peripheral time', living examples of the past that had, unlike the metropolis, failed to progress.[39] New Zealand used the metropolis to invert this image. London's history and heritage on the one hand, and modernity on the other, were appropriated to create a 'new' New Zealand. Chapters Three and Four sketch out New Zealand's movement away from colonial time and space using the experiences of travellers and expatriate writers and some of the literature they produced.

The remaining chapters consider factors instrumental in drawing New Zealand more tightly to London. Distant time and space give way to propinquity and simultaneity. 'London's Farm' (Chapter Five) and 'Produced by Britons for British Homes' (Chapter Six) explore the ways New Zealand's changed economic relationship with London helped redefine its cultural identity. Propinquity, in both its senses of proximity and kinship, came to characterise this version of New Zealand. The advent of an export market built on refrigerated pastoral products led New Zealand to reconfigure itself in relation to the metropolis as a modern, white, British, farming hinterland. To sell its produce at Home, New Zealand used the latest forms of commodity displays to make itself Homelike. Chapter Five follows this transformation through New Zealand's appearances at international exhibitions, locations usually interrogated for signs of emergent national identity. Chapter Six examines the phenomenon using primary – produce advertising, possibly New Zealand's largest modern marketing campaign until the rise of tourism marketing in the 1970s, and one that has been entirely overlooked.

New Zealand's farming image was as much metropolitan fantasy as hinterland reality, another strand in a complex web of cultural interdependence. 'London's farm', the rural hinterland, complemented the development of an 'imaginative hinterland', created by the new mass media emanating from the metropolis. This imaginative hinterland is the last of London's New Zealand landscapes explored here, and reflects the further distorting effects of time and space. The new forms of media specialised in creating a heightened sense of reality, in part because they emphasised simultaneity. Colonial forms of media, often aged by travelling long distances, were joined from the 1880s by new media like radio, cable, news and film, which acted like drawstrings to bring New Zealand into line with metropolitan time. They are often implicated in the retreat of the metropolitan relationship, but the combination of realism and immediacy they provided may also have kept this relationship in place for much longer than we have thought. This idea is explored in Chapter Seven, through the contribution of the press in sustaining links with the metropolis. Chapter

Eight uses an unlikely medium – film – that is commonly associated with the transmission of American culture, and analyses the role of short films in particular in sustaining images of London on the periphery. But eventually, the new media were also part of the dissolution of New Zealand's London. Chapter Nine considers the effects of television, the most powerful of all of the new media, on the gradual and equivocal disassembling of this long cultural relationship.

All of New Zealand's London landscapes examined here reconceptualise the impact of time and space in the colonial setting. The familiar 'tyranny of distance' was imaginatively overcome as New Zealanders reconstituted themselves as metropolitan, not colonial: time was reorganised to diminish the old colonial version of the past, and metropolitan space was appropriated too. This appropriation was both an imaginative and physical act. London existed imaginatively as part of New Zealand's cultural landscape, at the same time that it was city market and cultural capital. The new and powerful packages of cultural transfer might have come from anywhere, yet the system and its virtually exclusive trade network with Britain, centred on London, led to a disproportionate British influence. This was not unchallenged or monolithic – as we will see, America was to become the world leader in the new media, and New Zealand also sought to position itself within the broader 'family' of empire – but British influence was dominant. Neither Sydney, nor New York, despite their cultural power, could ever be Home. However, New Zealand's relationship with London was as much a city system as an imperial one, and, as a result, the 'sentimental' yearning for Home, with its sense of nostalgic 'return', had firm roots in the modern present. Through its reconfigured links with London, New Zealand changed, from old colony to up-to-date metropolitan hinterland. In 1840, it was home to the New Zealander on the bridge; by 1940, it had become a place to which he could never return.

CHAPTER ONE

NEW ZEALAND'S
LONDON

A whirl from Liverpool Street. 'We're in the City', declares a guide. 'This is Threadneedle Street. That's St Paul's.' Through Ludgate Circus and on up Fleet Street. What a ride! Ten minutes of marvels that the brain could not assimilate. Lunch at the 'Cheshire Cheese'. This really was London .... From a railway station in New Zealand to the 'Cheshire Cheese' was the distance I had come to see this country so often dreamed about.[1]

IN BREATHLESS PROSE, New Zealand journalist and sometime poet Ian Donnelly described the climax of his 'joyous pilgrimage' to England. At the Cheshire Cheese, in the heart of the imperial metropolis, he had found his Mecca, and in pilgrimage fashion, a journey of 12,000 miles was rewarded by the merest glimpses on a ten-minute ride through the heart of London. Eating lunch in the same room as Dr Samuel Johnson, surrounded by the iconic monuments of the metropolis, Donnelly had reached 'the focal point for numberless dreams and anticipations borne across the seas'.[2] His version of London, vividly imagined on the periphery, was mapped over the actual metropolis: he was now 'really' in London.

In the outwardly banal, worn and repetitive language of tourists like Donnelly lies a complex piece of cultural geography. His first impressions seem to trace a route through the actual geography of the metropolis – 'through Ludgate Circus and on up Fleet Street' – suggesting a journey through a literal landscape. In fact, through its selections and omissions, his account records an imagined, not actual place. It describes London as it existed in New Zealand. Donnelly expressed it as 'really' London, but it is better described as New Zealand's London. New Zealand's London is composed of specific geographic places – buildings, monuments, streets – and specifically located performances – parades, people, activities – that had coalesced in what might be termed the peripheral imagination as representative of 'London'. This imagined geography was loaded with symbolism, not for its own sake, but as important constituent elements of New Zealand's culture at this time. One of its functions was to minimise the idea of New Zealand as colonial periphery anyway. New Zealand's London may have been imagined on the edge of empire, but it functioned to pull New Zealand closer to its centre. More than that, its imaginative presence allowed New Zealanders to possess the metropolis too. This was not simply a sense that buildings belonged to them, but that the values these places came to embody were also shared by New Zealanders. In London, New Zealanders could become Londoners, members of the metropolis, and partners in empire as they incorporated London within their cultural landscape.

New Zealand's London was formed in two ways: first, by the imaginative construction of London in New Zealand, and second, by actual appropriation of London space. New Zealand's imagined London was created and sustained by constant repetition and reinvention through cultural channels, channels that became considerably more powerful from the last part of the nineteenth century, with the development of telegraph, sound recording, film and the expansion of the press. Together, they helped keep London familiar to New Zealanders, a familiarity that helped excise the 12,000 miles that lay between New Zealand and Home. In return, New Zealand extended its borders into London itself, and the 'familiar London' of the New Zealand imagination could be traced onto the city. This process took physical form: through maps and guides, on the wharves and in the markets, in New Zealand House on the Strand and through the iconic monuments of the city, New Zealand made itself at home in the heart of empire, colonising and appropriating metropolitan space.

We can follow this process through the experiences of some of those Britons on London Bridge. Their stories, whether published or unpublished, have fallen out of our cultural and literary histories, perhaps because travel in the first part of the twentieth century has been characterised as an elite activity, and therefore prone by its very nature to suspect Anglophilia.[3] Its close cultural cousin was imperialism, another elite idea that Keith Sinclair has argued 'belonged to an official rhetoric, to newspaper editors, to school teachers, to politicians, to Governors and Governors-General'.[4] By extension, then, it could be argued that stories of travel Home map cultural elitism rather than any more authentically rooted sense of identification. But as it happens, although there were a few travelling newspaper editors, the largest collection of visitors to London over this period was a considerably more diverse group. They were 'Bill Massey's tourists', thousands of ordinary New Zealanders who ended up in London as part of their service in World War I. New Zealand sent more than 100,000 men to war, some 9 per cent of its population. London became the main place of leave once the war effort moved to Europe, and although numbers are not officially recorded, it would be safe to assume that more than 60,000 passed through. These 'soldier-tourists', a cross-section of New Zealand's community, were also prolific producers of travel tales, mostly in the form of private correspondence. They too had an imagined London, although this might have been shaded and shaped a little differently from that of a touring newspaperman. Overturning assumptions of Home as retrograde cultural elitism, their diaries, letters and postcards also bear the imprint of London's place in New Zealand's cultural landscape.

The popularity of published pilgrimages also suggests that Home was not the narrow obsession of a few. Between 1927 and 1937 there were at least ten published – one a year, some by reputable companies like Longmans, Dent, Reed, and Whitcombe & Tombs, while serialised tales of travel in London were also common newspaper and magazine fare.[5] The master of the genre was Alan Mulgan, a prolific writer. *Home: A New Zealander's Adventure* became his most popular book, first published in 1927 and reprinted twice after that, in 1929 and 1934. The two reprints, evidence of its success, were issued under a new title. It became a 'colonial's adventure', probably to increase its sales in Britain and the rest of the the empire, 'colonials' being more numerous than New Zealanders. Further proof of the popular market for pilgrimages, the trip was supported financially by Mulgan's employers.

Imagined London: a woodcut by Clare Leighton.
Alan Mulgan, *Home: A Colonial's Adventure*, London, 1929, p.25.

The *Auckland Star*'s publishers paid him during some of his year's absence, and gave him £300 towards travel expenses.[6] It made good copy. His adventures were excerpted in the *Auckland Star*, the *Press*, the *Evening Star* and the *Christian Science Monitor*.

The little surge of published pilgrimages Home from the end of the 1920s have been considered out of step with the contemporaneous development of literary nationalism in 1930s New Zealand, and this may be another reason why they have been neglected. Mulgan's work has been critically dispatched as the epitome of 'late-Victorian moral conservatism, Empire loyalty, and a sense of England as "Home"'.[7] However accurate this assessment, books with titles such as *The Joyous Pilgrimage* and *Let's Go Home* are not anomalous with the development of literary nationalism. Like other better-known or better-written work, they are reflections of the culture that produced them. Combined with the experiences of the soldier-tourists, they provide an entry point into the imagined geography of New Zealand's London.

FAMILIAR LONDON

Like Donnelly's breathless whirl through the streets of London, travellers' tales trace out the shape of an imagined London, constructed in New Zealand and ready to be laid, like a template, over the metropolis itself. In part, this template was produced by personal and familial ties, often represented as nostalgia and sentiment. For travelling doctor Robert Noble Adams the source of imagined London was literally familiar, constructed from family stories.[8] Newspaper proprietor T. C. List, exactly the type of imperialist Sinclair had in mind, travelled to London for the Imperial Press Conference of 1930. He also had imagined London through the tales of his family. When 'confronted with the stately pile of buildings on the water's edge at Westminster . . . [he] knows they are the House of Lords and the House of Commons because he has seen pictures of them from infancy and has heard so much of them from his parents'.[9] For another traveller, H. K. Sumpter, London's churches acquired the 'added charm of recalling old nursery rhymes, photographs of fashionable weddings and other diverse and dormant memories with which we in the outposts of Empire have to be content'.[10]

But memories – the legacy of emigration – were not the only sources of an imagined London. Family stories and other private constructions of London were bolstered and transformed by public versions that reproduced a consistent version of the metropolis. The spread of modern technologies like film, radio and photography, along with rapid expansion of the press, subjects of a later chapter, ensured that London was constantly in front of the New Zealand public. These technologies would 'keep the empire more or less in place', although Edward Said did not have the white settler colonies in mind when he argued this.[11] In the modern world of shrinking space that such innovations created, a sense of propinquity – both cultural and spatial closeness – could be produced. When the self-titled touring pastoralist A. W. Rutherford arrived in London, he claimed, 'The illustrated papers had made me fairly familiar with London, so the buildings did not greatly astonish me.'[12] Alan Mulgan, whose family migrated to New Zealand from Northern Ireland, cited the *Boy's Own*, novels, and 'the big illustrateds – the *Graphic* and *Illustrated London News*, with their fascinating pictures of the Great World . . . . All this fed our love of Home and especially of England.'[13] Enthusiastic readers of *Home* agreed: one claimed 'your longings and experiences almost exactly duplicate mine – I grew up with a steady desire to go "Home" and that longing was fed on the English "illustrateds" and magazines like the *Captain* or the *Strand* with its blue cover with a drawing of the Strand'.[14] This desire was the product of media, not memories. Once finally in London, Margaret Johnson, who published a memoir of her trip, found it 'impossible to believe that I am really here, and seeing with my own eyes the things I've read about and seen so often in photographs'.[15] In his diary, journalist Ian Donnelly described his first sight of England: 'How often I have dreamed of seeing this storied and well-beloved country.'[16] It is no surprise, then, that he imaged the first days of his visit as the 'vast tome of London . . . opening'.[17]

This shared blueprint made travellers feel familiar with London before they even arrived; it shaped their expectations, itineraries, emotions and reactions. The familiar effect began with the first glimpses of England. These were loaded moments, as travellers imbued England's landmarks with cultural resonances: 'Britannia was all there – invisible, yet invincible – we could feel her strength along the coast, and feel, in a sort of subconsciousness, the sense of security that came as a moral atmosphere from her historic shores.'[18] The predetermined first glimpse was to be the white cliffs, as it was for Johnson: 'And then, late in the morning, came my first sight of England itself – Beachy Head, its grey white cliffs rising noble and beautiful out of the soft mist. Now Julius Caesar and I have something in common besides our noses – we have both seen the white cliffs of England.'[19] Beachy Head was a reasonable alternative for the real white cliffs of England, at Dover. Yet appropriate substitutions were not always possible, as Ian Donnelly noted when his first glimpse of England turned out to be Eddystone lighthouse: 'The pilgrim coming to England should see first the chalk cliffs of Dover. They should be his landfall, but it is not always practical to arrange things so.'[20] Nor was it always quite as expected: Gladys Luxford, a Voluntary Aid Division nurse, described getting to England 'at last'. Like other travellers, part of the trip was as expected – she saw Land's End. But part was unexpected: 'oh, oh, the cold wind going up the Channel'.[21]

Fond expectations of 'homecoming' were frequently tempered by reality. Mulgan had 'pictured' his arrival, yet his first glimpses were lost to fog. 'Were we to be denied the entry we had pictured to ourselves as perfection – coasting up the Channel on a clear day.'[22] His experiences deviated from

'The Magnet': albums of scenic photographs like this were widely available, reinforcing familiar London iconography in the colonial imagination. 582-Album-96, Sir George Grey Special Collections, Auckland Libraries.

the perfect pilgrimage script, one that, given his Irish Protestant heritage and avid reading of *Boy's Own*, was formed from public, not private, ties. This pilgrim experienced a miracle: appropriately, the weather changed, and 'we had our desire fulfilled, and in a manner so completely marvellous, so miraculously charged with wonder and beauty, that no man could fully deserve it'.[23] Even the momentous act of stepping on to English soil did not always meet the expectations of the visitors. A. W. Rutherford, arriving from what he had found to be a very foreign France, was 'predisposed to be sentimental about first setting foot in England, the home of the Briton, but Dover isn't attractive'.[24] The homecoming template did not extend to cover customs checks and queues, unromantic impositions on people who felt they were essentially Britons too. 'The thrill of stepping on to English soil was short-lived for we were soon lined up in a long queue filing past passport officials and customs men.' However, for Sumpter, the budget traveller, the gap between rhetoric and reality was soon neatly closed as he stepped 'into our first English train and away through fair Kentish hops towards the heart of the world!'[25]

These moments of disappointment and dreams fulfilled point to the strong grip of an imagined Home. Travellers simply expected a great deal from the 'heart of the world'. Indeed, contrary to assumptions of a naturally increasing sense of national identity, it seems that this grip strengthened over time. Voyagers writing between 1880 and World War I, although affected by their arrival Home, are relatively restrained in their descriptions of it. Russell Carr, a young woman travelling in 1886, wrote what feels like an almost cursory description: 'The first sight of England was beyond expression delightful and very impressive.'[26] Forrestina Ross's arrival, in 1912, is lyrical, but not overwrought: 'England – our first peep – grew out of the mist... those of us to whom England is an unvisited land have already felt its glamour, when Devon's rose red cliffs and tree crested capes grew out of the horizon.'[27] The unsentimental pastoralist, Rutherford, journeying in the same period, adopted an unimpressed posture. Later writing from the interwar period changes tone: for travellers like Mulgan, arriving Home, more than 'delightful', was nothing short of a miracle. Disappointed Australian tourists also start in this era to be outnumbered by enthusiasts, whose first sightings of England are marked by exclamations over 'land! dear English land!' and 'my beloved English soil'.[28] Later New Zealand writing likewise changes form. Typically, travel books move from the grand tour model of earlier writers, with England just the most significant of several countries visited, to tales dedicated to pilgrimages Home. In these later tales, even shipboard life and exotic stopovers almost disappear as 12,000 miles are telescoped into a few pages or less. List and Johnson dispense with any mention of travel at all, Donnelly spares one and a half pages, whilst Mulgan spins the journey out over two and a half. As actual distance disappeared from their narratives, the imagined closeness of New Zealand and London was emphasised.

While trips to England were being presented as pilgrimages Home, London was the main attraction. The city colonised images of England, and not only in the imagination of New Zealand travellers. At the turn of the century, London's Lady Guide Association made London '"chief representative" of England and the "pride" of its "countrymen"', whilst a later Ward Lock guidebook explained that the visitor to London would notice 'that the special aspects of many of the other great towns are reflected here', implicating Manchester, Liverpool, Oxford and Cambridge in forming London as epitome of the nation.[29] It is, then, less surprising that London could act as synecdoche for England for travelling New Zealanders. A young soldier, George Knight, subconsciously made London stand for England when he wrote from Boulogne: 'Oh England, I've always longed to go there. I hope I can see something of it. I'm longing to see Nelson's Monument, The Abbey, The Zoo and The Gardens. These are the chief things that have fixed themselves in my mind for London.'[30] A later tourist made London's symbolic role explicit, identifying Home with London and telescoping the attributes of England and empire into one place: 'To me it seems it must be because London is not only the heart of England, but is, to the British person, no matter where in the world his interests lie, the very heart of Empire. We learn this at our mother's knee, and to every loyal son, some day or other, the urge speaks with insistent voice and we come "Home".'[31] London's predominance could be expressed without pretension. One newly arrived soldier wrote: 'The impressions [of England] were all thrilling to us, to be in the Old Country. In due course we were given leave to go where we liked, and backpay too. So we all made for London.'[32]

'A DREAM COME TRUE': LONDON IMAGINED

'Making for London' meant glossing over its outskirts, which again were not part of the imagined template. They were, at best, 'the drop-curtain before the mise en scène in the great drama of London town'; at worst, 'a sorry introduction to the excitements and picturesqueness of the city'.[33] The proper arrival was supposed to be something like this:

> Evening was closing in as we neared London, and we saw it first through that blue misty light that is its own. After this day of quickened emotions, Chelsea and the oft-dreamed-of Thames were blurs. Fortune, however, was not yet satisfied. After supper I was driven to the city – Westminster Abbey, the Houses of Parliament, Whitehall, the Strand, Fleet Street – we even stopped at the Cheshire Cheese for a moment – St Paul's, the Bank; in a half dream I heard my host indicating these jewels of London. The evening ended with a visit to Waterloo to retrieve my luggage, and there I had my first experience of a moving staircase. And so to bed, and do you wonder that, tired as I was, I could not easily sleep?[34]

'Really in London': a New Zealand tourist's photograph of St Paul's from Bankside. O.031861, Harry Moult Album, Museum of New Zealand Te Papa Tongarewa.

This, not the outskirts, was the London fashioned – 'dreamed of' – in New Zealand.

First glimpses reveal its 'familiar' outlines. 'Our drive from Victoria to Piccadilly Circus, where the Regent Palace Hotel is situated, was one of the most thrilling of our lives, for we were continuously recognising such famous buildings as Buckingham Palace and St James's Palace. The way one recognises so readily historic buildings and monuments and buildings is one of the charming surprises of London.'[35] These buildings were, as Donnelly put it, 'really London'.[36] Where imagined London was given substance, it was a 'dream come true'.[37] St Paul's was a sacred site for London pilgrims, a visual icon of arrival: 'when we crossed London Bridge, and looking back, I caught my first glimpse of St Paul's dome, a deeper grey through grey mist – then I knew I was really in London'.[38] It was a crucial part of the familiar London template: 'The sight of St Paul's from Fleet Street is the view of London strangers know well.' Donnelly 'knew it long before [he] saw it in reality'.[39] Its iconic status was almost too well-rehearsed. Soldier Hugh Grierson, on leave in 1918, 'went over St Paul's Cathedral it is very fine, but just what I expected, I had seen so many illustrations of it that it was like looking up an old friend'.[40]

London was treated like an old friend in other ways. Travellers expected to be able to navigate its streets, as if they would be as familiar to them in reality as they seemed to be in their imagination. This was not always the case: soldier Stan Chester was 'lost most of the time' one day in March, whilst an officer, Captain F. S. Varnham, was 'bewildered at first, huge crowds and dazzling lights and noises'.[41] But even being lost is transformed into a 'familiar' experience. Varnham later wrote, 'Easily lost in London – turn around twice and I am lost. Then simply ask a policeman or take a taxi.'[42] One policeman claimed he 'too oft found himself astray in less-known parts', suggesting being lost was a typical experience for all 'Londoners', including those from the colonies.[43] However, others wrote proudly of mastering the city. World War I nurse Ella Cooke spent 'a few days piloting Nurse Eddy around. She thought I found my way around splendidly.'[44] Soldiers were masters of casual familiarity with the capital, as they 'roam[ed] about', 'knock[ed] about', 'potter[ed] about' and, in one case, 'had a good old loaf around' the heart of empire.[45] In part this reflects soldierspeak of the time; patrols were 'picnics', attacks were 'stunts'. Slang has a number of functions, including group identification, but it also works to minimise the events themselves, to keep them human-sized and under some sort of control. A casual reference to 'roaming about the big smoke' is a way of bringing the capital down to size, a cultural bridging strategy with swagger for colonials who felt they had a stake in the imperial capital too.

Although soldiers have usually been conscripted into narratives of New Zealand's developing nationalism, it is possible that the thousands who went to London may also have helped maintain familiar London. It is difficult to demonstrate this conclusively, but on leave amongst London's iconic geography, they too were tourists, taking photographs, writing letters and sending postcards to families. These images, which recycled a shared imaginary, sustained London's imaginative presence in New Zealand.[46] Photographs were cheaply and readily available, especially as postcards,

'This monument looks very high from the street': New Zealander Leslie Carrick Hewson's postcard home. Leslie Carrick Hewson Correspondence, 21 October 1917, Leslie Carrick Hewson Papers, MS 89/158, Auckland Museum Library.

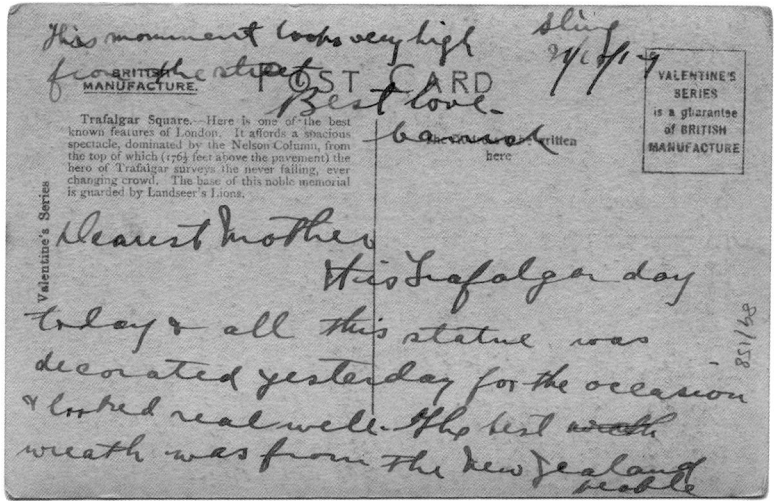

and one traveller 'bought views of London and England gardens and posted them to Alice', while another 'sent home some book views of London'.[47] A number of the archived postcards are not postmarked or addressed, so they were either kept as souvenirs or enclosed with letters in envelopes. Leslie Hewson sent postcards of France, Sling, British hospitals, London Bridge and Nelson's Column. On the back of this last he wrote, 'Dearest Mother, It is Trafalgar day today and all this statue was decorated yesterday for the occasion and looked real well. The best wreath was from the New Zealand people. This monument looks very high from the street.'[48]

Soldiers' letters about London are overwhelmingly positive, no doubt in part because the soldiers at last had something to write about that their audience would understand. Imagined London, unlike the unimaginable warfront, could be shared. Their intense experiences, often lasting only a few days, tended to focus on the historic centre of the city, reflecting and reinforcing the familiar template. On his first leave, Captain Herbert King had only two days in London: 'It is a large place as you know and one cannot see everything in two days but I did my best and had a look at the Houses of Parliament, St Paul's, Westminster Abbey, Tower of London, Hyde Park, the Row, Serpentine etc. It is all very interesting and wants to be seen to be appreciated.'[49] Nurse Ella Cooke, writing to a young relative, described London's iconic monuments carefully:

> Well now I must tell you a wee bit about London although it is hard to describe. Perhaps the first thing that strikes me is these smoke begrimed large buildings towering up into the skies. The streets are mostly narrow, often only just admitting two carts at a time (one each way). Some of the old architecture especially (Wren's) works most wonderful. Wren's work is perhaps best known in the building of St Paul's Cathedral, Houses of Parliament, Westminster Abbey and St Alban's cathedral and Abbey. The outside of these places one could look at for hours but I think some of the domes inside are most wonderful. I can't describe the work, it is quite beyond me. Just to think they have stood for some hundreds of years, it is marvellous.[50]

Cooke's letter not only demonstrated the careful cataloguing of London sights integral to maintaining the imagined metropolis on the periphery, but also brought to life another important set of images. The narrow streets and smoky buildings evoked the 'Londons of Dr Johnson, Charles Lamb, and Charles Dickens', and these, as much as famous monuments, came to be considered the '"soul of the city"'.[51] They too formed part of London's history and heritage. Indeed, through the grime of its haphazard streets, London was unequalled as a place where the past might be observed.

Private P. G. Williams' letter gives an account of the 'principal sights' a soldier might see:

> By the way about a week before we left Sling we went on our four days' draft leave. I went to London for mine and had a look around. Went through the Tower of London, St Paul's, Westminster Abbey, the King's Stables saw the horses he rides at reviews etc. Went through one of the museums and in it among other interesting things is the skeleton of Napoleon's horse. Saw Madame Tussaud's waxworks. The figures are that lifelike that I was very nearly asking a policeman to a certain part of the building. There are several tableaux including King John signing the Magna Charta . . . the murder of the Princes in the Tower (I saw the room where this happened when I was through the tower the day before also the place where their bodies were hidden in the wall for nearly 100 years.) The Babes in the Wood with the birds covering them over with leaves. The execution of Mary, Queen of Scots and Jack the Giant Killer settling a giant with a pick. I was stopping at a YMCA in Holborn Street. It cost me 1/6 for 3 nights (6d per night) and meals average 1/- each. You could live in London (in uniform) and have a bit of a look around for 5/- a day. But to have a decent look around you would want from 15/- to £1 per day. Well this is all the news of importance right just now.[52]

Private Williams' sights took him into the past. Like the Londons imagined by readers of Dickens or Lamb, they shift almost imperceptibly between fact and fantasy. The fairytale presentation of Jack the Giant Killer merges with the real story and setting of the princes in the Tower, or Mary Queen of Scots. This was part and product of London's existence in the imagination as well as in reality, where multiple cultural threads were merged.

While in some ways London was treated as a gigantic version of Madame Tussaud's, with various monuments and buildings plucked out to exemplify 'British' history and heritage to tourists, it was not all waxworks. New Zealand's London was also located in the activities of the city: like the tourists themselves, familiar London had a performative aspect.[53] Mulgan knew he was 'really' in London at Whitehall with the changing of the guard: 'This was truly London!'[54] Another visitor had 'to drive through the City proper to London Bridge Station, and it was almost necessary to hold me down in my excitement at seeing the funny little streets in grey old London,

and men walking unconcernedly about in silk hats when they aren't going to a wedding or a garden party, and London buses and a hundred other things'.[55]

London was, though, more than a history lesson come to life. 'Historic' London's spaces were partnered with 'modern' London. Visitors expected to experience modern life there; they expected to be overwhelmed by its size and pace. Experiencing London's traffic, policemen, underground trains, even the process of arriving in London by steamship, positioned these travellers as participants in the modern world. The pastoralist on tour, Rutherford, was neither astonished by the buildings, nor daunted by traffic, as 'it is common knowledge that the control of street traffic by the police leaves nothing to be desired'.[56] Johnson took a tour as 'the lights were coming out, and the city was crowded', and she 'didn't feel a bit overwhelmed by the traffic of London', and 'as for the crowds – I quite felt I was amongst "my ain folk"'.[57]

Modern London could, however, fail to live up to its thrilling reputation. High expectations of the capital were not restricted to a cultural elite, but were broadly shared amongst ordinary New Zealanders. World War I soldier Private Herbert Gill, writing to his wife Sophia, asks her to –

> Just picture me sitting in the heart of a small village called London. Dropping you a few lines to let you know I've been out in the country ... here I am in the city of the big smoke.[58]
>
> Soph, disappointed with London, I thought it would take an hour to cross the streets here but I have seen as much traffic in Wellington if not more. Was in the busy streets last night, the Strand and so forth and I did not see any difference from Wellington, some very fine buildings, am going around to Westminster Abbey in the morning, have passed pretty close to it, been across the Thames a few times some great sights to see quite easy to find your way about, pretty dark at that, very few lights. The people about here amuse me, ask where a certain place is they don't know, never heard of it and it would only be a couple of miles off, they want waking up, thousands and thousands of big able-bodied men knocking about in civic clothes.[59]

'A London policeman': another icon photographed by a travelling New Zealander.
O.032075, Harry Moult Album, Museum of New Zealand Te Papa Tongarewa.

New Zealand soldier-tourists in Piccadilly Circus, probably on Peace Day, 28 June 1919. O.032003, Herbert Green Album, Museum of New Zealand Te Papa Tongarewa.

Gill expected more from New Zealand's modern metropolis: overwhelming scale, the bustle of a fast-paced city, the bright lights of peacetime, not the dark afternoons of a wartime winter, and certainly not somewhere like Wellington. He also expected more from its citizens. Australian soldiers made similar comments. Some of these have been attributed to colonial brashness, but others to 'disillusioned Anglophile colonials who had expected to be more impressed'.[60] Gill's letter, though, is neither brash nor Anglophile. Instead, it speaks to the strength of that 'familiar' London template, and its broad reach among ordinary New Zealanders. Gill's London is a 'small village', easily conquered by a travelling New Zealander. Yet it would be wrong to minimise his experience. Reaching the heart of London, mastering its busy streets and passing 'pretty close' to Westminster Abbey remain significant achievements, even if his personal style is to play them down. In a way, this makes London seem even more accessible, both to the traveller and to his reader. His time in London remained a memorable experience for him, and a treasured one for his reader. The letter made it home, although Gill himself, like so many other soldier-tourists, never would.

LONDON APPROPRIATED

New Zealanders not only recognised the metropolis, they also appropriated parts of it. Indeed, they even had some encouragement in their imaginative possession of the metropolis. A. Staines Manders' *Colonials' Guide to London*, written for visiting soldiers in 1916, claimed 'the Tower, the Abbey, Westminster Hall and St Paul's appeal to the imagination of the peoples of the Dominions as no novelty however brilliant can appeal. For these are theirs and ours, and in the shadow of the Abbey or the White Tower, we are Londoners all.'[61] Some twenty-one years later, another guide written for the 'white colonials' of Australia, South Africa, Canada and New Zealand was still remaking London as a joint possession. In *The Empire Comes Home*, author, actor and 'white colonial' himself W. S. Percy wrote, 'No nation possesses a capital which has such a hold in the hearts and imagination of the people as London. It has over the English a fascination almost as strong as Mecca has for the Moslem. In London the Colonial feels he can enter into his heritage as freely as those born within the sound of Bow Bells.'[62]

New Zealanders were quick to appropriate iconic London as part of their heritage. In doing so, they once again inverted the usual direction of imperial power, turning the imperial gaze, with its ability to 'passively look out and possess' back on the centre itself.[63] Johnson was moved to tears on viewing the Houses of Parliament: 'It was the realisation of all I'd read and heard. And I felt so completely at home, as if I belonged there, and it was all a part of me.'[64] These same buildings were appropriated for all 'colonials' by List:

> Here is the seat of the supreme Government of the British Empire, the Mother of Parliaments, the shrine of the world's liberties, the last word in political tolerance and democracy.... He is filled with pride, tinctured with gratitude – pride that he, an inhabitant of the most distant post of Empire, can share in this possession of this wonderful institution that has

it roots so firmly fixed in the past, and in the habits and instincts of the nation; and gratitude in that he has attained his childhood ambition of viewing this part of his wonderful heritage.[65]

Traversing time and space, List travelled from 'the most distant post of Empire' 'down the ages' to view 'this part of his wonderful heritage'. Historic and imperial London are collapsed in the Mother of Parliaments, which is regarded as a colonial possession: 'they, the descendants of Britons who years before had emigrated overseas to found new nations and extend Britain's dominion, all sharing in the possession of this historic building and the other historic architectural treasures at the seat of Empire'.[66] List called his book *The Briton at Home*, and it is difficult to know whether the title describes the people he was visiting or himself.

Westminster Abbey was another appropriated treasure, not as church, but as shrine of a literary kind. Cultural reconnection occurred for H. K. Sumpter by 'Poet's Corner, where only plain marble slabs mark the resting places of our greatest writers and poets. It was not until I stood in this hallowed spot that I felt that deep emotion which is closely akin to tears.'[67] These are not simply great writers: they are 'our' writers, whilst being explicitly British. 'I had dreamed of the day when I would be able to stand in Poet's Corner, paying my tribute to the sleeping dust of men whose labours have coloured so gloriously the English heritage. They toiled more magnificently than they knew. Songs tossed off for the pleasure of the "Mermaid" lived on to bring joy to British hearts in remote realms unknown to rare Ben Jonson and the rest.'[68] In fact, the Abbey may literally be a colonial site. At the Unknown Warrior's tomb, Mulgan wondered whether the soldier beneath saw 'the summer sea sparkle under the dark green and red of the pohutukawa on a Christmas morning, or breathe[d] the sharp dry air of tussock lands? Each Dominion will ask a similar question.'[69]

Like the Abbey, the magnetism of St Paul's, the empire's church, was not, as Mulgan also acknowledged, really religious. He was more entranced by the Gothic architecture, 'so intimate a part of our English heritage', and the abbey's role as 'a national and Imperial burial place [that] . . . is second in interest to Westminster Abbey only'.[70] Which nation, or rather, who belongs to it, is again not quite clear. Certainly Sumpter, when he visited the 'tombs of Nelson and Wellington . . . felt such a flood of emotion as to stir [him] to the depths'. So stirred was he, in fact, that he wished to have seen it at ten

'Our heritage': a visiting New Zealander takes photographic possession of the Houses of Parliament. O.032045, Harry Moult Album, Museum of New Zealand Te Papa Tongarewa.

years of age, and so 'render for England a service so great that I would be forever remembered in this sacred place'.⁷¹ Nelson in particular was connected to New Zealand as what Mulgan called 'the greatest seaman the world has known': 'We New Zealanders may say without impropriety that, like the English, we are what the sea and winds have made us and here lies the greatest of these who bent the strength of the sea and the winds to the tremendous purpose of our race.'⁷² Tenuously, then, Mulgan connects landscape, heritage and race to repossess an imperial hero. He finds that 'the Englishman is still by far the most important "national" in the Empire. He supplies Britain with most of her wealth, enterprise and character. What is more, he is still the world's chief champion and expositor of freedom and tolerance, good humour, justice and fair play.... He is the playing field boy of the Western youth.'⁷³

Other travellers also found 'British' values embodied in the tombs, churches, monuments and buildings of their metropolitan centre. Not all of the buildings were conventional monuments: Donnelly found 'familiar' London in the literary associations of an old eating house, the Cheshire Cheese: 'London stood for Johnson, for Lamb, for Wells, a hundred others, and in the first hour the "Cheshire Cheese" stood for them all.'[74] And in the shadow of these monuments, New Zealanders did indeed become 'Londoners all', as they read their own history and values in the landscape of the imperial metropolis. They also embodied these values themselves. Noble Adams came to the end of his journey Home 'very proud to know that I am a Britisher, living under a flag that stands for Truth and Righteousness'.[75] In this way, the values of empire and nation encapsulated in the London landscape were also located in the travelling 'Britons'. Like the landscape, they figured themselves as ideal expressions of a cohesive empire, cultural exemplars, not cultural dependants. New Zealand was 'British', so its heritage and history were therefore quite logically located off shore, where it was available for enthusiastic acquisition by colonial co-owners.

'SUPER-BRITISHERS'

If New Zealanders could use London to redefine their status as metropolitan, they could also use it to confirm their place within empire. A regular feature of the journey to London included leaving the boundaries of historic London for an 'exotic tour' through parts of the centre's own periphery, visiting different ethnic neighbourhoods or the equally foreign-seeming slums of the East End.[76] In this part of the empire's heart, New Zealanders could assume the more conventional imperial gaze, fascinated by the transgressive elements of race, sex and class. Donnelly, whilst generally disapproving of London as a 'liberaliser' (he viewed barmaids, banned in New Zealand, with some suspicion, seeing 'rather more than tap-room conviviality in their good fellowship'), took 'an excursion to the Limehouse' within two days of arriving in London:[77] 'Children quick to pick strangers, and as remorseless in quest of pennies as the coloured gamins of Colombo

The Westminster Abbey Tower from the Dean's Yard.
O.032072, Harry Moult Album, Museum of New Zealand Te Papa Tongarewa.

and Port Said . . . . Not an almond-eyed beauty anywhere, not a sinister yellow man. One Lascar lounging under a street lamp.'[78] Under the guise of emigration research, Rutherford 'engaged a taxi for an afternoon's exploration of the slums of London', evincing particular interest in the condition of Jewish women.[79] Women did the same: Ross went south of the Thames – 'in the heart of the poor part of London – beyond Blackfriars Bridge' on the invitation of the Women's University Settlement to observe work done to raise 'boys and girls from the slough of despond they are apt to sink into'.[80] Johnson took an exotic tour to the Jewish community in Berwick Street, and 'soon we found ourselves in a smallish shop full of jabbering Jewesses with their make-up very plenteously and sketchily applied'.[81] Travellers may also have practised this imperial gaze on the trip over when their ships docked at places like Port Said. As Angela Woollacott has observed, 'Australian women viewed their own status in the British Empire at least partially through the knowledge they gleaned of the empire's constituent parts on their passages "home".'[82] Although exotic tours taken on the voyages Home did not feature in New Zealanders' published travel tales, this does not mean New Zealand travellers were immune to their effects in reinforcing the imperial hierarchy and their place in it.

London was a place where metropolitanism could be created and experienced, where New Zealanders could participate as members of the first-world 'white empire', not the dependent empire.[83] But while there was some ambiguity in the status of white colonials, New Zealanders frequently experienced a form of metropolitan superiority. World War I nurse Ella Cooke wrote heatedly, 'As regards my opinion of English people it's quite altered now that I have lived amongst them. They seem to think the people in the colonies are not up to much and really don't know anything never the less at a time like this they ought to send all the men they can to defend England. That's all very fine but why can't more be sent from here? . . . . You never in your life saw more "rotters" or "slackers" than I have come across.' She added, 'Believe me Florrie, Eaddy and I were happier in France with foreigners than being here with our own flesh and blood.'[84] Another writer disowned the Londoners entirely, preferring the 'sensible shoes and colours' of Glasgow to London. (He was not reborn as a New Zealander,

New Zealand soldiers explore Petticoat Lane, part of the 'exotic' East End, during World War I. Album 413, p.39, Auckland Museum Library.

though, commenting 'I felt at home in Scotland – think I must really be Scotch.')[85]

It was disappointing to find feet of clay amongst the English, and the defensive tone suggests the regard in which 'Englishness' was held. Similarly, it was unpleasant to be labelled 'colonial' when you felt you were part of the same extended family and might even be a better version of it. Yet stressing subordination oversimplifies the complexity of the cultural relationship, and obscures the role of whiteness in creating London as Home and New Zealanders as special members of the 'family of empire'. This is clear in the case of Indians travelling to the 'heart of empire'. They inverted the idea of imperial spectacle, creating a spate of Indian-written travel guides to the metropolis.[86] Yet these imperial visitors were not recreated as heirs to London's history and heritage. This was a dominion privilege. *The Empire Comes Home* and *The Colonial's Guide to London* were written specifically for the white dominions, and 'there were no systematic commercial guidebooks written specifically for non-white tourists until after World War II'.[87] Dominion visitors were features of the fomer type of guidebook, but Indians were included only 'occasionally as comic interludes where it was made clear that there were limits to who was at home in London'.[88]

New Zealanders' appropriation of London was at least partly built on their similarities to, not differences from, other 'proper' metropolitan citizens. Soldier Charles Spragg saw it this way. After being wounded at Gallipoli, he was sent to Greece to convalesce. 'Most of my pals here are English officers. They are all good company and a change from colonials, though we have some of them, and good chaps too, here.'[89] While being to some extent inclusive, Spragg's letter inscribes an imperial hierarchy, in which the white settler societies form a unique group. The unique status of white colonials is indicated by writer Jane Mander, who clearly differentiates between dominion visitors to London who make up 'Empire' and 'others': 'One does not have to be a Londoner long to be able to pick out the outsiders. I do not mean the obvious foreigners, like the Hindoo law students . . . . I mean rather the Empire visitors, who come branded with a different cast of face, freer movements, a less blasé air, and varied intonations. One can pick them anywhere.'[90] In this redefinition of empire, even the jewel in the imperial crown, India, is overlooked.

Whiteness was an obvious expression of New Zealand's assumed metropolitan-ness. Travellers themselves did not tend towards accepting a position of subordination, but nor was it appropriate to adopt a position of superiority. Donnelly cautioned visitors not to 'be arrogant', suggesting with a useful simile that it is better to be 'rather like country boys come to town, and trembling to hear brave tales from the lips of miraculous uncles'.[91] While attention has been paid to the origins and prevalence of colonial cringe, less credence has been given to the notion of colonial superiority, and certainly New Zealanders were lively contributors to the debate about British 'degeneration' exposed by the Boer War. Rutherford felt it was 'only reasonable' to suppose the British were degenerating, as 'an inevitable corollary' of the colonising process that left only 'inferior stock' in the country: 'As corroborative of this, in what branch of athletics does Great Britain hold the championship? – None.'[92] Rutherford's comments may seem cranky but attitudes like these were even more common on the battlefield, applied to soldiers rather than athletes. That New Zealand soldiers outclassed their British counterparts was the stuff of popular legend, regularly evoked in comments like 'a tommy is a poor class of chap compared with any colonial'.[93] Often perceived as an expression of nationalism, the firm belief in the superiority of the colonial soldier also suggests limits to the idea of colonial subordination. However, these expressions might be better understood as another part of the imaginative extension of New Zealand's borders. White settler societies recognised the connections between themselves and Britain, even going so far as to position themselves as arks for 'Britishness' against the rising tide of the debilitating consequences of modernity and urbanisation.

The inheritors of the civilised centre were quick to invoke the privileges of metropolitan-ness, and to use London as the locale for metropolitan performances of their own. Rutherford decided 'there seemed to be an all-round conspiracy to give us a great time in honour of the auspicious occasion – the crowning of the King. Of course we were not all invited to Buckingham Palace, but it was a poor creature who hadn't the honour of shaking hands with a Duke. One lady applied to our High Commissioner for names. He sent her a hundred. She said, "That won't do, send me two hundred".'[94] It seemed the metropolis held 'many Aladdin's caves [for which] there is an open sesame in London in the password, "the Colonies"'.[95] And not only in London: on the return trip to New Zealand, twenty-five years after the coronation, Noble Adams 'realised we were looked on as super-Britishers. The name New Zealander was even a better "open sesame" than that of Englishman.'[96] Indeed, Noble Adams had already used his magic powers to be whisked to the front of the Jubilee procession crowd. Telling a policeman that they couldn't see and were all the way from New Zealand, the policeman replied, '"that's good enough for me" and grabbed us both and placed us right in front of the line of police, and we were home and dried'.[97] Ewen Allison tried the same thing at the theatre – 'Excuse me, I come from New Zealand. I am a new chum in London and I have not much money' – but does not report on his success.[98]

However, criticism was sharp when New Zealand failed to live up to its status at official occasions in London. The 'super-Britishers' who were such a feature of the writings of travelling New Zealanders, and in the reported affectionate responses of the British to the New Zealand presence in their midst, were not in evidence at the coronation of George V. Rutherford noted the 'sorry display' New Zealanders made with 'our few uniforms plain' and the 'tin shop appearance' of 'our "orders"'.[99] Johnson was disappointed with a later New Zealand Trafalgar Day effort, which disconcertingly reflected something of New Zealand's actual size: 'Most of the wreaths had already been placed in position. In front were those from various parts of Empire, those from India and Canada being especially magnificent. That from the New Zealand Government looked like a poor relation beside them, but then we are much smaller.'[100] It was not only in comparison with the rest of the empire that New Zealand looked insignificant. At a New Zealand Day service, the New Zealand car, waiting beside the Lord Mayor's coach, looked 'about as exciting as a boy's trolley'.[101] New Zealand's participation in these events was premised on its sense of metropolitan citizenship, which created a sense that its stature would be greater than that of 'poor relation'.

These experiences indicate the ways in which familiar London existed and functioned within New Zealand culture. Its imaginative existence was enhanced, not diminished, by the experience of travellers, whose journeys through the metropolis helped map London as part of New Zealand's cultural landscape. As 'Londoners all', lost and found, they laid claim to a metropolis they had imagined from 12,000 miles away. They would also make it Home. The next chapter explores the business of making New Zealand's soldiers of World War I feel at home in London while on leave, and the development of a 'New Zealand House' and Home in the heart of empire. 'Familiar' London was imaginatively constructed in New Zealand, but Home – no simple sentimental expression – was also constructed in the metropolis itself.

CHAPTER TWO

AT HOME IN LONDON

IN 1921, THE IMPECCABLY imperialist Lord Meath came up with a new way to perpetuate and articulate the bonds of empire. He had already popularised Empire Day, which was held on 24 May and marked by celebrations across the empire. Now, he had a new plan which would celebrate the heart of that empire.[1] In a contribution to a collection of essays on the development of the metropolis entitled *London of the Future*, Meath called for London to be officially recognised as the capital of empire. In return, representatives from the dominions, India and the colonies would be co-opted onto London's civic bodies. This was a very formal attempt to capture a very informal phenomenon: the 'homeliness' of the imperial metropolis. Meath claimed, 'There is an attractive force which London possesses in a greater degree than any other city, and which causes British citizens all over the world to love the Empire's capital above all other cities, and to return to it, whenever the opportunity offers, with never failing joy and delight. It is, I venture to think, its homeliness which is London's greatest attraction.'[2] For all Meath's encouragement, London never became the official 'home city' of empire. But it hardly mattered. The dominions did not require any official sanction to make themselves at home in London, because they already considered it to be their city too.

This chapter looks at two ways New Zealand's London took physical form. Perhaps the most important marker of New Zealand's place in London was the New Zealand High Commission, known colloquially as New Zealand House.[3] As its name implies, New Zealand House converted metropolitan space into New Zealand place. Originally envisaged as a place where New Zealand's interests might be represented in London, it evolved to become an important portal into the metropolis itself, a place where New Zealand's appropriation of London was physically and imaginatively embodied. Like the shadows cast by the Abbey, New Zealand House helped transform travellers into Londoners, and made London a 'familiar' place. That role would take on increased importance during World War I, when thousands of New Zealand soldiers found themselves in London on leave. The experiences of those soldiers, and the efforts of official organisations to create the metropolis as a 'home away from home' for them, are the second way to explore New Zealand's physical co-option of London space.

Together, New Zealand House and the experience of New Zealand soldiers in London during World War I complement the earlier discussion of travellers and their imaginative appropriation of the capital's space. They are a physical manifestation of the same possessive impulse. But whilst they are separated out here, it is better to consider the imaginative and physical appropriation of London as intertwined. New Zealand House's functions were shaped in part by the demands of tourists, whilst the needs of soldiers were catalysts for the formation and operations of volunteer organisations. Unlike Meath's failed plan, where formal machinery could not capture informal relationships, here they work together. They are small examples of the more general difficulty of separating empire's formal 'systems' from culture's 'shaky "networks"'.[4] For both tourists and soldier-tourists alike, official constructions of London overlaid, intersected with, amplified and sometimes contradicted a collection of more informally developed conceptions of the metropolis. Home, even in its physical form, remained a co-production, this time between the official and informal imagination.

A HOUSE IN LONDON

New Zealand House was located in the Strand, a part of central London that members of the empire, especially the white dominions, helped to construct. With its theatres, hotels and restaurants, the Strand was a tourist destination. 'In tourist literature ... the Strand was a place of familiarity and relative safety, and a starting place for tours of the city.'[5] It was also an area where London's status as the 'home city' of empire – again, particularly of the white empire – was on display. Jane Mander, New Zealand novelist and long-term Londoner herself, claimed 'the Strand is known in the summer as the Dominion Promenade'.[6] By 1937, the Australian guidebook writer W. S. Percy, who had already interpreted England and Scotland for antipodean audiences in books like *Strolling Through Cottage England*, described the Strand as 'the heart of Empire where you have but to stroll along its pavements to meet men to whom the words Camloops, Calgary, Ronderbosche, Kaitangata, Hokitika, Murrumbidgee and WaggaWagga are familiar names, and not simply unintelligible jargon'.[7] Percy's colourful choice of places names may have evoked a little colonial exoticism, but they belonged in the far more familiar locales of Canada, South Africa, Australia and New Zealand.

The dominion 'houses' formed part of that imperial display. During World War I New Zealand moved its office, choosing the Strand, with its proximity to tourists, over its old location in Victoria Street, which was closer to colonial administrative offices. Australia House was opened in 1918 in Aldwych, and the Canadian High Commission moved to Trafalgar Square in 1923. A new South Africa House opened in Trafalgar Square in 1933, replacing their old building with a suitably imposing structure in the same location. The choice of location was no small matter: one Australian Member of Parliament pointed out that the negotiations over an appropriate site for Australia House in London had overtaken the search for the new federation's own capital.[8] Setting up house on and around the Strand, the dominions literally cemented the relationship between themselves and the heart of empire, and, at the same time, helped constitute it. One writer has imagined the area's impact in imperial terms: 'a young Londoner, moved and inspired by the statue of General Gordon in Trafalgar Square, decides finally ... to emigrate to South Africa. Twenty paces from him he sees South Africa House, which will furnish him with information about the colony: a dozen steps beyond are the offices of the steamship line which will take him there.'[9] In another reversal of metropolitan influence, it was Australia that brought civilisation to a little piece of London, as its classically designed High Commission – 'the Epitome of the British Empire in

Aldwych' – was built over what had a been a vacant lot covered in wild flowers.[10] The Kingsway–Aldwych redevelopment, where Australia House was built, was 'presented simultaneously as a rational modernisation of London's street pattern and a fitting monument to Edwardian high imperialism'.[11] The physical clustering of the 'houses' recognised, reinforced and reified London's role as the centre of empire. At the same time, their imposing preferences for architecture demonstrated the extent to which the dominions considered themselves partners in that empire and members of the metropolis.

It is possible to misread these aspirations in the centre. Dominion displays gave London an imperial character, but individually they were not to be characterised as part of an amorphous and undifferentiated empire, as Lord Grey discovered in 1914. He was the enthusiastic promoter of a collective 'Dominion House' to be built alongside Australia's new premises in Aldwych. This plan to incorporate all the dominions in one place, and 'cause the attention of the home consumer to be focussed effectively and impressively on the products of the Dominions', was, like Meath's official version of London, yet another imperial unity scheme doomed to failure, not least because it misread the purpose of the 'houses'. However much they might have agreed that 'London has no building suggestive of the great and rapidly increasingly importance of the self governing dominions', Canada, New Zealand, Australia and South Africa were also imperial competitors.[12] Australian building efforts had been hurried along by comments like those of former Prime Minister Alfred Deakin, who claimed that little New Zealand had somehow managed to 'cut a figure in the Mother Country enabling her to appear as if she could offer the same opportunities for development as the whole of this continent'.[13] Canada also suffered from a little dominion status envy. Upon the opening of the new Canada House in 1923, the *Liverpool Journal of Commerce* noted, 'Many a time I have seen John Canuk looking enviously at Australia's splendid building in the Strand and bemoaning the fact that Canada must be asleep to have tiny offices tucked away in an old building on Victoria Street when Australia with not much more than half Canada's population has one of the most imposing buildings in Great Britain.'[14] It was the envy of John Canuk, not the

New Zealand's House on the Strand: the New Zealand High Commission in London in the 1930s. S. R. Skinner, *My Life with the Kiwis*, London, 1962, image page following p.22.

'The Epitome of the British Empire in Aldwych': Australia House.
London, Ward Locke & Co., n.d., n.p.

buying power of John Bull, which the reporter commented on. Dominion high commissions promoted their own countries within London, which included an individual relationship with the metropolis against the rest of empire. New Zealand's only purpose-built High Commission, opened in 1962, provided one of the last examples of this mindset. Although its controversial glass tower was an architectural expression of modernism, it was otherwise only an updated version of dominion house-building from the turn of the century.

Similarly, it is possible to misread dominion intentions from the edge. New Zealand House and its displays may appear to be symbols of nationalism, yet for most of the twentieth century the doorway to New Zealand House in fact opened into the heart of the imperial metropolis. Reflecting New Zealand's appropriation of the centre, the High Commission was as fully involved in mediating the metropolis for New Zealand visitors as it was in pursuing New Zealand's interests there. It worked to make New Zealanders at home in London. This began with its facilities for travellers. New Zealand House offered reception and reading rooms, a library and *poste restante* service, functioning like a democratic version of that London institution, the club. The High Commission's own guidebooks advised visitors not to worry about having New Zealand papers sent to them, as they could read them on site. Combined, these services created what one touring Presbyterian minister called 'a convenient and most congenial meeting place', frequented by thousands of New Zealanders each season.[15] The Australians had a similar arrangement: visitors could 'make Australia House their headquarters, and utilize the library, sometimes daily, to read the papers, generally seek information, and meet old friends'.[16] Settling in as the third New Zealand High Commissioner in 1913, Sir Thomas Mackenzie wrote, 'The busy season for callers at the Office is again beginning, and I think it will soon be necessary to make some announcement and fix certain days for being available to callers. I am told that later on there will hardly be a moment free during the day and that quite a number of people call, as they say, merely to "yarn".'[17] More than one report notes the pressure of callers during the 'season'; in 1909 Sir William Hall-Jones cancelled all leave, and the 1931 report notes 'in summer particularly, the staff works at high pressure'.[18] Sir James Parr, who was on his second round as High Commissioner just a few years later in 1935, struck the Jubilee, and 'with four times the number of New Zealand visitors than in any previous year ... and Forbes and Coates demanding my presence ... I feel thoroughly tired out and wish I were in my bungalow on Takapuna Beach for a month or two'.[19]

One of the tourist services developed by the High Commission was a guidebook, *Handbook for New Zealand Visitors to London*, which was initially produced to assist soldiers on leave during World War I (and part of that wider project to configure London as Home, discussed later). By 1924, the High Commission was publishing a version for all visitors. Following the general trajectory of New Zealand travel writing on London, the handbook's heyday was the 1930s when it was reprinted every year (except 1933), including a special 1937 Coronation edition, complete with illustration of Westminster Abbey. Printing was suspended during World War II, although handbooks in various versions, and with decreasing tourist content, continued to be printed until 1972, when it seems the High Commission finally broke the habit of acting as representative of London for New Zealanders.

Edward Said has argued, in an imperial context, that 'All cultures tend to make representations of foreign cultures the better to master or in some way control them.'[20] Whilst the metropolis was hardly foreign to New Zealanders, the *Handbook* nevertheless represents a form of control and appropriation. Evidence that the colonising power of cartography was

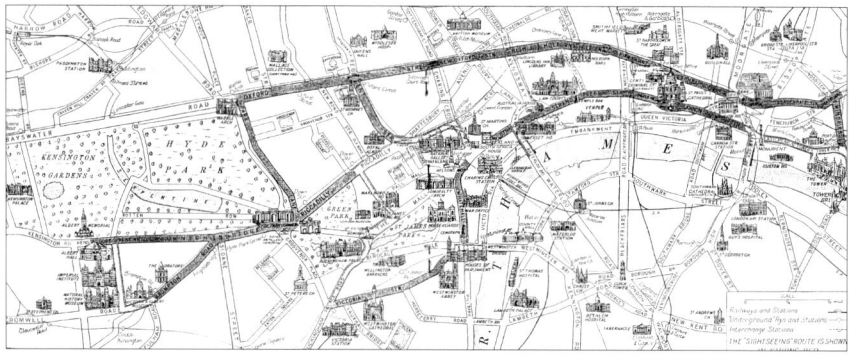

Mapping the heart of empire: a 'Map of London for New Zealand Visitors' with the recommended sight-seeing route in 'strong red'.
Handbook for New Zealand Visitors to London, London, 1934, n.p.

not confined to metropolitan mapmakers, the *Handbook* marks out a particular version of London in its two-page 'Map of London for New Zealand Visitors'. This 'London' is the city's centre: it runs from Tower Bridge to Kensington Gardens, from Westminster to Oxford Street. All the sights considered worth seeing – palaces, churches, monuments, art galleries and museums – are within this area. The map traces a route, appropriately enough 'in strong red', so 'the visitor may see all the important sights of London'. In doing so, it transforms London itself into a proper sight. For, as anxious commentators at the time noted, 'despite its peerless status as the world's greatest imperial metropolis', architecturally, London lacked imperial gravitas.[21] There were no sweeping boulevards with their triumphal arch focal points as might be found in rival capitals such as Paris. Instead, as Jonathan Schneer suggests, a visual sense of London as the heart of empire had to be consciously produced in other ways. Streets were widened to create properly imperial vistas of the city, while civic parades were organised to follow routes that showcased architectural evidence of London's imperial power.[22] The *Handbook*'s sightseeing map helps construct just such a vista, creating an imperial landscape that city planners could not. All small streets have been cleared away and there are no anonymous buildings to obstruct the view. Instead, detailed, larger-than-scale drawings of certain London buildings and monuments dominate the map. As an example of just how impressively these buildings figured in the peripheral imagination, on this map Nelson's Column is a little under quarter of a mile high!

48

Making imperial London: New Zealand Divisional troops in a victory march, London, May 1919. Thomas Frederick Scales, G-14228-1/2, Royal New Zealand Returned and Services' Association Collection, Alexander Turnbull Library, Wellington, New Zealand.

Nestled amongst the monuments at the heart of empire was New Zealand House. It too was a London sight, and it was considered 'wholly desirable that as many New Zealanders as possible should become acquainted with the extent and character of the Dominion's representation in Britain and with the work that is carried out'.[23] The *Handbook* also singled out New Zealand-run establishments, such as tearooms, that visitors might find useful, further extending New Zealand's reach within London. These interpolations of New Zealand space double as familiar territory and as markers of more repossessed metropolitan space. However, other important sites of New Zealand's relationship with London are overlooked, notably Smithfield and Tooley Street. These two key sites of New Zealand commerce are shown on the map, but omitted from the sightseeing route, and their absence points to an important erasure in the construction of New Zealand's London. New Zealand's most significant material contribution to the metropolis was to its food supply, and Smithfield was the principal destination for New Zealand meat, whilst Tooley Street handled New Zealand's dairy produce. These were certainly familiar places to New Zealanders: one farming publication, the *New Zealand Dairy Exporter*, sent free to every dairy farmer, ran regular full-page advertisements promoting visits to Tooley Street and Hay's Wharf. But they did not form the basis of New Zealand's imaginative possession of London. Despite the fact that most tourists came to London on vessels designed to carry meat and butter below, and passengers above, those travellers were encouraged to view their relationship with the metropolis via the family bonds of empire, not the cold calculus of economics. New Zealand House and its handbook were part of that imaginative process.

Underlining the dual character of New Zealand House in London, the majority of the staff were English, making them perfect guides for the metropolis. One visitor wrote to the Minister of Internal Affairs to 'mention Miss FitzGerald with whom probably visitors are brought mostly into contact. Not only is she a veritable mine of information she was not only ready but keen to help us in every possible way to visit the many places of interest which we desired to see.'[24] However, English staff were less useful for intending tourists to New Zealand. One local paper complained that New Zealand's exhibit at the 1908 Franco-British Exhibition was staffed by someone who 'knew nothing at all about New Zealand. Presumably he was a clerk in the High Commission Office, a place where they seem to know less about New Zealand than anywhere else in London.'[25] This was a familiar complaint. A travelling clergyman, the Reverend Dr Whitley of London, found the staff 'knew nothing and were not at all helpful'.[26] The publicity officer conceded the point, responding, 'as many of the assistants in the High Commissioner's Office are English and have never been to the Dominion it is only natural that it would not have been possible for them to supply detailed information of the nature required'.[27]

As early as 1912, the High Commission was starting to sag under the weight of visitor numbers and expectations of its tourist services for London. 'It cannot be adequately realised the amount of time taken now by the work involved in meeting New Zealanders and assisting them when in the Old Country . . . everything is done to assist them in seeing as much of interest in this country as possible. This of course involves a very great amount of work and correspondence in obtaining special permits for places of interest, and in furnishing of very many letters of introduction. During the year, 1,897 orders were obtained enabling 2,185 New Zealand visitors to see over various places of interest in London.'[28] Careful record-keeping was required to stay on top of visitor requests for privileged access to various London institutions. In 1916, nine hundred tickets were issued by

New Zealand House just for 'the House of Commons, Tower of London, Royal Mews, state apartments of Mansion House and other places of interest'.[29] These numbers had more than doubled by 1926.

New Zealanders also expected privileged access to various city, state and imperial occasions. Tickets for these events were highly sought after. Sir Thomas Mackenzie wrote:

> Another difficulty here is the matter of tickets for important functions and the somewhat unreasonable demands that are made by all and sundry for admission to such functions. Take, for instance, the Opening of Parliament on the 10th instant. Four tickets were granted to this office by the Lord Great Chamberlain for that function. I gave two to the Wards and two to the Allens. Other New Zealanders actually demanded tickets which we had not the power to obtain, but we were able to make some other arrangements for them for seats at windows. These seats were scornfully rejected by some, who talked about making it clear when they returned to New Zealand how their wishes were neglected.[30]

One visiting Member of Parliament complained bitterly that he had not been invited to the Empire Dinner. By way of defence, High Commissioner Sir Thomas Wilford agreed, but added that the MP had been invited to Lady Jellicoe's reception, the British Empire Academy Tea Party, the Royal Agricultural Show opening, Lady Clarendon's reception and the Trooping of the Colour.[31] Nor were receptions limited to visiting Members of Parliament at the expense of other New Zealanders. Sir James Allen's report of 1926 noted that over 3000 people were invited to two receptions, and over 1200 attended the Royal Garden Party of 1925.[32] Balconies and windows were reserved for visiting New Zealanders to see the annual Lord Mayor's Show, and High Commissioner Sir William Jordan fought it out with the other dominions to secure seats along the 1937 Coronation route: 'We are endeavouring to secure 3,000 seats to be made available from this office, but the chances are not very hopeful.'[33]

As time passed, New Zealand demand for favoured access to imperial and metropolitan occasions did not diminish. As late as 1953, the High Commission guidebook warned, 'In 1952 only one invitation was received for every 15 New Zealanders who applied' to attend a Royal Garden Party.[34] (Numbers were down in 2011, but there were still three applicants for

An imperial occasion: the Strand decorated for King Edward's coronation, 1902. AWNS-19020821-8-3, Sir George Grey Special Collections, Auckland Libraries.

every ticket, and New Zealand House still furnishes them.) Sir William Jordan wrote in 1938, to no less than the Prime Minister, Michael Joseph Savage, regarding complaints over access. A Dr G. Phillips of Feilding wished to attend the Trooping of the Colour and the Royal Garden Party. 'Miss Fitzgerald informed Dr Phillips that as the number of applications far exceeded the number of invitations allotted to New Zealanders she could not promise that they could all go.... Dr Phillips became abusive ... [and] claimed that as he had been thirty years in the Dominion he was entitled to whatever was going, and as his daughter had been granted the Jubilee Medal he thought the family was entitled to first consideration.... I pointed out... that we could not give preference to anyone... as all visitors from New Zealand rightly considered themselves entitled to invitations to functions.'[35] New Zealanders insisted upon their rights within what had been configured as their metropolis too.

New Zealand House predated Lord Meath's vision of London as the 'home city' of empire, but in many ways it conformed to it. At the same time, it restated New Zealand's relationship to that centre as a constituent part of the metropolis, through its role as interpreter and gateway to the centre. Within the prescribed boundaries of the heart of empire, and using its well-established iconography, New Zealand extended its borders to co-opt a version of London as Home. However, New Zealand's home in London was not always built on such conventional foundations. A more complex and contested version was produced during World War I.

HOME DURING WARTIME

At no time was a home in the metropolis needed more than during World War I. Over 1.3 million dominion troops were mobilised during the war: New Zealand's contribution numbered over 100,000. Although New Zealand's initial involvement was in the East, by early 1915 its centre of wartime operations had shifted from Egypt to Europe. The shock of Gallipoli was to pass into the unrelieved attrition of trench warfare on the Western Front, and this is where the majority of New Zealand troops would serve. Consequently, military infrastructure was concentrated around London. Military headquarters and hospitals were based there, and the main New Zealand camp, Sling, was just 74 miles away from London on the Salisbury Plains. This led to a singular cultural experience little considered in New Zealand, or metropolitan, histories: although soldiers' experiences overseas, notably at Gallipoli and in Egypt, have formed a strong strand of nationalist historiography, the more numerous experiences at Home have not. In one four-year period, tens of thousands of 'Bill Massey's tourists', most of whom had never been overseas before, roamed the high streets and back streets of their cultural capital. The scale and location of war meant that this Home would have to stand in for the other when soldiers had leave. 'Britain was the New Zealander's place of respite from the horrors of war, and as such it will always be remembered as a half-way Home, or as the undemonstrative New Zealander sometimes described it, "A Home away from Home".'[36]

The configuration of London as Home during wartime has two related elements. First, parts of London were physically transformed into New Zealand space to provide the infrastructure for New Zealand's occupation of London. Thousands of soldiers needed to be accommodated in the heart of empire: just one London club, the New Zealand Soldiers' Club, recorded 67,483 bed nights in 1918 alone.[37] But it also quickly became apparent that soldier-tourists needed more than just somewhere to stay. Some of the social and cultural controls of home also needed to be reinstated.

The military turned for assistance to volunteer organisations, at a time when volunteerism was gendered and closely associated with maternalism and domesticity.[38] As a result, 'Bill Massey's tourists' experienced London configured as a Home, and another element in New Zealand's continued cultural engagement with the metropolis was created.

Soldiers, of course, are a special kind of tourist, and the conjunction of the terms may seem to trivialise soldiers' war experiences. However, there is some evidence that travel may have been a motive for enlistment, particularly in the early stages of the war. In Australia, where conscription was never introduced, 'recruiting committees were not backward in advertising enlistment as a "Free Tour to Great Britain and Europe – the Chance of a Lifetime". Great enthusiasm was felt for seeing the Old World and many men felt that enlisting was worthwhile just to see Europe. A number of men had relatives in England and took the opportunity of visiting them and re-establishing family contacts. For some, it was a matter of visiting their own families and returning to their homeland.'[39] In New Zealand, motivations for volunteering for the war were complex, and grew more so as conscription was introduced.[40] But as in Australia, Defence officers in New Zealand claimed that most volunteers were motivated by 'adventure, travel, curiosity and the colonial love of a fight'.[41] These motivations undoubtedly changed in the light of growing casualty lists, yet it seems that travel remained, if not an incentive, then at least a bonus, of war service. In 1917, as the war ground on, and no one could possibly harbour illusions of a quick or easy victory, one Australian soldier wrote, 'Everybody is anxious to get to England and get things over, but we all thought it would be just as well to see as much of the world as possible.'[42]

First recruits expected to go to England, 'every loyal tourist's preferred goal'.[43] One New Zealand soldier wrote from on board ship on 25 November 1914, 'we are looking forward to a good Christmas Dinner in England'.[44] Australian soldiers felt the same. 'The first contingent had been expecting to go to Britain: the decision to offload them in Egypt was made at the last minute, to general disappointment.'[45] For soldiers who did make it to England, London was the principal destination. William Malcolm wrote to his brother, 'Well Andy, I scored my trip to London.'[46] Before being sent to France, soldiers encamped at Sling could expect draft leave, usually of four days. Most went directly to London; even those with relatives to visit elsewhere in the country (another important part of Home) could make rail connections through London that allowed them to see the sights. Leave, as Richard White has noted amongst Australian soldiers, was 'central, sacrosanct: the army was expected to accommodate the needs of the tourist'.[47] Captain Herbert King, part of the 2nd Otago Battalion, arrived in Sling on 30 October 1916, and was off to London promptly: 'Leave for Friday and Saturday was granted and everyone was taken to London.'[48] Realities of life in camp made London even more attractive, a 'perpetual call to the exile in training'.[49] The perpetual call led to perpetual leave extensions. On 13 November 1916, Captain King wrote, 'I had exactly 14 days in England but managed to spend 6 of those in London and saw a bit of the great city.'[50] Owen Clark 'reported to the Army Police in London whilst on leave and asked for an extension of three days as some of my leave had been spoiled by a touch of the flu'.[51] Some didn't even bother with an excuse. 'Came to London and had a roam around. Viewed inside St Paul's Cathedral. Very fine building. Due back in camp but overstayed a day or two.'[52]

Like other tourists, the soldiers brought an imagined London with them, and this may have made them feel more at home there than in other places they visited. A veteran of the Western Front wrote to his wife from hospital at Brockenhurst: 'I have had a good trip around France although I was not able to see much of the places however I called at Roura [Rouen?], Grouaville [?] and Le Havre and as nice as these places are there are none equal to Blighty.'[53] Part of feeling 'at home' was a function of race. Just being in London confirmed the privileged status of white New Zealanders within empire. Lord Meath might have envisaged a London that included the dependent colonies along with the dominions, but that vision was not apparent in the wartime metropolis. White and non-white troops had fundamentally different experiences of the capital. During wartime, white colonials became spectacles of empire too, but this enhanced the special status of the white dominions. White soldiers were treated as the archetypes of imperial manhood, 'irreproachably masculine', endorsing already existing beliefs that New Zealanders were of superior stock.[54]

As metropolitan citizens, perhaps even superior ones, they were relatively (in fact, given their actual behaviour, surprisingly) free from constraints while on leave in London. Wounded New Zealand soldiers, dressed in distinctive blue uniforms, were fêted, with special trips organised for them. One recalled an outing to the 'Eccentric Club' where they were 'placed at small tables seating four only – two "blue-boys" to a table and

Citizens of the metropolis: New Zealand soldiers and officers join civilians to watch a parade, possibly the Lord Mayor's procession. Photograph probably taken in November 1918 by Thomas Frederick Scales. G-14090-1/2, Royal New Zealand Returned and Services' Association Collection, Alexander Turnbull Library, Wellington, New Zealand.

something feminine opposite. The club members did all the waiting.'[55] The blue uniforms constituted a form of social control, intended to restrict some of the soldiers' activities – in particular, it prevented them entering public bars.[56] But non-white soldiers required greater restrictions, and in the metropolis they were monitored as racial anxieties usually reserved for the periphery were transferred to the centre. 'Indians were closely supervised on Western soil, and never more so than in Britain', with even wounded Indian soldiers restricted to the grounds of hospitals rather than being given leave.[57] These rules were clearly based on fears of miscegenation, and its attendant subversion of imperial order: 'If a rumour circulated that an Indian battalion was to be housed in a camp close to the residential quarters of British women munitions workers, protests were strenuous.'[58] So while New Zealand troops could roam the heart of empire, Indian soldiers were allowed only supervised access to the metropolis, in specially created Hindu or Moslem Cook's Tours that might include an hour's shopping.[59] As the guidebooks mentioned in Chapter One suggested, only some colonial soldiers could be truly at home in the heart of empire.

While race and its relation to empire was a confounding problem for the military during World War I, it was not the only one to be managed. War, by its very nature, upset conventional social relationships and the conventional social controls they enforced. In the New Zealand Main Body, 56 per cent of soldiers were under twenty-five years old, and 85 per cent were under thirty.[60] As one observed, 'to a soldier, city life is like champagne', and they took advantage of London's theatres, restaurants and bars.[61] This was particularly so for those soldiers on leave from the Front: 'Jack and I are on leave', wrote one soldier, 'and you can understand it is like fourteen days in Paradise after being over in France for 13 months, and I may tell you that we are living every hour of that 14 days.'[62] Dominion soldiers were 'described as strolling around London, hands in pockets, cigarettes in mouth, woman on arm', 'effective bachelors for the duration'.[63] Sex was, along with drunkenness and gambling, considered part of city life. The white archetypes thus had a darker side. But in their case, it was the metropolis and, in particular, metropolitan women rather than the soldiers who would be policed.[64] New Zealand troops were not 'gated' in London, unlike troops of the dependent empire. Instead, London would be made more homelike, and its unruly elements contained.

The construction of wartime London as Home for New Zealand soldiers, to counterbalance the darker side of the metropolis, was largely the work of two volunteer organisations. At the outbreak of war, the New Zealand Young Men's Christian Association (YMCA) already had a connection with the military, having been involved with territorial camps. The YMCA was 'an essentially peaceful organisation, concerned normally with the social welfare of the citizen; but here at one stroke the particular class of citizen with whom it had to deal, the young man in civilian life, had been called away en masse to the battlefield'.[65] After some initial resistance from the military, the YMCA became closely involved with all aspects of the soldiers' lives. The three points of the YMCA's red triangle representing 'mind, body and spirit' came to stand for 'troopship, training camp, and trench'.[66]

'Like fourteen days in Paradise': London leave. *Chronicles of the N.Z.E.F.*, 5, (54), p.125, Special Collections, University of Auckland Library.

In London the YMCA quickly focused its activities on entertainment and accommodation, ministering 'to the comfort and social welfare of the men'. Home was to meet physical needs and protect the soldiers' social and moral welfare.

The second organisation, the New Zealand War Contingent Association (NZWCA), was formed by the High Commissioner of the time, Sir Thomas Mackenzie, at a meeting on 14 August 1914 at the Westminster Palace Hotel in London. 'The Meeting was remarkably well attended, and most of the prominent New Zealanders in England at that time were represented.'[67] The list of attendees was a notable cross-section of New Zealand high society already happily resident 'at home'. Reflecting preconceptions about the nature of the war, the organisation's initial aims had a personalised character: 'their services would be required to assist New Zealand soldiers by providing them with comforts, visiting them in hospital, securing accommodation for convalescents after they had passed through hospitals so that

A home away from home: the YMCA Club on the Strand. The sign reads, 'You Cannot Spend Any Money Here. It is Your Home. Come Right In.' *The Triangle Trail*, No. 10, 8 June 1918, p.6.

they might be taken in hand and gradually brought back to health, also by keeping in touch with the soldiers and their relatives'.[68] Reflecting something of the genteel nature of the organisation, the first general meeting, at the end of 1915, also thanked Lord Ranfurly for his 'many kind gifts of game' to the Walton-on-Thames hospital.[69] However, the grim realities of Gallipoli, combined with military administration moving out of Egypt into London, expanded the role of the association considerably. By the middle of 1916, there were thousands of New Zealand casualties in England, and 'the condition of the early arrivals from Gallipoli (officers and men were in a truly terrible plight, possessing little, if any, clothing, and being unable to obtain authority to purchase kit) was deplorable. Someone had blundered in the Dominion in not anticipating the requirements of these men.'[70] The association began handing over its responsibilities regarding casualties to both the military and the New Zealand Red Cross, which remained an affiliated organisation. The focus of the NZWCA now turned to more general hospitality and comforts for men on leave and convalescents. The result was organised entertainment, clubs and canteens, and a 'home' in the metropolis.

Clubs became the physical location and manifestation of New Zealand's home in London. Seventy-nine clubs open to soldiers were listed in the *Overseas Club Map and Guide*, integrated into the iconic geography of central London. A number of these were defined by certain brands of soldier – Canadian, South African, officer, even 'colonial'. The YMCA's Shakespeare Hut and the New Zealand Soldiers' Club (the NZWCA's residential club) marked New Zealand soldiers' metropolitan presence. These venues were clustered around Russell Square, also the location of New Zealand's Military High Commission at 8 Southampton Row. Shakespeare Hut was in Keppel Street, on the corner of Russell Square, and the NZWCA residential club was there too, around the corner from its clubrooms in Southampton Row. They were handy to Simpson and Edwards, Colonial and Military Outfitters, at number 98 (for replacement New Zealand uniform buttons). It was a straight line from here to Aldwych and the Strand, where the High Commission was located, and the Australian YMCA hut, Aldwych (which was also popular with New Zealanders). When, after the armistice, the New Zealand YMCA required even more beds for men on leave, one hotel in Southampton Row was commandeered, another hotel one street further west in Torrington Place, and some more space in Little Russell Street. It was a New Zealand neighbourhood, located in the heart of empire: 'we caught a bus here to the NZ Pay offices in Southampton Row to draw some money: the NZ Association Rooms under Mrs Empson and Wray are just opposite so I looked in but they were out. Taxied to Peel House in Regency Street – not far from Westminster Abbey – to leave our luggage and book rooms.'[71]

Within this 'neighbourhood', soldiers would find clubs fashioned as homes. In one sense, this was implicit in their function, for the clubs provided meals and accommodation. But homeliness was also reflected in the nature of contemporary volunteer work. At the turn of the century, it was women's work; its emphasis on maternalism and domesticity leveraged women's private roles into the public sphere.[72] War created greater scope for this work and emphasised these values. New Zealand's soldiers' clubs were often staffed by New Zealand women, which increased the homelike atmosphere and acted as a reminder of family left behind in New Zealand.

New Zealand soldiers in a sightseeing tour outside Shakespeare Hut.
George S. Richardson Album, Album 413, p.30, Auckland Museum Library.

But these women were given a greater significance: like the soldiers, they too were created as archetypes. Cooking, cleaning and helping the soldiers, they were 'mothers' in the metropolis. Women at the New Zealand Soldiers' Club were, it was claimed, 'only too pleased to do anything they could for the boys in the mending and darning line. Lucky are we boys from New Zealand. We are fairly what I might term "carried about", we seem to have most of the good things going, in fact the club is, I have often heard it termed, a "regular home away from home".'[73] Clubs were presented then as familial places, with the comforts of home and its conventions too. Within the club setting, soldiers engaged in the world's bloodiest war became 'boys', to be looked after by women who were characterised as motherly. The YMCA referred to the Shakespeare Hut as 'The New Zealander's "Home Away from Home"', and the success of the NZWCA clubs was put down to the 'homely "atmosphere" caused by the presence of New Zealand ladies among the "boys"'.[74]

The club environment, where women were mothers and soldiers were innocent boys, was at once a return to an imagined familial home and a reconfiguration of metropolitan experience, with a didactic purpose. The maternal archetype was set against its obverse, the prostitute. The public and the military were anxious about the sexual behaviour of soldiers, a concern that was warranted given the high rates of venereal disease amongst troops, even if this concern was not matched by any realistic measures to prevent its spread. The New Zealand YMCA approached the problem of metropolitan temptation with a letter tucked into each of their *Blighty* guidebooks. Addressed 'Dear Friend', its avuncular tone occasionally slips into the slightly hysterical, revealing the great anxiety these organisations felt about soldiers loose in London. It also reveals that the soldiers themselves were not seen as responsible for their own behaviour. Instead, they are portrayed as victims both of the effects of life on the front, and the depredations of decidedly non-motherley, disreputable women in the metropolis:

> No doubt a portion of your leave will be spent in the Metropolis of Empire – London. In this city, a soldier, particularly a colonial soldier, is up against a set of conditions such as he has probably never faced before. Unfortunately London swarms with women, many of them hopelessly diseased, who live by trading what we have been taught to regard as woman's most sacred possession . . . . It is good advice to avoid these women, but difficult to follow when the matter has to be decided on the streets of London. Somehow or another, the reaction after life in France seems to render reason and self control ineffective . . .[75]

Although women of all classes were initially afflicted with what was termed 'khaki fever', in time the problem came to be associated with working-class women and prostitutes.[76] Philippa Levine has suggested that 'these sentiments struck a chord in the popular imagination, strengthening the opposition between moral innocence and depraved knowledge and perhaps hinting that the white settler required a little longer the protection of the mother country'.[77] The New Zealand High Commissioner, Sir Thomas Mackenzie, saw it differently. Britain needed to curb its predatory women. He urged the British government to segregate infected prostitutes to 'preserve our men', reconstructing the innocent and archetypal dominion soldier by relocating the blame within the metropolis. He paralleled prostitutes with enemy torpedoes, both submerged dangers: 'Germany depends on the submarine for victory; perhaps she is trusting to the submarine plus the evils wrought by diseased women for the realisation

A group of New Zealand War Contingent Association canteen workers.
I. W. Raymond, *New Zealanders in Mufti, 1914–18*, London, 1924, p.16.

of her hopes.'[78] The officer responsible for the New Zealand Division in Britain agreed: 'military men had to be protected "from the results of indulgence"'.[79] Having framed the problem as between the innocent boys and the evil sirens of the city, making a 'home' staffed with archetypes of womanhood becomes a more comprehensible, if not particularly useful, attempt at control. At Shakespeare Hut's canteen, which seated two hundred, the soldiers were 'waited on by the lady workers in their crushed-strawberry coloured frocks which helped to make the hut bright and attractive. These ladies, numbering 450 in all, are voluntary workers who do duty in different shifts for the whole 24 hours of the day. They have always got a word and a smile for the men, no matter how busy or hustled they may be.'[80] It 'should have been always a comfort to the mothers, wives and sisters of the soldiers to know that such an enticing home was provided in the midst of London, with its temptations and its great loneliness'.[81]

There is evidence to suggest that, amongst the official vilification of metropolitan women and the imposition of maternal archetypes, the soldiers themselves considered sex at Home quite differently from other overseas experiences. The New Zealanders' attitude towards prostitution in Egypt was infamously exposed in a riot started in a brothel in the Wazzir, Cairo's red-light district, officially said to have been caused by 'accumulated contempt for the Egyptians themselves'.[82] This is consistent with attitudes of later travellers through the East. One writer called Port Said 'an evil town', while in Nicholas Boyack's study of soldiers and prostitution in Egypt, France and London, racial distinctions were made.[83] One soldier, on arriving in Britain, wrote, 'most of us had got such a thorough sickening of the importunities of the filthy Arabs and Egyptians that it was a very welcome relief to find ourselves again in the company of nice girls'.[84] Nice girls in this context could still be prostitutes, or the more fluidly categorised 'amateurs'.[85] Some took on a domestic role, 'required to act as tourist guides, wash clothes, provide homely meals and offer companionship during a soldier's period of leave as well as looking after sexual needs'.[86] One such account was given by Stan Stanfield, who was in Brockenhurst hospital when the armistice was declared. On leave in London, he 'got drunk this day and two women picked me up. One was a war widow and the other one, I don't know what she was. I spent the afternoon and the night with them, you know; and these women, they just looked after me, one thing and another, saw that I got a good feed and put me on the train the next day ... I'm quite sure that I was picked up by London prostitutes for the mere company. A good-looking, clean-looking young soldier from New Zealand, good company.'[87] In contrast with the 'others' of Egypt, sex in this city is domesticated. Stanfield is even slow to identify his companions as prostitutes, preferring to couch his experiences in familial terms. He becomes an innocent abroad in the metropolis, where even prostitutes mother him, feed him, look after him and make sure he returns safely to where he came from.

This, of course, was not the sort of domesticity that volunteers were attempting to construct. Both the YMCA's International Hospitality League and the NZWCA had programmes to introduce New Zealand soldiers to the British, through dinner invitations and visits to private homes, and for longer home stays. The YMCA claimed that thousands of introductions of this type were made, although the NZWCA noted that guests could be in short supply, the main obstacle being 'the New Zealander's aversion to making appointments to go to a stranger's house at such and such a time. He is afflicted with a natural shyness and a certain unwillingness to tie himself down to times and places', a shyness apparently lacking at other times on the streets of London.[88] A YMCA publication, *The Triangle Trail*, 'reported' one of these experiences:

Speaking of home, my thoughts have been drawn nearer to the old folks by the little homely touch shown to me during the most pleasant part of my leave. I was invited to spend the afternoon at a lady's house together with half-a-dozen other chaps; and for a right royal welcome and enjoyable time, lead me to one of the hostesses of the Hospitality League. We hardly got seated when cigarettes, etc, were handed round. Under the influence of the soothing weed, comfortable chairs, a gracious and interested hostess, we were soon at our ease ... we all felt better for that little sympathetic home touch which drew out the best in us.[89]

Home is once again conjured up for the lonely soldier. The organisations' hopes for these programmes went beyond keeping these soldiers out of temptation's way. The YMCA considered they had 'set up a new bond between the overseas soldier and the people of the Home country'.[90] The *Chronicles* described these visits as 'the best sort of hospitality, and through it many friendships will spring up between old country folk, and us across the seas'.[91] Some of these visits revitalised family links, as New Zealand soldiers often used part of their leave to make connections with family and friends elsewhere in England. Reflecting the dual sense of propinquity in the New Zealand/metropolitan relationship, Gordon Harper wrote to his mother 'the likeness between you and Aunt Fanny is wonderful in all sorts of ways, so you can understand what a great thing it is to come across such beautiful associations with our whole life at the other end of the world'.[92] This was the sense of family and home that the volunteer organisations were working to create.

Similarly, soldiers' access to undesirable types of homes was actively proscribed. Both the YMCA and the NZWCA met the soldiers at train stations, to avoid 'the activities of well-dressed people who meet these trains and did their utmost to induce the men to accept the hospitality of those homes, mostly dens of iniquity, which had sprung up in London'.[93] The International Hospitality League, concerned that hospitality could be carried too far, organised street patrols, in action 'between 7pm and 2am'. One of a number of similar schemes, their work 'was of a delicate personal nature requiring the utmost tact to separate men from women of known disreputable character. Its success was so distinct that before long Great Britain, Canada, United States, Australia, and New Zealand were engaged in it.'[94] Once again, it was the unruly London with its 'disreputable' women

New Zealand International Hospitality League workers. *The Triangle Trail*, No. 15, 17 August 1918, p.4.

that was to be policed. New Zealand women were members of the patrol, complete with their own uniforms and armed with sticks for 'delicate' separation.

The creation of homely clubs and home visiting had its counterpart in the guidebook configuration of the metropolis as a familiar space. The New Zealand YMCA published both *The Soldier's Guide to the British Isles* and *Blighty* to make soldiers feel at home in the 'Old Country'. The *Soldier's Guide* made it clear: 'We know of no better means of maintaining the Bonds of Empire than for the "Children of Empire" to be familiar with the scenes and historic incidents of the great Motherland.'[95] Disreputable London was to be overlaid with the 'historic' motherland, and soldiers were once again transformed into the 'children of empire' (a transformation made acceptable in this instance because it was within the context of a white colonial guidebook). London was the principal sight, and the soldier had a duty to see it. 'Leave at last! How are you going to spend it? Have you seen London? If you have, go straight to Scotland, or Ireland, to Devon or to North Wales; or to any of the delightful beauty spots in Great Britain. If you have not seen the capital of the Empire, make the most of your first few days in seeing the chief places of interest, and then get away to your friends in the country or wherever they may be.'[96] There is a hint of the dangers lurking in London

Respectable London on show: YMCA Tour Party in Trafalgar Square.
The Triangle Trail, 16 February 1918, p.3.

in the booklet's urging for soldiers to see London, then move on to the rural 'beauty spots': both the *Soldier's Guide* and *Blighty* provided information on the key London sights, including a four-day sightseeing itinerary, and pictures of the Tower, St Paul's and Westminster Abbey.

But the volunteer organisations did not leave the important business of presenting 'familiar' London just to guidebooks. Like New Zealand House, they were interpreters and guides. The International Hospitality League opened booths all over London to provide information to soldiers, so they could 'obtain reliable information instead of appealing to strangers, who might or might not have been reliable'.[97] Both the NZWCA and the YMCA ran escorted tours from their clubrooms, using 'London gentlemen [who] acted as honorary guides and thousands of New Zealand soldiers were shown around at no cost to themselves'.[98] This was historic and respectable London on show, reinforcing that template of 'familiar' London: 'Four of us went with guide Mr Bernays M.A. to see London sights. We saw through Royal Exchange, Guildhall, (Library and Art Gallery attached), St Lawrence Jewry, Bow Church, Boy of Penger Alley, Paternoster Row,

Stationery Hall.'[99] Albert Newton recounted a similar experience to his family: 'Every day some men or ladies come here and take parties around to see the chief places of interest and pay all expenses as well. Already I have been to the Zoo, Parliament Houses, Westminster Abbey, the King's stables, Buckingham Palace, the Royal Academy and the waxworks besides the theatre three times. It is well we have someone to guide us about as otherwise we would spend half our time looking for these places.'[100] Such tours could be difficult to avoid: 'We were walking around when a YMCA manager seized hold of us and put a guide in charge of us.'[101]

Richard White has argued that the mass tourism of this era heralds the start of 'self conscious' cultural tourism, which led to those greater displays of cultural affinity amongst travellers in the 1920s and 1930s. War had meant the 'great cultural wall between those who could expect to travel and those who could not was breached for a time. One way for the travelling class to repair that breach was to turn travel after the Great War into an even more self consciously "cultural" experience.'[102] However, in mediating the soldiers' experience of 'cultural London' the organisations were also proscribing their access to disreputable London. For one soldier, proscription was the biggest part: 'We got a little book telling us about some of the things that we were going to encounter – in London in particular. You know – always to remember we have the honour of New Zealand to uphold. The main thing in London of course was prostitution .... Being a soldier in uniform, you were easy prey. And you couldn't go anywhere in London, anywhere at all at nighttime, without being accosted. And of course a lot of our chaps fell for it. Fortunately I didn't – that's not to say I wasn't accosted on many occasions.'[103] A crammed four-day itinerary of churches and museums was designed to keep the soldiers away from the temptations of the metropolis, although the greatest success of these tours may have been reinforcing the version of London existing in the peripheral imagination.

Although expressed through the conventional discourse of London as a centre of history and heritage, and charting the same tourist maps, New Zealand's wartime London was in fact built upon aspects that could have destabilised empire. It was a moment when New Zealand's conception of London as Home might have been upset. The iconic geography of monuments, the safe displacement of history and heritage, the privileged access to institutions and the careful hierarchical positioning of New Zealand within metropolitan displays of empire might not have been reinforced.

New Zealand's wartime experiences, for instance, are conventionally considered to have undermined imperial ties. The argument runs that New Zealand's disappointment in British military command, and the recognition that New Zealand soldiers had distinctive characteristics, provided a platform for an emerging sense of nationality. It seems, paradoxically, that the darker side of the wartime metropolis instead served to reinforce London's role as New Zealand's metropolis. Soldiers on leave brought 'familiar' London with them and, like other tourists, used it to chart a course through the city as a centre of heritage and history. Their presence led to this conventional form of London being reinforced, not only in situ, but, through the transmission of their experiences back to New Zealand in letters, postcards, photographs and stories, in the peripheral imagination as well. Some of their experiences fell outside the preferred 'familiar' pattern, yet this led to a greater emphasis by officials in creating London as Home.

Home was also created, in a less anxious form, in the activities of the New Zealand High Commission. Like participation in war, New Zealand House appears outwardly a national symbol; yet its role in the metropolis was not so simple. If London was New Zealand's metropolis too, then New Zealand House was the official point of entry, mediating the metropolis and providing privileged access to it. Like the travellers themselves, New Zealand House constituted the metropolis as imperial centre. But it also made the metropolis familiar, and homelike, playing its part in the imaginative appropriation of New Zealand's London.

CHAPTER THREE

A 'NEW' NEW ZEALAND

WHEN NEW ZEALANDERS travelled to London, they were making a journey back to the 'Old Country'. As journalist, writer and outstanding Anglophile Alan Mulgan reached England as part of his 'colonial's adventure', bad weather lifted, and suddenly, 'A door had been opened and England was before us – old, gracious, and lovely.'[1] Other writers evoked similar images of their first sightings of 'old' England. One selected an atmospheric stone village that 'fitted so exactly into the scene that it caused no surprise. It was just what I had expected to find in any watered corner of England.'[2] Wounded soldier Charles Spragg, waiting to be transferred out of a hospital in Greece in 1915, dreamed of 'dear old rural England'.[3] Mrs Leo Myers made her way to London in much more pleasant circumstances. As she travelled, she crossed fields that seemed to have been 'combed and brushed each morning for 1000 years; as if [they had] been washed and ironed by nature's rain and dew and sun every Monday morning for 1000 years'.[4] Mrs Myers' trip to England, like the others', was a journey through space and time, simultaneously covering a distance of 12,000 miles and going back in time a thousand years.

This trip back in time to the metropolis marks a neglected imperial journey, for it is usually the trip to the colony from the centre that has been associated with time travel. Colonies, it has been argued, were generally figured as backward places, for spatial distance from the centre could also be considered temporal difference, and both were used to maintain the distinction between the civilised metropolis and its not-so-civilised colonies.[5] Anne McClintock has described dependent colonies as 'anachronistic spaces', places thought to exist 'in a permanently anterior time within the modern empire', inhabited by people who are 'the living embodiment of the archaic "primitive"'.[6] Yet here was Mrs Myers, dweller in peripheral New Zealand, abroad in ancient England, steeped in a past that 'we moderns value only so much as it contributes to the present . . . our heritage of ages of which we are the complacent heirs'.[7] In this moment, colony and centre have changed symbolic positions: old New Zealand, the colonial periphery, has become home to the 'moderns', as England retreats into the past. At the same time, in a swift piece of cultural appropriation, Myers has become the 'inheritor' of that past.

Mrs Myers' inheritance forms another strand in the transformation of New Zealand's culture and identity that occurred around the end of the nineteenth century. These changes – characterised as 'something close to a collective identity crisis', and symbolised by the arrival of 'Better Britons' on London Bridge – may, in part, have been resolved through the formation of a new identity in conjunction with the metropole.[8] When New Zealand travellers traipsed through London's historic buildings to find their 'heritage', they were borrowing the past; when they were overwhelmed by London's traffic, they became part of its very modern present. Time joined space as a dimension of New Zealand's London, with the same effect. Just as London's space was an important factor in reconfiguring New Zealand as a modern member of empire, so too was its time. Past and present played different roles, explored in this and the following chapter, but both would be used to recreate the former colony as a 'new' New Zealand.

Finding the past in the metropolis rather than in New Zealand does not seem all that strange for a British settler colony, given its migrant origins and relatively recent settlement. However, this 'natural' feature of settler culture, like nostalgia for Home, was not merely a passive phenomenon. A borrowed metropolitan past replaced New Zealand's indigenous and colonial pasts, which, within the hierarchy of empire, could limit its own projection as modern. By the turn of the nineteenth century, there were signs that New Zealanders were ready to distance themselves from the old, colonial, version of New Zealand. One obvious sign was the change of the country's official title, from Colony of New Zealand to Dominion of New Zealand in 1907. Although this shift is now considered only of slight constitutional interest, its architect, Prime Minister Joseph Ward, had greater aspirations for it. Dominion status was supposed to signify the end of New Zealand's colonial existence and the unfortunate connotations of backwardness that went with it. Indeed, Ward claimed it was 'more important than the mere change of name that we should get out of the ruck of dependencies which call themselves colonies'.[9] New Zealand's new official status initially received a lukewarm reception from the public.[10] But the change it was meant to capture was broadly apparent in other ways. At a time of intensified contact with the metropolis, Maori were widely considered to be dying out, a useful fiction that persisted for some time after it ceased to have any basis in fact. In part this reflected the grafting of social Darwinian ideas over earlier race-based discourses, but these alone cannot account for the persistence of the myth, as it was matched by a surge of interest in another dying race, the pioneer. What Maori and pioneers shared was not race, but a role as markers of the old colonial past. In 'new' New Zealand, they were anachronisms.[11]

The desired passing of 'colonial' New Zealand was also captured in changing ways of writing about it. Non-fiction writing shifted from what Peter Gibbons has termed the 'literature of invasion' to a 'literature of occupation'. Books written for intending migrants or on Maori culture, for example, made New Zealand 'known', and were instrumental in the 'imposition and extension of European power'. This 'literature of invasion' was superseded by writing that worked instead to render '"native-born" colonists . . . as the indigenous people', like the first New Zealand histories or inventories of its flora and fauna.[12] These changes were followed by the demise of another creative celebration of anachronism, the literature of 'Maoriland'. Drawing on romanticised images of sublime landscape, myth and Maori, this strand of New Zealand created a fictional version of the 'occupation' impulse. It was a flourishing form of literature from the 1870s until at least World War I, surviving after that in what has been termed a 'pan-British literature'.[13] From the 1930s onwards, however, this first, self-conscious attempt at national literature 'occasioned embarrassment and contempt'.[14] It was quarantined by a group of writers later known as 'literary nationalists', who would form the backbone of New Zealand's literary

Time travelling in New Zealand: a 1930s tourist poster designed for the British market. Carl Thorwald Laugesen, Eph-E-TOURISM-1930s-08, Alexander Turnbull Library, Wellington, New Zealand.

canon, and who favoured a 'hard and sinewy' version of New Zealand over Maoriland's romantic myth-making and outdated English conventions.[15] Their literary quarantine was repeated in geography, as anachronistic space in 'new' New Zealand was reduced and re-zoned – for example the tourist resort 'Rotorua', with its wild geothermal landscape and contrived Maori villages. The tourist industry kept time travel available there and in a few select areas of sublime scenery like the West Coast of the South Island.

Borrowing the metropolitan past meant New Zealand could distance itself from its own colonial past, and this process went beyond the acquisition of history and heritage. Metropolitan industrialisation, urban decay and poverty could form the backward backdrop to settler colonial progress, one that threw the colony's sense of modernity into sharp relief. Angela Woollacott has argued that when Australians travelled to London at the turn of the nineteenth century and beyond, they were able to figure Australia as 'modern' by comparison. With imperial time running in reverse, London in effect became Antipodes and Australia could more confidently be projected as the modern nation.[16] Yet it was not simply the metropolitan past in its various forms that could make colonies such as Australia and New Zealand seem new. Modern London was appropriated along with the older version, part of a suite of cultural interrelationships that shaped both New Zealand and London. As a consequence of borrowing time, New Zealand was increasingly imaged as rural, 'new' and 'uncultured' space. The complements to these – urban, 'old' and 'cultured' space – were accessed via the metropole. This had a reciprocal effect. 'Old' England could be constructed, not just visited, by the colonies: England as garden was not solely produced by landscape artists and romantic poets; nor was the Great Wen only to be vivified by Dickens. These meanings were carefully calibrated. Even where New Zealand might choose to appear more modern than London – for example, colonials in London often complained about its antiquated and inadequate plumbing, claiming higher colonial standards in this and its associate, bathing – these meanings remained within the boundaries of reciprocity. Colonial brashness was quite subject-specific. For example, farming in New Zealand was modern and productive; in England, it was quaint. This reciprocal imagery did not always carry necessarily positive or negative associations. 'Old' England was home to both rural virtue and social ills; 'new' New Zealand might boast superior material living conditions yet lack the cultured nature of its Home.

When New Zealand borrowed metropolitan time, it inverted the imperial journey back in time. In the process, it also inverted the use of that journey's defining tropes. The metropolitan past is not simply analogous to British or English history. The 'old' metropole is feminised, atavistic and rural. At the same time, it is imagined as cultured and urban, industrialised and degenerating. The instability of these images is resolved by their place in time. For example, archetypal rural England exists as the past, in a form of essentialised Englishness that New Zealand can adopt as part of its heritage. Rural New Zealand, on the other hand, was a contemporary creation, formed in the present as the reciprocal image of modern London.

In a complex series of exchanges, New Zealand could be remade afresh, a 'new' haven for old rural virtues somehow lost to modern England.

However, 'new' New Zealand, product of shifting time zones, belongs to a distinct historical moment. New Zealand had, as a result of rapid colonisation, changed in character. Progressive social legislation, improved standards of living and growing urbanisation – the hallmarks of New Zealand's identity as social laboratory of the world – meant that, in many respects, 'new' New Zealand was actually modern. Conventionally, this has made these changes part of the narrative of national progress. But the timing and nature of that shifting character can be linked to important changes in metropolitan imagery. Contemporaneously with New Zealand's recolonial era, Britain was rearranging its own past for more optimal interpretation. The creation of an authentic location for English identity is theorised to be the product of anxiety over the linked processes of modernity and imperialism.[17] New Zealand's appropriation of metropolitan historic time was a reinforcement of this process, whilst at the same time it helped to construct New Zealand's own identity. New Zealand's imagery during this period is discontinuous; there are reversals and reworkings that are difficult to view as progressions. 'New' New Zealand grew younger, not older. The uncultured landscape, the empty land, the rural antidote to metropolitan urban ills and the 'modern' nation may well have had a peripheral existence. But here, 'new' New Zealand is a collaborative metropolitan creation.

MAKING 'NEW' NEW ZEALAND IN THE OLD COUNTRY

Mrs Myers, 'inheritor' of the metropolitan past, might also be considered one of its inventors. The retreat of England into the past was a process observed, owned and constructed by travellers such as her. They helped construct England as a place where the past could be safely located. It formed a metropolitan version of anachronistic space, one that, in this case, did not carry the same overtones of primitiveness as colonial pasts did. But it carried some of its markers. Home was old, its pastness – 'old, gracious, and lovely' – forming a striking feature of travellers' first impressions. It was also, like other anachronisms, feminine. The 'Old Country' was 'Mother England'; Mrs Myers conjured up 'Britannia'. When Alan Mulgan was asked about his first glimpses of England, he replied, 'you might as well ask a man what he thought of his wife'.[18] This is not quite as odd as it sounds, for gendered characteristics of the 'Old Country' were often extended into the family trope of empire. London was the 'mother city', a mythical homeland to which return was possible, even for those who had never left.[19] This mythical homeland was atavistic, in the sense that rural England was the ancestral home of essential Englishness. It was a cultural touchstone, a place where England could 'secure and locate its identity'.[20] There, just as with colonial time travel, you could experience the past in the present. For young Charles Brasch, who was later to become a significant literary figure in New Zealand, the countryside was 'densely populated, not by people so much as by what they have made over many settled centuries'.[21]

However, for all this ancient aura, the construction of 'dear old rural England' was actually a contemporary metropolitan phenomenon. The claims of the thatched cottage and tiny fields to represent an immanent, unchanging Englishness have been seen largely as the product of nineteenth-century anxieties over industrialisation, urbanisation and imperialism.[22] The essentialising of rural England, in particular the landscapes of the south, as the wellspring of an authentic British identity developed rapidly from the 1870s, when a 'flood of repetitive images of "a" rural England (in new versions and old – republished, reproduced, endlessly anthologised)' appeared. This flood washed away other competing rural scenes and other potential challengers to the idea of rural England as icon of national identity.[23] One of the most popular sources of this torrent was John Constable, a painter who predeceased his popularity by some decades.[24] His paintings of southern English countryside became 'beloved talismans of an English homeland', recruiting rural locales as national icons.[25] The old English cottage in *The Haywain* was claimed as 'the most typical thing in England': unlike noble mansions or modern houses, 'the old cottage prefers to nestle snugly in shady valleys. The trees grow closely about it in an intimate way.'[26]

Obviously England is constructed here as 'old', and at one with its surrounding nature. But Constable's England, with its cottages, mills and farm scenes, was, appropriately enough, also an example of the feminine picturesque. Alun Howkins has noted the development of this archetypal landscape, which shifted away from an earlier, romantic emphasis on Wordsworthian sublimity. Like Mrs Myers' combed and brushed hills, the picturesque created a rural England 'rolling and dotted with woodlands.

Merry Olde Nelson: English-like imagery in John Saxton Waring's panorama of the Nelson settlement in 1842, part of a collection of illustrations made to accompany Edward Jerningham Wakefield's *Adventure in New Zealand*. PUBL-0011-06-2, Alexander Turnbull Library, Wellington, New Zealand.

Its hills are smooth and bare, but never rocky or craggy.'[27] Constable's construction of an old and feminine rural England was complemented by its unmatched potential for atavism. *The Valley Farm*, a painting of an old stone cottage, had, by 1877, come to be an 'emblem of the sturdy English yeoman'.[28] Yeomen or indeed any rural workers were not common subjects for landscape artists, and if they did appear, it would be in an idealised form.[29] However, *The Valley Farm* featured in a book, *Home Life in England*, which proposed just this sort of yeomanry as ideal breeding stock for the colonies. Even Constable's style was perceived to reflect this essential Englishness: he was described by one turn-of-the century writer as having worked with 'John Bull conscientiousness' over the details of one painting.[30]

These images, and others, became what Elisabeth Helsinger has termed 'portable icons of England for those who have left home – urban dwellers with real or imagined rural origins, colonists and imperial administrators in South Africa or India, soldiers in the trenches of World War I'.[31] But these 'portable icons' of an imagined and essentialised England did not simply journey out to reform settler landscapes as models of Home. They made a round trip, tucked safely in the imaginations of white settler colonials travelling to the centre. New Zealanders found the essence of Englishness in thatched cottages and tidy fields just like actual metropolitan citizens, and in doing so, they furthered its reification. This is suggested in two ways. First, although metropolitan historians have noted the flood of rural

English imagery that gained volume from the 1870s, this did not include the waves of rural English-*like* imagery produced by British colonies in the preceding years. Merry old England, recreated, was a feature of New Zealand's emigration propaganda, whether in a bucolic panorama of settler Nelson in New Zealand Company publicity, or in a handbook encouraging settlers to New Zealand, the 'Britain of the South'.[32] Such characterisations provided the metropolis with another source of idealising images.

Second, white settler colonies grappling with being 'modern' had a greater investment in discovering the source of their own 'reconstructed ruralism with its yeoman hero' and locating themselves within it.[33] Certainly, visiting 'rural' England was an important part of any New Zealander's journey Home. William Malcolm, a soldier-tourist caught up by the Great War, arrived in the depths of winter. On the journey to the camp at Sling, he 'managed to see a good deal of England before dark. It is grand agricultural country, very closely farmed. Tiny paddocks and all farmed to perfection.' It was dark when he finally arrived at camp, but he was 'luckier than George who passed through it all in darkness'.[34] For another soldier, an afternoon in 'lovely England' turned a route march into '"a real treat"'.[35] Even without a route march, 'rural England' was an obligatory experience: 'I must arrange to get a turn away some Sunday to see the surrounding countryside. These English woods are very beautiful right now.'[36] For Australian travellers, like their New Zealand counterparts, the ideal landscape was English, specifically, the 'idealised images of gentle green fields and pretty family farms of pre-industrial England'.[37] Margaret Johnson, whose 'dreams came true' in London, felt the same. 'Today I set off to see England. London is fascinating . . . . But I really think that the English countryside, with its trees and birds and ridiculously neat fields and meadows, its churches and villages, lies nearer to my heart.'[38]

When the metropolis was figured as 'old', the colonies could appear 'new'. This took a variety of forms. With London and its landscape of monuments imagined as the centre of a shared 'British' heritage, New Zealanders could embrace the idea of their country as a 'new' land, unencumbered by the primitive past. Consider the self-description of traveller Ewen Allison, who asks us to 'Just fancy a raw New Zealander for the first time in Westminster Abbey with all its historical associations. I shall never forget the occasion.' Allison, the 'raw New Zealander', is detached from history, and so is his version of New Zealand: 'having come from a country which

Discovering 'old England':
two New Zealand World War I
soldiers outside a small church in
Burford, near Sling camp.
nla.pic-vn3314627, National
Library of Australia.

had little history but Maori tradition – a new country in the making – and to be in Poet's Corner . . . was wonder itself'. In this description, he separates the indigenous past from history proper, clearing the landscape of Maori history by containing it as tradition. Yet, reflecting the dual nature of settler colonialism, the same process can also be put to work in the 'old' metropolis. Allison is struck by the customs at the Tower of London because he is an 'Antipodean with no history behind me'. Here, it is the Tower's traditions that exist in that 'permanently anterior' time, appearing 'strange to the person from overseas who has been trained in the utilitarian, practical school which takes no account of precedent or custom'.[39] Allison's role as a 'new' New Zealander in this instance provides a touch of colonial superiority, as precedent and custom in heritage London are reminiscent of 'old world' social ills such as the class system, ills that are not to be found in modern New Zealand. In both cases, though, when confronted with London's history, Allison and his New Zealand are 'raw', 'new' and with 'no history'.

English charm: a rose-covered cottage door, photographed by a New Zealand tourist. O.032113, Harry Moult Album, Museum of New Zealand Te Papa Tongarewa.

The entangled imaging of Old World and 'new' periphery is especially obvious when the two rural worlds are compared. Alongside the auratic space of rural England, the New Zealand countryside seems immature and uncultured. Whilst travelling through the English countryside, one writer found 'plenty of authentically older places for a New Zealander – fresh from ephemeral residences of wood and corrugated iron, with no associations and no beauty – to be charmed with'.[40] In comparison with rural England's 'charm' and 'beauty', New Zealand appears masculine, with nothing soft or alluring in its wilderness. New Zealand as 'man's country' is often seen as a 'natural' consequence of the settler past, part of the pioneering myth of the frontier. Masculinity has also been at the heart of studies of New Zealand identity, exemplified in Sinclair's *A Destiny Apart: New Zealand's Search for National Identity*, where he describes a 'male oriented society' in which the 'centralist nationalist ideals were male'.[41] Yet the man's country may be as much an imperial invention as a local one, for New Zealand's relationship with the 'old' metropolis helped forge this image. McClintock

'Rural England is very beautiful': a tourist's photograph of an old English cottage.
O.032131, Harry Moult Album, Museum of New Zealand Te Papa Tongarewa.

argues that, as part of nationalist ideologies, time is gendered. Women are associated with the past, and men, 'by contrast, represent the progressive agent of national modernity'.[42] New Zealand as masculine nation, 'hard and sinewy', was a modern reaction to the romantic mistiness of Maoriland. Romance retreated into rural England, leaving New Zealand's landscape to be sparsely furnished with the raw pragmatism of 'baching'. In the ideal old English landscape, houses 'with centuries enfolding them like ivy, look like homes' and are 'part of the landscape's beauty', but in New Zealand, they lack 'charm'. 'The New Zealand farm-house too often looks like a hut.'[43]

'New' New Zealand was then, by its very nature, reimagined as uncultured, uninhabited space. One traveller wrote, 'I have often noticed how much less straggly are English towns than New Zealand ones – the houses group closely together, and the fields come right up to the town, instead of there being a no-man's land of scattered dwellings between town and country.'[44] Ngaio Marsh, on first seeing England 'close at hand' was struck by the difference: 'For a moment I remembered the West Coast of New Zealand as

I'd seen it one evening nearly three months ago: remote, bereft of humankind, so old and so lately born out of primordial time. It astonished me to see now how the South East Coast of England bore an almost unbroken chain of habitation.'[45] In the raw New Zealand landscape, there was no proper past to be found, no picturesque scenery. 'Rural England is very beautiful – far beyond what we in Australasia can show.'[46] Having stripped culture from one landscape, travellers indulged in the construction of culture in another. They made their imagined England not only symbolic but also productive. It was 'a new delightful experience for the overseas visitor to be a guest at an English Country home . . . the English man and woman in such an environment are at their best'. Despite its potential to be a home that would emulate English rural values, the 'new' landscape of New Zealand could not yet produce such a cultured experience: 'compared with them we of the Dominions are rough, unpolished, sometimes discourteous without meaning to be. We are the product of a newer country, the natural forces of which we and our fathers have been engaged in shaping and taming to our needs. We shall in time develop conditions making for culture and fullness of living.'[47] Time again was to be the solution.

'DARKEST LONDON'

The discovery of 'dear old rural England' was confirmation and complement to New Zealand's new and uncultured space. That newness would be given a more positive rendering by another discovery, this time of 'darkest London'. Reversing the imperial journey again, the dark sides of London's modernity were considered anachronisms, and figured in language usually reserved for the colonies themselves. In guidebooks, 'anxious connections were made between the empire and its capital, from William Booth's appropriation of the language of missionary exploration in his attempts to civilize the "darkest England" of the East End to concerns about London's environmental effects created by the physical condition of the troops in the Boer War'.[48] The dark side, like rural England, formed another aspect of the metropolis's pastness, and like rural England again, it was partly a colonial construction: 'The problems of urban life, its noise, poverty, pollution, and crowds, the size and gloominess of London, its industrial fog and murk, its packed streets, its square miles of slated hideousness, its foul slums – these have been emphasised to a colonial all his life.'[49] Within Britain itself, rural virtue was marshalled as counterbalance to images like these and the anxieties they elicited about the degenerative effects of urban life.[50] As we have seen, one product of this was the Constable country of the south. A less obvious byproduct was 'new' New Zealand, although in this instance, New Zealand would be an active participant in its own refashioning. As with other, more positive versions of the metropolis's past, such as its heritage and venerable history, darkest London allowed colony and centre to change symbolic positions. With London imagined as Antipodes, New Zealand could position itself as new, forming another counterbalance to the disturbing aspects of modern metropolis.[51]

An entry point into this idea is to consider New Zealand travellers' reactions to poverty, one of the most disturbing features of the metropolis. Against a background of 'square miles of slated hideousness', antipodean pride in social advances and the idea (if not reality) of New Zealand as a rural and thus socially, morally and physically healthy place were thrown into sharp relief. The contrast helped New Zealand forge what Lawrence Jones has characterised as the dominant cultural myths of the period, as 'Pastoral Paradise' and 'Just City'.[52] In London, touring journalist Forrestina Ross 'wonders what the little ragged beggar child, barefooted and hungry, must feel as she watches the pampered poodle on the carriage seat'.[53] She worries for the poor in midwinter, and is 'glad that in our newer, happier land such conditions are unknown'.[54] Similarly, Allison was 'surprised to see so many people begging in the streets of London. No one is allowed to beg in New Zealand.'[55] Such attitudes were also shared by Australians. They 'almost unanimously considered Britain to be historically lagging behind Australia, to be riddled with an anachronistic class structure and system of social deference many Australians found offensive'.[56] Here the centre is 'historically lagging' behind the colonies. Colonial advances were couched in social terms, whilst they remained the product of the natural environment: 'Real poverty, and therefore real class consciousness, could not exist in a country where the sun shone so brightly.'[57] New Zealand was 'a land of sunshine, and has the lowest death rate in the world', a shining opposite of darkest London.[58]

Signs of antipodean superiority in response to London's flaws can be seen as a platform for nationalism and self-definition. With 'darkest London' as backdrop, Australians, for example, could be defined as 'appropriate

The 'glorious open space' of London's parks. 'Hyde Park, London', Eric Lee-Johnson, O.007391, Museum of New Zealand Te Papa Tongarewa.

proprietors of the new nation rather than either metropolitan Britons or Australian Aborigines'.[59] Yet antipodean superiority was constructed in the metropolitan context. When compared with the real Antipodes, London needed to be dragged out of the past towards their future. Rutherford took his pastoralist's tour in 1912, noting 'London is fortunate in its parks which are extensive and well laid out . . . it is a pity so many . . . are disfigured by the recumbent city loafer. He is to be seen lying in the parks in hundreds, after the manner of his kind in past years in Sydney Domain. He has been removed from there, why not from here?'[60]

Underlining the contingent nature of identity, writers in the 1930s were not so quick to offer newer, sunnier lands as a solution, perhaps because their own experience of the Depression in New Zealand made them less confident that poverty could be consigned to the past as an 'old world' ill. When 'new' lands seemed to be historically lagging too, writers dealt with metropolitan poverty by simply turning away. Journalist Ian Donnelly actively sought out the 'dirt and danger' of the metropolis on his *Joyous Pilgrimage*. But there was no sunny southern solution offered: 'For a

Quaint English farming. O.032128, Harry Moult Album, Museum of New Zealand Te Papa Tongarewa.

stranger, unaccustomed to these frank and terrible avowals of poverty, there is an impulse to help such people. It is an easy business to make a beginning with charity of this kind, but here can be no end to it. One battered match-seller has no better claim to consideration than another. The simple solution is to ignore them all.'[61]

When metropolitan poverty is no longer a problem the colonies can solve, it must be de-emphasised. But in either case, imagery of the colony and the metropolis remained intertwined. Parks, metropolitan pockets of English rural virtue, were used as ways to ameliorate poverty and to lessen its effects. 'I had always read that London parks were beautiful; but their beauty has to be seen to be properly appreciated. No longer do I feel sorry for the poor children of London. Hungry and cold they may be at times; but no matter where they live they have near them a glorious open space.'[62] Mulgan relied on rural virtue too. At pains to correct any impressions of lingering Victorian industrialism, whilst at the same time sustaining them, he suggested that the visitor 'goes Home, therefore, perhaps prepared to find England crowded with factories almost to overflowing'; instead, he finds 'a vast garden with industrial towns here and there'.[63] He insists that these 'beautiful surroundings [are not] a substitute for an adequate wage and decent conditions', and they are not.[64] They are compensation for the visitor from 'new' lands. Like other later visitors, he minimises the issue: 'England's poverty is blight, but I must say that what I saw of the slums did not reach the depths of expectations.'[65]

The Just City and the Pastoral Paradise could also be produced by more trivial metropolitan experiences. In London, travellers complained about the weather ('simply damnable'), living conditions, and price and quality of food.[66] The metropolis was a marvel in many respects, but there were 'no tea-rooms equal to those in New Zealand'.[67] London aside, rural New Zealand was much more up-to-date than rural England. The 'travelling pastoralist' claimed British farming was 'what the prosaic call slovenly', and London wool stores 'are not for one moment to be compared with the wool stores of Australasia'.[68] Mulgan, man of letters not sheep, and thus tempted to be even-handed, was nevertheless struck by the inefficient and outmoded practices of shepherds and their crooks, whilst noting the progressive use of telephones by New Zealand farmers.[69] But rural superiority could be taken too far. He also recounted an unattributed account of 'the grandson of a colonial who, on being shown Westminster Abbey, exclaimed, "But you ought to see my father's woolshed".[70] The woolshed and the abbey is a cautionary tale: 'new' New Zealand's pastoral prowess might make English farming seem quaint, but it was comical in comparison to the capital's culture. Visiting Australians who tried the same thing, comparing Collins Street in Melbourne with London, were considered guilty of committing a 'definite *faux pas*', which 'seems to have disappeared' as a cultural practice particularly after World War I.[71]

THE MODERN METROPOLIS

New Zealand appropriated the metropolis's present as well as its past, and this too worked to make it seem 'new'. 'New' New Zealand was a product of synchronous time: when modern Mrs Myers left the ancient atmosphere of rural England, she arrived in London where 'strange thrills fly up and down our colonial backbones; something stiffens way up the spinal column, grips the brain, jingles the eyeballs, sharpens the ears, flexes the fingers,

London's 'maelstrom of traffic'. This picture comes from the *Auckland Weekly News* around the time of Mrs Myers' visit. *Auckland Weekly News*, 21 May 1908, AWNS-19080521-16-2, Sir George Grey Special Collections, Auckland Libraries,

tightens the muscles. It is the electric life of the greatest city on earth. It pulsates powerfully, it fastens and fascinates.'[72] In synch with the metropolis, New Zealanders would participate as modern, not peripheral citizens. One traveller noted, 'to walk or drive in the West End is thrilling but not awe-inspiring. A New Zealander, no matter how fresh from the tussocks, need have no fear that he will be overwhelmed with dismay at the vastness of London.'[73] But others were shocked by 'modern' London: 'Sometimes she frightens me with her noise, her appalling size, her never ceasing work and energy. After a day spent in the city she seems to get on your nerves, she tires you out, she is never still. You feel you want to get away from it all and yet – London calls you back.'[74]

London could be an exemplary modern centre: 'How things run so smoothly and efficiently amidst such congestion and inconvenience is amazing. It is just London! It could not happen elsewhere.'[75] Some writers enjoyed the dirt and danger, and were quick to display their mastery of modernity too. Allison took a 'little continental trip', but 'the call of London was in our veins. It felt good to return to the "Big Smoke" and to the roar of London's traffic.'[76] Myers headed out into the 'maelstrom of traffic', even though 'the ruralised New Zealander will shy at the wicked whizzing motors that whir in and out of the ceaseless stream of traffic'.[77] Her choice of words is apt, for in the urban centre New Zealand's rural character was emphasised. But it was 'ruralised' not only in the sense of playing country to the city: it was, once again, an uncultured space. In London, the urban mob becomes the model crowd, as the writers commented on the comparative lack of drunkenness and its good manners and behaviour. Crowds at King Edward's funeral procession displayed 'quiet restraint' and 'splendid orderliness', with the only display of bad manners from a 'foreigner', and it was 'suggested pityingly that she couldn't be expected to understand British courtesy'.[78] At Hendon Airshow, 'there did not seem to be a single ill-natured, disgruntled person in the crowd. Would that I could say that about a New Zealand gathering.... We have a long way to go before we are as courteous and good-natured as the people at Home.'[79] The rough diamonds from the colonies were not only so in relation to the essentialised Englishness of rural space, but in the heart of the modern metropolis as well. This too was a cultured landscape, the home of heritage. Part of that heritage was high culture, and an exploration of the reciprocal nature of this metropolitan relationship follows in Chapter Four. As such, there remains just a grain of truth in Ewen Allison's ingenuous observation that: 'In New Zealand we milk cows and make butter, at the same time producing beef, mutton, lamb, and wool. This is really our first consideration in life. Consequently, when I found in London that books were written and published, it was a business quite new and foreign to me.'[80]

FROM MAORILAND TO EMPTY LAND

The experiences of travellers in the centre sketch out a significant, but overlooked, shift in New Zealand's identity, one worth testing in some other facet of New Zealand culture. It happens that, despite Allison's claims to an uncultured existence, the self-fashioning of 'new' New Zealand can be demonstrated quite clearly within the history of New Zealand's literary culture, although this history has more regularly been used to chart New Zealand's disconnection from, not connection to, the metropolis. Yet the conventional histories of New Zealand literature offer only an equivocal guide to any growing sense of national identity, as the development of a 'New Zealand' literature fails to conform to what may be imagined as an incremental path to independence. Instead, a brief bloom of local turn-of-the-century literature 'petered out in frustration and indifference', and the establishment of a lasting local canon was, in histories at least, postponed until the 1930s.[81] To allow for this deviation in trajectory, Sinclair termed this early failure a 'variety of premature nationalism'.[82] But there are difficulties with this approach. First, the criteria for a sufficiently local literature are subjective cultural projections, often of an elite nature.[83] As an example, in 1936, in a speech at the first New Zealand Authors' Week, well-known writer Jane Mander, whose own work is hard to categorise using a progressive approach, picked 1934 as the beginning of 'what may in the future be called the New Zealand Renaissance. After G. B. Lancaster's *Pageant* . . . we had Mr Alan Mulgan's *Spur of the Morning* in 1934.'[84] Neither of her choices would be current critical favourites for the opening of a 'New Zealand Renaissance' today. Second, linear cultural progression is an unlikely concept, its nature obscuring and erasing outliers rather than explaining them.

These subjectivities have led to the critical dismissal of 'Maoriland' literature, an important part of that 'premature' literary bloom. Maoriland literature celebrates the archaic: it works as a literary form of anachronistic space. A recent study has traced its origins to 1872, and its end to around the beginning of World War I, although some of its thematic strands had longer literary life in New Zealand; it also survived as a form of colonial exotica in pan-British literature.[85] It has been considered as a 'first' national literature: however, as we have seen, those normally associated with that title, the writers of the 1930s, were hostile towards it.[86] Their construction of an 'authentic' New Zealand literature strongly rejected the mythic borrowings and scavengings that characterised Maoriland writing, especially elements lifted from what they considered outdated English literary conventions and from fanciful imaginings of a romantic Maori past. Maoriland writing was 'old': theirs would be 'new'. What follows is not a detailed critique of these genres, but an attempt to align their trajectories with the broader recolonial impacts of the metropolitan relationship.[87] It is an historical, not literary analysis, arguing that the timings of these literary shifts – the rise and fall of 'Maoriland', and its replacement by the 'empty land' of the later literary nationalists – are part of a more general shift away from old colonial New Zealand to its 'new' version. This is not just a traveller's tale, but a story played out in two outwardly 'local' literatures.

Maoriland on the margins: in this postcard from the 1910s, the romantic past, denoted by the Maori maiden, frames 'New' New Zealand – in this case, modern Christchurch – with its male figure and English architecture. A. J. Gudopp Collection, Eph-B-POSTCARD-Vol-2-17, Alexander Turnbull Library, Wellington, New Zealand.

In 1910, Edith Searle Grossman published *Heart of the Bush*. An example of Maoriland literature, it is set in New Zealand but, significantly, has London as antithesis. Essentially a romantic fiction, it follows the relationship of Dennis and Adelaide. Adelaide, although New Zealand-born, has spent several years living in London. Dennis, on the other hand, is ambiguously native-born, and is as closely identified with Maori as convention will allow. As a child he 'swam about with the agility of a fish or a North Island Maori'.[88] As an adult, 'her bridegroom was such a barbarian sometimes, and she felt as if he were literally bearing her straight out of the civilised sphere into his kingdom'.[89] The farm, 'Haeremai' (a Maori term for 'welcome'), is surrounded by sublime landscape, the third omnipresent character in the book. There are undiscovered valleys, an 'impenetrable jungle' of native bush, 'white peaks rising out of the mists and a wide river of turquoise rolling unsullied out of a glacier'.[90] As we should expect in this space, Adelaide imagines Maori fairies live in the woods, along with what Grossman terms a 'tohunga' (an adept or shaman): in fact he is something

'New' New Zealand: a contemporary freezing works set in a cleared landscape. Tokomaru Sheepfarmers' Freezing Company Ltd works, at Waima, Tokomaru Bay. 1/2-000272-G, Price Collection, Alexander Turnbull Library, Wellington, New Zealand.

like a white bush hermit.[91] Even an encounter with an ox is imaged as a 'taniwha' (a monstrous or mythic being).

Adelaide is enchanted by this landscape, and rejects metropolitan life (although she cannot quite let go of metropolitan high culture), symbolised in the book by her rejection of a 'cultured' suitor fresh from England and her preference for Dennis, a man of the land. Indeed, the land literally captures her: whilst on a honeymoon trip into the surrounding mountain ranges, Adelaide is swallowed up in a mountain chasm, only to be discovered by their dog, 'Tane' (the Maori forest deity). However, this Maoriland idyll is threatened by modernity, represented by Dennis's increasing interest in 'modern' farming. As Adelaide is captured by the bush, he is drawn into the modern world of business. He starts a district freezing works, and his time is spent less and less with Adelaide. The narrative condemns this choice – their baby dies, and their relationship is strained – then offers redemption. Dennis, when forced to choose between the modern world of the farming industry and a retreat into Maoriland, chooses the latter. He sells his shares, and the two withdraw back into the sublime landscape, 'the immortal childhood of nature [coming] back to the spirits of the two who were children and lovers together for life'. They go again into 'the upper valley of the Waoini and explored the hills around'.[92] Confirmation of their choice, the book ends with Adelaide pregnant, and Dennis reconciled to the loss of his wealth.

With the death of the freezing works dream and the impending birth of a child conceived in nature, *Heart of the Bush* claims an unambiguous victory for 'old New Zealand'. It is anachronistic space, a 'permanently anterior time', located in, and accessed through, a sublime landscape. As Adelaide's metropolitan suitor points out, there 'isn't a castle or an old cathedral, or even a thatched cottage in the whole colony'. However, it is not yet an 'empty landscape', for it remains populated by a primitive, if appropriated, totemism. Indeed, Adelaide replies to this that she is 'only a child of nature after all'.[93] This tale pitches the redemptive qualities of the anachronistic periphery against the dubious benefits of modernity, imaged in London, and in the local freezing works that helped sustain that metropolitan connection. It exhibits what Jane Stafford and Mark Williams have outlined as the main characteristics of Maoriland literature: its dependence on Maori sources, making it thus 'both fantastic and encyclopaedic', its use of sublime landscape and the difficulties of 'forging a relationship with that sublimity'. Finally, they characterise it as 'quintessentially Victorian', a meeting place between the archaic and a growing sense of colonial modernity. In this respect, it is a transitional literature, where it is suggested 'we might come to see Maoriland as having been part of the solution of being modern'.[94] However, if we view this literary form through the prism of the imperial hierarchy and the metropolitan relationship, it is more problem than solution. Maoriland prolonged New Zealand's existence in peripheral time. It continued to identify New Zealand with markers of the periphery, long after the New Zealander on the bridge had become a 'Briton'. Whilst *Heart of the Bush* neatly summarises the elements of the recolonial transition, it remains out of step with it, choosing anachronism over modernity. The periphery was to be memorialised, not revivified.

It may be that the keenest observers of this lingering anachronism were its successors, the 'literary nationalists' or 'Provincial' writers of the 1930s, who, as Lawrence Jones has observed, were engaged in creating 'anti-myths' about New Zealand and its 'community mental complex'.[95] Yet they also existed within this complex, for 'in the process of revolt they almost inevitably accepted the myth's categories of significance'.[96] This is evident in the literary nationalists' strong rejection of Maoriland and other later writing that shared some of its time-bound characteristics. Their judgements in some cases are undergoing a critical re-evaluation – for our purposes, however, it is the nature of their criticism, rather than its appropriateness, that matters. For in the Provincial rejection of Maoriland writing, we see the rejection of anachronism and confirmation of the construction of 'new' New Zealand already observed amongst travel writers. 'Old' New Zealand, banished by the Provincial writers, reappears as a place we are increasingly familiar with: raw, empty, uncultured, masculine New Zealand.

How fitting, then, that John Mulgan's novel, the archetypal Provincial fiction, should be titled *Man Alone*. Mulgan's hero Johnson, and the New Zealand he inhabits, stand in direct contrast to Grossman's world. Johnson's travels around New Zealand as an itinerant labourer reveal an uncultured landscape, of small towns, work camps and failing farms: 'Leaving the green Waikato . . . was like going out of a land of plenty into desert. On the scrub hills there was little grass and no life.'[97] Johnson cannot settle – there is no 'Haeremai' here – and the farms he works on barely function as homes. His illicit relationship with the wife of one of his employers, which leads to Johnson shooting the man, is a spectacular representation of the unravelling of one of these dysfunctional homes. Rua, the employer's Maori wife, is variously referred to as a 'bitch' and a 'half caste', undercutting any sense of indigeneity and belonging.[98] Indeed, it is suggested that she had 'advanced herself' by marrying the farmer, Stenning, a 'real white who worked and kept to himself', not a 'poor white . . . who would one day come back and live in the *pa* with them'.[99] Should any lingering thought of Maoriland romance or even older fragments of peripheral native exoticism have needed further demolition, Mulgan provides it with Johnson's assessment of his sexual relationship with Rua: 'It wasn't anything special.'[100] Johnson hides in the bush, but it is hardly the refuge of Adelaide's imagination. In the cold and wet Kaimanawa ranges and 'the dark loneliness of the bush', he almost starves.[101] Neither picturesque nor sublime, the bush is simply hostile and empty. The sullen land is mirrored by its inarticulate inhabitants: in this uncultured landscape, the characters barely speak. Even the cities lack culture. Again, in direct opposition to Grossman's formulation of the metropolis, it is New Zealand that suffers in comparison with

'A fragment of Piccadilly': Queen Street on a wet night around the time Mulgan's *Man Alone* saw it. Arthur Ninnis Breckon, DU436 1214 Q3 5A, Auckland Museum Library.

London. Johnson arrives in Auckland for the first time with a returning New Zealand soldier who remarks: 'It's not a bad little town – nor a bad little country. It looks small after London though don't it mate? It looks different to me now to what it did.'[102] As Johnson walks through empty, wet, city streets at night, he is drawn to 'an electric light sign of a kettle pouring tea [which] sat the bottom of the street, like a detached fragment of Piccadilly'.[103]

Although Mulgan's book frames wider issues of social criticism than this reading engages with, it nevertheless reveals its contribution to the construction of 'new' New Zealand, shared more generally with the Provincial writers. That Maoriland writing was an anachronism is clear in their criticisms of it as old-fashioned: 'The forms and values of colonial literature are, of course, Victorian, and in the past, Victorian literature was viewed through the lens of a disdainful modernism.'[104] This was as true of the form as of the material, for Provincial writers were more interested in English modernism than the Georgianism of their predecessors. Its backward-looking adoption of indigenous icons was scorned as the 'tui and treacle' school.[105] More notably, it, and later forms, were subject to extreme gendered criticism. Rua was not a lone example. Rex Fairburn derided the 'menstrual school of poets', whilst Eric McCormick specifically criticised Grossman's work as 'didactic, moralizing and melodramatic, all of them charges levelled more often at female writers than male ones'.[106] Having cleared the bush of Maori pixies, these writers were free to indulge in ideas of land as empty, uncultured, masculine space, again echoing its metropolitan construction. Effacement and erasure, a feature of Provincial writers, created most famously 'a land of settlers with never a soul at home'.[107] This was particularly so of Maori, who generally failed to feature in this writing, turning up occasionally as 'ghostly presences' or as 'a verbal equivalent of a Goldie painting'.[108] The empty landscape was indifferent and sometimes hostile, but this made it more clearly a masculine rather than primitive space, especially in comparison with England: 'The alienation of the New Zealander from the land . . . [was] partly a matter of the nature of the land itself, so isolated, so relatively unhumanised, not like England "smooth and rounded with the passing of unnumbered generations" (as John Mulgan put it).'[109] It was, like the farms Johnson works on, without 'charm'.

Provincial writers, having created a 'new' and uncultured land, were wary of too great a cultural dependence on Home. Yet they too would continue to access modernity and culture via the metropole, reifying the cultured/uncultured divide of their fictions within the cultural landscapes of New Zealand and London. The new literary movement's magazine *Phoenix*, first published in 1932, symbolised the shift away from Maoriland's anachronistic approach and its ambivalent incorporation within recolonial culture: the new literary scene was 'to be a high-culture oriented, Eurocentric, male-dominated movement, all of which qualities strongly influenced its cultural nationalism'.[110] Here was a New Zealand literature that, having banished the past, might exist in synchronous time with its metropolis.

Despite their resistance to Home, then, the writers of the 1930s were participants in a recolonial cultural project. They sustained, created and reflected the same 'new' New Zealand that travellers had discovered in the metropolis. The reciprocal imagery of 'Old Britain', with its rural, immanent Englishness, the dark heart of empire and the modern metropolis, helped form a raw, new, empty and uncultured land, that otherwise can seem a 'natural' product of colonial experiences. Yet the existence of a cultural form that imaged New Zealand as an archaic space in opposition to modernity demonstrates that newness was contingent, and, in this case, it was at least in part contingent on a metropolitan collaboration. 'New' New Zealand contained only a 'fragment of Piccadilly' – as the next chapter shows, the rest had to be borrowed.

CHAPTER FOUR

LONDON LITERATE

New Zealand Writers in London

IN 1928, EXPATRIATE writer Jane Mander published an article on her experiences in London. First-hand accounts of metropolitan life, society gossip and 'London letters' were common and popular content for local newspapers, joining formal news items as important threads drawing London into New Zealand's cultural landscape.[1] Mander had previously written on topics like London's new underground stations, summer weather in London's streets, nightclubs and new plays, her articles interweaving episodes of metropolitan life into the busy daily pages of provincial newspapers. She had even acted as tour guide, inviting readers to 'Come Round London with Me!'[2] But in this latest story, written for a British paper, she brought New Zealand and London together in a more interesting way. Called 'My Life in Two Worlds', Mander described her London life as a counterpoint to life in New Zealand. At a London orchestral performance, she recalled 'the Maori band, the bush workers' accordion, the magic of the first violin brought by an Englishman into our starved solitude'. In metropolitan streets, looking 'enviously upon some lovely old London house, I visualise a four-roomed shanty'. In London bookstores, and in the libraries of London friends, she remembered 'that funny little collection we put on the mantelpiece of the sitting room, when we had a sitting room . . . "Villette", "Wuthering Heights" and "Vanity Fair", Shakespeare, "The Pilgrims' Progress", and Cruden's "Concordance", Collier's "History of England" and a small life of "Alexander the Great"; two improving little books, "Line upon Line" and "Peep of the Day", a verse anthology from which my father use to recite Tennyson, Longfellow, Mrs Browning, Mrs Hemans, and Couper, in gift bindings'.[3]

Mander's story, crossing and recrossing between London and New Zealand, uses time and space to construct both places in familiar ways. London, with its bookstores and orchestral concerts, forms a cultured present. New Zealand, with its shanties and 'starved solitude', is the opposite, its backwardness imprinted clearly in the titles on the spines of texts ranged along the impoverished shelf of 'Victorian' books.[4] Some years later, Eric McCormick, New Zealand's first literary historian and critic, described two similar worlds. In the officially commissioned 1940 centennial survey into New Zealand's progress in 'arts and letters', he described a cultural life that overflowed national borders. It was spread across London and New Zealand, shaped into what McCormick called 'two hemispheres'.

This chapter examines London's impact on New Zealand through its high cultural life. In part it does so by mapping the ways in which New Zealand writers used London as their metropolis too, forming another instance of the imaginative expansion of New Zealand's cultural borders. It is perhaps the most obvious one: of all the attractions the metropolis held for New Zealanders, none was more self-evident than its role as the home of high culture. London was simultaneously the world's publishing centre, the heart and home of English literature, and the literary landscape of many of its best-known novels. Just as other travellers 'knew' and appropriated London, so too did aspiring New Zealand writers, for whom it had special resonance as the epicentre of a wider colonial writing world.[5] However, the relationship between New Zealand writers and the metropolis has usually been thought of as a bordered experience, with writers living between the 'two worlds' of New Zealand and London. Mander's 'two worlds' and McCormick's hemispheres seem to emphasise this divide. But both also express something different. Despite their obvious contrasts, Mander lived 'in', not 'between', two worlds. Likewise, McCormick's hemispheres are connected spaces, part of a whole. London was one of 'New Zealand's two hemispheres', the cultured metropolitan complement to what he called the 'native' hemisphere.[6]

For McCormick, this hemisphere was exemplified by H. Guthrie-Smith's *Tutira*, a natural history of a colonial farm. In its own way, Guthrie-Smith's careful record of the ecological changes on his farm illustrated the productive, if not always positive, tension between the endemic and the introduced.[7] But although *Tutira* was an outstanding book, the native hemisphere had 'disadvantages' for the production of literature. McCormick considered that it limited the potential of some writers, whose work was 'evidence of the lack in New Zealand of all but the minimum conditions necessary for the creation of literature'.[8] Those were to be found in New Zealand's other hemisphere, the metropolis, and its exemplary New Zealand product was Katherine Mansfield. In the cultured space of the metropolis, 'New Zealand's greatest writer found the conditions she needed for self-expression'.[9] It cannot be said that McCormick approved of this relegation of culture to the centre. He was as interested in locating an authentic national tradition as any other literary nationalist, and an official centennial publication seems a likely place for such sentiment to flourish. Critical of writing that merely mimicked English writing, and invested in the idea of 'adaptation', he insisted on the productive benefits of New Zealand's two hemispheres, not as separate entities but as a shared landscape. He claimed that 'the single ticket to England (as distinguished from the return passage) has proved itself the entrance to a blind alley'.[10]

As the nature of McCormick's hemispheres suggest, the way writers used London buttressed the idea of New Zealand as 'new'. I suggested earlier that the nationalist writers of the 1930s reflected and constructed 'new' New Zealand through their approach to writing. Here, we examine how writers would also construct it through their perceptions, experiences and use of London. Time remains the organising idea. Literary London's heritage and history made New Zealand 'uncultured' by comparison: the 'native hemisphere' is reminiscent of the backward, colonial periphery. Yet as we have seen, the terms 'new' and 'old' work reciprocally between metropolis and hinterland, and their meanings are not always positive or negative. Writers, like travellers, shifted their meanings. They also used London synchronously, as a place to live and work as writers. London's 'homeliness', the bane of literary nationalists and putative obstacle to cultural progress, facilitated the process. Familiarity with the metropolis and its literary culture made it easier to get by in the city. These writers were 'London literate'. It also may have helped them when they returned to New Zealand. London remained the acme of cultural success and, although writers may have been amongst the first to reject its cultural implications, they also understood that their familiarity with London could be converted into New Zealand capital. But although it was used in extraordinarily repetitive ways, the London connection was no guarantee of success. For many writers, life was harder and their work was less, in quantity and quality, than they would have liked it to be. The attractions of the metropolis were not necessarily equivalent to its rewards. Even so, in this historical, not literary analysis, New Zealand's relationship with London, if unequal, is symbiotic, and expatriatism is a productive, boundary-blurring activity. Yet even as boundaries blurred, their significance did not: the cultured space of London reinforced the uncultured space of 'new' New Zealand. There were two hemispheres, but McCormick's insight is correct: both were 'New Zealand hemispheres'.

TWO HEMISPHERES

It is perhaps no coincidence that Jane Mander named *Villette* as one of the books on her colonial bookshelf. Like Mander, *Villette*'s heroine went to London, proclaiming 'who but a coward would pass his whole life in hamlets and forever abandon his faculties to the eating rust of obscurity?'[11] Some years before Mander's article, a young Katherine Mansfield left her life in the 'hamlets' to discover the cultural capital. In 1903, aged fifteen, she wrote:

> I wish that I could give you an idea of London. It is totally beyond description. It is most marvellous!!! The traffic is so astounding. There is none other way to have a really splendid view, than to sit on top of a bus, with a piece of strong elastic on your hat; Then it is superb . . . . My dear, I wish that you could see Westminster Abbey. It is so lovely!! It is utterly impossible to rush the Abbey, because immediately you enter you are held enthralled by some marvellous work of sculpture, and so it is the whole time you are there . . . . We went to St Paul's Cathedral last Good Friday . . . . The building of St Paul's is fine but I don't like all the pigeons

that are constantly flying about.... How interested you would be in the British Museum. My dear, you could see enough Julius Caesars to last you a lifetime. With noses, and minus noses, according to B.C. and A.D. .... On Bank Holiday Father & I did the correct thing & went to 'Appy 'Ampstead Heath. When we arrived there it grew most fearfully cold, and we had a bad snowstorm. I loved it. The whole place looked like a picture postcard. A place I <u>am very</u> fond of going is Hyde Park. The carriages, horses, and babies are most lovely, especially the last named .... The motor cars are very fascinating. You see hundreds dodging about everywhere.[12]

Mansfield's impressions are a notable fusion of the attractions of the cultural hemisphere. At one level, she provides a route map through the iconic landscape of 'familiar London' – St Paul's, Westminster Abbey, Hyde Park and the British Museum. Between them they create a sort of 'best of British' heritage park, marking the most important elements of culture to be appropriated: religion, history, knowledge and examples of the civilised 'British' way of life. Indeed, they have already been appropriated on the periphery: she goes to Hampstead Heath and finds it looking 'like a picture postcard', while real flying pigeons at St Paul's are a contrast to those rendered motionless in postcards and pictures, and disrupt her expectations. However, other parts of London in motion are in keeping with its role as 'most marvellous' metropolis: the 'astounding traffic', the holiday crowds on Hampstead Heath, the 'fascinating' motor cars. On return to the capital of the native hemisphere, Wellington, she would write: 'Isn't it terrible to love anything so much. I do not care at all for men but London – it is life.'[13] Wellington itself was renamed 'Philistea', and she began to plot her escape from it.

Many other writers were also planning their escape. Although a stronger local literary culture would develop in interwar New Zealand, the grip of the cultural hemisphere was also strengthening. As the identity of 'new' New Zealand developed, culture was increasingly seen as a metropolitan attribute. The metropolis held a cultured form of the 'past', and it was the home of modern cultural forms. Writers were attracted to, and appropriated, both, using the capital's present while continuing the process of incorporating London as the home of a proper past. Literary nationalist Rex Fairburn's first impressions illustrate the latter. Upon arriving in

'Appy 'Ampstead Heath, photographed by Herbert Green in 1919.
O.031995, Museum of New Zealand Te Papa Tongarewa.

London, he wrote to fellow writer R. A. K. Mason, that 'I feel as if I were in a dream. I don't know how the legend of London's ugliness sprung up. It's a *lovely* old place – my breath is taken away a hundred times a day by its sheer beauty.'¹⁴ London here is old, lovely and legendary, conforming to the precept of anachronistic space as old, feminine and atavistic. Charles Brasch, arriving a few years earlier in 1927, found the cultured past in a small cloister at Westminster Abbey: 'It was pure London, plane tree and fountain humanised its cloistral reserve, it wore anonymity which set it outside particular ages and customs, freeing it for anybody to consider his own. There was my first foothold and point of rest, in England, in the old world.'¹⁵ Here the old world is permanently anterior, 'outside particular ages and customs'. It is also free for colonial appropriation. Frank Sargeson referred to this as the 'first stage of London – simply gaping'.¹⁶

That writers expected to find the past is another indication of London's imaginative presence in New Zealand. Ngaio Marsh, destined to become an internationally successful writer of mysteries and a serial expatriate, arrived in London in 1928:

My childhood dream of London is in some ways clearer in my memory than the events of that first morning: they, indeed, have a dreamlike, wavering quality.... I remember being told to look up out of the car window and there was the dome of St Paul's.
Up the hill to Ludgate
Down the hill of Fleet.
I thought, and the words jingled confusedly in my head. As if in answer there were bells, high in the air, clanging away above the roar of London
'That's St Clement's Dane.'....
'We'll have breakfast somewhere. There's a new place in Piccadilly we might try.'
The smell of the West End in the early morning. Hot bread. Coffee. Freshly watered pavements. Hairdressing parlours.... Eggs and bacon are ordered and then we are driving up a beautiful wide street.
'Do you know what that is?'
'Buckingham Palace?'
But it flashes up and is gone and so is the whole of the journey into Buckinghamshire.[17]

Marsh's London has been inculcated from childhood: she incorporates lines from Walter de la Mare's poetry collection for children, *Peacock Pie*, regularly reprinted after its first edition in 1913. Underlining 'familiar' London's presence, Marsh's childhood dream of London is in 'some ways clearer in [her] memory' than the actual first experience of it. However, like Mansfield, Marsh's London has two dimensions. She intersperses old London, imaged by St Paul's and the landmarks known through childhood nursery rhymes, with the 'roar' of the modern metropolis. This dual rendering of London as past and present is also maintained by what is omitted from their recollections. Marsh's sharp recall of the West End, its sounds, sights and smells, contrasts with her vagueness about the East End: 'of the long drive through the East End into the City I remember little except, again, names. "Limehouse" and "Poplar" for instance, in those days evoked wonderfully sinister references to opium dens, gas lamps wreathed in fog, and wet stone stairs. The Commercial road looked drab, broad, and bald on that bright summer morning and held no romantic overtones.'[18] Charles Brasch also edits his first glimpses to reify New Zealand's cultural capital: 'Dora and Esmond took Lel and me for our first view of London. We walked

'A foothold in the old world': entrance to the cloisters at Westminster Abbey.
O.032063, Harry Moult Album, Museum of New Zealand Te Papa Tongarewa.

in the damp mild grey air through Trafalgar Square, down Whitehall, into Westminster Abbey; then through Westminster School, past the Houses of Parliament, and back across St James's Park.... Much of this was half familiar, from photographs, but the reality was totally different. My response, I think, was too breathless, too greedy, to be more than naïve.'[19]

London's 'pastness', however, was not always so romantic. Like other travellers, writers edited the landscape to reduce its undesirable anachronistic elements and enhance its cultural status. In one of many radio talks Jane Mander made after her return to New Zealand (usually on the self-consciously high cultural 1YA network), she advised listeners 'you will be sorry to know that the nice old-fashioned organ grinder has almost disappeared from the London streets. He may still linger with the poor in the East End for all I know.'[20] In this instance, East End streets do not belong in London proper; like the outdated organ grinder, they belong to another world, one closer to the four-roomed shanties and bush bands of the native hemisphere than the metropolis. Likewise, she claimed to have no

knowledge of London's vast suburbs: 'Now, I suppose a greater number of the business girls who are seen in the City and West End sections of London during the day come from the enormous suburbs, that is the towns that lie on the fringes of London . . . . I have travelled sometimes with thousands of these girls in the evening rush hours and have wondered what sort of homes they went back to and what they did with their evening.'[21] Listeners could only continue to wonder with her, as Mander's radio shows preferred exploring the cultured metropolis to venturing out to the suburbs. Her audiences would learn instead about London's parks (she listed twenty-seven in a row), the 'Feeling for Beauty in England', literary London, the Temple, Hampstead and Chelsea. Cultured London was even conjured up for children, in a talk about the statue of Peter Pan in Kensington Gardens.[22] Nor was Mander the only author to shape the metropolis in this way. Marsh wrote articles about Piccadilly and various 'vignettes of London', while Rex Fairburn's selections included 'Merrie England', 'English Villages' and 'London Fatalism'. In this last article, traces of undesirable 'old' England appear, as Fairburn describes living conditions in Depression-era London, where people 'are destined to live for the term of their natural lives in a condition which would drive the average New Zealander to drink or suicide within the week'. But this picture of metropolitan poverty is redeemed by history: 'I may appear to have painted a desperate picture of London under the blight of unemployment. But in spite of the misery that exists, there is nothing like despair in the minds of the people. London still stands on the Thames; and underneath the depressing appearance of things there is still a rock-like solidity.'[23]

'Philistea', on the other hand, was not created simply through the absence of high culture, but by the lack of 'sympathetic and stimulating surroundings', which might be found instead in the metropolis.[24] Indeed, the chances of such surroundings developing in New Zealand seemed to have decreased in the first part of the twentieth century. Belich has described changes in social attitudes in New Zealand during the interwar years as the 'Great Tightening', a period of increasing pressure for conformity within a narrower range of social attitudes. Within literary culture, Jones identifies New Zealand's 'own particular variety of Puritanism' as one of the

The 'real' St James's Park, photographed by New Zealand visitor Harry Moult in the 1920s. O.032083, Museum of New Zealand Te Papa Tongarewa.

'anti-myths' writers existed within and worked against.[25] Expatriation was one form of liberation from it; when we consider the experience of soldiers in the capital, perhaps London's role as antidote to puritanism deserves greater emphasis. From the vantage point of the metropolis, New Zealand seemed narrower and London's cultural sophistication greater. The modern metropolis offered all kinds of freedoms: 'You can look anyway you want in this comfortable town';[26] and Mander claimed that the 'mental horizons here are immeasurably wider then they are in New Zealand or Australia'. In suggesting London has wider mental horizons, she seems to acknowledge puritanism's influence, defending England from 'people from the Dominions' who 'come Home and pick holes in this and that'.[27]

Fairburn's anti-puritan epiphany is clearly the result of arriving in London: 'My God, I've changed my notions since I landed over this way! What a flaming innocent I were!'[28] He thought New Zealand looked 'a bit tawdry and fusty and nonconformist [puritan] from a distance', compared with a place where 'it is unnecessary to begin a discussion on James Joyce by determining whether or not he is pornographic. Intelligent people raise their eyebrows and gape blandly if you come out with irrelevancies of that sort.'[29] He openly embraced the metropolis's sexual freedom, particularly through his friendship with Geoffrey de Montalk who 'further reduced the pangs of idealised love by acquainting him with women who insisted on realized loving'.[30] He in turn recommended the life to Clifton Firth: 'oh hell, England's the only place for a chap like you.... The freedom here is wonderful. You can talk to the women about homosexuality, and fucking (by that name).... without a trace of self consciousness.'[31] Frank Sargeson took the opportunity to go beyond talk about homosexuality, and 'in London he discovered what had previously been closed to him elsewhere; doorways into a private world of homosexual culture and activity'.[32] Eric McCormick hoped to do the same, but returned with 'the girdle of chastity... dented but... still unbreached'.[33] Fairburn was later famously antagonistic towards homosexuality, yet its comparative visibility in London served to prove how fusty New Zealand was: 'God, they're a sophisticated lot over this side of the water. Every literary and artistic club is a hotbed of perversion, not merely homosexuality, but the most luscious variations on the theme. At the same time it is impossible to be depressed by it. Life here is so different from Auckland. There is none of that seriousness and sombre Puritanism.'[34]

A young Edith Searle Grossman, later a participant in New Zealand's London-based literary world. Macmillan Brown Library, University of Canterbury, no. 13450.

London as liberation from puritan attitudes was just as important for women. For Katherine Mansfield, the 'impulse to escape the provincialism of New Zealand and the bourgeois values of her parents was as significant as her need for sexual expression'.[35] Along with a greater degree of sexual freedom, London seems to have provided a common escape route from puritanism's emphasis on family and domesticity. Louisa Baker and Edith Searle Grossman both managed to leave their husbands behind when they moved to London, whilst Bridget Griffen-Foley, writing about Australian expatriate journalists, notes that 'other Australian journalists, particularly women, were escaping from or delaying marriage', citing Louise Mack as an example.[36] All Mander's novels were written in London: on her return home, 'Jane's own artistic struggle was bogged down by domestic and family interference. The energy she poured out in assisting others meant her store was depleted. By the end of 1933 she still had not managed to complete any new work which she could regard as "serious".'[37] The strictures of family life may well be a sympton of the age difference between men and women writers travelling to London: women were generally older, usually in their thirties, while the men were in their twenties.[38]

Having escaped the puritan confines of the 'native hemisphere', writers quickly joined the vibrant metropolitan cultural milieu. They published books, took tea with Walter de la Mare, met artist Jacob Epstein (everyone met Jacob Epstein!) and one even played the piano for Edward Elgar using his nose.[39] There might be some cringe here (although apparently Elgar enjoyed it), but it is not cultural cringe, for the New Zealanders often actively sought out these encounters. George Bernard Shaw and G. K. Chesterton, whose profile would have been enhanced through his regular column in the *Illustrated London News* between 1905 and 1936, are, like Epstein, regularly name-checked in biographies of New Zealand writers. Sargeson sought them both out in London: 'I was off very smartly to any place where such as Bertrand Russell or Bernard Shaw would speak ... not to mention places where I could listen to G. K. Chesterton and Hilaire Belloc.'[40] Sargeson literally ran into Chesterton once and Shaw twice, on one occasion in Italy. Alongside the past, writers appropriated London's present. Novelist and biographer Hector Bolitho –

> ... walked along the Embankment to Battersea Bridge .... We returned along the river bank and I noticed three exciting protests that London makes against its morbid light: the red of the 'buses, the red of the pillar boxes, and the red coats of the Chelsea pensioners .... I ate my first English tea, with scones and honey, at the Blue Cockatoo .... Later in the evening we drove from Chelsea to Piccadilly .... We dined at the Café Royal, amid the old gilt and red velvet that have since disappeared. Angus pointed discreetly across the room and said, 'There's Augustus John' then, 'That's Jacob Epstein.' I watched the great men, smelled the port in my glass and had no complaint against the world.[41]

However, writers could also be overwhelmed by the cultural centre. Bolitho felt 'intellectually afraid' of D. H. Lawrence, Sargeson was 'too shy' to speak to George Bernard Shaw in Stresa, and Fairburn recognised his 'flaming' innocence, underlining a sense of inadequacy they felt in the world in which they found themselves. On Brasch's first evening in London he went to dinner at a house near where 'Coleridge had pressed Keats' hand

and felt death in it. The talk after dinner turned to Picasso and modern art; most of it was over my head, but it would not be so for long; that was the world I was seeking; I recognised it at once, but did not know how unready for it I was.'[42]

The two hemispheres were not always delineated in London's favour. Fairburn was frequently critical of metropolitan life – it hardly treated him well – but these criticisms still reveal the different construction of the two hemispheres. He claimed 'no sympathy' with the cultured English landscape, preferring a 'smelly tidal New Zealand creek'.[43] However, when he toyed with the idea of returning to New Zealand, going to 'a really dirty, tough hole like Taumarunui', it was 'the people [he was] afraid of'.[44] A distinction between cultured and uncultured remained.

'LONDON LITERATE'

The native and the metropolitan hemispheres may have been different, but the gap between them should not be overstated. London, even if overwhelming, was still a New Zealand hemisphere, and it could be viewed as a useful and productive extension of New Zealand's literary landscape. As a recent study has suggested, New Zealand's connections to a wider colonial writing world meant that even those who didn't leave New Zealand could use London in this way.[45] But Jane Mander did leave, and when she went to journalism school in America in 1912, she carried the manuscript of a book with her. 'I never mentioned my novel, but I suggested I come to London first, as it seemed a kind of treason not to.'[46] She had in mind, I think, two kinds of treason. The first would have been not going to London before travelling on to her journalism studies in America; the second would have been passing up the opportunity to get her book published there. Even when writers didn't pack a manuscript along with them, their major objective in London was to write and be published. Fairburn wrote a novel whilst in Wiltshire. Bolitho carried one with him. Sargeson worked away on one after his walking tour. Marsh wrote her first detective story. Even though Mander could be pessimistic about 'colonial' possibilities in the metropolis, she did not rule out colonial success: 'it takes us longer of course to get the best publishers . . . when you are depressed remember that Conrad and H. H. Richardson had to wait for 20 years'.[47]

For London remained the cultural acme. Nothing could beat the imprint of a London publishing house for an aspiring writer. 'The mass of people who read novels can never know, and old novelists may merely remember, the ecstasy that a young author enjoys when his first book is published in London', claimed Hector Bolitho.[48] Should this be seen as a reflection of his particular Anglophilia, it also appears to be true of Australian Henry Lawson, who 'berated "the mighty Paternoster Row Machine" for eschewing true Australian literary talent ... [but] was contented to have Methuen produce his *Children of the Bush* in colonial edition form after visiting London between 1900 and 1902'.[49] The imprint itself mattered, and not just to the writer, but also to the reading public: in Australia, 'the British imprint on a book ... added to its authority, popularity, and sales'.[50] Edith Lyttleton put up with 'devious' dealings in order to maintain her relationship with the 'prestigious' imprints of the Century Company and Allen & Unwin.[51]

As a result, numerous writers arrived in London with little but their ambitions and their pens. Fairburn borrowed £50 from his aunt for boat fare; Bolitho arrived in London 'solvent', but not much more than that. Sargeson, on the other hand, was comparatively well off, with over £200 from the sale of a section in Hamilton, after paying £40 for his fare.[52] However, he did not expect to work in London. Mander received a small allowance from her father that 'did mean she was able to have a roof over her head and some food on the table'.[53] Marsh was also partly supported by her father – he paid her boat fare – but she had saved money from her painting and newspaper articles.[54] In addition, she lived for some time with a well-connected English family, the Rhodes, whom she had come to know when they lived in Christchurch. Iris Wilkinson (Robin Hyde) came with £150, and 'when she was almost penniless, Sir William Jordan, the New Zealand High Commissioner in London ... advanced her a timely £5'.[55] But London did not guarantee success. Mander complained, 'For nearly a year now I have been listening to pathetic stories of the destitution and heart-breaking struggles of overseas artists who come to make their way in London. "For God's sake," said an English artist to me the other night, "do what you can to stop them coming unless they have money".'[56]

Although Mander wrote despairingly of the natural advantages of English writers, 'born with technique in their pens. They inherit it', she may have overstated the case in suggesting 'we overseas people do not and

A colonial network: Ngaio Marsh on holiday in Kent with the Rhodes and Plunket families. PAColl-9232-08, Margaret Lewis Collection, Alexander Turnbull Library, Wellington, New Zealand.

nothing in our youth helps us'.[57] English literary traditions were strong in New Zealand, evidenced in later criticism of 'Georgian' poets and, more generally, in the reading habits of New Zealanders. They were steeped in British literature, in all its forms. Newspapers ran serialised fiction, bought from the same British syndicates that supplied British provincial papers.[58] Public libraries flourished from New Zealand's earliest settlement, and by the end of the nineteenth century the country had the highest density of libraries per head in the world.[59] For commercial as much as for cultural reasons (notably the advent of the colonial edition, a special cheap edition of a metropolitan book that was made available in the colonies), it is likely their catalogues were dominated by British literature.[60] A private lending library at a Wairarapa farm had just 140 American authors in its two-thousand-strong collection of titles.[61] No wonder a Gallipoli veteran arriving in England claimed that 'everything English bears the same air of familiarity due beyond question to the thoroughness with which her life is portrayed in her novels'.[62] These arrived in New Zealand in great quantities: employing a suitably recolonial metaphor, the London managers of

Gordon and Gotch remarked in 1906 'that literature in the colonies is sold very much like butter – by weight'.⁶³ Writers had more up-to-date links in the form of London magazines. The Auckland Public Library carried plenty of them including, *Punch, The Illustrated London News, The Spectator, The Strand, The Windsor, Harpers, London Times, Blackwoods, Athenæum* and *The Times Literary Supplement*.⁶⁴ We can safely presume that the writers who took themselves to London had grown up reading them. Marsh recalled finding a stash of them one wet day: 'they were of two kinds. *The Windsor* . . . and *The Strand* . . . . All day I hunted and devoured, tracing the enchanting series from one edition to the next. The rain beat down, not on the windows of a New Zealand house but across those of a gas-lit upstairs room in a London street.'⁶⁵

This background, combined with New Zealand writers' literary and metropolitan aspirations, meant that they could speak something of the language of the cultural capital before they arrived there. It made them 'London literate'. Two other factors assisted New Zealand writers in London: their own New Zealand-based literary networks, and the connection between these and London-based versions. The small society of New Zealanders became even smaller if you were interested in cultural matters. Connections between New Zealanders were easy to make, both at home and in London, and these provided all kinds of support in the struggle to make a living. Work could be drummed up on each other's behalf, publishing contacts passed on, living quarters shared. Fairburn asked Mason to help him sell articles to the New Zealand press; de Montalk introduced Fairburn to Charles Lahr, whose Blue Moon Press would print his poems. Lahr's Progressive Bookshop was a radical node in London's literary networks and beyond, and its reputation and connections meant it was 'haunted by a number of expatriate New Zealanders'.⁶⁶ Dennis McEldowney hints at the possibilities of connections amongst other London publishers, noting that some 'seemed readier than others to publish New Zealand authors. It is tempting to look for associations in explanation', and he finds two. Sir Stanley Unwin, of Allen & Unwin, had three brothers living in New Zealand, and Dent, of the eponymous firm, had a brother there too.⁶⁷ We might add that the Edward Garnett who read Frank Sargeson's manuscript was the same man who earlier read Mander's *The Story of a New Zealand River*, and passed it on to John Lane, of the Bodley Head (who also worked with New Zealand poet D'Arcy Cresswell). Marsh benefited from her contact with the Rhodes family, but also with Alan Wilkie and his touring Shakespeare company, for whom she worked as an actress. Wilkie would not have selected Marsh had it not been for her family's involvement in the local arts scene. Wilkie also proved a lynchpin for Hector Bolitho. The two met in a restaurant, and the meeting ended with Bolitho taking on the job of starting the Australian periodical *Shakespeare Quarterly*, which was, of course, reviewed in London. Shared cultural aspirations and a small society worked together to help these writers establish themselves in the metropolis.[68]

The second factor was a colonially inflected version of metropolitan networking. Being 'London literate' meant the writers were well positioned to take advantage of any introductions they received. Hector Bolitho, whose unflattering critical reputation as a 'royal biographer and apologist' may be unsalvageable, is nevertheless the king of expatriate networking, which he describes, with a slightly regal air, as a 'multitude of kindnesses'.[69] Not only did he manage an Augustus John and Jacob Epstein sighting on his first night, he also managed to get a job interview for the next day. On the way to it, he bumped into that magnet for New Zealand expatriates, George Bernard Shaw. The job interview came from a chance meeting, supposedly facilitated by the fact that he 'had arrived from New Zealand only a few hours before'.[70] However, the 'open sesame' effect of New Zealand takes more credit than it should, for the circumstances of Bolitho's meeting with Shaw are framed by Bolitho's cultural aspirations. First, he was met by a friend, a fellow New Zealander who had stories 'accepted by *The Spectator*; he had spoken to G. K. Chesterton on the phone and had seen D. H. Lawrence eating a boiled egg at the Trocadero'.[71] This friend (probably Angus Wilson) took him to the Café Royale and Oddenino's, where the chance meeting occurred.[72] In effect, Bolitho was placed in the right cultural context, and this, along with his cultural conditioning in New Zealand and his cultural aspirations, gave him an advantage in the metropolis. From this one meeting came a long series of opportunities that culminated in his living and writing in Windsor Castle.[73]

Bolitho may have been the master, but he was not the only example. Fairburn developed a patronage relationship with an avant-garde art gallery owner, Lucy Wertheim, based on their mutual interest in art, and, apparently, his habit of sleeping on park benches.[74] Wertheim had earlier befriended Frances Hodgkins, and then introduced Fairburn to her and to

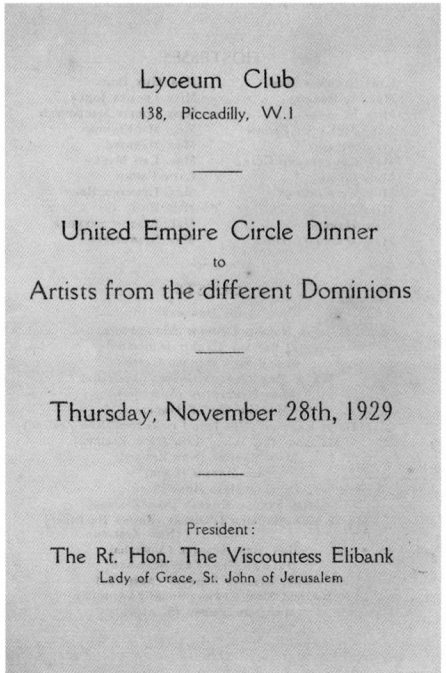

London literati: Jane Mander's invitation to the United Empire Circle Dinner. NZMS 535, Sir George Grey Special Collections, Auckland Libraries.

other modern artists. As a published author, Fairburn also had the advantage of making literary connections through his publisher, Charles Lahr. When Mander first arrived in London, she met some 'Victorian' writers through her publisher, John Lane, and his wife.[75] She moved on to various literary functions, including the United Empire Circle Dinner to Artists from the different Dominions, in 1929, where she joined other 'colonials' like David Low, and the Women Writers Dinner in 1930. Mander's table included Naomi Mitcheson (also at the dinner were Vita Sackville West and for a change, Mrs G. K. Chesterton).[76] In 1924, Ward Lock hosted a party especially for Isabel Peacocke, whose children's books were bestsellers in Britain, at the Waldorf Hotel.[77] Journalist and writer Nelle Scanlan was invited to become part of the London P.E.N. Club after her first book was reviewed, meeting some of the same people Mander did at her first P.E.N. gathering in 1923. None of this is to suggest that the writers felt able to storm the capital but, rather, to show that the combination of their colonial background and metropolitan aspirations worked together to give them access to the literary heart of London. Being 'London literate', the by-product of high cultural dependence on the metropole, could make the capital more accessible.

For some writers, it seemed to be London itself, rather than its connections or opportunities, which made them productive. Ngaio Marsh is a particularly interesting example of this. She returned home to New Zealand in response to her mother's illness, and stayed to look after her father when her mother died. While Marsh continued to write in New Zealand, she hoped to return to London, for 'you get a certain freshness of impact each time you come. The London feeling which I get very strongly to an extraordinary extent, starts me off writing every time as soon as I come to England.'[78] It has been argued in the case of Katherine Mansfield that 'as much as she turned against London, she still knew the secret of its attraction to her and its power to inspire her. It was in London that her talent was ripened and sharpened; it was there she developed the techniques that allowed her to express her unique vision.'[79]

Yet metropolitan success could be elusive. Mander observed: 'It is true that manuscripts had left New Zealand for London. That is, their authors had duly posted and insured them . . . . But one never knew what happened to them in London. About the adventures of those brain children in the Empire capital there was a great and persistent silence.'[80] Those based in London also met with a great and persistent silence. Mander, Fairburn and Sargeson failed to get their first efforts published. Earning a living required considerable ingenuity and compromise, and the most common fallback was journalism, both for London and New Zealand papers. The small outlets for writing in New Zealand meant that most writers already had experience in this area, which was fortunate because journalists had 'the best chance, even though every journalist in England wants to come to London'.[81] Mander had edited her father's paper, *The Northern Advocate*, and had attended a journalism course at Columbia. Bolitho had worked at the *New Zealand Herald* and the *Auckland Star*. Scanlan began at the *Manawatu Times* and freelanced in America. Expatriate writers also contributed those regular columns of news and gossip about London found in New Zealand newspapers. Marsh became a 'New Canterbury Pilgrim' for the *Christchurch Sun*, contributing regular articles on her travels. Mander wrote for the *Auckland Sun* and the *Evening Post*, whilst Fairburn had some success with the *Auckland Star*. (Sargeson, living off funds, did not take this approach, but tried to use his travel experiences later. One piece was published in the *Waikato Times*.)

The realities of writing for a living in London meant inevitably that novels and poetry took a back seat to more prosaic assignments, literary and otherwise. As Mander noted, 'The result of all this enormous activity in books has been various sidelines. And as only a few writers comparatively make enough to live on out of novels, and as the freelance work is a precarious business, for the taste of editors is very fickle, a surprising number of writers keep the pot boiling by hack work, by reading manuscripts for agents and publishers and by translating foreign books.'[82] Hack work probably included short story writing, by which popular author Edith Lyttleton was able to earn a living. It would most certainly have included Bolitho's publicity work. Mander worked at book production and reading manuscripts. Marsh ran a decorating shop. Fairburn tried to sell paintings to earn money to keep the London dream alive. Even being published did not lead to the financial freedom they hoped for. As Mander would later report, 'I am supposed to have had a considerable literary success in both England and America.... I have written three novels, and I am today hundreds of pounds in debt.'[83]

However, being 'London literate', once demonstrated as 'success' in London, boosted writers' reputations in New Zealand. They could be popularly claimed as part of New Zealand (even if, like Hector Bolitho, they would not later form part of the story of literary nationalism) and as local examples of metropolitan acculturation. This, more than their actual work, made them interesting. Bolitho, returning to New Zealand briefly in 1934, basked in the reflected warmth of recolonial success. He was invited to a ball and a lunch at Government House, and 'with the trophies of my little success, I was permitted to dance with Lady Bledisloe, and when I spoke at the Town Hall, I sat between the Governor-General and the Mayor'.[84] Such success was part of a general, national expression of connection with the cultural capital. In 1928, the proudly parochial *Auckland Sun* ran a double-page spread, titled 'Aucklanders Who Have Won Fame in London'. The introduction effortlessly spans 12,000 miles to reconnect hinterland with the metropolis:

> London, for most of the world, is the city of dreams. In that crowded metropolis of the British Empire statesmen, and artists, singers and poets, authors and actors hope for the reward which will crown them with fame.

London is the Mecca of those who wish and work for success. Her acclamation sets a standard by which the greatest endeavour is judged; her plaudits are echoed by the rest of the world.

Auckland is definitely linked with the Empire metropolis. Among London's millions some of Auckland's sons and daughters are firmly established – their ability acknowledged by the most severe critics. Most have gone Home with little or nothing except the spark which urges them to dare the whole world; their record is a memorable one.[85]

Going Home with 'nothing except a spark' then succeeding in the face of 'the most severe critics' exemplified the distinct yet connected nature of the two hemispheres, emphasising both 'new' New Zealand's latent ability, and the overwhelming importance of London as yardstick of success. The local habit of lauding overseas success had a practical benefit for the writers, for the added cachet of London may have made them more desirable as writers of articles and givers of talks. The prestige value was not lost on Fairburn (who benefited very little from it in other ways). When attempting to sell some paintings in New Zealand he wrote with some sarcasm, 'I think I'll send three or four watercolours out to the next Socy. of Arts show in Auckland. They might hang one or two – seeing that I'm living in England and not in N.Z.'[86] Mander was somewhat more pragmatic. On considering returning to New Zealand, she wrote, 'I do need the publicity of a book or two to start me off as a writer out there, and so I am hoping to get another book that I have started finished before I come.'[87] The newspapers had not been slow to latch on to her 'success'. One of her local newspaper articles was sub-headed as follows: 'This interesting review of new developments in London has been written for SUN readers by Miss Jane Mander, the New Zealand-born novelist who has found marked favour in England.' At the time, that meant so much more than the same favour in New Zealand.[88]

EXPATRIATION

The London lives of New Zealand writers redraw the relationship between the two places as integrated and productive, which is at odds with nationalist narratives, where expatriation is a barrier to the development of an

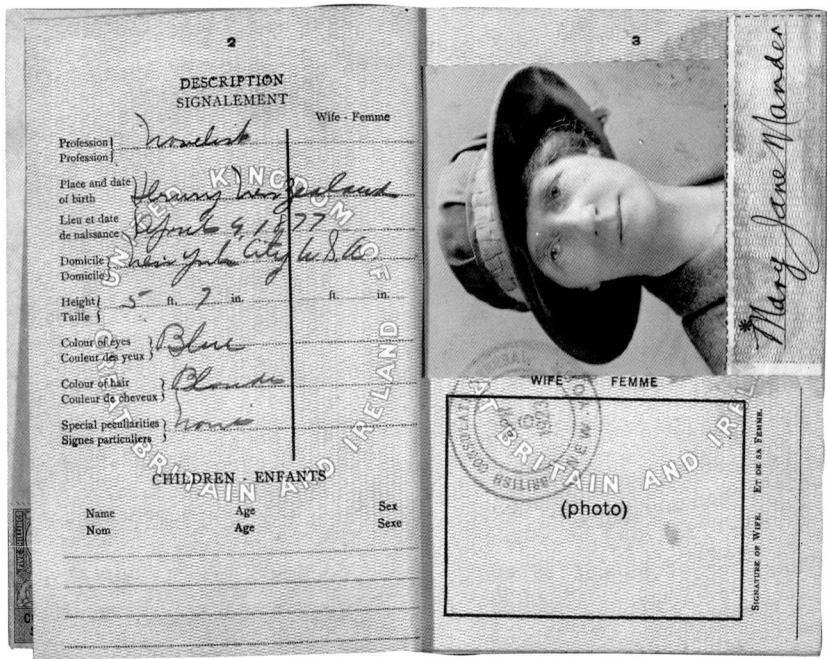

Jane Mander's passport: a gateway not only to London, but also to literary recognition. NZMS 535, Sir George Grey Special Collections, Auckland Libraries.

authentic cultural voice.[89] It has been argued that 'the literary nationalism of the 1890s made little headway partly because so many of the writers left the country'.[90] It is certainly true that many writers left: *The Oxford Companion to New Zealand Literature* lists some 120 writers of various types active in the period 1900–1940.[91] Of those, at least forty-nine spent considerable time in London. A recent study of New Zealand writers working between 1890 and 1945 comes up with an even higher ratio: 65 out of 118. Characterised as escape from the wastelands of colonial culture, this outflow of talent is also conventionally considered to have stunted the growth of that local culture. Yet expatriation's negative effects may be overstated.[92] Leaving the country seemed to be no barrier to Jane Mander in publishing novels about New Zealand, novels that were less than enthusiastically received here. Lawrence Jones notes that the period 1890 to 1934 is 'marked by a series of separate struggles by talented individuals to become New Zealand novelists, with each finally withdrawing into silence or expatriation'.[93]

Whilst struggle was certainly a factor for many writers, the association of expatriation with 'silence' and 'withdrawal' is not necessarily an accurate reflection of their experience. If we consider Mander again, silence and withdrawal, at least from the perspective of writing novels, came on her return to New Zealand.

Further, although we are accustomed to the idea of expatriation as a physical and cultural divide, it is not clear that the writers themselves felt that way. London was an extension of their world, not an exile from it. Fairburn felt a kind of reverse homesickness when he stumbled onto a fragment of the 'native hemisphere' in the form of New Zealand flora in Kew Gardens. He wrote: 'I know what it is now, to be an exile. It brings, not the unhealthy melancholy I've suffered from occasionally when I've been away from home in New Zealand, but a feeling of romantic dignity. It may sound strange, but I don't feel nearly as remote from home now as I have done before on occasions when I have been out of Auckland.'[94] Stephen Alomes notes that in the case of some expatriate Australians, 'being a Londoner was a kind of resolution. It did not require them to cease being Australian and to become English.'[95] Here, London mediates between oppositional identities. But it could also integrate them. Fairburn, later a staunch 'literary nationalist', gazed at William Blake's house and, thinking of a time when London was not 'the dirty, hopeless hole then that it has since become', wrote to Mason that 'you can't imagine how one comes, over here, to think of oneself, not as a dweller in the England of 1931, but as part of a nation, a part of its history. It's like being one of a large party on board a steam-roller which is rushing down a slope.'[96] Marsh became 'part of its history' on seeing the Tower of London, 'where a New Zealander began to feel London in her blood.... I had the first taste of extraordinary buoyancy, the sudden quickening of all one's perceptions, the sense of belonging to, and being carried high, on the full tide of London; an experience that sooner or later comes, I think, to almost everyone who stays there.'[97]

Writers, whether or not they were engaged in the project of literary nationalism, were in this way no different from other travellers to the centre already discussed: in the shadow of Westminster Abbey, they too were 'Londoners all'. This was obviously so in relation to the rest of Europe. Sargeson's famous phrase, 'I had to visit Europe to discover that I was truly a New Zealander: I felt myself weighed down by so much civilization', is generally taken as evidence of his growing 'New Zealand' identity.[98]

'Where a New Zealander began to feel London in her blood': the Tower of London. O.032056, Harry Moult Album, Museum of New Zealand Te Papa Tongarewa.

However, his disorientation occurred in Europe, where things were truly foreign, not in London. Although he recounted his travels confidently at the time, in retrospect, Sargeson believed he had only 'ignorantly imagined' walking in Switzerland.[99] But then, Switzerland was not 'familiar' to New Zealanders in the way London was. After his European experience, London became a place of refuge. He did not return to New Zealand immediately, but instead attempted to redress the cultural balance by devoting the rest of his trip to study in the British Museum library. Similarly, Fairburn retreated to London after a disillusioning experience walking in France and Spain. In Paris, 'his morale was shaken at being so alone in a foreign city'.[100] Barcelona proved worse: 'he had had enough; he was going back to London'.[101] On his return, he wrote to Mason that he 'no longer had any scrap of belief in' such things as modern French painters, modern English painters, novels and T. S. Eliot.[102]

Repositioning London as part of New Zealand's cultural landscape modifies nationalist interpretations of expatriation. But the idea of the hinterland also highlights the commonalities between the experiences of colonial and provincial British writers. Some of their common cultural capital, in the form of shared literary influences, has already been noted, and they may have shared more. In an echo of Jane Mander's colonial 'starved solitude', one provincial British writer, Patricia Williams of Flixton, complained of the lack of literary congeniality for those sentenced to life in the 'wilds of Manchester . . . . In London there are clubs, societies, etc for the meeting of writers and journalists; in Manchester there appears to be nothing of the kind.'[103] She might as well have been in Rex Fairburn's tough and dirty Taumarunui. For this writer, as much as for her colonial counterparts, London was the cultural centre. This equivalence, between provincial metropolitans and white settler colonials, raises the difficulties of attempting to apply postcolonial approaches to these colonial writers, just as it would be difficult to apply them to provincial British writers, based as they are on an assumed opposition between colonised and colonisers. White colonial writers were not, as postcolonialists might describe them, mimics of the centre, acting as ventriloquists of a culture that did not belong to them.[104] Instead, they were active participants in this culture they felt was theirs too. This is a challenge to the theoretical assumptions of postcolonialism, but it offers interesting possibilities for metropolitan literary histories. For example, colonial writers may have had their part to play in the democratisation of literary culture, a feature of cultural life in the interwar metropolis.[105] Life as a writer there had previously been a reasonably elite preserve, but from the turn of the century, more and more middle and working class Britons were not simply audiences for the burgeoning print culture, but producers of it. Patricia Williams, lonely in Flixton, was one of these, and colonial writers could be considered in the same way. For whilst writers like Rex Fairburn, Hector Bolitho or Frank Sargeson might have been more middle than working class, it remains true that, like working class provincial writers in Britain, few colonial authors came to London with the 'social advantages' typical of successful metropolitan writers.[106] Authors in London's British and New Zealand provinces had this in common too.

Most writers, especially those who now form part of the cultural canon, eventually returned to New Zealand. Expatriation was for most of them a temporary state: 'it was rare for a writer to leave New Zealand and never come back'.[107] Although some would go on to write against the idea of England as Home, London retained its role as metropolis to hinterland, providing a necessary extension of narrowly drawn local cultural borders. Mander, in her twenty years away, seems to have exhausted both herself and London. New Zealand now seemed to offer freedom: freedom from financial pressure, freedom from the 'noise and dirt' of the city and, although it did not eventuate, freedom to write.[108] Fairburn claimed he wanted to 'live in the backblocks of N. Z., and try to realise in my mind the real culture of that country. Somewhere where I might escape the vast halitosis of the Press, and the whole dreadful weight of modern art and literature. Because we really are people of a different race, and have no right to be monkeying about with European culture.'[109] Here the native hemisphere is resurrected as antidote to European culture. But when he came to leave, biographer Denys Trussell notes, 'Rex was certain they would return to England', and Fairburn himself suggested his 'return will be an Emergency Measure'.[110] There is no ambiguity about the location of culture, only uncertainty as to how it might exist in the backblocks of 'new' New Zealand. After his return to New Zealand, Fairburn continued to 'monkey about' with European culture, writing for the *Phoenix* and maintaining a cultural life that was in parallel with that of the metropolis.[111]

For these 'brain children of empire', London was an extension of New Zealand's cultural landscape that should be more properly considered a productive not proscribing influence. Mander wrote, 'On the whole, I find life easier and more diverting in London. There are days, of course, when I think that the sight of a kauri tree ... but when I feel like that I walk around Westminster Abbey.'[112] The nature of the two icons signalled the cultural dependence on London. New Zealand was represented by nature, London by a cultural, historic and religious monument that is also, significantly, the location of Poet's Corner. New Zealand's past had indeed shifted, and in its place was the raw and empty 'new' New Zealand. Some writers produced this place in their work and in their lives. Through their experiences in the centre, they participated in and produced the two hemispheres of New Zealand, one cultured, the other uncultured. Even among those most committed to producing a 'national identity', 'new' New Zealand was a collaborative construction with the metropolis. The following two chapters consider how time and space could be transformed to produce another identity that also had implications for the location of culture: New Zealand as 'London's Farm'.

CHAPTER FIVE

LONDON'S
FARM

IN 1885, THE ANNUAL Lord Mayor's procession in London had an unexpected antipodean addition. Two enterprising meat salesmen from the New Zealand Loan and Mercantile Agency Company Limited, with cart, carcasses and a banner reading 'New Zealand Frozen Mutton – the Meat of the Future', crashed the rear of the parade, making both the procession and the papers in an improvised attempt at meat marketing. This brash intrusion into a metropolitan, imperial spectacle caused mixed reactions. 'Excellent as was this advertisement, it did not end with the mere exhibition of the meat in the streets of the City for the morning papers of the following day all commented upon this novel feature of the Lord Mayor's Show, some treating it as part of the authorized procession, and others indignantly inquiring how it was a lorry with its burden found its place in the time-honoured pageant.'[1] However, proof that advertising can pay, the carcasses went on to be sold above market price the next day.

Frozen mutton was considered out of place in the Lord Mayor's parade, and it may seem out of place here. Meat, butter and cheese are not the usual staples of cultural history, although their role in reshaping New Zealand's economic history is well known.[2] With the advent of refrigeration in 1882, pastoral production of these consumables grew to become, alongside wool, the mainstay of the New Zealand economy. This economic transformation reconfigured New Zealand's landscape too. As the new export trade made small-scale dairy and sheep farming viable, the quintessential New Zealand farm was brought into existence. This in turn transformed the cultural landscape.[3] The farm has become one of New Zealand's most powerful and enduring identities. Firmly entrenched in the national imagination, 'rural New Zealand' and its virtues have regularly been preferred to the social realities of New Zealand as an urban nation. It has become an example of 'second nature', a human intervention in the landscape that comes to be considered as 'natural'.[4]

This 'rural myth' has long and diverse roots, but here the emphasis is on the crucial but neglected role of the metropolis in constructing it.[5] This and the following chapter trace the construction of New Zealand's identity as farm in London: first, in exhibition space, and in Chapter Six in advertising. Together, they argue that the development of New Zealand's farming identity was not just a natural consequence of economic change. For the transformation of New Zealand's physical landscape, created in response to the needs primarily of London consumers, was paralleled by a reshaping of the cultural landscape in the crucible of metropolitan commodity culture. From the late nineteenth century New Zealand functioned as a farming hinterland of London. But it was in the new spaces of metropolitan mass consumption that it began to consider itself to be one.

This transformation involved another of the distortions of time and space that characterise the relationship of New Zealand with London. The new export industry was enabled by refrigeration, another technological contribution to the era's compression of space and time. Refrigeration halted decay: it suspended time. But the greatest distortions appeared in advertising space. The farm, constructed in imperial exhibition halls and on city billboards, in shop windows and parades, was a particular place. It was a familiar, 'British' farm. Surprisingly, this familiar farm no longer appeared as a far off colony. New Zealand as 'London's farm' emphasised propinquity, in two ways. Not only was it culturally close – 'British' – but it seemed also to have come physically closer. In the discourses of metropolitan commodity culture, the old colony would be recreated as neighbouring hinterland, and it would be imaged by its similarity to the centre, not its 'otherness'. Difference vanished with distance.

Not so shabby: a scene from Samuel Brees' promotional work, *Pictorial Illustrations of New Zealand*, London, 1847, drawings from which provided the basis for the later 'Colonial Panorama' exhibited in Leicester Square. With ships in the harbour, smoke from the chimneys and busy streets, along with markers of civilised settlement such as gardens and a courthouse, Brees created a lively and 'settled' Wellington. Courts of Justice, Wellington, c.1843, B-031-009, Alexander Turnbull Library, Wellington, New Zealand.

Like 'new' New Zealand, the creation of London's farm transformed an older colonial identity: New Zealand as settler colony. This earlier version of New Zealand was also created in metropolitan commodity culture, in part through the diverse and extensive advertising campaigns for emigration. But there was a crucial difference. In this earlier form, New Zealand itself was the commodity, rather than a producer of them. The migration campaigns of the nineteenth century seem to have been neglected by historians of advertising, despite their unparalleled success in rebranding penal colonies and wild frontiers as potential homes, then persuading millions to move to them. 'Advertising scarcely existed' before 1851 and the Great Exhibition at the Crystal Palace; it was 'only a rather shabby last resort' limited to cheap handbills and posters, and small newspaper advertisements.[6] Or at least that is the claim. Yet at the same time that the Great Exhibition was supposed to be inaugurating commodity culture, a spectacular version of New Zealand as emigration destination was available, twice a day, at S. C. Brees' 'Colonial Panorama' in Leicester Square.[7] It was more than a shabby handbill. Over two hours, a version of New Zealand 'glided' before the public gaze in a series of twenty-six painted sections, in an exhibit that *The Times* claimed would 'do more to promote emigration than a thousand speeches and resolutions'.[8] From harbour to hinterland, spectators travelled through a New Zealand marked by energetic settlement and described as a 'touching illustration of the inroads made by civilization on the wild solitudes of nature'.[9] Banks, government offices, mills, 'merchant's offices' and churches were depicted, along with 'every building of note' in the colony.[10]

Here, land was the commodity, and although existing histories of commodity culture overlook this, the emigration schemes of the nineteenth century did not. Promoters both created and assuaged metropolitan 'land hunger' (an unmistakably commodified term) by producing potential farms and town lots from 'empty' lands. Using surveys, mapping and some considerable stretching of imagination and faith, these promoters sold the idea of prospective paradises to be created on the periphery. This required the mediation of the uncivilised aspects of frontier life, which Brees had experienced as a surveyor for the New Zealand Company. A promotional poster for the panorama featured a Maori and settler shaking hands surrounded by a transliteration of the welcoming words tena koe and haere mai, in 'an image of harmony and amalgamation that no doubt would have been reassuring to potential investors and immigrants'.[11] However, the images of civilisation in the panorama itself were the most convincing. After seeing the paintings, which made colonial Christchurch 'bloom as a rose, though at that time it bloomed with nothing but tussock and flax', Edward Seager, Ngaio Marsh's grandfather, set aside his 'vivid picture' of 'ferocious cannibals' and decided to emigrate.[12] The 'New Zealand' of migration advertising reversed the expected use of imperial time. Usually colonies appeared as wildernesses that confirmed the centre's more civilised status. But settler colonies worked differently. New Zealand was given the attributes of the centre, making it appear civilised.[13] However, this process also had consequences for the centre. When migration advertising borrowed signs of civilisation – government, religion, commerce – to construct their 'civilised' colonies, they were also defining what those signs should be. In this way, settler colonies were not only borrowing Britishness, but collaborating in its construction.

As Seager later discovered, 'blooming' Christchurch was '"made in London" and existed inside Mr Brees' panorama, but nowhere else', which is probably the best confirmation that the spectacular panorama should indeed be considered an advertisement.[14] But while histories of immigration schemes recognise that 'their representations were as much expressions of metropolitan concerns as they were of interactions with distant landscapes and their indigenous inhabitants', they tend to analyse the promotional material as literature.[15] However, panoramas, 'puffs', propaganda, pamphlets, handbooks, guides, lectures, lithographs and landscapes of emigration and settlement schemes are advertisements by other names. They have a great deal in common with the semiotic system Thomas Richards identifies as arising from the Great Exhibition, although they predate it. Richards' scheme enumerates six characteristics: autonomous iconography, descriptions of objects with 'an intensity out of all proportion to their use or value'; commemoration, which revises 'the past to make it wholly present'; a democratic ideology of consumerism, where everyone wants the same things; the transformation of commodity into language; the figuration of the consuming subject; and the myth of abundance.[16] All of these occur within migration advertising's attempts at reforming the frontier. Diverse colonies shared similar iconography that served a commemorative function. Mythic pasts of Arcadian England or classical Greece were pressed into service as the promised future of new settler colonies. Athens, Georgia and Cambridge, New Zealand, share an impressive aspirational iconography, if little else. These colonies also prefigured the democratic ideology of consumerism by appearing to offer opportunity to all, whilst carefully configuring their own consuming subject through the characteristics of 'ideal' colonists. Even that figuration seemed democratic: fitness to be a colonist was more a matter of character than status or position, and handbooks went to some trouble to describe just what personal attributes were required to handcraft your own paradise. Finally, the myth of abundance, so easily identified in shopping arcades, was also integral to the utopian, Arcadian and paradisiacal imagery of emigration literature.

All these elements were presented using techniques akin to the spectacular ordering of the Great Exhibition. Complementing panoramic views of the periphery in the metropolis, handbooks included large maps, charts and decorative globes, providing 'all-encompassing vistas with the power to collapse the global into a single volume or volumes'.[17] Settler New Zealand was also subject to these processes, neatly encapsulated in evocations of it as 'Greater' or 'Better' Britain. This appeal to Britishness, common amongst settler colonies, was indeed somewhat out of proportion with reality. At the same time, the creation of New Zealand as a new and improved version of Home served a commemorative function, simultaneously placing Britain in the past and giving it mythic power as the model for a new society. The emphasis on Britishness also prefigured the ideal consumer of 'New Zealand', acting as an appeal to, and a sifting device for, its settlers. Finally, Greater Britain's promise of abundance was made self-evident in its name.

Yet there was always tension in this portrayal. Greater Britain remained a promise, not a place. In emigration material, New Zealand, like 'blooming Christchurch', remained a prospective paradise, and even later promotional material needed to balance the 'savage' and 'civilised' aspects of colonial life, albeit in new ways.[18] Still, the colony as commodity remained pre-eminent until the 1870s, the peak period of immigration and its image-making.[19] From the 1880s, both slowed in the face of a declining economy. Government schemes were dismantled in 1891, and from then, immigration became a 'spasmodic' affair.[20] New Zealand as a commodity initially had no replacement in the metropolis, but from 1882, when the first shipment of New Zealand frozen meat arrived in London, a new image of the country as producer of commodities would fill the space. Accordingly, from that time, the number of exhibitions held in New Zealand began to increase sharply, with at least nine held before 1900; previously there had been just two, one in 1865 and another in 1872.[21] Likewise, New Zealand's international appearances were sporadic until the 1884 International Health Exhibition held in South Kensington. From then, exhibition halls replaced emigration propaganda to form a new version of New Zealand, one that eventually would move from the confines of exhibition courts and cabinets into the streets of the metropolis and the windows of the new chain stores (called multiples) before being reflected back to New Zealand itself. From 1882, butter, meat and cheese, along with wool, would come to stand for New Zealand, as the colony became London's farm.

COLONIAL ENCOUNTERS NEW ZEALAND AND METROPOLITAN COMMODITY CULTURE

The arrival of colonial commodities in the metropolitan marketplace disrupted more than the Lord Mayor's procession. It changed the nature of commodity culture. From the last quarter of the nineteenth century, a new range of produce from settler colonies like New Zealand began to flow into the centre. It was a second wave, following the earlier arrival of exotic commodities such as tea, coffee and sugar, and like them, it changed the nature of metropolitan consumption. However, the new commodities were anything but exotic. From the first decades of the nineteenth century, Britain had begun importing basic foodstuffs to feed its growing population, first from Ireland and then from Europe. Around the last quarter of the century, this was supplemented, and then eventually supplanted, by familiar farming produce from America and the settler colonies.[22] Meat, butter, cheese and wheat – in larger qualities, at lower prices, and sometimes in new, frozen form – expanded the market for these products among British consumers.[23] At the same time, prices fell across almost all foodstuffs in Britain by 25 per cent, whilst real wages were increasing.[24] Butter consumption rose by 15 per cent per capita from the late 1880s to the turn of the century, and by 1908, 87 per cent of this butter and 76 per cent of cheese were imported.[25] Meat consumption rose by almost a quarter between 1870 and 1896. However, the increase in the rate of imported meat consumption was more dramatic, rising eighteen-fold in the same period.[26] This increased supply of refrigerated meat came with lower prices, initially ranging from 2½d to 3d per pound compared with 9d to 1s for home-produced meat.[27] One survey of the weekly per capita consumption of a selected range of common foods indicates that whilst consumption of older commodities, particularly tea, continued to grow in the period 1860–1913, there were rapid rises in the consumption of meat and butter.[28] Milk consumption also increased, as the metropolis's own dairy farmers turned to town milk supply, insulated from import competition, while the virtual metropolitan farmers of the colonies provided cheaper butter and cheese.[29] Although the first wave of colonial commodities brought an exotic empire home, new colonial produce made greater consumption of 'British' food possible.

But the impact was not restricted to dietary change. As the flow of commodities grew, new types of distribution developed. The 1880s were marked by the growth in new retailing forms, which, among other developments, took advantage of cheap and plentiful produce. Co-operative societies, for example, were established during the first half of the nineteenth century, but they boomed on the back of cheaper food, purchased with higher wages. The 600,000 members of co-operative societies in 1880 had reached almost four million by 1914.[30] Multiples, or chain stores, on the other hand, were a new form of retailing altogether, and they too began to expand rapidly in this period. Footwear, books and sewing machines were the first products to be sold in this way but, from the 1870s, they were joined by food retailers. Grocers, previously serving the upper classes with luxury goods, 'were forced to extend their range of goods to compete with "the stores" and the growing number of provisions dealers'.[31] Even so, in the ten years from 1885 to 1895, the number of multiple stores in Britain with ten or more branches more than doubled, from thirty-one to seventy-two.[32] Lipton's, the 'King of the Dairy Provision trades', was founded in 1880; a group of older stores was rebranded, appositely enough as 'Home and Colonial Stores', from 1888. At the same time, they turned their focus from selling an older colonial commodity, tea, to selling butter, one of the newest. By 1895 they had more than two hundred branches.[33] The Maypole Stores, established in 1898, could survive carrying just four lines – margarine, butter, condensed milk and tea – in their 800 branches as late as 1922.[34]

London was the epicentre of this expansion, reflecting its greater reliance on imported food. Britain's twenty-three large frozen meat firms, for example, had 3828 outlets by 1910. The highest concentration of these stores was in London; housewives in areas like Yorkshire and Scotland considered buying imported meat a 'very last resort'.[35] Indeed, by 1919, multiple stores of all types in London attracted 50 per cent more customers than the average for these stores in Britain generally. By then, some of the stores were almost completely dependent on colonial, not just imported, produce.[36]

The second wave of colonial commodities thus brought massive market expansion, but in Home-style farm products. Their familiar nature may be the reason why effects like these have gone largely unnoticed.[37] Although the Great Exhibition of 1851 is often seen as the fulcrum of a new commodity culture, Thomas Richards concludes that 'it was not until the 1880s that commodities were again able to achieve a monopoly of signification in the public sphere'.[38] This may be because the range of mass marketable commodities was too narrow until the arrival of the second wave of colonial produce. Certainly, some food was more expensive during the years before 1880 than previously, final tariffs on sugar and tea were removed only in the 1870s,[39] and mass production of branded food products like bread and biscuits was only beginning.[40] Just as settler colonies themselves may have predated the Great Exhibition as commodity spectacle, so it may be that new opportunities for that 'monopoly of signification' really began to appear in the metropolis with their produce from the 1880s.

Ranges of provisions expanded in the last quarter of the nineteenth century, and 'in contrast to the preparation of the grocers in the middle of the century, were often ready-packed by the manufacturer and advertised under a brand name'.[41] In this same time period, multiple stores, novel themselves, used 'ingenious and startling advertising campaigns', ranging from 'posters, leaflets, handbills, and free gifts, to elephants pulling outsize cheeses through the street and processions of men dressed as coolies carrying chests of tea'.[42] The spectacular displays of department stores, mid-century archetypes of consumption, would be reproduced in the rapidly growing number of shop windows oriented towards working class and, later, middle class customers. 'In practically all trades and among nearly all types of retailers emphasis had begun to be placed on window display, on salesmanship, and on advertising.'[43]

At this point too, advertising began to be professionalised, handled through agents rather than by manufacturers themselves. Products, not yet consumers, lay at the heart of the advertisers' messages, and increasingly those products would be endowed with greater symbolism, creating a phase of 'product idolatry'.[44] Newspapers began to accept illustrated advertisements, poster art became more sophisticated, and commodities spawned their own collectibles in the forms of cigarette cards, postcards and other ephemera.[45] Exhibitions, perhaps the most innovative feature of late Victorian commodity culture, show this transformation towards a new discourse in commodities clearly. Whilst the Great Exhibition and others began by featuring the 'gadgets' of an industrialising world,[46] 'their theme was gradually transformed from the international industrial exposition as in 1851 and 1862, to imperial and colonial display'.[47] This is, of course, because within the discourse of metropolitan mass markets, colonies largely bereft of industry could speak only through their commodities.

New Zealand's shift from colony to commodity producer was part of this broader metropolitan change, meaning the development of the new pastoral export industry was more than a locally based historical discontinuity provoked by the ingenious application of innovative technology. Refrigeration reconnected New Zealand directly to the heart of the metropolis's rapidly changing commodity culture, and it may well have helped change it. As markets took over from migrants, familiar farm products from New Zealand became the principal vehicles for forming 'New Zealand' in the increasingly sophisticated metropolitan world of mass consumption. One migrant to New Zealand at the turn of the century claimed, 'My knowledge of the country was lamentably sparse. New Zealand's sole function to my uneducated belief was to produce the accompaniment to green peas and new potatoes. Canterbury lamb was as familiar to the English dining table as the Mother Country's roast beef. I had also seen a "New Zealand" sign on the large mounds of butter in the Maypole shops. A land flowing with butter and inhabited by gambolling lambs was my new address.'[48] What he knew about New Zealand was learned through a display of its commodities in a multiple shop window and not through an immigration handbook.

In this new mass market, the much anticipated 'Britain of the South', finally freed of frontier economics and imagery, could now emerge. It did so by taking advantage of the shifts in time and space we have already encountered. Marketing imagery borrowed metropolitan historic time and reinvented a timeless, idealised English rural past. Milkmaids would exist in New Zealand advertising, if not actually on New Zealand dairy farms. At the same time, the imagery shunted New Zealand forward in time by taming and domesticating the landscape. Markers of the past, like Maori, were removed, in favour of 'gambolling lambs'. Like 'new' New Zealand, 'London's farm' was characterised as a masculine place, not because it necessarily was, but because metropolitan commodity culture portrayed the dependent colonies as the feminine 'other'. Tea remained considerably more exotic than prosaic mounds of butter. Potentially unfavourable aspects of modernity were likewise carefully managed. New Zealand's 'industry' was limited to farming. Even the industrialised processes of refrigeration, dairy factories and freezing works that underpinned recolonial trade were minimised, as meat production was symbolised by images of Arcadia rather than abattoirs. New Zealand produce came 'direct' to London tables, and it was produced for them by 'Britons'. Propinquity was produced in surprising ways: *The Times* claimed that the frozen carcasses in the first shipment of 1882 were in as 'good condition as if they had been slaughtered in some suburban abattoir'.[49]

Some remnants of the older frontier version remained embedded in the imagery of the farm. A thread of rural British virtue linked the old and new versions, although, as part of the recolonial shift, the farm was now complement, not competition, to Britain itself. Other, less compatible, legacies existed in tourism marketing, where New Zealand itself remained

A familiar farming hinterland: tourist publicity for the British market, c. 1935–49.
Tourism Department, printed in England by Sun Printers Ltd, London and Watford.
Eph-D-TOURISM-1940s-06, Alexander Turnbull Library, Wellington, New Zealand.

a saleable commodity. Although publicity for tourism, agriculture and immigration continued to be intertwined during this period (notably, but briefly, as the Department of Agriculture, Commerce, and Tourists, and in the multipurpose scenic films produced by its successor department in the 1930s), tourism's preference for the sublime and the archaic emphasised differences between New Zealand and metropolitan time and space, rather than similarities.[50] However, it was increasingly the poor cousin of export marketing efforts. The majority of tourism expenditure was on local infrastructure, and while there was growth in the domestic market, tourist flows from Britain remained low throughout this period: total overseas tourist numbers were fewer than 20,000 per annum until 1955.[51] In 1924, organisers for the New Zealand display at the British Empire Exhibition at Wembley noted 'New Zealand is too far from the United Kingdom to attract tourists in any considerable numbers.'[52] By 1940, a Wellington schoolteacher visiting London could claim that 'posters advertising New Zealand produce were far more frequently seen than those advancing the Dominion as a tourist centre'.[53] Posters were one factor in the rise of New Zealand farm identity. It began in earnest in exhibition space.

'POLISHED TO SUIT THE LONDON TASTE'
CONSTRUCTING THE FARM AT EXHIBITIONS

In 1890, professional exhibition manager and showman Jules Joubert had an ambitious new plan.[54] He proposed following up the success of the New Zealand and South Seas Exhibition, just held in Dunedin, with a New Zealand exhibition in London. His appeal was compelling, if just a little slighting: 'Enlarged and elaborated, but a little more trimmed and polished to suit the London taste, what a revolution this Exhibition would effect in the popular impressions of New Zealand, if it were held in the world's metropolis instead of at the Antipodes!' A revolution, it seems, was needed, for 'despite the efforts of lecturers and agents, despite, and in fact partly because of, the exhibits New Zealand has sent to previous European exhibitions, the impression remains amongst the masses even to the well-to-do middle class at Home that New Zealand is a very beautiful but very barbarous country, producing gold, wool, ferns and cannibals and that the shepherd tends his sheep, or the miner delves for the unwilling gold, if not at risk of his life, certainly amidst the rudest surroundings. The ignorance regarding New Zealand at Home is positively inconceivable.'[55]

Joubert's plan marks a transitional moment, both in the nature of 'New Zealand' in the metropolis, and in the manner of its construction. First, it is apparent that, even as late as 1890, New Zealand in London was still endowed with anachronistic frontier characteristics. 'Beautiful but barbarous New Zealand', peopled by shepherds, miners and cannibals, was reminiscent of the old New Zealander on the bridge. Lingering like this cliché, echoes of old colonial New Zealand remained. Even allowing for an element of showman's exaggeration, this was hardly appropriate imagery for a white settler colony with ambitions as a neo-Britain. Accordingly, Joubert prescribed a change in the nature of 'New Zealand' and the mode of its presentation. In place of gold and sheep, he recommended a tourism court, a restaurant, a fruit stand, fernery and working dairies. Maori were to be incorporated only 'to a very limited extent', making mats and kits, although a haka troupe might be included if 'used with caution'. Finally, he recommended that this revised New Zealand be created using that spectacular method of metropolitan commodity display, the exhibition. In this space, a New Zealand 'polished to suit the London taste' could be constructed.

Jules Joubert's revolutionary London exhibition was proposed for 1890, and had it proceeded, it would have been yet another in a sporadic series sparked by the Great Exhibition at the Crystal Palace in 1851. One examination of English, Indian and Australian exhibitions suggests that there were more than fifty major exhibitions involving these countries between 1851 and 1914.[56] These spectacular displays have become rich sources for cultural historians, who have found that imperial power and its construction, mediation and contestation were also on show in the exhibitions' plaster pavilions, native villages and display cases.[57] At the same time, others have found nascent national identities articulated in exhibition space.[58] Interestingly, commodities themselves – the heart of the exhibitionary spectacle – have played the least part in these analyses. Inadvertently, the commodity has been cut adrift from its own cultural form, so whilst we can follow the forms and fissures of imperial power or national identity through ethnographic displays and art or exhibition architectures, the meanings of wheat, gold, butter or meat are unexamined.[59] One consequence of missing the main attractions has been to overlook their role in forming identity. Wool mountains and cows made of butter were not only the most significant features of exhibition space, they were also the defining features of New Zealand's identity. They overshadowed other elements routinely associated with the formation of a distinct 'New Zealand', such as Maori culture, curious fauna or scenic wonders. Instead, these became increasingly marginalised motifs of difference for an essentially familiar British farming image.

EXHIBITING THE FARM

For all that exhibitions were intended as expressions of an imperial order, early examples were not always orderly sites.[60] The 1851 Great Exhibition presented a chaos of foreign and colonial produce. India was given a separate court, and British exhibits were categorised by type, but foreign and colonial exhibits were blended together and 'the effect must have been extraordinary confusion'.[61] Over time, that chaos would be ordered, not only by region or into nations, but also into a proper relationship of resources to empire. John MacKenzie has shown that imperial content increased in exhibitions over time, and that the meaning of empire was constructed in them in a particular way. The metropolis was the centre of consumption and secondary industry, whilst the colonies were portrayed as sites of primary production. This sense of the empire as 'a great interlocking economic unit', along with a greater emphasis on empire itself, was a powerful combination that also acted on New Zealand.[62] However, early New Zealand enthusiasm for the modern exhibition was not matched by anything particularly modern to exhibit. New Zealand's first appearances at exhibitions, naturally enough, were as part of Australasia, and it was characterised by its frontier, not farm, experiences. In 1851, amongst the chaotic displays of the Great Exhibition, the 'Greater Britain' of Edward Gibbon Wakefield's imagination was represented by a small number of commercial and ethnographic exhibits, including a model of a 'New Zealand war pah' and a lithograph of a native village.[63] The country's appearance was 'best described as miscellaneous'.[64] Eleven years later, at the 1862 London International Exhibition, little had changed. Export commodities were limited to small amounts of gold, kauri gum, flax and wood, which were exhibited alongside scenic photographs and paintings, including Charles Heaphy's *The Tarata*

Old New Zealand: a lithograph of J. A. Gilfillan's 'Interior of a Native Village or "Pa" in New Zealand'. An identical lithograph was displayed at the 1851 Great Exhibition. E. Walker, lithr., Day & Son, 1850. C-029-001, Alexander Turnbull Library, Wellington, New Zealand.

Boiling Springs, Roto Mahana, New Zealand.[65] These types of displays were often recycled or supplemented by the contents of ethnographical collections of New Zealanders living in Britain: Julius von Haast's moa skeletons, first reconstructed for an exhibition in Vienna, were a regular feature. But exhibitions were primarily trade shows, and with the demise of gold and the downturn in wool, New Zealand was short on material for the capital of consumption. In the new spaces of metropolitan commodity culture, the 'Britain of the South' had little new to offer.

However, by 1884, just two years after the inaugural shipment of frozen meat, the fledgling industry provided a new basis for New Zealand at the International Health Exhibition at South Kensington. Over 100,000 chops were sold there, a fitting prelude to the development of New Zealand as metropolitan farm.[66] The 'New Zealand Grill' sold eight hundred to a thousand cooked chops each day, and the butcher's shop was also 'doing a roaring trade: in fact, many residents of South Kensington have taken season

New Zealand's pavilion at the Franco-British Exhibition. *Auckland Weekly News,* AWNS-19081001-11-1, Sir George Grey Special Collections, Auckland Libraries.

tickets to the exhibition solely in order to be able to buy mutton there'.[67] (Further evidence of the ways in which metropolitan consumer culture was being shaped by the new produce, the newly established National Training School of Cookery showed how to cook New Zealand frozen meat, consuming another 1400 New Zealand sheep.)[68] In 1886, at the Colonial and Indian Exhibition, both New Zealand and Australia provided frozen meat and produce for the exhibition restaurants, although these were sited at the Colonial Market rather than within the New Zealand exhibit itself.[69] Still, the New Zealand exhibit was more comprehensive than previous iterations. Commodities now mingled with curios: the catalogue acknowledged the growing importance of New Zealand's farm products, alongside displays of birds, ethnological collections, lizards, moa, 'Maori curiosities', geology, fish, invertebrates, tuatara and a red cod.[70] The guidebook noted New Zealand's mineral wealth, but concluded that 'farm products form the chief source of wealth of the colony, the export of wool in 1884 having reached £3,267,327, the frozen meat trade . . . £345,129'.[71]

New Zealand had its first outing as a dominion at the Franco-British Exhibition in 1908, and here the farm began to hold sway. Publicity described New Zealand's exhibits as 'organised mainly to demonstrate the natural resources and productive economy of the Dominion. That the exhibits of products of this class reflect on solid achievement is shown by the value of export trade of New Zealand, which amounted in 1907 to over twenty millions sterling – all but a small part was derived from the country's pastures, fields, mines and forest.'[72] The photographic display emphasised this, with 'enlargements [that] were typical of the agricultural, pastoral, and industrial aspects of the Dominion, as well as the scenic'.[73] Even the dominion's own advertising for the exhibition echoed this farming image, by calling for migrant farmers, shepherds, agricultural labourers and men able to milk cows, albeit alongside an advertisement for tourist and health resorts.[74] By 1911, at the Festival of Empire, New Zealand was represented by four courts – 'Sport and Tourism', 'Timber and Minerals', 'Wool, Grain, and General Exhibits' and 'Refrigeration' – two of which focused on the farm.[75] Visitors who took a ride on the festival's 'All Red' railway saw a Maori village and geysers, but also docks 'where steamers may be seen taking cargoes of grain, wool, and mutton for shipment to Great Britain'.[76] Through the 'perfection of the scene painter's art', they would also see the 'sheep farms of New Zealand', which became part of a bucolic imperial blend as 'the flock and herd would stretch away beyond them. The apples would be plucked from the trees, and the orchards would stretch away into the distance.'[77] Slowly, the frontier fragments that kept New Zealand as colonial space were replaced by images of an improved Arcadia, a hinterland that could co-exist with its metropolis in modern time. Touring All Blacks and colonial soldiers reinforced this, their impressive physiques assumed to be products of an idealised rural existence.

War interrupted the great progress of exhibitions, but they returned in spectacular form in the British Empire Exhibition, held at Wembley from 1924 to 1925. New Zealand was to spend £100,000 on Wembley. After a slow start, around thirty million visitors came to the exhibition, of which the New Zealand pavilion attracted around eight million.[78] In an interview with the *Daily Telegraph*, Special Trade Commissioner Colonel Roberts explained that 'the whole reason [for exhibiting] . . . is to be found in our desire to increase our trade with Great Britain, not only by means of our exports, but by a large increase in the materials we buy from you . . . . Although we may be a small market, we are anxious to do our bit to help empire trade.'[79] This was, of course, the New Zealand version of 'empire trade', where the metropolis was, to all intents and purposes, the empire. The souvenir handbook continued the new trend of equating New Zealand with commodity production, lauding New Zealanders as 'the world's crack-a-jack traders. With a population of 1,300,000 their exports and imports exceeded in value £96,000,000.'[80] This was no peripheral existence, but a partnership in the modern consumer society.

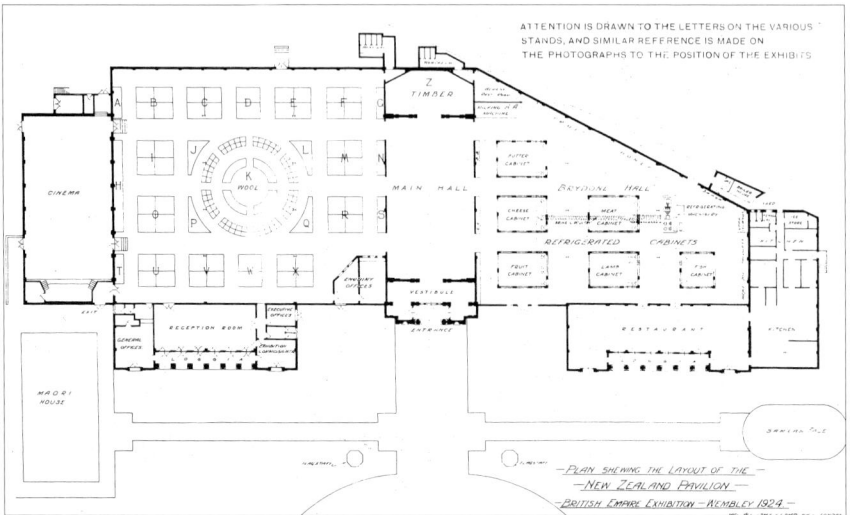

Plan for New Zealand Pavilion, Wembley, 1924. The South Court, to the left of the main hall, featured wool, and the North Court, to the right, featured refrigerated produce. *Souvenir of the New Zealand Pavilion at the British Empire Exhibition*, Wembley, London, 1924, n.p., Alexander Turnbull Library, Wellington, New Zealand.

Fittingly, at Wembley the frontier was no more. The majority of the New Zealand pavilion focused on farming products – butter and cheese, mutton, lamb and wool. The pavilion was designed around two large courts, the North Court being 'devoted almost entirely to a display of primary produce – mutton, lamb, butter, cheese, fruit, and fish, exhibited under frost in refrigerated cabinets.... Nearby and overlooking the lakes will be a restaurant where, as far as practicable, New Zealand products will be served. The main feature in the South Court will be the wool exhibit.'[81] Given the 'British' nature of New Zealand's produce, the restaurant's culinary contribution to any 'New Zealand' distinctiveness is hard to quantify. Toheroa soup, made from a local shellfish, came off the menu amidst fears of ptomaine poisoning, and the restaurant was run by well-known British catering company Lyons. However, the final report for the exhibition claimed that 'so far as the display of Primary Products were concerned, the general consensus of opinion was that in both 1924 and 1925, the New Zealand display was the finest in the exhibition. This was eminently satisfactory when we consider that the chief value of the exhibition to the Dominion was the opportunity for advertising our Primary Products to the consumers in the United

Maori on the margins: decorative motifs in the New Zealand tearooms. IA 10/2/2/15, Archives New Zealand The Department of Internal Affairs Te Tari Taiwhenua.

Kingdom.'[82] The exhibition layout made it clear that the farmers had taken over. Previous exhibition mainstays, minerals and photographic displays, were, like Maori culture, pushed to the margins, with scenic photos lining the walls of New Zealand's shrine to refrigeration in the North Court, the 'Brydone Hall'. Here, spectacular scenery would be overshadowed by the spectacle of commodities, and New Zealand's most prominent mountains were no longer the Southern Alps but mountains of wool, meat and butter.

New Zealand's new exhibition wonders were butter sculptures, products of the farm. Enclosed in 'immense refrigerating cases' were a life-size cow and a New Zealand farmhouse made of butter (fortunately not to scale).[83] New Zealand was literally molded by the metropolis: little butter sailing ships linked butter relief maps of England and New Zealand, exemplifying 'the Dominion's claim that she is the dairy farm of the Empire' even though all the ships were headed for London.[84] The developing 'empire's farm' was in fact a metropolitan one, although the term remained useful within the imperial hierarchy. Imperial farm outranked imperial plantation.

New Zealand's butter exhibit at Wembley, 1924. *Souvenir of the New Zealand Pavilion at the British Empire Exhibition*, Wembley, London, 1924, n.p., Alexander Turnbull Library, Wellington, New Zealand.

Other dominions also used exhibitions to tame their wild frontiers. Over in the Canadian Pavilion, three tons of butter were used to express empire loyalty in the form of a life-size sculpture of the Prince of Wales posed on his Canadian ranch. Later the Canadians recklessly attempted to assert Canadian 'uniqueness' whilst preserving an essential Britishness. They re-sculpted the Prince as Big Chief 'Morning Star', posed amongst butter members of the Tschantoga tribe, horses and dogs.[85] The Prince liked it, but some of the Canadian press and public did not. One paper claimed, 'certainly it is time that Canada should cease to be advertised by representations of Indians in war paint'.[86] Canada, like New Zealand, would rather have been modern than distinctive, particularly if distinctiveness referenced its peripheral past. New Zealand organisers did not risk mixing their metaphors in this way. They preferred sculptures of Alice in Wonderland over any from Maoriland. Despite Canadian competition, results in the butter section were satisfactory, and the New Zealand exhibitors claimed 'there is no doubt that this section of the Primary Products of the Dominion benefited more than any other from the publicity at Wembley ... butter lends itself to artistic molding and ... a really attractive exhibit can be designed.'[87] The exhibit included a machine to cut one-pound packs of butter, which visitors could buy for themselves or post to friends from a kiosk in the court. This version of New Zealand was easily consumed; profits from sales covered the salaries in the section.[88]

The trade in butter: butter relief map of New Zealand, complete with ships and cows (top); and a butter Wonderland (above). *New Zealand Farmer Stock and Station Journal*, 1 September 1925, pp.1358 and p.1359..

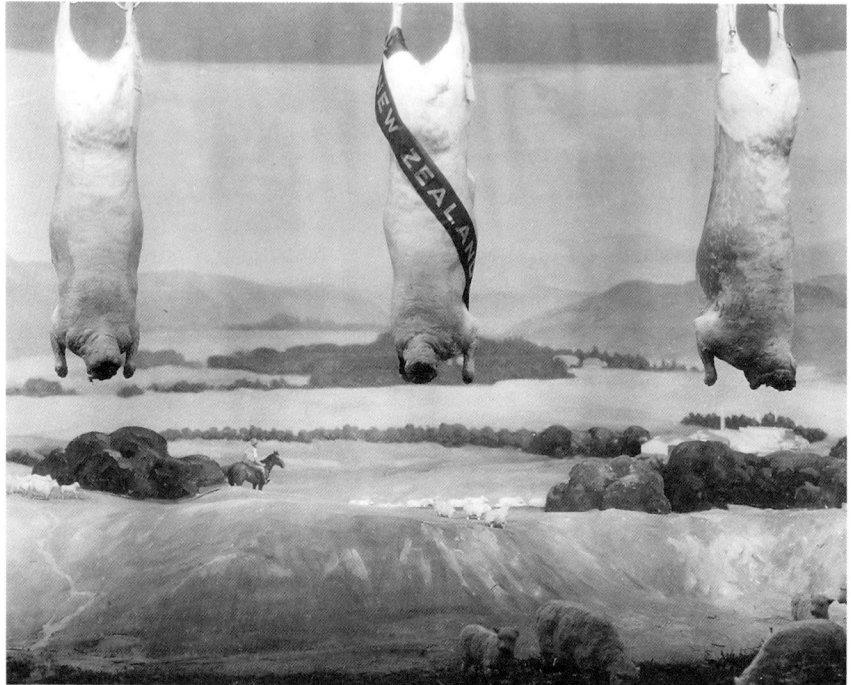

Making meat palatable: a display of carcasses hang over an idyllic farming scene.
IA 10/28, Archives New Zealand The Department of Internal Affairs Te Tari Taiwhenua.

New Zealand's metropolitan farm was built from more than butter. Meat mountains were an enduring aspect of New Zealand's metropolitan image, which, if nothing else, stressed the farm's bounty and reconnected New Zealand with migration literature promises of an everyman's paradise. Organisers avoided 'making it repulsive by too much mass display', using the services 'of the most expert men in the art of meat display' and by introducing 'some novelty in design which will attract attention and detract from the actual "meaty" appearance of the product'.[89] The meat itself was less important than the image of an abundant farm.

The focus on the farm continued in the south court, which featured a wool mountain, topped by a sheep. The problem for organisers here was not so much disguising the product as disguising its utter dullness and ubiquity. They argued, 'it must be realized . . . that the Wool business is now very highly organized and with buyers from all parts of the world attending the sales in New Zealand, our wools are well known to those interested in

The Wool Mountain, South Court, Wembley, 1924. *Souvenir of the New Zealand Pavilion at the British Empire Exhibition*, Wembley, London, 1924, n.p., Alexander Turnbull Library, Wellington, New Zealand.

the trade'.[90] At the heart of their concern, I think, was the fact that wool was akin to an extractive industry, a raw material processed in the centre. The products manufactured from it were therefore harder to identify as 'New Zealand' for consumers. Live sheep made a more interesting alternative and, in 1925, quarantine issues were overcome to allow six Corriedales to vivify the farming imagery.[91]

If wool was dull, it at least added weight to the metropolitan version of New Zealand as improved arcadia. Industry, it seems, did not. Secondary industries, located in the South Court, were overshadowed in every way by the wool mountain. Wembley organisers advocated reducing displays of New Zealand's industrial production still further on the basis that it did not sustain comparison with British manufactures. This reflects the influence of imperial debates on national displays. Exhibits of manufactured products were often used emblematically, as proof of a colony's self-sufficiency and prospects, even of modernity and metropolitan-ness. Dominions, in order to rank above the dependent colonies and to maintain their roles as replica British societies, needed to display some industrial prowess. But imperial preferences tended to define and then present colonies as primary producers; inevitably, secondary production, signifying advancement, was a metropolitan characteristic. The 'great interlocking unit' of empire could be put together only in one very specific way. This formed a significant part of imperial mythology and its hierarchy of colonies, whilst creating a paradox to be resolved by the dominions.

One potential way for New Zealand to tackle this was in its emphasis on the development of the farming 'industry' and its focus on mechanisation. By underlining farming technology, rural New Zealand avoided being seen only as an underdeveloped backward periphery, whilst appearing to remain uncontaminated by the evils of industrialisation that marred the modern metropolis. This nuanced representation was apparent twenty years earlier, at the New Zealand International Exhibition in Christchurch, 1906–7. Analysing the Department of Labour's Court, John E. Martin suggests that it promoted the 'social laboratory of New Zealand' more than its secondary industries, and that 'only in the case of the woollen mills and the manufacture of ammunition was an impression given of a large, mechanized, and organized workplace'.[92] However, there were also displays of timber milling, dairy factories and freezing works. These suggest a way in which New Zealand's exhibitions could be contained within the prevailing imperial imagery, while at the same time asserting the requisite modernity required to maintain dominion competitiveness.

Although mediated by the metropolis, this version of the farm remained important in New Zealand as well. In the Christchurch exhibition's official record, James Cowan describes 'gardens a mass of glowing colour, orchards rich with bending clusters of fruit, haystacks and cornrick; homesteads embowered in evergreen shelter – trees, fields ripe for harvest stretching far and fallow to the sun, now and again the whirring of artesian wells; trucks upon trucks loaded with wheat at the station sidings in transit to the holds of some great London-bound tramp'. Jock Phillips suggests that this image was at the heart of the exhibition, found 'not in the Machinery Hall, but just to the west in the Department of Agriculture's display. The emphasis was very much upon New Zealand's agricultural, rather than industrial progress, for the country presented itself to its overseas visitors as a supplier of agricultural goods and a market for the products of foreign factories.'[93]

As Cowan's orchards, haystacks and cornricks suggest, the New Zealand farm was given an English ambiance, in a reinvention of the mythic and timeless 'dear old rural England' for the modern consumer. Exhibitions emphasised this farm, with its borrowed overtones of the metropolis's past, over New Zealand's own colonial past. Its 'British' nature was also developed through the ordering of exhibition space itself, a process that made good use of modern techniques to remodel time and space. Metropolitan exhibitions of this period were explicitly imperial in their design. The 1911 Festival of Empire was promoted as an 'Imperial "At Home", hosted by the "Mother City", London, as the "Mecca of Empire", the heart and home of the British Race'.[94] The implications of exhibitions as shaping forces for the centre are clear. They reify the role of London as the modern imperial metropolis. The 1911 exhibition featured a train ride round the 'All-Red Route' that encircled the empire in just twenty minutes, taking visitors from Newfoundland to South Africa, via the scenery of Jamaica, a Malay village, 'the oriental splendours of the native bazaar', Australian sheep farming and the Parliament House at Ottawa.[95] For an even faster survey of the empire, visitors could view a model of the exhibition at Aldwych, a Lilliputian version of empire located appropriately enough within another miniaturised version, the imperial heart of London with its colonial 'houses'.

The act of recreating empire in the metropolis, separated only by avenues and not oceans, displayed the ordering power of the centre and allied it with modernity. But it also risked disordering the empire.[96] The white settler colonies, their special relationship formalised in the 'Dominion' title, were presented with particular challenges when contextualised as part of a disparate, largely 'dependent' empire. Their response was to present themselves as distinctive, yet coherent, parts of this whole. Individual displays therefore took place within arguably national frames, symbolised in their 'national' pavilions. But these were always incomplete; or, rather, 'nation' was completed by appearing within the context of empire as created in the metropolis. In a cultural form of symbiosis, the metropolis was complicit in, not oppositional to, the production of a complete nation. Whilst the pavilions and their contents can be seen as metonyms for nations, they also express imperial concerns, or a dominion's role within the 'world order' created on site.

The separation of the 'white dominions' from the rest of the empire is further illustrated in the arrangement of the pavilions and courts. At the multi-imperial Franco-British Exhibition of 1908, the dominions were arranged together, even if along the unfortunately titled 'Avenue of the Colonies'. Rivalry could be fierce: at the same exhibition, Australia paid an 'exceptionally large rent on the understanding that the view of the Pavilion façade would be completely unobstructed', and subsequently took court action when the Commissioner General allowed another building to block part of it.[97] The 'white' or overseas dominions would commonly be grouped together, as would colonies and crown dependencies. India was its own category. This 'opposition between the "races of the jungle and the moor" was a persistent element in British imperial discourse', and an obvious feature within the exhibition halls.[98] At the Colonial and Indian Exhibition of 1886, visitors could move from the exotica of India to the Australasian sections, which offered 'science, landscape painting, manufactures, minerals, wool, and wood' and in which 'one met with no Oriental, but a sturdy British element'.[99] These distinctions were writ large in pavilion design. Whilst local architectural styles could be included in dependent colony pavilions, the dominions preferred to promote 'civilisation'. Their pavilions for the 1911 exhibition were based on three-quarter scale models of their parliaments, classically styled buildings embodying the very nature of 'self-governing' dominions, relentlessly positioning their present in a civilised, not primitive, past. In 1924, the dominions appeared as calm embodiments of 'timeless' western civilisation, with white, neoclassical facades, classical sculptures and frescoes as decoration. These plaster claims to a proper past and position within empire had their permanent equivalent in the High Commission buildings found around the Strand.[100]

Reordering imperial space and time contributed to New Zealand's manifestation as a white settler society, represented with, but apart from, the exotic members of the 'dependent empire'. The opposition helped reinforce the difference. However, New Zealand also needed to be differentiated from the rest of the 'overseas dominions' to attract immigrants, promote trade and satisfy local pride. The need for both separation from and identification with the other white settler dominions was a general problem: New Zealand largely resolved this paradox by promoting 'settled' New Zealand, imaged by its essentially 'British' character, but buttressed and most widely promoted through its developing role as Britain's farm. On the other hand,

The main entrance of the New Zealand Pavilion, Wembley, 1924. *Souvenir of the New Zealand Pavilion at the British Empire Exhibition*, Wembley, London, 1924, n.p., Alexander Turnbull Library, Wellington, New Zealand.

Maori culture, which we might have expected to see serve as a symbol of 'New Zealand', was, in this context, problematic. A touch of indigenous culture provided differentiation, whilst, as the Canadians found in their butter sculpting, too much endangered the image of a progressive 'Great Britain under the Southern Cross', threatening to reposition it as a frontier fragment. This tension may account for the myriad presentations of Maori culture discussed in the extant exhibition and tourism secondary literature. They were largely attempts to contain and domesticate unsettlement – the same techniques came in handy for geysers, so it is perhaps no coincidence that wild landscapes and people were merged in the tourist spectacle of Rotorua, and then kept at a safe distance from the rest of the country.[101]

As New Zealand began to re-envision itself in the metropole, different strategies emerged to contain Maori and to preserve a 'settled' landscape in which their presence was reduced.[102] The *Colonial and Indian* guidebook of 1886 minimised, contained and normalised Maori culture in New Zealand, claiming 'there are, it is estimated, about 44,000 Maoris or aboriginal inhabitants. A great part of these are given to the same peaceful pursuits as the European settlers – growing wheat, potatoes etc and keeping cattle. Every year is increasing this. Schools are everywhere established for the Maori children; they have their own churches and Christian ministers, and the possibility of any disturbance with the Maori has passed away, and life and property are as safe in New Zealand as in England.'[103] The 1886 exhibition court continued to include Maori exhibits but only 'so as to show what New Zealand was like in the Old Maori times and then to show what it is doing now'.[104] Accordingly, organisers chose to surround pataka Mataatua, a carved house that had been used regularly in other overseas exhibitions since it was completed in 1875, with wax figures, rather than use live exhibits of native people as other colonies did. This and a carved tomb placed in the fernery were illustrative of Maori as a dying race, belonging 'to a past which is as dead as the age of the cave-men and lake-dwellers'.[105] Despite a presentation more sepulchral than savage, however, it seems that any appearance by Maori could have threatened to reanimate New Zealand as periphery. One writer at the time, John Bradshaw, felt the New Zealand Court was a failure for reasons entirely consonant with New Zealand's new relationship to the metropole: 'stuffed birds and tall tree ferns may be the products of an uninhabited island; the native whare and Maori curios referred to an almost forgotten past than to the present'.[106] It is hardly surprising that in 1890 Joubert would include Maori only 'with caution'. Maori were to function like ferns, picturesque exotica that might be found only at the margins of the farming landscape.

Clearly, the presence of Maori in metropolitan versions of New Zealand remained troubling, remnants of the old colony conflicting with the image of a progressive and 'British' settlement. A live troupe, led by Maggie Papakura, was incorporated into the 1911 Festival of Empire, despite the misgivings of organisers. As was usual at exhibitions, they were supposed to live within a replica village and this was situated at some distance from the New Zealand pavilion. The troupe was literally required to live in the past. Although popular with visitors, the living Maori village concept foundered, and the troupe abandoned both the village and the festival, moving on to another exhibition at the White City. There they were housed beside another one of empire's symbols of the past, a replica Irish village.[107] They may have appeared in the Festival's *Pageant of London*, where Maori were converted into proof of the value of the colonising project and New Zealand's progressive social conditions, and also as 'the solitary example of a dark race surviving contact with a white, and associating with it on terms of mutual regards, equality, and unquestioned loyalty'. The aptly named masque was, after all, 'an allegory of the advantages of empire', and New Zealand was represented in the pageant by the signing of the Treaty of Waitangi, a notably conciliatory experience that ended with Governor William Hobson's famous phrase 'he iwi tahi tatou' (we are one people) and the flying of the Union Jack.[108]

The 1924 Wembley Exhibition pageant was more elaborate, creating a benevolent empire suffering from amnesia, although it dispensed with real Maori and used Londoners dressed up instead. However, Cook's arrival was added to the treaty set piece, with facsimile natives at 'a respectful distance', along with the 'strangely chivalrous' 'war with the Maoris, 1864', which ended when confiscated land was returned, and 'under tolerant and tactful administration, their troubles were soon forgotten'. With the past sealed, Maori return as proof of imperial unity in the last scene, 'The Call to Arms'. 'The Union Jack is unfurled, and men of all kinds and classes, including the Maoris fall into rank together and march off to martial music in answer to the call of the Empire.'[109] Here, having located Maori within an historic and imperial context, they were then made to vanish in the accompanying publicity: 'it must be realised that the native race of New Zealand is after all an unimportant element in the life of the Dominion. New Zealand is emphatically a white country populated by British people. This will be understood when it is stated that the British population is more than one and one quarter million, whereas the Maoris number only 50,000. The New Zealand section of the British Empire Exhibition aims to demonstrate what are the contributions to the common civilisation of the British Empire made by this essentially British Dominion.'[110]

This, surprisingly enough, is not to suggest that Maori culture had no place in exhibitions, but that it was difficult to find an appropriate role for it within this newly envisioned 'white country populated by British people'.[111] Thirty years earlier, in 1890, the Chief Representative of Thomas Cook and Son, Ernest Bilborough, argued for Maori inclusion in Joubert's proposed exhibition, claiming it would strengthen New Zealand's position, 'especially when the attractions that the Maori and the South Sea Islanders presented to Englishmen is considered'.[112] These were, of course, historicised and romanticised Maori and South Sea Islanders, which, as in the pageants, were civilised through colonisation, then contained safely in the past. Still, even then others remained opposed, claiming 'our exports on the English markets are the best proofs of the fruitfulness of our soils ... not Mr Joubert's score or two of half-clad Maoris and his other showman's devices'.[113] Organisers at Wembley would have agreed. Including Maori in that exhibition could 'undermine "the idea of the Dominion being up-to-date"'.[114] The meeting house Mataatua was included but, significantly, it was placed outside the main exhibition hall. There, it acted as a symbol of

Outside the modern dominion: Mataatua was located alongside the official pavilion. IA 10/1/1/6, Archives New Zealand The Department of Internal Affairs Te Tari Taiwhenua.

the past, in contrast to the 'timeless' pavilion filled with the products of the modern farm. Emphasising its role as a cultural sarcophagus, the meeting house was 'to contain fine specimens of Maori carvings and other relics of the aboriginal natives of New Zealand'.[115] But even this role was short-lived. In Wembley's second year, Mataatua was replaced by a pen of live sheep.

The strict identification of Maori with a vanishing frontier past and the overwhelming presence of the 'farm' were instrumental in the process of creating a 'British' New Zealand, emphatically part of the dominions, and not part of the exotic empire. This process would be extended by primary produce advertisers, considered in the next chapter. At Wembley, although the 'Rotorua Diorama was undoubtedly one of the star attractions of the whole Exhibition', it was ultimately a safe box for old, wild New Zealand.[116] The official souvenir guide felt 'it cannot be too strongly emphasized that changing one's home to New Zealand is not the same as wandering to a foreign country; it is simply paying a visit – more or less prolonged – to

Mataatua's replacement: a pen of New Zealand's very own Corriedales. IA 10/2/2/21, Archives New Zealand The Department of Internal Affairs Te Tari Taiwhenua.

another relative in the same old family; for New Zealanders are more British – if one may seek to use an anachronism – than the British'.[117]

By 1925, then, a new version of New Zealand had developed, its raw materials transformed by the combined pressures of metropolis as metonym of empire and as centre of the new commodity culture. After the exhibition gates closed, London's farm would be created through new means, on a scale that would make the eight million visitors to Wembley seem small. In the commodity capital, 'London's farm' would be configured and disseminated through mass advertising created by producer boards and the Empire Marketing Board. In these sites, we find further evidence of a transnational cultural conversation, its reciprocal imagery creating a New Zealand truly 'polished to suit the metropolitan taste'.

CHAPTER SIX

'PRODUCED BY BRITONS FOR BRITISH HOMES'

ALTHOUGH IT WAS NOT clear at the time, the British Empire Exhibition at Wembley was to be the last of the great imperial exhibitions.[1] But the New Zealand commodity spectacular lived on. It moved out from the tight space and time constraints of an exhibition site and into the much more broadly dispersed spaces of mass consumer advertising. 'New Zealand' was relocated from pavilions to billboards, from display cases to press advertising, as representations of commodities came to consumers, rather than, as at exhibitions, the other way around. From the 1920s, the metropolis's mass consumption of New Zealand produce would be complemented by the mass marketing of New Zealand as farm.

Exhibitions had contained commodities within a 'New Zealand' pavilion. But in the new spaces of mass marketing, commodities could theoretically be set free of their association with New Zealand. Butter, potentially, could stand for itself, or indeed anything, rather than become a sculpted version of

New Zealand. Yet primary produce continued to be co-opted as the central actor in the performance of New Zealand in London. In primary produce advertising, largely undertaken in the metropolis by government-formed producer boards, 'New Zealand' became the brand under which all produce was advertised, and London remained the major market. To borrow the words of one advertiser, the Empire Marketing Board (EMB), butter, cheese and meat were the commodities, but 'New Zealand' was the idea.[2] Whilst technology like refrigeration made it possible for New Zealand to function as a rural hinterland, new technologies of consumerism helped dictate the outlines of that place.

Three key factors converged to shape commodity culture's version of 'New Zealand' and to keep it central. First, advertising itself was changing. Its emphasis shifted from what a product could *do* to what a product could *mean*. Second, the rise of producer boards changed the nature of commodity marketing and concentrated marketing around a national brand. Finally, the market itself changed. Free-trading Britain turned to imperial preference, meaning the image of the 'Empire's farm' had considerable economic, not just sentimental, benefits.

Early advertising emphasised a product's usefulness, whether this was real or imagined. Advertisements for Victorian-era patent medicines, with their extravagant lists of claims, are good examples of this. From the early twentieth century, however, advertising began to shift away from emphasising a product's usefulness, towards a greater emphasis on its symbolic qualities or associations.[3] It was the idea, not just the product, that was to be marketed. In New Zealand's case, the idea was 'the farm', and the brand was New Zealand itself. So advertising, developed to sell meat and dairy produce in the metropolis, also created a national identity. Combined, they constructed New Zealand as British farming hinterland.

This new approach to advertising was one marketing innovation; producer boards as clients were another. Producer boards and their advertising have not generated much historical attention, even in economic history, and New Zealand's dependence on the British market is more likely to be condemned as shortsighted than examined for innovation.[4] But in this chapter, we will find plenty of new ideas. To begin with, producer boards were novelties themselves. Although they were concerned with practical marketing matters like controlling supply, shipping rates and quality, by the 1920s New Zealand's newly formed producer boards were working with

London advertising agencies such as S. L. A. Mastin (SLAM!), creating and participating in the newest forms of commodity discourse to create a New Zealand for metropolitan consumption.[5] In the case of the dairy industry, producer board promotions were augmented and outpaced by the industry's most effective marketer, the New Zealand Co-operative Dairy Company. However, they too marketed 'New Zealand'. These intense efforts to build and secure markets for primary produce in Britain are grounds on their own to re-evaluate our cultural history. Interwar New Zealand has long been portrayed as a cultural wasteland, not least by literary nationalists who were engaged in forging their own version of New Zealand identity in this period. However, viewed through the lens of commodity culture rather than high culture, the years after World War I become one of the busiest periods of New Zealand's image-making, although they were not images those nationalists would like. Commodity advertising refined and redoubled the presentation of New Zealand as settled, Home-styled farm, not distinctive nation.

Finally, these developments occurred against a background of fundamental economic changes that significantly impacted the choices New Zealand marketers made in presenting their primary produce. During the interwar years, Britain steadily retreated from free trade towards a protected economy. Faced with reduced industrial dominance, increasing international competition, economic decline and depression, and constant pressure from the dominions (who stood to gain most from the change), Britain finally turned towards imperial economic unity as a solution. Tariff reform, including imperial preference – the pet scheme of ardent imperialists – had a longer history, but these changing conditions meant that preferential, reciprocal trade amongst members of empire finally looked like a feasible option.[6] It became an economic reality at the Imperial Economic Conference held in Ottawa in 1932, after a good deal of bad-tempered bickering between the dominions and Britain over the nature and scale of preferences to be offered.[7] Whilst historians remain unclear about 'who fooled whom' in Ottawa's negotiating rooms, the longer-term impact of a greater economic emphasis on empire played out in the articulation of New Zealand's identity.[8] John Darwin has suggested that the 'popular image of Empire as the source for Britain's food and raw materials ... was really fixed in the 1930s even if its roots were laid earlier'.[9] New Zealand had been working on that for a bit longer, but imperial preference reinforced the existing division between the primary-producing rural hinterlands of empire and the secondary industries of the metropolitan centre.[10] Farm and city were constructed again, metropolis and hinterland re-emerging, this time in imperial guise. Although empire was the context of New Zealand's appearances at exhibitions, in commodity advertising it became explicit in content as well. Empire and Britishness became integral parts of New Zealand as farm.

MEAT MARKETING 'BRITISH! NEW ZEALAND'

The first shipment of frozen meat from New Zealand to London in 1882 was successful enough to be reported as a 'prodigious' fact.[11] The second arrived with mildewed cargo, during a glut, and was sold at a loss. Like the two meat salesmen at the back of the Lord Mayor's parade, meat marketing in the metropolis began in an improvised and disorganised fashion. Lamb, not mutton, was to be the 'meat of the future', and 'frozen' was not an adjective that marketers would later choose to attach to New Zealand meat. By 1922, with the establishment of the New Zealand Meat Producers Board, spontaneous improvisation in marketing was to be a thing of the past. Inaugurated in response to New Zealand fears of overseas 'meat trusts' entering the local trade, the board's establishment also reflected concern over a price slump that occurred in 1920, directly after the end of Britain's wartime commandeering of all New Zealand's food exports. The board's primary concerns were to regulate shipments to avoid gluts and shortages, and to reduce freight charges. However, they quickly turned to problems of market competition and expansion. London was their main market. In the first annual report, the board was 'strongly of the opinion that special advertising of New Zealand lamb and mutton throughout Great Britain should be undertaken, and the newly appointed London Manager, who has recently left New Zealand to take up his position, has received instructions on the matter'.[12]

From the board's inception, then, New Zealand meat would be promoted by associating it with 'national' characteristics, a selective process that would create a particular version of New Zealand in the metropolis. Much of the board's work concentrated on London: in 1930, New Zealand still supplied 63 per cent of Smithfield's imported mutton and lamb, and

'The best in the world': New Zealand lamb in Mr J. Hammond's shop window, Gosport. New Zealand Meat Producers Board, *Annual Report and Statement of Accounts, 1928*, Wellington, 1928, p.10.

only 46 per cent of the rest of the United Kingdom's supply, a share hardly different from that of 1910, when New Zealand supplied 66 per cent of London's mutton and lamb.[13] The Meat Board spread its marketing net wider, constructing New Zealand in sites ranging from the inside covers of British stamp books, to an electric van that toured seaside resorts, flashing messages about New Zealand lamb a thousand times a day. However, the centrepiece of the board's marketing was the butcher's window, a spectacularly ordinary approach to us now, but one that was innovative at the time. As butchers, once wary of frozen meat, began to carry it, the board was first to utilise butchers' window spaces for promotional purposes, developing a network of 20,000 participating stores.[14] These windows acted as mini exhibition spaces: little New Zealands could be liberally sprinkled throughout London and greater Britain, mini arcadias interwoven amongst the arcades of the modern metropolis.

One of the earliest was Mr J. Hammond's Gosport shop. In 1927, his window display was limited to a poster, claiming New Zealand lamb as the best in the world, and a row of hanging carcasses. These carcasses were members of a select touring team of 650 frozen lambs purchased for

'PRODUCED BY BRITONS FOR BRITISH HOMES'

Advertising for New Zealand lamb in the Home and Colonial Tea Stores. Note the Union Jack and 'British New Zealand' map. New Zealand Meat Producers Board, *Annual Report and Statement of Accounts, 1930*, Wellington, 1930, n.p.

promotional purposes. They were displayed in central London department stores and then Smithfield market before touring suburban London butchers' shops and finally reaching provincial outlets like Mr Hammond's. The lambs signified not only quality but abundance, and mammoth meat displays reminiscent of exhibitions were to remain central to meat advertising in the metropolis. By 1930, the touring team was over one thousand strong (with a few wax reserves) and increased promotion was accompanied by increased sophistication in point of sale material.

A Home and Colonial Tea Store window inaugurated two key themes in the development of New Zealand as familiar farm: health and Britishness. Window cards stressed that meat was produced 'under PERFECT hygienic conditions and strictest GOVERNMENT VETERINARY INSPECTION. Every carcass is officially GUARANTEED PURE.' The emphasis on hygiene, purity and cleanliness reflected late Victorian and Edwardian debates, revived in the 1930s, over the perils of modernity and urbanisation, both of which were held to have impacted on food quality.[15] Lower quality was suspected to be a product of rural decline in Britain, accompanied by a greater quantity of prepackaged and imported food.[16] Manufacturers used advertising to mount their defence: Huntly and Palmers 'portrayed its factory as pursuing a "Cult of Perfection"', while 'Smithfield meat market advertised the benefit of its large scale operations and strict inspection regime'.[17] The practice of displaying whole carcasses, even if made of wax, reduced the appearance of processing and helped sidestep concerns over adulteration and negativity around 'factory' food.

Images of freezing works and abattoirs, although crucial to meat exporting, could therefore be counterproductive in meat advertising. So the idealised New Zealand farm appeared, rather than the freezing works. Nor did the meat appear to be advertised as frozen. 'New Season's lamb' was a more useful marketing approach, as it artfully managed seasons and temperatures to evade the issue of freezing altogether. Weeks of icy transit (and possibly even longer storage) were excised in a 1938 press campaign, when 'frozen England' received lamb from 'summer pastures'. 'Winter in England is summer time in New Zealand and here is NEW SEASON'S MILK-FED NEW ZEALAND LAMB direct from those sunbathed pasturelands for you today. Rich in vitamins, delicious in tenderness and flavour, economical – a treat indeed and so good for you.'[18] Imagery of 'sunbathed pastures' could mitigate any residual stigma associated with freezing, particularly when combined with promotional cookbooks, information booklets and cooking demonstrations. As late as 1930, forty-five years after the Colonial Grill's 'roaring trade' in chops, cooked joints were still being made into lamb sandwiches and given away. 'In this very effective manner the prejudice against frozen meat is being broken down.'[19] For similar reasons, the board had developed the 'Lamb Presentation Scheme', whereby friends could send gifts of legs of lamb to British homes.

Beneficial in deflecting attention from freezing, sunshine imagery also linked New Zealand meat with contemporary scientific ideas about health. In a reversal of late Victorian fears about sun exposure, sunlight was now considered health-giving. People were encouraged by organisations such as

'Sunshine Products': New Zealand meat and dairy products are promoted in Liverpool. New Zealand Meat Producers Board, *Annual Report and Statement of Accounts, 1934*, Wellington, 1934, n.p.

the Sunlight Leagues to expose themselves to sunshine.[20] Board advertising suggested that New Zealand meat, product of an apparently endless summer, was therefore better for consumers, and advertising could actually revolve around the sun. In 1933, the New Zealand High Commission's window on the Strand, often pressed into service for commodity promotions, featured the sun as its centrepiece 'around which orbited some half dozen of our model carcasses with black velvet draped in the background' and some lambs grazing on imitation grass. In 1934, a joint promotion with the New Zealand Dairy Export Produce Control Board in Liverpool combined butter, cheese, lamb and mutton under the banner of 'Sunshine Products for Merseyside'. This theme was repeated in promotional posters, featuring sheep spelling out 'N.Z.' on a hillside, against the backdrop of an enormous rising sun.

The emphasis on 'Britishness' may also have been related to issues of health and purity. Race and food had been connected in debates that associated poor quality food with racial degeneration.[21] However, mutton

A new cross-breed: the 'British' New Zealand Lamb. Point of sale material for butcher-shop windows. New Zealand Meat Producers Board, *Annual Report and Statement of Accounts, 1930*, Wellington, 1930, n.p.

and lamb were British, not 'foreign' produce, and New Zealand meat could be positioned as a substitute for meat already familiar to British consumers. Serendipitous consumer confusion over the true origins of Canterbury lamb only emphasised New Zealand's similarities to Home, and 'prime Canterbury Lamb' signs were commingled in shop windows with the 'British! New Zealand' campaign. Nor was this confusion simply apocryphal: a survey conducted by the Empire Marketing Board in 1930 in Colchester noted that 'one butcher mentioned a customer who had asked for Canterbury lamb, and said she would prefer it killed the previous week as she liked her meat to have been hung a day or two. He seems to have told her she would be lucky if it was killed the previous year.'[22]

However, the most likely reason for the development of the British New Zealand farm was the increasing importance of the work of the Empire Marketing Board, which, from 1926, ran publicity campaigns to promote the purchase of British produce first.[23] It is likely that these campaigns led to the otherwise geographically curious labelling of the map of New Zealand as 'British!' featured in the Home and Colonial Tea Store's display, and the subsequent development of a suite of 'British New Zealand' marketing material. The 'British!' New Zealand map of 1930 was incorporated in 1931 into window friezes, window streamers up to six feet long, window discs and cut-out lambs in two sizes, bearing the legend 'British

'Produced by Britons for British Homes': New Zealand High Commission window on the Strand, London. New Zealand Meat Producers Board, *Annual Report and Statement of Accounts, 1931*, Wellington, 1931, n.p.

New Zealand Lamb – the Best in the World'. In New Zealand's commodity culture at least, colonial cringe is notably absent. Although it is hard to imagine a poster design that could outdo 'New Zealand Lamb – British to the Backbone', especially when propped in front of hanging carcasses, in 1932, 'an even more elaborate and attractive range of material [was] prepared for issue to retailers'.[24] This range included rosettes proclaiming 'I am British from New Zealand.' In 1934, 310,000 of these were issued, along with 2,500,000 similarly inscribed joint seals that would be attached to the meat itself.

Themes of purity, health and Britishness were integrated in the window of the New Zealand High Commission for four months in 1930, which on this occasion was turned into a replica butcher's shop. Hygiene and purity were emphasised directly, with cut-out lambs and a showcard printed with 'guaranteed pure'. These qualities were also symbolised in the clean, modern shop that located modernity firmly in the metropolis, and the model female shopper labelled 'discerning'. 'Sunny New Zealand' could also have modern connotations, given the new science around sunshine. Like the idea of a 'farming industry', it negotiated a space between the evils of modernity and its benefits. (The connection with New Zealand and health also resonates with earlier emigration imagery of New Zealand's health-promoting climate, and as a rejuvenating destination for invalids.) The farm shown through the window is typical of primary produce advertising, harnessing the contradictory images of emptiness and abundance to portray the antithesis of urbanisation. It is at once empty of people yet abundant, its productivity obvious in the flock of sheep and the show card advertising ten million carcasses sent to Britain. The mannequin butcher seems to be pointing to this landscape, rather than to the hanging carcasses, focusing the viewer's attention whilst suggesting that New Zealand is just through the window. Helpfully, distance between London and its faraway New Zealand farm is excised in the prominent tagline, 'Direct from New Zealand's sunny pastures to your table.' Propinquity, of course, denotes kinship as well as closeness, and the recreation of the farm in London supported the window's primary message: 'New Zealand lamb. Produced by Britons for British Homes.'

A passerby in the Strand eight years later might have noted a shift in the imaging of the metropolitan farm. Whilst New Zealand lamb was still the 'best in the world', it was not marked 'British'. Further, the usual meat mountains had disappeared – just two carcasses adorned a window that was devoted to a diorama of a farmhouse, rolling hills, cabbage trees and flocks of sheep. Four smaller dioramas featured tourist views of New Zealand scenery. Despite what seems to be an apparent lurch towards a more 'authentic' portrayal of New Zealand, this window is as much a creation of the metropolitan, imperial context as its predecessors. From 1935, the Meat Marking Order required all imported meat to be branded as 'empire', 'foreign' or with the name of the country of origin. 'Empire' could, of course, denote the suspect dependent empire, from which New Zealand had spent considerable effort separating itself. Further, because most of New Zealand's meat competitors were empire-based (over half of British meat supplies were still produced in Britain), the soundest strategy to protect market share would have been to brand with country of origin, especially given the previous investment in developing the British New Zealand connection. It seems it was worth forgoing some imperial identity to avoid being lumped together with Australia. From 1935, all marketing material 'was specially designed to draw the attention of the public to the fact that all New Zealand meat is branded New Zealand and that NO New Zealand meat

Safely at the margins of the English-style farm, cabbage trees, geysers and Maori figures provide distinctly New Zealand iconography to meat marketing in the New Zealand High Commission window on the Strand, London. New Zealand Meat Producers Board, *Annual Report and Statement of Accounts, 1939*, Wellington, 1939, n.p.

would be branded Empire'.[25] Thus, the High Commission window added small touches of distinctiveness to the metropolitan farm's landscape, without endangering the familiar nature of the rural idyll. Exotic cabbage trees were counterbalanced by a very civilised-looking farmhouse, and the scenic additions were ranged around the edge of the display. One view featured two Maori, traditionally dressed, positioned beside a pair of active geysers. As we might have expected from the sparing and cautious co-option of Maori in exhibitions, they remained as historic fragments, remnants of a wild frontier once again safely corralled in a three-dimensional box on the margins of the farm.

By virtue of the Meat Marking Order, 'New Zealand' was even more firmly connected with its farming products and the iconography used to promote them. These images became ubiquitous. By 1932, the board was able to boast, 'No other meat receives anything like the publicity in Great Britain given to New Zealand meat, and in fact there is no other empire product which is better known or more widely advertised.'[26] In the interwar period, the relentless promotion of the farm subsumed New Zealand's other identities in the metropolis. While just £3,000 was spent by the board in 1926, through the 1930s direct marketing expenditure increased tenfold – and this does not include High Commission expenses.[27]

The board proved adept at generating free publicity too, using carefully staged promotions. Publicity drives were often accompanied by window-dressing competitions, which were rapidly extended to include other events. Children's colouring competitions, designed, then as now, to ensnare parents as well, were popular, with over 200,000 'skeleton' painting sheets of New Zealand lamb advertising distributed to retailers in 1935. Small cash prizes would be awarded, and all entrants were invited to a free cinema show, which included the New Zealand meat industry film 'From Meadow to Market'. Local dignitaries such as the mayor and mayoress awarded the prizes and even the High Commissioner for New Zealand might attend. In 1938, the board noted that 'sometimes the entry is so large that we have to book two large cinemas to accommodate the children.... This is an eminently effective type of publicity not only for New Zealand meat but is good publicity for New Zealand.'[28]

Adults could join the fun by decorating vans or bicycles, and even themselves, in New Zealand point of sale material. The 1932 Meat Producers Board annual report noted, 'A large and wide demand has been experienced for the Board's general advertising matter for making up into fancy dress costumes for Empire Shopping Weeks, Dances, Carnivals, and Fêtes which are regularly held all over Britain. Many traders request special material for decorating vans and lorries, and full advantage is taken of these offers.'[29] The decorated bicycle competition, devised in 1935, 'proved an instant success. The entrants are obliged to utilize the advertising with which we supply them and the decorated machines are paraded though the town for a distance of, say, two miles, to a central judging point.'[30] In the coronation year of 1937, special red, white and blue crepe paper was printed with an advertisement for New Zealand lamb in gold lettering. Rather than ornamenting shop windows, this was to be used for fancy dress costumes, and 'retailers were circularized as to the availability of this material and supplied with sketch designs showing not only how the material could be used for fancy costumes, but also for decorating motor cars and/or vans and cycles for carnival purposes'.[31]

A rise in mass consumer advertising complemented the expansion of public relations activities. The board had previously engaged in wholesale

A parade of British butchers' bicycles decorated with New Zealand lamb-marketing material. New Zealand Meat Producers Board, *Annual Report and Statement of Accounts, 1935*, Wellington, 1935, n.p.

advertising, using trade journals, and circulating hotels and boarding houses with information booklets. In 1932, butchers distributed three and a half million postcards featuring 'six different scenes of typical New Zealand farm country'.[32] Reinforcement came in the form of sample menu cards featuring pastoral scenes circulated to 12,000 hotels and boarding houses. By 1934, half a million had been distributed. Schools also received 'a set of twenty five miniature cards with a pastoral view of New Zealand on one side, and a question relative to New Zealand on the other'.[33] However, the greatest innovation was the development of magazine advertising. Reflecting the rising recognition of the importance of women as purchasers, the board's advertisements featured in publications such as the *Ladies' Home Journal* and *Woman's Weekly*, estimating appearances in twenty-six million copies between May and September of 1934, rising to fifty-seven million in 1939.[34] A smaller press campaign ran alongside this, using 179 of the leading evening papers, 'including all the large London evening papers,

The first-prize-winning window display of a Monmouthshire butcher. New Zealand Meat Producers Board, *Annual Report and Statement of Accounts, 1939*, Wellington, 1939, n.p.

and local papers circulating in Greater London, and the Home Counties and the Provinces'.[35]

New media prompted new approaches. For the first time, consumers were featured, as smiling families pictured eating 'Delicious New Zealand lamb'.[36] These advertisements themselves reflected little of the farming iconography developed in other spaces, yet images of whiteness, familiarity and domesticity remained attached to the New Zealand brand. Further, the board's reports carry only a sample of the advertising used: it is likely that other advertisements continued to carry messages about rural, healthy New Zealand. Indeed, in the board's approach to marketing, we have a case of evolutionary identity. Whilst changes in emphasis did occur, during the period from 1923 to 1939 new themes joined, rather than replaced, earlier versions. A final shop window helps illustrate the point. In Monmouthshire, in 1939, purity, sunshine, health, a happy consumer and the modern craze for crossword puzzles come together to create a 'New Zealand' – branded product, which remains 'British to the Backbone'.

DAIRY MARKETING THE ANCHOR AND THE FERNLEAF

If the work of the New Zealand Meat Producers Board could create an idea of New Zealand through the marketing of a commodity, then it seems reasonable to expect that the work of the Dairy Board, formed just one year later in 1923, would work in much the same manner and that the following discussion of dairy marketing would reveal a similar series of shop windows, dressed with 'Cheese made by Britons'. Yet the story is not quite the same, reflecting differences in the industry's internal structure and its external competitors. I also need to note the inadequacy of both primary and secondary sources for developing this story of the marketing of one of New Zealand's agricultural mainstays and so my conclusions must be tentative, perhaps even speculative. Whilst there has been some interest in the history of dairying, particularly in local dairy factory histories, discussion has been largely restricted to its economic or industrial development.[37] In addition, no attention has been paid to the ways in which New Zealand's dairy brands have been developed or used. When we consider that the New Zealand Co-operative Dairy Company (NZCDC) was, even as early as the 1920s, one of the world's largest dairy exporting companies, this is a significant omission.

The strange tale of dairy marketing reflects the internal divisions within the dairy industry itself. From the outset, it was marked by the proliferation of small factories. Unlike frozen meat processing, dairying infrastructure required a relatively small capital investment: in 1891 there were seventy-four factories, with an average investment of £1,357 and an average staff of just four (in 1886, the average investment in meat processing plants was ten times that).[38] Contention between North and South Island producers, between co-operative and proprietary companies, between the NZCDC and others, also made industry co-operation difficult. Dairy companies sold their produce through individual competitive contracts made with agents based in London's Tooley Street. For a brief moment, the industry was able to agree on the formation of the New Zealand Dairy Export Control Board. But accord quickly descended into acrimony over the idea of absolute control, introduced in 1926. To the great pleasure of Tooley Street agents, free marketing returned after thirteen months and was maintained until the advent of state marketing under the Labour government from 1936. The

London's farm in action post-war: *The New Zealand Journal of Agriculture*'s August 1946 cover reminds farmers exactly where their produce is going. Maurice Conley, *New Zealand Journal of Agriculture*, Hocken Collections Uare Taoka o Hākena, University of Otago.

fate of general advertising under this guaranteed price scheme is unclear, but war again led Britain to commandeer New Zealand's food exports, and advertising was rendered unnecessary after 1939.

Further twists in the tale are created by the nature of New Zealand's dairy produce competitors. New Zealand's main rival for market share was Denmark. Danish butter exports to Britain had once been used as machine lubricants and as a parasite ointment. But by the 1880s, Denmark had become not only a symbol of premium quality but also Britain's largest source of imported butter.[39] However, although physically closer to Britain, and an 'Anglo-adapted food supplier', it was still a 'foreign' country.[40] Presenting New Zealand butter (and to a lesser extent cheese, as Canada was the most significant competitor in this market) as an 'Empire' product was therefore an option, especially in light of Empire Marketing Board activities detailed below. But most significant is the role of the NZCDC. Responsible for over a third of New Zealand's dairy exports, and with the strength and unanimity of purpose not possible amongst the fractious industry in general, it created a separate brand identity for New Zealand in the London marketplace. (It also initiated Empire Dairies to purchase and resell Australian butter.) Its brand, 'Anchor', drew upon British iconography to establish itself as 'the superfine New Zealand butter' in spite of the development of an official Dairy Board icon, the silver fern.[41] In the campaigns of the anchor and the fern leaf, farm and frontier, there was a winner and a loser, and the dominance of the 'Anchor' brand ensured New Zealand's continued imaging as familiar Home farm.

The development of a 'National Brand' was a task for the inaugural board. The fern leaf with 'New Zealand' along its middle rib, adopted in 1925, was the result of a public competition. Initially, its use was limited to a stamp on butter boxes, replacing the estimated 600 different factory brands, although a space was retained so that each individual factory name could be added. This would have little impact on metropolitan consumers. Butter was sold by weight from casks or boxes, so its national origins were not necessarily clear. They were also not particularly relevant, as various butters might be blended before reaching the retailer. Even so, a year later little actual progress had been made, as the board waited upon new season's stocks to begin the stamping campaign. Perhaps signalling the board's lack of direction, a further series of public competitions was run in New Zealand to provide marketing material, as the second *Annual Report* felt that 'inspiration and enthusiasm for New Zealand can render us a service in this direction'. These included a photographic competition, along with a slogan competition, which was 'unfortunately, without any fruitful results'.[42]

Not all the board's efforts were homespun, though. By 1927 it had begun to advertise in earnest, allocating £20,000 to shop window displays, posters and general newspaper advertising. These techniques are reminiscent of the work of the New Zealand Meat Producers Board, with shopping weeks, decorated vehicles, and even a Boy Scout street display that was somehow ingeniously 'linked with a display of New Zealand Butter and Cheese'.[43] The board initiated a 'gift butter' scheme, 'vitalizing connecting links between the two countries'. Whilst it was claimed that 'the stimulating power of [this] is immeasurable', we do know that in its second year of operation, nearly two thousand four-pound cartons were dispatched.[44] Sculpted butter links were being superseded by the real thing.

Dairy produce publicity also incorporated themes familiar from meat advertising. Butter and cheese were promoted as nutritious sunshine products: the 1934 Royal Commission into the Dairy Industry noted that 'the medical profession in Great Britain has paid tribute to the high and uniform potency of our dairy products, especially butter, in Vitamins A and D. This potency is due to the plentiful sunshine and rich, unfailing pastures of the Dominion.'[45] It was certainly not due to the addition of adulterating chemicals: pushed by British restrictions on the use of preservatives in butter, the board urged manufacturers to end the use of boric acid, as 'to definitely dispense with it will frustrate the attempts that have on occasions been made to create a prejudice against Colonial butter because of its use'.[46] Prejudice also meant cheese labels avoided the word 'factory', for 'that word in Britain connoted a second-grade article'.[47] The greater processing involved in dairy produce made it more difficult to overcome some of the negativity attached to this aspect of modernity. However, New Zealand's essentially rural character was reinforced by the liberal use of model cows in window displays, whilst posters of cheery milkmaids with silver ferns on their aprons overlaid the reality of the New Zealand dairy industry with the patina of Arcadian England.

This was not consistent, though. A Wolverhampton shop window in 1927 incorporates the fernleaf and Maori motifs, in a marked contrast to the contemporaneous 'British! New Zealand' campaigns of the New Zealand Meat Producers Board. Yet the Dairy Board's own attachment to a distinctive New Zealand character seems to have been short-lived. By 1930, they had begun joint marketing with Australia as 'Empire Butter'. The first butter cargoes of the season were given a special welcome by the Lord Mayor, accompanied by trumpeters and dairymaids.[48] In 1931 it was time for the Lord Mayor to 'Welcome Cheese!'[49] The arrival of New Zealand 'Empire' cheese was spectacular, especially for its reintegration of dairy produce into 'British' New Zealand. As a decorated bargeload of cheese arrived at Hays Wharf,

> ... dairy maids wearing sashes denoting various English cheese advanced ... while a toastmaster declaimed an invocation in rhyme to 'ye brethren of the cheese' welcoming the newcomers to the fight against foreign cheese:
>
> From full creamy pastures drenched in sun,
> Full of vitamins they come,
> To fight the fight as you yourselves,

Of 'British cheese' for 'British shelves'
And make it every day much harder,
For foreign rinds to fill the larder.⁵⁰

One of the casualties in the fight against foreign cheese and butter may well have been the 'National Brand'. Empire Marketing Board displays used the fernleaf, but empire marketing in general may have reduced opportunities for distinct 'New Zealand' branding. The 1934 Dairy Industry Commission noted 'there is evidence that customers who ask for New Zealand butter are told that "empire" means the same thing, and it is probable that cheaper Empire butters are sold as New Zealand butter. However, the London committee expressed the opinion that the publicity given by the Empire Marketing Board had helped New Zealand by encouraging consumers to buy Empire goods, but that New Zealand had recently tended to lose by merger of its identity.'⁵¹

In fact, the fern leaf was considered moribund by some as early as 1932, having become 'a quality mark . . . [with] no sales value as far as the public is concerned'.⁵² Its relegation to quality mark only was assured when the Dairy Board was unable to find a way to use the mark on the newest form of butter marketing, the pat, or packet. Wrapped pounds and half pounds were becoming an increasingly large part of the trade, particularly in London, and the board's especially appointed investigative committee was 'unanimously of the opinion that the selling of butter in pats in Great Britain would provide wider consumption and greater popularity of New Zealand butter'.⁵³ They would also provide pound and half-pound advertising opportunities as consumers would buy prepacked butter, wrapped by the producer, not scooped out by the grocer. Yet the board was unable to take advantage of this new consumer marketing opportunity. By 1932, they had 'come to the conclusion that the sale of New Zealand butter in pats under the existing Fern Leaf Brand or any similar brand . . . is not a proposition that can be put across in this country'.⁵⁴

This left New Zealand dairy produce associated not with the indigenous fern leaf, but with the British symbolism of the NZCDC's 'Anchor' brand. Already a de facto quality standard for the wholesale trade, 'Anchor' patted butter was available to consumers from 1926, when 811 tons were sold in London, rising to 1316 tons in 1929.⁵⁵ By 1932 the NZCDC had established their own packaging plant in London, which probably wrapped butter as

Anchor advertisement for wrapped patted butter. *New Zealand Dairy Exporter*, 1 October 1932, p.54.

shown in the 'Anchor' gift advertisement, above. The fouled anchor, the symbol of the brand, is generally believed to have been inspired by a tattoo on a factory worker's arm, and this may well be the case. However, as Richard Wolfe notes, 'Britain has been the single largest external influence on New Zealand trademarks – reflecting the origins of over 90% of our non-Polynesian population. Various symbols of the British Isles were appropriated, presumably to act as reminders of Home.' But this particular symbol had additional salience: 'New Zealand's isolation and vulnerability to attack by sea meant images of British naval superiority were welcome reassurance to New Zealanders.'[56] In this case, the fouled anchor was even more reassuring, for, as the top-ranking naval symbol, it adorned the Admiralty flag from 1856.

At some point in Anchor's marketing, the 'sailor boy' complemented the fouled anchor, again tapping into British imperial symbolism to sell

Imagining London's farm: an Anchor marketing poster. The New Zealand Co-operative Dairy Company, *New Zealand Dairy Group, 1919–2001*, Hamilton, 2001.

New Zealand produce.⁵⁷ This fusion of Britishness and New Zealandness, already encountered in that strange crossbreed, the 'British New Zealand lamb', forms the central idea in an extant Anchor marketing poster that probably dates from the mid-1930s. Here butter is transformed from a commodity to an idea, a set of interlocking images about two places and their complementary cultures. New Zealand's version of London appears as the iconic St Paul's, appropriately set, dreamlike, in the clouds. Similarly, New Zealand appears as a farm, its frontier past replaced by a domesticated rural scene. More hinterland than colonial periphery, its geographical distance from Home is diminished by the striding sailor, who travels on foot, not by boat, and the words 'Direct from New Zealand'. On the idealised New Zealand dairy farm, there are neither fern leaves nor factories, just symbols of Britishness and its epitome, London. These ideas would form the core of propaganda developed about New Zealand for the Empire Marketing Board.

'ASK – IS IT BRITISH?' THE FARM AND THE EMPIRE MARKETING BOARD

Whilst meat and dairy marketers remade New Zealand as familiar rural hinterland, another marketing body made sure it was 'British'. In 1926, the British government formed its first peacetime propaganda body, the Empire Marketing Board, as a means of encouraging empire trade without having to legislate for it.[58] Over the previous thirty years, preferential trade schemes between members of the empire had often been suggested as the solution to improving the economies of both the metropolis and the different parts of its empire. The rise of other industrial powers, including the United States, threatened Britain's status as global power, and in the difficult postwar and Depression years, an economically united and insulated empire seemed both attractive and feasible. In 1930 New Zealand's High Commissioner, Sir James Parr, enthused 'the Empire will become an economic unit like the forty-eight states of America, exchanging on a free footing with each other, and erecting a tariff wall against foreigners'.[59] However, when the Conservative government had actually tried to introduce preferential tariffs in 1923, they promptly lost office. This left successive governments in a difficult position, as the dominions in particular wanted to secure special access to the British market. It was crucially important to them; by 1910–12, 60 per cent of all settler colony exports went to Britain, as 'feeding Britain in general and London in particular, had become . . . the white empire's main business'.[60] But free trade and cheap food remained popular with the voting public.

In this political climate, the EMB was a creative compromise. Rather than impose tariffs, it was developed as a way to implement imperial preference by proxy. With funding of up to £1 million a year (roughly the amount the dominions would have gained through the introduction of tariffs), the EMB hoped to use scientific research, improved marketing and, most notably, the persuasive powers of publicity to convince British shoppers to choose empire produce over other kinds. Persuasion, not preference, was to preserve free trade whilst giving the dominions a bigger share of the market. In their first 'Message to the Shopping Public', published in metropolitan newspapers, the EMB carefully outlined what this meant. Where at all possible, shoppers should 'choose goods produced at home or within the overseas empire in deliberate preference to goods of foreign origin'. The campaign's tagline was simpler: consumers just needed to 'Ask – is it British?'[61]

Although this question seemed to make all of the empire generically 'British', in fact, the EMB made a very clear distinction between the economic roles of the metropolitan centre and its colonial peripheries. Britain was the centre of both consumption and of secondary industry, whilst the colonies were conceived of largely as sites of primary production. Together, they formed the 'great interlocking unit of empire'. Economic realities contradicted this idealised compatibility: Britain had its own farmers, the dominions had their own secondary industries, and 'Home' still relied on 'foreign' produce too. Yet empire as interlocking unit remained the basis of the EMB's ideology.

Nor was this fantasy of a compatibly structured empire the only wishful part of the board's economic thinking. Although the EMB co-opted marketing luminaries William Crawford and Frank Pick onto its board and invested more than one-third of its funding in publicity, the organisation found it hard to justify its existence on the evidence of increased empire trade.[62] One curt summary has concluded, 'It is hard not to laugh at these pathetic efforts to create "non-tariff preferences" for Empire goods.'[63] Still, some tried to take them seriously: in the lead-up to the 1930 Imperial Conference, an editorial in *The Times* noted sympathetically that 'publicity work is seldom susceptible of exact measurement, and critics have not been lacking to suggest that the posters of the board, however ornamental as additions to the amenities of the streets, could have little practical effect on sales', before announcing twenty-two new records for consumption of empire foods, including Palestinian grapefruit and New Zealand butter.[64]

Publicly, New Zealand's primary producers seemed well-disposed to the EMB's work, but a report prepared for the same Imperial Conference in 1930 described the poster series as 'ineffective as sellers of produce and of little practical value'. 'The whole empire propaganda work is carried out from the political angle of impressing the dominions with what it is doing rather than from the point of view of selling Empire produce.'[65] Interestingly, board members would have agreed. Chairman William Crawford, also managing director of one the two largest advertising agencies in Britain, scrapped one New Zealand poster campaign after it had been printed because it was too produce-oriented, causing a less than dutiful response from the representative of the most dutiful dominion, R. S. Forsyth, who 'did not feel able to agree' with the decision.[66] However, Crawford insisted, claiming that the campaign, featuring piles of meat and cheese, threatened 'to destroy the whole character of the Board's poster campaign'.[67] The EMB 'interpreted their mission as also having long term ideological and educational aims. Immediate sales were not their only aim, and they tuned the content of the posters and their distribution accordingly.'[68]

Poor vehicles for increasing sales, the EMB's campaigns are nevertheless potent sites of imperial ideology. The EMB chose to speak through commodities, not about them, using them to develop ideas about empire that, like exhibition space, influenced the ways empire's constituent parts could be displayed. Stephen Constantine has catalogued some of these tropes, such as 'the empire as family', largely from the point of view of the British consumer.[69] But it is clear that not all members of the empire's family were the same. In the board's signature poster campaigns, the dominions appeared almost twice as often as the dependent empire. Further, although these posters cast both dominions and dependencies as centres of primary production, the imagery created a clear distinction between the two types. If all of the empire was British, some members were more definitely British than the others. Whether depicting Canadian wheatfields or New Zealand paddocks, EMB images emphasised dominion similarities with the metropolis, and downplayed differences.[70] The countries shown in these pictures appeared as white and bright farming extensions of Home, not colourful producers of exotic commodities. Using imagery that we can describe as rural, racial and replica, EMB marketing created New Zealand as a British farming hinterland.

'Rural' New Zealand was developed in several interlocking ways. First, the commodities themselves were farm products. New Zealand was constructed out meat, butter, cheese and apples; and had the 'Imperial Bee' campaign not been cancelled, it would have appeared as a land of milk and honey.[71] Second, mountains of meat and piles of cheese and butter were almost always pictured within a rural setting, referencing a form of immaculate production from a generally empty landscape. Although, as we have noted, one campaign took this too far, a sense of abundance from emptiness was a key characteristic of the EMB's approach to the dominions generally, and this echoed the earlier colonial version of New Zealand and other settler colonies as the migrant's 'promised land'. One press advertisement described them as the British citizen's 'great inheritance', 'containing

The abundant yet empty farm. 'Empire Marketing Board to New Zealand Meat Producer Board', Carlton Studio, CO 956/229, National Archives (U.K.).

resources of inestimable value still untouched – immense areas still awaiting settlement by men and women of our own race'.[72] Through the genius of modern technology, however, even those who never left the metropolis could benefit from the products of the promised land. The domestication and sanctification of former frontiers of empire continued in references to the 'Empire's garden' and 'fields and orchards'. That empire was a special creation was promulgated by its supposed harmony with nature and the seasons: 'Never was there a people who owned such a garden as our Empire garden – a garden in which everything grows from rhubarb to rice, from corn to coco-nuts. Spring is busy in one corner of our garden when autumn is at work in another.' This promotion featured Australian and New Zealand apples, preparing London for the arrival of an 'Empire Shopping Week' in which 'the colour and sunshine of Empire fields and orchards will flood the windows of the Empire's capital'.[73]

New Zealand, the abundant rural paradise, was also New Zealand the non-urbanised, unindustrialised nation. Empty rural landscapes were one way to signal this; another was to remove urban and industrial activity from the landscape. The EMB's 'Map of New Zealand' was hardly empty, with almost every inch of its surface covered by recumbent cows, apple orchards and sheep.[74] However, excision needed to be handled carefully, lest New Zealand be banished to the status of a backward colony: as we have seen in exhibitions, the rural hinterland needed to exist in the same time zone as its metropolis, and therefore some concessions to modernity were required. Although people, urban centres and industrial activity were removed, dairy factories remained. A dairy factory is also the subject of one of only two posters used to illustrate New Zealand through anything other than maps, rural landscapes and piles of produce.[75] The poster is also distinctive because it is the only one to feature a group of people (out of just three that feature any people at all), and because it seems to have included a Maori worker at the right-hand side of the picture. It is difficult to be sure, but such artistic assimilation is not out of keeping with the more general racial discourses of absorption and assimilation. Less subtle is the artist's metonymic reproduction of New Zealand as British farm by naming the factory the 'British Empire Dairy Factory'.

Empire Marketing's emphasis on trade reciprocity enforced the rural/urban divide, as advertisements linked consumption of New Zealand produce with benefits to British manufacturers. Contracts from New Zealand for British factories became the basis for advertisements. One asked, 'A contract for New Zealand is now in hand at these works. Question: how can you help to secure further contracts from NZ?' The answer supplied was 'by buying and getting your wife to buy the produce NZ is sending us', namely meat, butter, cheese, honey and apples.[76] Press advertising reminded the British public that 'in New Zealand a family of five will spend on average at least £90 a year on buying goods imported from the United Kingdom. Foreigners spend nothing like that.'[77] Dominions in general were positioned as 'our best customers', and consumers were urged to purchase from them because 'then some of your money will come back certain and sure, in the shape of an order for something British-made which someone out there wants and would rather buy from us'.[78]

An advertising sequence in 1930 interpreted this idea with greater clarity. The EMB had introduced huge poster frames, around twenty-five feet in length, capable of carrying a set of five images, topped by a five-foot-long caption. In keeping with the board's 'high class' approach, they were erected in prominent positions where they would not have to compete with other advertising.[79] By 1928, there were 1500 in 270 towns, rising to 1800 in 450 towns by 1933.[80] Each set would be replaced after three or four weeks.[81]

Making butter and cheese at the 'British Empire Dairy Factory', with what may be intended as Mt Taranaki in the background. 'Dairy Factory New Zealand', F. C. Herrick, CO 956/3, National Archives (U.K.).

In 1930, the board issued a new series of posters that focused on the idea of reciprocity, or the 'interchange of trade'. New Zealand's appearance in this series focused on wool, meat and butter, and featured a poster of a sheep station alongside British woollen mills. In between were two further posters that emphasised the rural hinterland, improved Arcadia interspersed with industrial modernity.[82] In the first, 'New Zealand Serves Our Table', a middle-aged man and his wife prepare to eat a meal of New Zealand meat, butter and cheese, whilst through their window we can see a grey sky and rows of chimney pots.[83] In the second, 'British Cloth in New Zealand', a New Zealand tailor measures cloth for a suit we can only suppose had previously been exported to Britain as raw wool.[84]

However, the central poster in this series is the most interesting. The campaign meant to emphasise trade reciprocity, but in this case, it sends a further message – that the ties were so tight, these countries were almost one. This was not just a metropolitan fantasy: the New Zealand Dairy Commission report in 1934 emphasised the integration of the two markets, concluding 'that New Zealand is economically almost a part of the United Kingdom'.[85] Copy running across the twinned maps of New Zealand

Britain and her rural hinterland: Empire Marketing Board poster promoting trade between the United Kingdom and New Zealand. CO 956/146, National Archives (U.K.).

and Britain balanced the value of frozen meat exported with the value of textiles bought from Britain, whilst reciprocity's cultural resonances were reinforced by the supporting posters.[86] A similar approach for India, pairing elderly tea-drinking ladies with Sikhs puzzling over yards of cotton, was less successful. In this instance, India's reciprocal economic relationship could not be remade as a familiar cultural one.[87]

The British Isles and New Zealand were more than simply drawn to the same scale: New Zealand was also portrayed as a replica British society. EMB campaigns (like those of the New Zealand Meat Producers Board and the New Zealand Dairy Board, which used London advertising agencies) were almost exclusively designed and executed by British artists.[88] Apples, cheese, butter, and artfully arranged raw lamb forequarters and sides of mutton were posed against idealised rural scenes that owed as much to the English countryside as to New Zealand. This, as producer board advertising suggests, would not have troubled New Zealand; indeed, the Meat Board's man in London doubled as New Zealand's representative on the Empire Marketing Board. However, anglicisation was more problematic in the case of Ireland, where rural Ireland was imaged in one poster by 'a classic southern English white cottage, replete with an orderly thatched roof. To add to the incongruity, the cottage's chimney spouts a flume of smoke featuring the artist's signature and the word "London".[89]

Just as it was in producer board marketing, New Zealand was 'British' in campaigns that urged consumers to 'Buy Empire – Ask – is it British?'[90] The thriving New Zealand dairy industry, in the EMB's hands, was literally Britain united and transplanted. In 'The Dairies of NZ' poster, which accompanied the image of the 'British Empire Dairy Factory', 'the men and women that built up the great dairy industry of New Zealand were Englishmen and Scotsmen, Welshmen and Irishmen. They were proud of their race. The men went from Home', overlooking the colonial reality of Chinese, Danish, American and Maori dairying. These British farms were also stocked with British cows: the poster continues to explain that 'about 100 years ago the first cattle were shipped to New Zealand. The great dairy herds of New Zealand have been bred from stock bought from the farmers of Britain. Today in New Zealand a million cows are milked every night and morning. The herds went from Home.'[91]

'British' values were also exported along with livestock to these replica societies. British dominions stood for peace, with 'the whole weight of their influence among nations . . . thrown in the scale of Peace'.[92] They also stood for fair labour conditions, a tradition that 'has gone about the world with your own people'.[93] It was claimed: 'The Dominions share with Great Britain the idea of securing and maintaining a high standard of living', and therefore 'food from Home or the Dominions is better and more wholesome than food from any foreign country which employs sweated labour and tolerates insanitary conditions'.[94] This inadvertently suggests some concern with the production from dependent colonies, concerns that can be found in other EMB advertising, and are discussed later.

The trope of the 'Empire family' also helped in the imaging of the dominions in general, and New Zealand in particular, as replica societies. Readers of Christmas press advertising in 1926 could imagine they were eavesdropping on a conversation as friends discuss their children farming 'overseas', and their intention to buy 'Christmas stores from the Empire'. 'For all I know', mused one, 'I may actually be eating stuff from their own farms or if not, it comes from their friends or from sons of my friends. Anyway, it's all in the family as it were. I always like dealing with my own people. Everybody ought to do the same.'[95] Whilst the 'Empire as family' could

Empire marketing imagery fit for the dependent empire – feminine, servile, decorative. 'Gathering Cocoa Pods', CO 956/5, National Archives (U.K.).

theoretically be stretched to include the dependent colonies, it is quite clear that this conversation had a more exclusive view of 'family'. Indeed, whilst EMB campaigns may stress what Constantine refers to as a 'people's Empire, hardworking, multi racial, harmonious, forming a partnership', it also reflected and constructed a racial hierarchy.[96] By attempting to recreate the empire in the space of the imperial metropolis, the campaigns subject it to exactly the same kind of ordering pressures present in the reified empire space of exhibitions. Here, the white dominions strove to separate themselves from the colonial empire, and race was both driver and indicator of this. That dominions were different was evident from the term's regular use in combination with the word 'colonies', so that empire buyers might buy from Home, dominions or colonies. One press advertisement was designed specifically to enforce this division. In 'How many British Colonies can you name?', readers were told, 'Everyone knows something of India and something of the great self-governing Dominions. But these are not the colonies.'[97]

The most striking differences between dominions and colonies were apparent in the poster series. 'Colonial' imagery was, David Meredith notes, 'striking for its racial stereotyping', including 'scantily-dressed female rice growers' and 'rather undernourished Ceylonese men . . . . In a series of tropical ports of the Colonial Empire, natives toiled while white officers lounged.'[98] Redolent of orientalism, colonies were depicted as the exotic 'other', servile, decorative and feminine.

Such images were inappropriate for a white dominion, and instead the exoticism of the colonial empire served to reinforce ideas of familiar

Empire imagery fit for a dominion. 'Mutton Lamb Apples', Frank Newbould, CO 956/304, National Archives (U.K.).

Britishness in New Zealand. Congruent with the replacement of frontier with farm, New Zealand's imagery was imbued with western characteristics – masculinity, rationality, whiteness and leadership – characteristics that are evident both in the style and content of Frank Newbould's 'Mutton, Lamb, Apples'.[99]

It is easy to overlook the deliberate adoption of an anti-colonial set of imagery. Meredith suggests that dominion imagery was 'considerably less stilted', when in fact it is simply an opposite rendering of the same ideology relating to 'dependent' colonies.[100] Women did not feature in depictions of New Zealand, and those few posters that feature men do so in a way that exudes authority, like the New Zealand farmer shown above. Seated on his horse, he reflects control not labour, a portrayal typical of white men in colonial posters. Similarly, as a 'white' dominion, no Maori appear (with the earlier possible exception noted), nor were Maori motifs adopted. The only attempt at creating a distinctive identity based on indigeneity was limited to a series of retail posters and showcards, on which each dominion was represented by a native animal. This approach, although popular with the EMB's members, may have had limited success. One store pasted an advertisement for Spratts' dog biscuits on the showcard featuring the Irish Free State's symbol, the wolfhound,[101] whilst the image of a kiwi above the words 'Buy New Zealand lamb' may not have helped sales much either.[102]

Race, like gender, worked to distinguish New Zealand from the dependent colonies and emphasise its 'Homeliness'. Rural New Zealand was a complement to the modern metropolis, not its opposite. Maori, markers of a 'colonial' past, had no place in depictions of 'modern' New Zealand: the past now existed instead in evocations of a mythic merry old rural England. Likewise, the ostensibly locally constructed 'man's country' created a masculine complement to a feminised old England, while 'empty land' was consistent with the relocation of real history and heritage to the metropolitan centre. Like 'new' New Zealand, the farm was not a self-contained creation, but a metropolitan co-production.

Empire marketing created propinquity on its edges as much as in its centre. The EMB sought quite deliberately to make a community, enlisting consumers as part of a community of empire defined through trade. The EMB's organisation, along with primary produce advertising in general, created a bridge between geographically distinct societies, reflecting the metropolitan farm back to New Zealanders. This was most evident in the continued reinforcement of New Zealand as primary producer for Britain and purchaser of British manufactures. Whilst reciprocal trade may have been controversial, it remained a pervasive issue which, by its very nature, reinforced New Zealand's role as farm. As the Lister Company reminded farmers, 'Britain buys your butter – let a British separator produce it.'[103] With a rather punitive approach to persuasion, one car advertisement announced, 'in the five years ending 1930 the Home Country took £81,005,062 more of New Zealand product than we did of hers. This cannot go on.'[104] The division between producer periphery and transformative centre was symbolised in the EMB's promotional coup, a ten-ton 'Empire' Christmas pudding, for which New Zealand provided two tons of beef suet. The pudding, of course, was made in London. High Commissioner Thomas Wilford attended the pudding stirring ceremony, for 'New Zealand loves to be associated with any movement which spells Empire . . . the slogan of New Zealand in regards to Empire is: "Keep the money in the family".'[105]

The insistence on complementary, reciprocal trade was briefly given official shape by an exhibition of the EMB's posters in Auckland in 1932,

'PRODUCED BY BRITONS FOR BRITISH HOMES'

Inappropriate indigeneity? 'Buy New Zealand Lamb', F. C. Herrick, CO 956/61, National Archives (U.K.).

which displayed over a hundred of them.¹⁰⁶ The Governor General, Lord Bledisloe, and the former High Commissioner to London, Sir James Parr, gave regular addresses during the show. Copies of the posters were made available to schools and demand for these exceeded supplies. But interest in empire trade was not limited to an imperially minded elite. Trade with Britain was a grassroots issue, and empire was a commercial reality, not an ideological abstraction. The Ottawa conference was featured in advertising for Johnson and Nephew fencing wire, where a pipe-smoking farmer announced, 'Yes boys! I'm smiling. Why not! Have not Downie Stewart and Gordon Coates gone to Ottawa to arrange with our Motherland to protect our products against foreign competitors?'¹⁰⁷

Trade issues did not always inspire consensus or even optimism – the same smiling farmer was using the fencing wire to further subdivide paddocks just in case – but they did prompt numerous editorials. Sheep farmers might have kept in touch with empire marketing issues through the *New Zealand Farmer Stock and Station Journal*, which covered all of the agricultural industries. Photographs of exhibits at Wembley, and pictures of the huge 'Buy British' lighting display in Trafalgar Square ran alongside advertisements that urged New Zealand farmers to purchase British manufactures. Likewise, the free journal of the dairy industry, the *New Zealand Dairy Exporter*, drew a scattered rural community together around the London butter market, creating an imaginative hinterland of about 61,000 subscribers. It reported monthly on what the EMB was doing, as well as the marketing activities of the New Zealand Dairy Board itself. Any EMB poster series on New Zealand was covered, alongside reports of events like 'Welcome Cheese', 'Empire Butter', and the multitude of Empire shopping weeks and activities held throughout Britain. The *Dairy Exporter* did not stop at marketing information: when Tui, doyenne of the *Exporter*'s women's pages, travelled to England, her readers followed her trip in monthly columns. William Goodfellow, chairman of the New Zealand Co-operative Dairy Company, not only founded this publication, but also planned a radio network for his isolated suppliers so that they might stay in touch with their co-operative and its London marketplace.[108]

London's role as New Zealand's most important consumer marketplace transformed the economic and cultural landscape of New Zealand, as advertising and exhibitions sketched out a whiter, brighter British farm that complemented the urbanised, industrialised metropolis. The partnership of Old England and 'new' New Zealand was joined by the modern metropolis and its farming hinterland. This reciprocal relationship produced 'London's farm' by changing perceptions of time and space, this time to create a sense of propinquity. It was also an imaginative extension of New Zealand's own borders in reverse. Implicit in the imagery of recolonial reciprocity was the sense that what the farm lacked, the metropolis could provide. The following chapters consider the ways in which the farming hinterland was paired with another: New Zealand as imaginative hinterland of London.

CHAPTER SEVEN

LONDON'S IMAGINATIVE HINTERLAND

Mass Media and Identity

L ATE ONE SUMMER evening in December 1932, metropolitan time suddenly arrived in hinterland space. From out of the crackle of shortwave came the chimes of Big Ben as the first broadcast of the BBC's Empire Service brought a distinctively London sound into New Zealand homes. Those sounds added a new aural dimension to an already familiar visual icon of London. For the short period of the broadcast – just two hours – time and distance were overcome as New Zealand, like an outlying suburb of London, was drawn within earshot of the centre. It seemed not to matter that reception was poor, or that on the other side of the world, in London, it was morning and winter. New Zealand was the first in the empire to telegraph London confirming a successful transmission, one that was considered so important that it was made widely available by rebroadcasting on the 1YA network.[1] Just six days later, this process was repeated in an even more remarkable way. Those same homes hosted the King for Christmas as George V broadcast the first Christmas message to the empire, an address in which he noted the 'immense possibilities' radio offered to create a closer union amongst the nations of the empire.[2] He might well have been referring to sentimental ties, yet live radio's simultaneity also pulled the hinterland and its metropolis closer. That same ability to transcend space was recognised in 1935, when, completing a trinity of sorts, the BBC added a 'spiritual link' to the rest of empire through monthly church services broadcast from St Paul's. Organisers of this radio-enabled virtual church hoped that 'a great many people who have relatives or friends overseas will help by their presence and by joining in hymns'.[3] By transmitting their presence from the pews of St Paul's, propinquity could again be produced.

In hindsight, the Empire Service has a *fin de siècle* quality about it, as a late attempt to sustain empire through the ether that was never very popular or even reliable.[4] But the Empire Service played a part in reconfiguring the relationship between New Zealand and London.[5] It meant that radio, once the most local of the new mass communications media, could span 12,000 miles to bring New Zealand in touch with the metropolis. Radio was the latest in a range of media that had, since the late Victorian era, set about changing the nature of time and space. It joined the telegraph, sound recording, film, and innovations in publishing and printing technology as supercharged versions of what Harold Innis has described as 'space binding' technologies, or forms of communication particularly suited to reproducing cultures over distance.[6] These new, more numerous and faster channels increased the volume and range of cultural imagery available. They also made greater claims to realism than previous technologies of replication. Radio and recording provided a verisimilitude of 'live' sound, and, in cinemas, pictures moved and eventually talked. Innis outlines their role in fashioning empires, but these powerful new conduits of culture have often been associated with the rise of nationalism: Benedict Anderson has famously argued for the press's role in drawing together those 'imagined communities' called nations, whilst closer to home Keith Sinclair has suggested that burgeoning communication networks within New Zealand at the end of the nineteenth century 'led a perceptible strengthening and extension of both the foundations and the structure of nationalism'.[7]

But their impact was not limited to nation-building or empire-making. The new media could have a transnational effect, binding the space between city and its distant hinterland, and creating an imagined community that

'Remembrance flashed from land to land, is like the pressure of a hand': a c.1910 postcard promotes the telegraph as a way to reaffirm relationships across the empire. Eph-B-POSTCARD-Vol-12-097, Alexander Turnbull Library, Wellington, New Zealand.

merged London and New Zealand. Film, radio and cabled news combined realism with a sense of immediacy that made them space-conquering technologies. They did not just bind space; they could make it disappear. Cable 'fundamentally altered the spatial relationship between core and periphery' as 'information could now travel around the empire in hours or even minutes'.[8] Simultaneity, combined with a flood of new content, made the new media particularly potent tools in the production of the imagined geography that allowed New Zealand to think of itself as integrated with the metropolis. Radio brought Big Ben right into the home, connecting metropolitan time with hinterland space, while film transported London streets to Queen Street. The virtual version could even have some advantages: film of the 1937 Coronation, rushed to New Zealand by air, meant 'here at the other end of the earth we have had to wait only about fifteen days to see a picture which, in its completeness, excels those mere sections of the picture seen by actual watchers in London'.[9] Cinema screens and the other new formats were sites where London could be recreated again and again, with increasing detail. As an early Empire Service listener from New Zealand wrote to the BBC, 'Your "This is London calling" has a wonderful tonic effect on our imagination.'¹⁰ This chapter, and the two that follow, explore that imaginative effect, with emphasis on the role of the press, film and TV. Just as mass marketing had helped create New Zealand as London's farm – the rural hinterland of the commodity capital – the new mass media would also shape New Zealand, this time as an imaginative hinterland, with London as its cultural capital.

COLONIAL FORMS AND RECOLONIAL CHANGE

From the very beginnings of the colony, London was New Zealand's crucial cultural source, so metropolitan influence, on its own, was nothing new.¹¹ But until the development of new, space-conquering technologies towards the turn of the nineteenth century, New Zealand's communications with the metropolis were irregular and limited in range of sources and volume. Most importantly, they were not current. Book imports into New Zealand in 1860 were worth less than £15,000, and attempts in 1843 and again in 1878 to create a specific colonial book market failed.¹² There were several reasons for this, but one was that the first colonial editions were predominantly old, non-fiction, titles. There was literally nothing novel in the print run of 1843.¹³ In 1860, around 500,000 copies of newspapers were distributed by post around New Zealand. A little over half of these were published in Britain, a little under half were local.¹⁴ The imported papers brought old news, and the local papers had limited distribution. News sent by ship was also laboriously reprinted in those local newspapers even if it was six months out of date. By 1872, Australasian newsagents Gordon and Gotch had opened a London office complete with hydraulic presses to compress bales of British magazines for more efficient shipping to Australia and New Zealand. But compression, unlike refrigeration, could do nothing to avoid spoilage by time. This was the limitation of cultural transfer by space-binding materials: they kept the colony 'colonial'. Mimicking the trip backwards in time to the periphery, out-of-date newspapers, bundles of old magazines and stale reprints of once-fashionable novels reinforced the metropolis as centre, whilst emphasising the colony's distance from it.

The new media, and their effects, were radically different. They were regular, high volume and high frequency. Most importantly, they would be current, de-emphasising differences in time and space, thus assuming and creating contiguity between metropolis and former periphery. The book market was transformed with the development of successful colonial editions that extended the reach of metropolitan literature. The year 1885 marked the beginning of this enormously successful trade, a trade that in Australia, at least, lasted in form if not name until 1972, 'when Australia came to be treated not as a remote province of the UK, but seriously as a large and special market in its own right'.[15] Like other new media, the new trade in books helped make Australia a province, not a colony, of the UK: colonial editions cost less, and were initially presented differently from their metropolitan counterparts, but the 'main purpose of "colonials" was to release new novels simultaneously at home and abroad'.[16] Alfred Wilson, export bookseller and newsagent, assured purchasers of 'the very latest in high class fiction immediately on publication'.[17] These new novels appeared regularly. Between 1886 and 1913, one publisher produced 624 colonial editions, a rate of one new title per fortnight.[18] During the same period, books as well as their reviews were increasingly carried in steamships that were both frequent and fast.[19] Metropolitan timing was eventually matched by metropolitan appearance, as outward difference in colonial editions disappeared. By the 1920s, colonial markings, let alone production differences, were rare. Over the same time period, New Zealand's book import trade had grown: a market that was worth less than £15,000 in 1860 was worth £500,000 by 1929.[20]

The press was also transformed over this period. The volume and frequency of newspapers expanded as synchronicity with metropolitan time increased, ushered in by the advent of cable. By 1910, twenty-three million papers were posted, news now came by telegraph, and it was increasingly printed in daily, not weekly, papers. By World War II news was beamed, complete with Big Ben chimes, direct from the BBC's Daventry transmitter where it might be heard on one of 345,000 licensed radios in New Zealand,[21] or screened as a newsreel in one of New Zealand's 721 cinemas.[22] These new communications technologies acted like drawstrings to pull metropolis and periphery together. But this was not just an imperial phenomenon. William Cronon has described the same effect in his study of Chicago's relationship with its hinterland. As rail links, and the information that travelled along them, extended into ever more distant rural areas, they created an 'informational hinterland'.[23] London's relationship with New Zealand was configured this way. But it was not only metropolitan

Former radio announcer for 2ZB Kingi Tahiwi broadcasts an episode of the BBC's 'Calling New Zealand' from London in 1942. *New Zealand Listener*, 25 September 1942, PUBL-0159-1942-001, Alexander Turnbull Library, Wellington, New Zealand.

influence, but the metropolis's imaginative presence, that was sustained by the new flows of information, making New Zealand an imaginative as much as informational hinterland.

New technologies and a shrinking world seem to belong to a twenty-first-century sensibility, rather than to the past. But they are more durable phenomena with a long history, and 'the language of contemporary globalization replete with claims of radical novelty, often simply replicates the ways in which Victorians articulated their understanding of global dynamics'.[24] The 'family of empire', with its ties of kinship, began its metaphoric rise in conjunction with the development and widespread adoption of technological innovations, particularly steam and telegraphy, and gave fresh impetus to older political ideas, such as imperial federation. 'Before about 1870 a global polity was never considered as a feasible political option: afterward, it became a common demand.'[25] Consumerism was even more responsive than politics: from 1851, exhibitions articulated this dynamic in their own way, even if the emphasis was more on model empire than global village.

Similarly, studies of imperial communication also note the new media's ability to 'annihilate distance'.[26] Yet, like globalisation today, the power of new media needs some nuancing. Older forms co-existed with the new, creating echoes of information across time. Newspapers could carry shorter, up-to-the minute cables alongside items of older news. Similarly, space in the new system was not excised evenly, reducing markedly between London and empire, but not necessarily between other members of empire.[27] For example, while New Zealand newspapers formed part of an imperial press grouping, its imperial membership was not matched by an imperial circuit of news. Dominion news could flow inwards, and be redistributed, creating a 'one-way flow which sustained imperial press dependency'.[28] It was a metropolitan news service, with hinterland contributors and, like radio signals from the transmitter at Daventry, the press system was primarily designed to radiate outwards.

LONDON CALLING

The transition to immediate media was coupled with a tendency towards concentration of sources of information, a factor that distinguishes these particular media from new media today, which tend instead towards fragmentation and have shifted frequency another gear, from regular to constant. Concentration allowed London to remain New Zealand's mass media hub of choice, augmented by Australia in some cases, and challenged by America in others.

America was pre-eminent in the supply of film, and initially provided New Zealand with a large amount of popular radio material. It was also home to popular new music styles like jazz, although America did not dominate the music sales market until 1967.[29] But its tight grip on mass media was only partial. In the period up to World War II, in its peak year, 1936, America supplied only 10 per cent of book imports by value, while New Zealand newspapers remained quite insulated within the imperial press system.[30] American influence fluctuated: over the same period, New Zealand government broadcasting policy ensured that American content in radio programming declined, while as late as 1953 Gordon and Gotch supplied 946 different magazines to the Australasian market, of which only 32 were American.[31]

Australia, on the other hand, could act as a cultural mediator rather than alternate metropolis. It provided radio soaps to replace American programmes that were deemed unsuitable,[32] whilst the latest in metropolitan news might appear in New Zealand papers courtesy of the Australian *Argus* press agency in London. From 1899, Australia also became Britain's largest book importer, and was soon re-exporting around 20 per cent of New Zealand's total book imports from its depots.[33]

The new media were often hybrid in both form and content, and in New Zealand's case this hybridity may also have helped sustain London's dominance. American films could be on British subjects, as we will see, while British companies like the Rank Organisation happily distributed American films for New Zealanders. Jazz may have been an American musical form, but it also slipped into New Zealand second-hand, through Australian or British artists. Even real American music entered New Zealand courtesy of the British: HMV, based in England, maintained close to a monopoly over record supplies until the early 1950s.[34]

In contrast, London remained competitive by concentrating its dominance. Fleet Street was the centre of the British newspaper industry, the 'spiritual and physical home' of journalism for colonials.[35] From the last quarter of the nineteenth century, 'the publication of periodicals became centralized in London to a greater degree even than that of newspapers'.[36] Broadcasting House, 'the great temple of wireless in London ... affirmed the BBC presence at the centre of the imperial capital', and London remained the core of the languishing British film industry.[37] Further, it leveraged the prestige it enjoyed in the dominions for high cultural production in other areas, like publishing, onto the new media, like radio, where the BBC became the quality standard. This association of 'British' with 'quality' was reflected in New Zealand's own two separate radio broadcasting strands: 'the "highbrow" strand, designated YA was non-commercial, instructive, morally uplifting, and British. The "lowbrow" strand designated ZB, was commercial, entertaining, less moral and less British.'[38]

London's dominance had another dimension. As we have seen in earlier chapters, London could telescope 'national' values. Within the BBC's British programming, London quickly came to stand for nation: 'It seemed self evident that London could provide better quality in musical performance, bigger stars for entertainers, more important speakers than the rest of the country. The national culture that the National Programme claimed to embody was of the educated, southeast English variety.'[39] The Empire Service, always under-resourced, began by using this material, 'sending out the best bits of the home programmes'.[40] It was 'London calling', not Britain calling, after all. The evocatively titled 'bottled' programmes of the BBC's new transcription service, which provided recordings as an alternative to the static of shortwave, continued this preserving and essentialising process. Early programmes included a collection of old English songs and choruses called *Cakes and Ale*, a children's show and a story called 'A Pageant of English Life from 1812 to 1933'. New Zealand's first broadcast of a BBC transcription, in 1933, was a play on the life of the great architect of the metropolis, Sir Christopher Wren, and it 'marked the start of a long reliance on Britain for radio programming'.[41] London's symbolic 'national' role in radio was repeated in the press and in film, discussed in more detail below.

In the changing world of new media, then, New Zealand's principal relationship remained with London, and it perpetuated the familiar, reciprocal imagery of city and hinterland. High culture was joined by mass culture in reinforcing cultured and uncultured space, whilst New Zealand's rapid uptake of new technologies underlined its position as a modern first-world nation rather than backward colony. The combined effects are explored first through newspapers. The press's ability to create what Benedict Anderson calls 'parallel lives' was revolutionised with the advent of mass circulation, cable-connected daily newspapers. They became emblems of metropolitan synchronicity whilst continuing to recreate and reproduce London on the colonial periphery. London news might always have been read in New Zealand, but from the 1880s onwards, it would be read in metropolitan time.

NEWS AND THE HINTERLAND

> We have nothing to communicate this week as we are without news either foreign or domestic.[42]

Nothing so completely symbolises the peripheral existence of early New Zealand as a newspaper without news. For the early New Zealand press, the ability to generate an imagined community of any sort was severely curtailed by its isolation. The bereft editor of the *New Zealand Spectator* in 1844 would, like others in his position, have happily taken news from anywhere. However, even at this stage, news from Home had a special importance: 'Local news seems largely to have been considered a poor cousin to overseas news.'[43] Material from abroad was keenly sought: press histories recount rowboat races to collect news from visiting ships and complex newspaper exchange systems that transferred overseas news throughout the colony. The *Marlborough Express* flew a white flag at half mast to let readers know when an overseas extra was being prepared, hoisting it to the top when it was ready.[44] As late as 1878, over a million copies of British newspapers were circulated through the New Zealand postal system amongst a population numbering around 400,000.[45] But as eagerly anticipated as this news was, it remained colonial in form. Old and irregular, early press links with London could only bind, not conquer, space. In 1850, one newspaper editor noted that it took 115 days for English news to reach Auckland, and in 1857, a new record of sixty-one days was set.[46] This old news appeared sporadically, cut and pasted into weekly or tri-weekly papers. Reflecting the unevenness of communications and population, weekly digests of the few daily papers were created to meet the needs of more isolated readers. Low frequency was matched by low volume. Despite the existence of some daily papers, one estimate of the circulation of all papers for the year 1865 averaged out at just twenty-nine copies per capita, or just over one paper a fortnight.[47]

As Patrick Day has demonstrated, the nature and function of newspapers shifted markedly in the 1870s as a commercially viable press was established, replacing the politically motivated press of earlier years.[48] Growing populations in urban centres like Dunedin were able to support daily papers, volumes lifted and circulation numbers were rising. The *Otago Daily Times* claimed a circulation of 3000 in 1876 (which a rival thought 'grossly exaggerated'), whilst the *New Zealand Herald* in Auckland estimated its average daily circulation at 2700.[49] Total circulation figures do not exist, although the number of newspapers posted within the colony provides a qualified indication, with volumes rising from around two million at the beginning of the 1870s, or eight papers per capita, to around six and a half million in total and double the number per capita, at its close.[50] Frequency also improved as daily papers were introduced, the first of which began in 1861, and the range of titles expanded, making the period the 'peak of newspaper pioneering'.[51]

Colonial news: the *Evening Herald*'s office in Wanganui. Window posters advertise the imminent arrival of 'valuable cows' from Napier. 1/1-000139-G, W. J. Harding Collection, Alexander Turnbull Library, Wellington, New Zealand.

These changes were supplemented by another. Just like the early papers, the commercial press needed news, and the new national telegraphic service, begun in 1861 and completed in 1872, would provide it. As the figures above suggest, it was not growing populations alone that led to larger volumes, as newspaper growth was disproportionately larger than population increase. The Wellington *Independent* became a daily in 1871, noting the 'recent extension of telegraphic communication' as a reason for the change.[52] The weekly *Timaru Herald* came out twice a week from 1865 when the telegraph line arrived.[53] Timing mattered: Patrick Day argues that 'the means given by the telegraph to send news rapidly was a major factor in changing the nature of the newspaper.... It was the provision of news which the newspapers increasingly perceived as their major service for the public.'[54] News was starting to be current, not just new, and this sense of simultaneity helped knit the nation together.[55]

Despite these significant and impressive changes, however, it may be that newspaper pioneering remains an appropriate term to describe the growth of the press in New Zealand over this period. Newspapers remained relatively small, infrequent and marked by old news until the 1880s. At this point, the press moved away from its colonial form. Volumes of newspapers circulating by post rose to thirteen million in 1882, and by 1911 there were forty-three million copies in circulation. This again outpaced population growth, rising from 26 copies per head to 43 over this period.[56] These higher volumes were accompanied by much higher frequency, meaning people were reading more papers, more often. Although daily newspapers appeared in the 1860s, the peak year for their production was much later, in 1910. At the same time, the total number of titles fell as news markets were consolidated, largely around mass circulation dailies, making, by 1953, 'the triumph of the daily paper . . . the outstanding fact of the last half century'.[57] This preference for immediacy was also reflected in the decline of special weekly editions aimed at isolated settlements. There were still twenty-two of these being published in 1900, but the number fell rapidly to sixteen in 1910.[58] Only one, the *Auckland Weekly News*, survived by 1958.[59]

The upsurge in frequency, volume, concentration and immediacy were hallmarks of the new media. They were complemented and perhaps stimulated by better access to news from London. The extension of overseas cable services to New Zealand in 1876, when coupled in following years with lower costs, meant local newspapers could now carry news in its metropolitan sense, reporting it as it happened, not just when it arrived. The press could escape peripheral time, a possibility already signalled in the changing shape of the information hinterland from provincial to national. This process continued into the 1880s as 'telegraphy and a single press association resulted in a uniform news service and newspapers played a role in establishing a national identity'.[60] Cabled news conquered space: it 'made it possible to know about situations existing simultaneously in a number of centres'.[61] Not only might they be connected across time and space, but readers could also feel more involved in events, as immediate news has an emotional force that 'old or irregular news does not'.[62]

Simultaneity thus encouraged an imaginative hinterland, and its borders were not co-terminous with the 'nation'. In the first edition of the Christchurch *Globe*, the writer justified the advent of a daily evening paper by arguing that 'telegraphy is fast becoming such an important institution in the colony that the news of the morning seems stale in a few hours.... It will probably be no long time before we are connected by cable with Australia, and then we shall of course expect English news of any importance to be transmitted daily.'[63] The *Globe* did not last, but the writer understood the emerging shape of the new media hinterland. Whilst historians have tended to focus on the formation of national consciousness, the papers themselves saw that exactly the same forces were in operation between New Zealand and its principal source of overseas news, London. For, 'while overland telegraphy allowed people to imagine themselves as members of national communities, undersea cables could help sustain imperial identities and an overarching sense of Britishness'.[64] The process was, however, gradual. Initially, cable could be unreliable, and prices were too high for much news to filter through, but just as rowboat races had provided a competitive edge in early years, overseas cable news, although expensive, became essential: 'Telegraph news is rarely mentioned as a feature of newspapers in the 1880s and 1890s, compared with early decades. It was taken for granted.'[65]

Reading in metropolitan time coincided with the rise of London as a subject and centre of overseas news. This rise was the result of several linked factors. Although Fleet Street was historically the home of the press, during the period 1873 to 1923 news about London itself began to increase within British papers. This was particularly true of the mass circulation dailies at the heart of the system. London 'was where news was made, news that was informative, entertaining, and easily gathered'.[66] The dailies had diverse interests: *The Times* preferred serious London news, whereas the *Daily Telegraph* featured more sport, theatre and 'a considerable amount of London gossip – frauds, robberies and suicides as well as balls and parties'.[67] These different emphases were united by generally shared imagery of London. London as 'heart of empire', with all its associated cultural and historical significance, became more prevalent from the 1890s, although it was forced to share space with the usual anxieties about the metropolis, including its lack of imperial appearance and the dangers of urban degeneration, particularly during the interwar period.[68] These familiar themes, in a variety of news guises, would then appear more frequently for New Zealand readers.

Telegraph played a complex role in concentrating London's influence, one that has little to do with technological determinism. Indeed, although dependence on London increased, cable theoretically could have made news from all sources more widely available. However, London's role as global financial centre, a position enhanced by cable communication in which the City itself was an important investor, led it to be 'particularly well-connected with the rest of the world', increasing its potential for newsgathering.[69] It was the logical place for special correspondents to be based, and *The Press*, along with three other papers, formed the London-based New Zealand Associated Press agency before the turn of the nineteenth century to share the costs of a correspondent.[70] The *New Zealand Herald* already had a London office, and a second agency was formed in 1893. Cable was not necessarily the medium for communication back the other way – the first *Press* correspondent was contracted to provide news in colonial form through monthly reports sent by ship; and correspondents' 'London letters' would remain just that – but London remained as news centre.[71] This centrality was remarkably persistent: the New Zealand Press Association's (NZPA) first permanent appointment outside Australia was to London during World War II, whilst an American correspondent was not appointed until 1970.[72]

The expense of reporting by cable also worked to concentrate London's predominance. Initially, rates for international cables were more than two shillings per word. The most practical approach to the problem of expensive news was the formation of local press associations, sharing news from one source to defray costs. In New Zealand's case, newspapers banded together to form the United Press Association (UPA) in 1880, with three important effects. First, it homogenised the news, an effect multiplied by the high volume, high frequency characteristics of the new media: 'One parliamentary representative complained that the telegraphic news published throughout the nation was "identical" and "bore the imprint of one mastermind who had control of the news".'[73] Second, it increased the volume of news. Competition between different cable services and press associations eventually led to price decreases. The rate per word dropped below one shilling a word in 1909.[74] Yet papers did not take advantage of the reduced price to save money. Instead, the importance of up-to-date news was such that papers preferred to spend the same amount and receive an increased volume of news. In New Zealand, 'between 1908 and 1912 the total number of words received nearly doubled'.[75] Finally, these greater volumes were distributed more widely. Press associations ensured that London and its news could appear in relatively small papers as long as they were paid-up members.⁷⁶ This combination of press associations and telegraphy allowed even isolated inhabitants to be able to read the news in metropolitan time: 'Thanks to this a paper in a little bush village publishes the cream of all the intelligence at the same time as their metropolitan contemporaries. Anywhere else they would have to wait until they could clip them.'⁷⁷

They would also be reading a particular form of metropolitan news. Exported news was subject to a selection process, which happened in London, although it would be incorrect to see this as hegemony imposed by the centre. Amongst the New Zealand press, the power of Reuters was actively circumvented from 1887, and the UPA insisted that 'all references to the agency should be banished from the cable service'.⁷⁸ Instead, cabled news from London came at lower cost courtesy of the London office of the Australian *Argus*. But it would be equally incorrect to see this as an expression of peripheral independence: 'Whilst the *Argus*' London staff and the UPA Sydney agent selected items according to their own criteria of newsworthiness, British journalists ultimately determined what news was available to choose from.'⁷⁹ Their choices were not always satisfactory, as some news sent was not considered relevant to New Zealand, and some events, like Sir Joseph Ward's speeches to the Imperial Naval Conference, were not covered at all.⁸⁰ But these were problems to be resolved within the system. The UPA's solution was to add wire sources, and these generally remained London-based.⁸¹ For example, in 1913 they added another source that guaranteed 6000 words a week from the London *Times*.⁸² Nor was London's concentrating effect limited to cable news. Press correspondents, who worked outside the telegraphic system, increasingly provided 'soft' news, less prone to spoilage by time. By the twentieth century, this was 'rarely' non-British, whilst stories on London itself became more prominent.⁸³

Indeed, London's role as the centre of news tended to marginalise efforts to create an imperial news network. Cheaper cable rates applied in both directions, yet at the press conference of 1909 there was 'little interest by British proprietors in balancing the flows of news'.⁸⁴ In 1931, news sent from the dominions to the British press was still considered 'meagre'.⁸⁵ This tendency had deep roots. Even during periods of high migration in the Victorian era, 'Australia, New Zealand, and America were not prime subjects in the overseas news columns', a complaint heard again at the 1925 Imperial Press Conference.⁸⁶ But once again, the press couldn't imagine

itself outside the system. New Zealand delegates at this conference are considered to have taken a 'broader view than their Australian counterparts' by promoting 'a cooperative interchange of cables news between colonies'.[87] Even so, the central node in that proposed network remained London. In the flow of news, it was less an imperial press system than a metropolitan one.

If news flowed outwards, people flowed inwards. Fleet Street was an important piece of 'familiar London', and it tended to be treated as a joint colonial possession by New Zealand journalists, newspapers and writers. Leslie Verry, aspiring writer, journalist and, later, head of the NZPA, made two pilgrimages to the 'home of the fourth estate', and would later 'haunt' Fleet Street looking for work.[88] This was an antipodean habit: so many Australian journalists travelled to London that it has been claimed to 'constitute a "tradition"'.[89] Like literary London, Fleet Street was extension, and pinnacle, of the local industry. However, the naturalised adoption of Fleet Street as news centre was not solely the result of the individual initiative of peripatetic journalists. As Simon Potter has noted, 'many big papers sent members of their editorial staff to London in rotation so they could gain experience of Fleet Street practices and knowledge of British affairs that would prove valuable on their return to the Dominions'.[90] In personnel, if not news itself, there was also a considerable reciprocal flow. *The Press*, first published in 1863, employed only English senior executives until 1904, when the first New Zealander, Guy Scholefield, was appointed.[91] However, whilst the mobility of practices, money and people around the imperial network demonstrates a mutual interdependence, the same cannot be said for the significance of the dominions within the system. Although journalists worked and travelled throughout the empire, there was never any question where the heart of the system lay.[92]

From 1880, an old colonial press system gave way to a new version, one that brought New Zealand into closer contact with the metropolis. A transnational system itself, it then created an imagined transnational community and London was at the heart of both. The power of that system and the nature of the community it created are the subjects of the following analysis.

Fleet Street, the heart of the imperial press system. O.032053, Harry Moult Album, Museum of New Zealand Te Papa Tongarewa.

IMAGINING A COMMUNITY NEW ZEALAND'S OTHER HOME FRONT

On 7 September 1940, the Battle of Britain entered a phase that would directly threaten the metropolis. The dogfights over the English Channel and above summer fields turned abruptly into a bombing campaign targeting civilians and buildings in the heart of empire.[93] This was the Battle of London, a campaign that would eventually segue into the Blitz, an event described by one historian as a 'particular national crisis'.[94] Yet New Zealand, and of course other parts of the empire, saw this crisis as theirs too. Such a response was by no means limited to some form of representational, imagined crisis: during the Battle of Britain, New Zealanders within the Royal Air Force formed the 'largest group of Commonwealth pilots in that action', and the key Fighter Command, 11 Group, was under the command of New Zealander, Air Vice Marshall Keith Park.[95] Meanwhile, out in the imaginative hinterland, 'Every bomb that falls on London [was] a blow at the heart of Empire – a blow at us.'[96] Nor was this simply reactionary hyperbole. As earlier chapters have shown, New Zealand had a complex cultural relationship with London that is too easily dismissed as a combination of elitism, imperialism and misguided nostalgia. Instead, analysis of press coverage reveals again the culturally constructed nature of this relationship, and its powerful and consistent renewal through new forms of cultural transfer. As news reporting detailed the bombing, it also outlined the extent of New Zealand's London. These buildings were New Zealand's too.

At the same time, the shift to reporting as it happened made a sense of participation possible. Shortly after bombing began, key papers began fundraising campaigns for London, creating an expanded New Zealand home front. These campaigns might be seen as reinvigorating a dwindling sentiment for Home amongst a public otherwise investing in a national consciousness. Yet, as we have seen, it was nothing new for London to be considered a joint possession. Rather, the press campaigns are another example of the new media's ability to shift time and space to create a contiguous imagined community. This means that whilst the circumstances of 1940 were extreme, and therefore led to an increase in the volume of news about London, the reporting was, in other ways, characteristic of the time. By 1940 generally, news coverage was homogenised, frequent and marked by its collection in, and concentration upon, London. It was also immediate.

'Familiar London' attacked: map illustrating the area of central London bombed in German air raids. *Auckland Star*/Fairfax Media, 10 September 1940, p.7.

Headlines like 'Score Rises Still Higher: Yesterday's Bag 144 Nazi Planes' and 'First Bombs on London' emphasised a temporal connection with the centre.[97]

Those first bombs hit Tilbury, which, as previous travellers had noted with disappointment, was not 'familiar London'. This idea was heightened by an accompanying map of the Greater London area, which, being devoid of much detail, had the appearance of being largely unoccupied. Headlines adopted the present tense to announce, 'War Comes to London in Earnest', in the *New Zealand Herald* on 9 September. From this point, the momentum of reporting did not decrease until the end of October, almost a month after the official end of the Battle of London, when papers were still reporting on the destruction of the high altars of St Paul's, and, emblematically, of Our Lady of Victories.

Immediacy was enabled by cable, but, as suggested earlier, this was not its only influence on reporting. The stories were collated in London by the British official wire service and concentrated through the UPA, although this could be supplemented by press correspondents. Copy was written as if for a British audience (which it probably was) and required a reasonable working knowledge of London in order to follow reports of buildings, stores and streets being hit. New Zealanders would have needed their mental maps of 'familiar London' to follow the stories. At the same time, the prevalence of this type of reporting indicates that New Zealanders were comfortable enough with London's geography to be able to imagine what had happened. Reports simply sketched in the location: 'In Central London, a high explosive bomb fell at the corner of two important streets', and 'valuable stained glass windows were blown in at an historic Central London church. One bomb blew out the interior of a bank a few yards away'.[98] When buildings and areas could be named, the papers then ran shopping lists. By 18 September, the *Auckland Star* advised: 'it is authoritatively stated that the areas bombed last night included Piccadilly, Park Lane, Berkeley Square, Bond Street, Oxford Street, Sloane Square, and Bruton Street. Other places damaged include the Royal Arcade, Burlington Arcade, St. Dunstan's headquarters, Radnor House and Twickenham.'[99]

The combination of cable and press agencies also increased the homogeneity and frequency of these stories. As morning and evening papers took the same news, readers might see the same story twice, albeit with different headlines. On the second day of press coverage, the *Auckland Star* ran a story 'Fifty Killed in Block of Flats', essentially the same piece that a reader of the morning paper, the *New Zealand Herald*, had seen as 'Blown to Pieces: Block of Flats: over 50 Killed'.[100] The concentration on the geography of central London also reflected journalistic priorities. The newspaper editing process meant press stories carried their most important information first, leaving lesser information to succeeding paragraphs. In bombing items, central London, or London at all, always preceded news from the coast, the midlands or any other part of Great Britain. The effect was for the bombing of London to predominate, even though other areas may have been more seriously affected as a whole.[101]

Whilst cable news kept pace with events, pictures did not. Pictures had been a relatively late introduction in some papers anyway: *The Press* did not start regularly including photographs until 1930 because pictures were considered 'a little frivolous and out of place in a serious daily newspaper'.[102] Pictures by cable were similarly novel and were not used within New Zealand until after the war. This, and the delays imposed by wartime censorship, meant that the first photos of London air raid damage, including an upturned double-decker bus, appeared on 16 September 1940.[103] Until then, papers ran large photo spreads of historic and heritage London, renewing a set of already well-embedded images. Occasionally the photos were annotated with arrows or hand-drawn information to improve the

This photographic news coverage of the Battle of London began by featuring iconic images of the pre-war metropolis. *Auckland Weekly News*, 18 September 1940, p.1, Sir George Grey Special Collections, Auckland Libraries.

relevance, but the overall effect, like all the extended coverage of the battle, was to make more visible that which was threatened with destruction. On 21 August, the *Auckland Star* ran pictures of Nelson's Column, Piccadilly Circus and Thames Embankment, under the banner 'London – Heart of the British Empire'; while in early September, the *New Zealand Herald* illustrated stories of air raids with views of central London, including pictures of St Paul's.[104] The first pictures of actual damage to St Paul's did not appear until 21 October, when a photo was sent by radiogram. They appeared even later in the *Press*.[105] This lapse in continuity with metropolitan time, part of the layering of older and newer forms, had the paradoxical effect of reinforcing the imaginative hinterland, as pictures repeated a set of well-known images. Like an echo, their delayed appearance meant London's dominance outlasted the battle itself.

It is possible to suggest in hindsight that there is nothing particularly remarkable in detailed reporting on what was a major new war offensive, and that the detail was commensurate with its importance. But comparison with reporting on other bombed cities suggests this is not the case. Almost a year previously, Warsaw was destroyed by Nazi bombing in the invasion of Poland. The press reported on Polish heroism and Nazi cruelty. Headlines like 'City Still Holds Out: Germans Defied: Warsaw Becomes Tiny Island in Enemy Sea' countered 'Refugees Massacred by Nazi Hordes: Slaughter of Women and Babies-in-arms'.[106] One report noted near its end that 'survivors from Krzemieniec tell of the destruction of the famous cathedral of St John, one of the most beautiful churches in Europe . . . . The Royal Castle, containing priceless treasures, was utterly destroyed.'[107] But there was no further interest in reporting the loss of Polish cultural treasures or, for that matter, shopping thoroughfares. That would wait until it was Britain's turn to be the 'tiny island in the enemy sea'.

Further, bombs on Poland were not 'blows at us'. When the historic buildings of 'familiar London' were hit, their importance as New Zealand buildings was emphasised. Buckingham Palace was one of the first casualties. On 10 September, just three days into the battle, it suffered minor damage from a time bomb, then was struck again twice in following days, once with the King and Queen in residence. *The Weekly News*, published on 25 September, combined all three attempts into one feature article, by local writer, Matanga:

> Buckingham Palace bombed! The London home of our King and Queen . . . attacked with murderous intent from the sky, again and again! A sudden throb girdled the Empire as the news travelled. This was the worst yet, the climax of a ruthless enemy's concentration upon British sanctities; Britain, London, Buckingham Palace – each step in the sequence a closer invasion of the Empire's heart; this last made it quiver with deepest anxiety and anger.
>
> Round that famous building British memories cluster. It is only one of many buildings cherished in affectionate thought, and among the Royal

residences it is not the most historic; but its situation in the centre of London and the place it holds in the lives of our present King and Queen make it of special importance right now.[108]

Attacks on Buckingham Palace might well have made an imperialist quiver. But although imperialist in language, the article actually emphasises the importance of the metropolis. Buckingham Palace is the 'London home of our King and Queen', appropriated as an iconic building around which 'British memories cluster'. These 'British memories' are, of course, New Zealand memories. Any attack on British sanctities – 'Britain, London, Buckingham Palace' – is an invasion of a joint possession, the 'Empire's heart'. Similarly, although this piece is largely concerned with claiming metropolitan space, it also makes use of synchronous metropolitan time. When the palace is attacked, 'a sudden throb girdled the Empire as the news travelled'. Employing an organic metaphor characteristic of the imagery of empire, the throb is felt throughout the whole, and immediately.

'War-scarred London' in the *Auckland Weekly News*, 23 July 1941. The view reprises a classic tourist view of London from across Ludgate Circus to St Paul's. AWNS-19410723-30-3, Sir George Grey Special Collections, Auckland Libraries.

Matanga's article goes on to employ one of the most common methods of imaginatively appropriating the metropolis during this period. Although memories are apparently already 'clustered' around the building, the remainder of the story is devoted to a short history of the palace. Exactly the same process was used for claiming St Paul's after it was hit. In the *Auckland Star*, the main story of damage was accompanied by four paragraphs of historical information on the building, an extension and repetition of information run to accompany an earlier time bomb story titled 'Wren's Gems'. This article claimed that St Paul's was 'such a lovely and familiar sight even to the untravelled that to describe it is like describing one's grandfather in his own house'.[109] The *New Zealand Herald* too had already run an historical feature, 'St Paul's Through the Ages', when covering the time bomb, but still added a half column on the history and features of the 'Parish Church of Empire', 'revered by British people everywhere'.[110] This included children: the *Auckland Star*'s children's paper, the *Enzed Junior*, made 'Stately Old St Paul's' its feature story at the end of October. Another example of the press's echo effect, it ran shortly after the first pictures of actual damage to the altar appeared.[111]

The practice of historicising buildings to enhance their significance to New Zealanders was not limited to the major icons of London. The *New Zealand Herald* noted damage to Holland House in Kensington in a column on general air raid damage, concluding with a long paragraph on the building's history that was probably taken from a contemporary guidebook.[112] The great hall of Eltham Palace, 'a famous historic fragment', was saved by firemen. Readers were reminded that, had it been lost, it 'would have wiped out the last vestige of the palace where Henry VIII was educated and where Edward III held his Parliament'.[113] The schooling of readers included buildings that New Zealanders weren't even expected to know much about. The Church of St Anne and St Agnes, another Wren church and spiritual home to the Worshipful Company of Cordwainers, was covered by the *Auckland Star* in a quarter-page story complete with photographs. Pointing to the demarcation lines of New Zealand's London, the feature writer believed the church 'means little' to New Zealanders, except those who 'know their London'.[114]

London's particular significance to New Zealand was also emphasised by coverage of soldiers on leave in London, in stories that treated the metropolis as joint possession. London was 'just "the town" to New Zealanders'.[115]

New Zealand Soldiers

Activities in England

Left to right: S. Thomson (Christchurch), A. E. Copeland (Nokomai), and D. White and T. Irvine (Dunedin) in Trafalgar Square.

New Zealand Soldiers in 'familiar' London. Cover of *The Weekly News*, 4 September 1940, Sir George Grey Special Collections, Auckland Libraries.

Like soldiers of the World War I era, members of New Zealand's Second Echelon, who arrived in Britain in 1940, went on leave in London through July, and used it 'to carry out, what for many of them, were life long ambitions'.[116] War heightened the importance of the famous buildings they saw. One report claimed, 'When I stood in Westminster Abbey at the Unknown Warrior's tomb I realised for the first time what England actually means. I went back into that Abbey three times in two days. I just could not tear myself away. It is the foundation stone of the Empire. Every New Zealander and Australian who went here felt the same.'[117] Maori troops, described as 'tough as steel warriors' (who, in the same description, happened to be 'bronzed'), were also positioned as participants in metropolitan culture: 'when a group of Aussies and Enzeders visited Westminster Abbey, on their first day in London, it took one of the Maoris to translate all the Latin inscriptions'.[118]

In some reports, visiting soldiers went beyond being proud co-owners of the imperial metropolis to claim that New Zealanders appreciated the culture and wonders of Britain more than its actual residents. 'Howard' and 'Alan', two New Zealand soldiers, could not understand 'why no Englishman seems the least bit interested in England. Here we are running around the country trying to see everything at once and not one of you appears in the least interested in what you have to show . . . I'll bet you'll find New Zealanders all the way from Lands End to John O'Groats looking at every show place they can find. We want to go round your mills; talk to everyone we meet. You people simply don't realise what you have here.'[119]

At the same time, New Zealand's own London buildings were under attack. But these attacks were handled quite differently: the relevant reports were short, informative, and generally dwelt on the stoic and steadfast nature of the employees involved. While they shared space with stories about the bombing of iconic geography, and thus reinforced the idea that this battle was New Zealand's too, stories about damage to actual New Zealand buildings were never as prominent as those about buildings only imaginatively possessed. On 12 September 1940, two bombs fell in the Strand, next to New Zealand House, blowing out the High Commission's windows and leading to the evacuation of staff. Carefully gathering up ciphers and codes, personnel shifted to the New Zealand Forces Club, 'thus returning the hospitality given when the club was evacuated the day previously when a time bomb fell opposite'.[120] Other attacks failed to interrupt the work of the New Zealand Fruit Sales Division, and 'in spite of air raids, public business continue[d] within business hours' at the Bank of New Zealand.[121] Responses to these attacks were similarly stoic: Prime Minister Peter Fraser was impressed by the 'steadfastness' of New Zealand House staff;[122] the shareholders of Milne and Choyce Ltd voted to include the London office in that year's bonus distribution;[123] and John Burns and Co. went one better and doubled the annual bonus of their London staff in 'appreciation of the resolution of the staff in remaining in what they

Bomb damage at New Zealand House on the Strand, London. DA-01113-F, War History Collection, Alexander Turnbull Library, Wellington, New Zealand.

describe as the front line of the battle'.[124] Some businesses offered practical and personal help more in keeping with a hinterland than a distant outpost of empire. Staff in a Wellington-based insurance firm cabled their London office to help, whilst local Bank of New Zealand workers offered to 'look after any children of London staff that might be sent out'.[125]

In these reports, a shared British spirit joined with shared metropolitan geography to emphasise contiguity between the two places. A *Woman's Weekly* editorial claimed 'Hitler expects to demoralise Britishers by vicious attacks . . . . The heroism and individual courage of our race is too great.'[126] Coverage on this topic was constant, merging the values of Britishness with the symbolism of London and coming up with a secret weapon against Hitler. A *New Zealand Herald* editorial on 23 September 1940 suggested that 'Nazi leaders may well feel baffled' that the Luftwaffe had not been more successful, concluding that 'no doubt this is partly due to the British spirit, its steadiness, its refusal to panic, and the long habit of people to think for themselves'.[127] Reports from New Zealand soldiers in London emphasised this shared Britishness. Some claimed they felt fortunate 'because it "sort of makes the war seem more personal"'.[128] World War I veteran Bill Gibson traced the outlines of the strange geography of the imaginative hinterland when he said, 'last time I fought over the most of France . . . and I didn't have the same feeling I've got now. Somehow, I sort of feel I'm fighting in New Zealand.'[129]

THE BATTLE AT HOME

That feeling was reciprocated back home in New Zealand, as the press offered another way for readers to participate in the trials of the metropolis. During August and September, newspapers ran two different fundraising campaigns, both of which reflected the significance of war in Britain, or more particularly, London. The Spitfire campaign began in August, and fundraising for London followed. But patriotic fundraising had very slow beginnings in World War II. Nancy Taylor suggests this was largely the effect of public resistance to the long arm of the Labour government, which set out to organise giving: 'There were backward glances to the stirring activity and generous giving of 1914, when women went into action with fairs, Paddy's markets, sales of work, flag days, and concerts; when churches raised large sums, when flags and livestock were auctioned.' Rather than fundraising being spontaneous and local, as it was then, people now felt restrained by government regulations: 'All money collected now had to go to the provincial authorities, which seemed very remote to small towns.'[130]

By September 1940, however, as Taylor notes, 'a fresh start was made', with better internal organisation, and new impetus for giving coming from the invasion of Belgium and the Netherlands, and the bombing of London.[131] But the 1940 invasion of Belgium and the Netherlands did not capture the public imagination as the attacks on London would. The German bombing of Rotterdam was, like the earlier bombing of Warsaw, unrelenting. Headlines were sympathetic, yet reactions were muted. Whilst New Zealand's first major fundraising campaign coincided with the invasion, it was not specifically in aid of the invaded countries. An *Auckland Star* editorial on the day the appeal opened underlined the general lack of fundraising enthusiasm, and, with one of those backward glances Taylor describes, noted that 'up

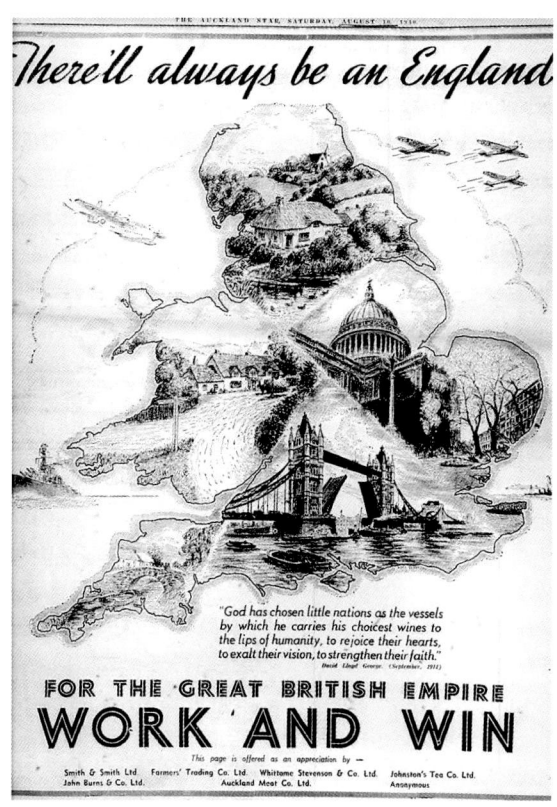

The iconography of England on the periphery: a full-page advertisement in the *Auckland Star*, paid for by New Zealand companies. *Auckland Star*/Fairfax Media, 10 August 1940, p.6.

till now there has been no response to appeals for patriotic funds in any way comparable with the efforts of a quarter of a century ago. The need has seemed less urgent and insistent.' The editorial went on to suggest that 'in a flash the whole position has changed'.[132] But it is not clear that anything had actually changed. Whilst the appeal may have been helped by public sympathy for the Belgians and the Dutch, it certainly did not exploit it, for advertising did not mention them. Rather, the appeal was a combined one on behalf of the Red Cross and the Order of St John, benefiting a wide range of causes, in particular New Zealand's own troops.[133] The 'brave little Belgians', centre of public sympathy in World War I, were yet to be replaced by the 'gallant little Londoners' of World War II.[134]

Bombs on the imagined metropolis turned the New Zealand public's attention firmly to war and triggered a will to give that the invasion of the Low Countries, with all its resonances from World War I, had not. The sudden local enthusiasm for buying Spitfires is best explained by the fall of France and the start of the Channel Battle on 10 July 1940. Actual danger to Britain was now apparent. The idea of paying for Spitfires was not foreign to New Zealanders. Because of the imperial press system of news flow, New Zealanders would have been aware of Lord Beaverbrook's 'buy a Spitfire' marketing campaign, which was so successful that 'virtually every major town in Britain had its "own" Spitfire'.[135] Like many towns in Britain, New Zealand districts began to raise funds for their own planes. Fundraising began in early July but gained momentum as the Battle of Britain progressed. The *New Zealand Herald* did not open its appeal for fighter funds until 16 August, and then the money poured in, with over £30,000 collected in three weeks. The New Zealand Meat Producers Board gave another £30,000. Eventually, enough was raised to purchase twenty-three RAF fighters, named after Taranaki, Northland and other regions, along with one named after the 'Country Women of New Zealand'.[136]

Whilst public interest in buying Spitfires was high, and remained so as the Battle of Britain progressed, government reaction to the campaign was at best lukewarm. The government played no part in initiating it, and while fundraising was authorised on 12 July, it was not clear that the money collected would go towards buying planes.[137] Both Peter Fraser and Walter Nash damned the idea with faint praise, claiming that whilst it was patriotic, it was not practical. In an unpopular decision, they set a limit of £100,000 on Spitfire fundraising. Then, when funds exceeded that figure, the government stalled on sending the full amount.[138] But there was no such parsimony or procrastination over funds for London. On 14 September, less than a week after the papers began to carry reports of the Battle of London, the government's National Patriotic Fund announced that £100,000 would be sent to London immediately for the relief of bombing victims.[139] This time, something had changed. New Zealand's London was under attack. There was no government quibbling over the use of sterling funds in this instance, as there had been over the Spitfires. Even more unusual, the National Patriotic Fund did not even wait for funds to be raised before sending the money. The *Herald* editor claimed that 'there would be universal approval' because 'nothing which has happened since the war began has so stirred the feelings of the English-speaking world'; he suggested that the government could do more: 'it sent money for the relief of the Finnish people in distress and of the victims of the Turkish earthquakes. Both were most worthy causes, but not so much as that of the suffering Londoners.'[140]

The press, already implicated in representing the bombing of London as a significant New Zealand event, now bolstered that coverage by running fundraising appeals that worked by emphasising the close ties between hinterland and metropolis. The *Star* got straight to the populist point by naming theirs the 'Heart to Heart' appeal. '"It cannot happen here", perhaps, but it has happened in the beloved heart of our Empire, and if our boasted ties of loyalty and kinship are to be more than intangible, our response to the cry for succour must, and will be open handed and speedy.'[141] Readers were reminded that every donation 'is a corpuscle of lifeblood to join the stream flowing along the arteries of the Empire to that sadly bleeding but still stoutly pulsing heart. Through that stream we can join in sacrifice of the people of London.'[142] Cash as corpuscles may be taking the metaphorical possibilities a step too far, but despite the hyperbole it seems the sentiments were sincere and shared, for donations reached over £6,000 in two days. The Auckland Harbour Board gave £1,000,[143] whilst the board of the Auckland Savings Bank gave £2,000, and the Auckland Transport Board gave £250 because they were 'sure the public would want the Board to contribute according to its means'.[144]

But donations did not come just from companies: the two papers stressed the importance of small donations as well. Both undertook to publish the name and amount of every contribution, and the *Auckland Star* also introduced runners to collect money. In just two weeks, the *Star* alone had raised over £22,000,[145] and by the end of the appeal, the two papers combined had collected over £40,000.[146] (An appeal for local orphanages run at the same time expected to raise £4,000.)[147] The published names provide some tangible indication of the nature of the giving, and the 'long list of contributors continues to show how anxious are firms and private persons to help the people of London'.[148] 'Old Age Pensioner' was a very common *nom de plume*, whilst many donations came from staff associations and social clubs, such as the Mt Albert Croquet Club, the staff of Bettine Crawfurd Gowns and Aluminium Utensils Ltd, along with Foot Glove Shu Factory employees.[149] Children's moneyboxes were emptied (although the children's feelings may only be guessed at), as 'Barbara, aged one' and 'Geoffrey, aged two' donated £1, and seven-year-old Desmond had his opened with a chisel.[150] Farmers sold stock to raise funds, and women sent in wedding rings. The *Auckland*

Star noted that 'many of the banknotes received have been carefully creased. Others gave off a faint perfume or smelled strongly of camphor. These were the donations made from the little hoard, the "rainy day" money of working girls and elderly women.'[151] These examples also give off a faint odour of promotional pathos yet the public continued to make donations to both funds long after they had closed.

The *Star* attributed the 'magnificent response' quite appropriately not just to humanitarian impulse, because this was not much in evidence in other worthy cases, but to the 'kinship with people of the Home Country, who are their own flesh and blood, bound by the ties of a common nationhood'.[152] Here, the *Star* may have overlooked its own role. Alongside the cultural ties of kinship – the 'ties of common nationhood' – ran other, quite different cultural ties, whose influence increased over time. The press produced the propinquity its fundraising reflected. However, Fleet Street's impact on New Zealand, if not much studied, is perhaps more easily accepted than the subject of the next chapter. It considers the role of film in creating and sustaining the imaginary geography that lies behind New Zealand's London.

CHAPTER EIGHT

HOME MOVIES

London on Film

THE ARRIVAL OF the King in New Zealand via the Empire Service ether had an earlier parallel: the 1897 film scenes of Queen Victoria's Diamond Jubilee. The footage was 'extremely popular throughout New Zealand, particularly the sections showing "the Maorilanders"'.[1] Audiences cheered and clapped so hard that exhibitors had to rewind and rerun the sequence, while some members of the audience stood and sang the National Anthem as the Queen's carriage passed.[2] This apparent confusion over representation and reality was perhaps to be expected: film and its new lifelike forms were still a novelty, for New Zealand had screened its first motion pictures only one year previously. However, there was no notion of peripheral backwardness or colonial form in this, as 1896 was the same year that films were first screened in New York and Paris.

For a few flickering moments, as the Queen's carriage passed through those crowded streets, London came to life in the colony. The very first film images that screened in New Zealand, just a year earlier, may also have included scenes of metropolitan street life.[3] Film's ability to dissolve distance in this way was unparalleled: 'perhaps the most far-reaching impact of the new simultaneity was due to the cinema, which was able to bring together an unprecedented variety of visual images and arrange them coherently in a unified whole. German audiences moved visually between Munich and the wild American west; French audiences travelled to the North Pole and the moon.'[4] New Zealanders left their seats to join in Victoria's jubilee. But the rise and dominance of the American film industry after 1917 suggests that London's presence might have been limited to a few flickering moments. By 1929, just 9 per cent of films screened in New Zealand were British. Consequently, the impact of film in New Zealand has largely been associated with the arrival of a competing American culture into '98.5% British New Zealand'. But while film was undoubtedly an 'American revolution', its cultural impacts in New Zealand were more nuanced.[5]

In part this was because British influence remained strong in other key areas. Radio, for example, when brought under state control, was quick to moderate American influence. The BBC was radio's exemplar, and there was no American equivalent of the Empire Service.[6] Even the old space-binding book trade remained dominated by London publishers and, as we saw in the previous chapter, American press influence was negligible. Further, American film was not automatically a vehicle for 'American' culture. In the 1930s in particular, Hollywood became an alternative source of images of London for New Zealand audiences. Importantly, these images portrayed London in familiar and consistent ways, reinforcing imagery created in those other media. Finally, film's power to excise space was not limited to feature films. Whilst America dominated the main features, British films successfully exploited other, less glamorous, viewing niches. These included the short feature, a staple of New Zealand's film-exhibiting culture for most of the twentieth century. Short features also became the staple of a newly emerging market: educational film. In both cases, familiar London themes were likely to be overrepresented, and film, conventional vector of Americanisation, became another means of capturing New Zealand as an imaginative hinterland of London.

'BRITISH' FEATURE FILMS IN NEW ZEALAND

Although this chapter focuses on the role of short films, some feature film context is appropriate. Whilst America's dominance is not in doubt, a recent study has demonstrated Britain's crucial importance as the profit centre for American movies.[7] As movies changed from silent to sound features, the associated problems of dubbing and subtitling different languages limited the interchange of film, reducing the scope of world markets.[8] In addition, a number of previously important European markets began to close. They developed their own industries in their own languages, and protected them with quotas, making them less profitable as markets even when they did import American films. Political changes in Europe further limited distribution, making some of these already less profitable markets disappear completely. Between 1933 and 1941, the number of cinemas worldwide that could, technically at least, screen American films almost halved from 62,000 to 32,500. Under these circumstances, the British market, already the largest importer of American film, and its related markets in the white dominions, took on an increased importance. In 1938, these countries plus America represented a market of some 25,000 cinemas. Their numerical importance was matched by their financial importance. In the 1920s, Britain provided 35 per cent of Hollywood's foreign earnings, rising to more than 50 per cent in the 1930s. With no need to subtitle or dub movies, the British and dominion market could increase a film's profitability too: 'Between 1930 and 1945, MGM's films, on average, made 66% of their total earnings from the domestic market and the remaining 34% from the foreign markets, only the final 19% of which were realized as profit.'[9]

It is not surprising then that, during this period, a new form of hybrid 'British' movie developed in Hollywood. These hybrids used British talent, British source material and British settings to cater to the 'overwhelmingly predominant' British taste in foreign markets.[10] New Zealand seems to have shared this taste: cinema entrepreneur Henry Hayward imported fifty British-made films in 1928 to play at the Strand and Majestic theatres, although his attempt at establishing the aptly named London Theatre in Auckland as an avenue for British films only was notably unsuccessful.[11] The fate of the London seems to confirm a widely held conception that British films were not popular with New Zealand audiences, or even British ones, in this period, being considered inferior to Hollywood's slick productions.[12] Yet Hayward was still operating the Majestic theatre as an 'All-British theatre' as late as 1933. Further, there is research amongst British viewers that suggests a revival of interest in 'home' movies. In particular, the introduction of a quota system in Britain in 1928 appears to have improved

New Zealand's premier 'All-British' theatre, the Majestic, c.1933, featuring *Tell Me Tonight*, a British remake of a German film, starring a Polish tenor. Stills Collection, New Zealand Film Archive Ngā Kaitiaki O Ngā Taonga Whitiāhua.

the quality of local films and the size of their audiences.[13] Correspondingly, New Zealand exhibitors persisted in attributing a fondness for British films to their audiences, claiming that 'the technique and artistry of American pictures is generally considered to be on the whole superior to the average British film. The latter, however, has a special appeal to British audiences owing to its national spirit and associations and is particularly successful in New Zealand.'[14]

The combination of both was bound to be popular. There was no apparent sense of contradiction in an Auckland cinema, the St James, claiming 'you'll be proud you're British when you see *Lives of a Bengal Lancer*', a film made in America about the British Raj featuring Hollywood star Gary Cooper.[15] Hybrid American/British films would also insulate Hollywood against losing market share to a slowly reviving British film market in the 1930s. Again, there is evidence of this rebound in New Zealand: by 1933–34, 29 per cent of films screened were British compared with the nadir of 9 per

A Hollywood hybrid: Paramount brings 'some of Britain's finest' to the screen at Auckland's St James Theatre. St James Theatre, scrapbook 193[?4]–1937, MS 91/20, Auckland Museum Library.

cent in 1929.[16] In the Upper Hutt's People's Pictures theatre, the preference was even more marked: a study of the top twenty movies screened there between 1931 and 1934 revealed that half were British, from the comedy *On Approval* to naval drama *The Flag Lieutenant*. (The most popular American-made film was a remake of Lewis Carroll's *Alice in Wonderland*.)[17]

The importance of the lucrative British market helped ensure a British presence in Hollywood films.[18] Some hybrid British films, reflecting an American version of cultural dependency on the old metropolis, were prestige productions with lavish sets and costumes and accordingly larger budgets, like early versions of the big budget blockbuster. Like blockbusters,

MGM's *David Copperfield*, complete with Hollywood's own 'whiter and cliffier' stand-ins for the white cliffs of Dover. St James Theatre, scrapbook 193[?4]–1937, MS 91/20, Auckland Museum Library.

too, they were not the most numerous form of feature film. One studio, MGM, made two or three a year out of a total of thirty-five. But they were financial and popular successes in both America and England. Films like *Mutiny on the Bounty*, *Tarzan the Ape Man*, *Lassie Come Home* and *Mrs Miniver* had roughly equivalent earnings in America and the 'foreign' markets dominated by Britain and the dominions.[19] In these prestige films, an idealised version of Britain appeared. The settings were remarkably consistent, resembling a 'tourist's view', as Britain was essentialised into a few familiar sets of images.[20] Authenticity was no substitute for this idealised imagery. In *David Copperfield*, the actual white cliffs of Dover were replaced by cliffs at Malibu beach because the director claimed they 'were better – whiter and cliffier'.[21] Higher and whiter cliffs surrounded an idyllic filmic countryside. Rural Britain became romanticised rural England, complete with manor houses, charming cottages and Elizabeth Taylor galloping along in *National Velvet*. These films also included opening shots of London and its landmarks, using familiar 'national' symbols like 'Big Ben, St Paul's Cathedral, Tower Bridge, and heavy and constant fog'.[22] Hollywood may have been the dominant location for production, but it allowed for many settings. One was an imagined London, 'deriving from travellers' accounts of London, the novels of Charles Dickens (particularly *Bleak House*), the Sherlock Holmes stories of Sir Arthur Conan Doyle and press accounts of the Jack the Ripper murders'.[23] Hollywood's London was not all gloom, though. An artificially sweetened version would turn in up in films such as *Mary Poppins*.[24]

These idealised images were compounded by the studios' predilection for historical and costume dramas, such as Warner's 'Merrie England' films that included *The Adventures of Robin Hood*, and extended by a continued interest in imperial tales including *Clive of India* and *Gunga Din*, as 'Empire throughout the thirties was big box office'.[25] Modern versions of Britain also appeared, especially in war movies, but 'even while portraying new England . . . the films do not stray very far from the characters and settings of the old England'.[26] That suited New Zealand audiences: it seemed a New Zealander would 'pay his one and six rather more readily if he thinks the history he is going to see is "British-made"', even if the production was actually American.[27]

Hollywood's British films 'centred on British literature, and history, its culture and heritage', thus claiming for themselves the kind of cultural prestige expected of actual British films.[28] This may not have been a sop solely to the British market. Hollywood required a little cultural elevation in American eyes. Small-town America felt threatened by 'East Side' film values, which were regarded as reflecting the tastes of an incompatible, urban and migrant population. From the late 1920s, these towns 'rejected early talkies drawn directly from hit Broadway shows resplendent with Yiddish humour and barely clad chorus girls, causing headaches for Hollywood film producers'.[29] Anxiety about movie morality and values culminated in the adoption of rules for film content, the Hayes Code, from 1930, a change that might have helped to keep the hybrid, with its cultural high tone, in production. Certainly, the connection between metropolitan cultural prestige and moral values was explicit in New Zealand. Following its British counterpart, the New Zealand government imposed a quota in 1928 to encourage the screening of British-made films.[30] In part, this was a response to imperial trade preferences; however, the root of this preference for things British seems to rest less in the idea of economic support than in the sense that the British product was of superior moral fibre. Sir James Parr found it 'horrible to think that the British Empire is receiving its education from a place called Hollywood. The Dominions would rather have a picture with a wholesome, British background, something which gives British sentiment, something that is honest to our traditions, than the abortions which we get from Hollywood', whilst noting rather more mildly that 'trade follows the film, not the flag'.[31]

Not all British/American films were so wholesome. The other hybrid was the 'quota quickie', developed by American film companies to fulfil their British quota obligations. New Zealand exhibitors considered them 'crude' and blamed them on producers catering for double-feature formats (which were also considered déclassé) and 'large industrial centres where certain types of cheap comedy film have an appeal'.[32] They belied the association of Britain and betterment, a reflection of the concentrated cultural power of the metropolis that was not isolated to film. British films, like other aspects of British media, were expected to have a higher cultural tone. Indeed, some New Zealand film exhibitors claimed that they reserved such films for their 'better class' theatres.[33]

BRITISH SHORT FEATURES

The production of consistent, idealised images of Britain, and Britain's association with improving culture, whether in American versions of British films or the real thing, tended to privilege exactly the same kind of themes we have already encountered amongst New Zealand travellers, writers and soldiers, and in the reciprocal imagery that developed between the cultured metropolis and its rural hinterland. It is likely film played a role in forming such images. A contemporary New Zealand critic claimed 'London – yes we'd probably know our way around Scotland Yard, St Paul's and Trafalgar Square, and we'd recognise No. 10 Downing Street if we passed it: those places are as familiar to us by sight as almost any place in New Zealand.'[34] British films and Hollywood hybrids were instrumental in creating this sense of familiarity, and they were partnered in the process by a rather more unassuming part of the film industry, the short feature. In this case, hybridity could occur in screenings and programming as much as in content and film type.

Short films were the only sort of film in which Britain remained competitive with America on New Zealand's cinema screens. Although between 1928 and 1949 just 18 per cent of the nine thousand feature films shown in New Zealand were British, the percentage of British short features shown in New Zealand increased to 48 per cent.[35] This was not the case in Britain itself: in 1939, just 27 per cent of shorts screened were British-made. The total number of British short films released that year was 275, whilst the total number of British shorts shown in New Zealand was more than double that number, at 576.[36] In short features at least, New Zealand was 'more British than the British', which casts some doubt on the findings of a New Zealand parliamentary report that stated 'it was thought that the tendency would be for British short films to be used in with programs with British features and this has proved to be the case in practice'.[37] No doubt they were; but as British shorts vastly outnumbered British features, some accompanied American films. In one theatre, Clark Gable's *After Office Hours* screened after pictures of the Jubilee celebration in London.[38]

New Zealand's preference for British short films was part of an unusual predilection for showing shorts at all and was confirmed by the 1934 Committee of Inquiry into the Motion Picture Industry, which noted that 'the general policy adopted in New Zealand differs from most other countries in that, as a general rule, only one "feature" or "long story picture" is shown'.[39] Short features around the world were challenged by the innovation of the double feature, which soon predominated, and one leading British short filmmaker cited New Zealand as 'the only part of the Empire that he knew had not introduced the practice of the double bill. There the demand for short films continued unabated.'[40] Lack of demand in the United States and Britain may have limited supply, and there was 'a real problem finding enough "shorts" of good quality to make up the supporting programmes which the bulk of our audiences demand'.[41] A single feature supported by a cartoon, newsreel and short (such as a travelogue) was characteristic of Auckland's St James in the 1930s. The combined programme may have enhanced the space-conquering capabilities of the short, its currency perhaps presumed by its being played with the latest feature. Although out-of-date newsreels were not uncommon, simultaneity was actively promoted: latest footage of the Battle of Britain was advertised as 'rushed by boat, plane, and rail' before arriving at the Century theatre.[42] Whether through the parsimony of cinema owners, the imagined moral malignancy of 'double features' or a more general culture of restraint, New Zealand's temperate habit of just one film per evening may have created another source of London imagery, courtesy of the continued presence of the short feature.

 # Theatre Royal

TO-NIGHT.   TO-NIGHT.

MR. JOHN FULLER,

MYRIORAMA

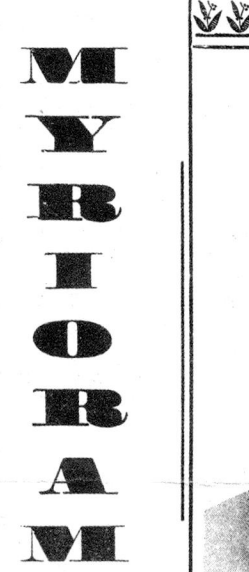

Travel,

Song,

Music

AND

Story,

Pictorially Illustrated

The Gifted and Popular Tenor Vocalist.

London Day by Day.

"The Audience, by means of a Magnificent Triple Optical Lantern, purchased by Mr. JOHN FULLER, from the Sydney School of Arts, are taken on a Pleasant Tour, Instructive and Entertaining. The Magnificence of the Views highly delighting those who witness them. The Audience are, for the time being, mentally transported to the scene of the tour and rapidly taken from one point of interest to another, the pictures are of large and life-like proportions, being projected on to and completely covering a screen stretched to the fullest dimensions of the stage. One picture melts away into another, handsome and imposing edifices being reared as it were before the audience in the space of a second. Famous thoroughfares appearing to the vision with startling realism, others coming into evidence before the preceding one quite disappears. Each scene is briefly described in terms that are well chosen and always interesting. The Company includes some exceptionally gifted Vocalists whose various Solos are enhanced by Pictorial Illustrations and effects, for instance in the song 'The Little Hero,' these are thrown on to the canvas appropriately to the lines and in a life-like manner, the Mate threatening the boy, giving him ten minutes to confess, the boy praying, and the Mate finally clasping the 'Little Hero' in his arms. The magnificent instrument used is not a 'Graph' of any description neither can an instrument that—with effects—cost upwards of £1,000, be called a magic lantern, as all that science and ingenuity can suggest have been brought together in this "**Myriorama.**"

   For Detailed Programme see over.

The Most Complete, Interesting, Up-to-date

Entertainment of its kind travelling.

"Lyttelton Times," Chch

Although we know how many were shown, it is harder to know what these short films were about. While undoubtedly covering a wide variety of subjects, records of their screenings are almost non-existent and there are few left to view.[43] But London was, for a variety of reasons, likely to be the subject or setting for shorts. In the very early period of film, at the close of the nineteenth century, London was the world capital of the emerging film industry and, reprising her role as entrepôt for any number of trading commodities, the 'world clearing house of open market films'.[44] In the era before studios, production houses were drawn to the south to take advantage of better weather. In London, they also had the added bonus of ready access to theatre district actors. Films could be shot in the street: as late as the 1920s, *Wonderful London*'s 'London's Free Shows' included a sequence filming the filmmakers, warning that 'around the corner you may come upon a horrible murder or a fiendish abduction . . . . It's all right – it's only for the pictures!'[45] London streets also abounded in 'actualities', the stock-in-trade of early filmmakers, and the picturesque. These factors would help keep the industry in London, and in turn keep London images in front of New Zealand audiences from the earliest of screenings. The Salvation Army Biorama Company's show in Christchurch presented, amongst items of religious and historical interest, 'some of the finest slides ever shown in Christchurch of scenes of the River Thames'.[46] Not only were they possibly the finest but, like other recolonial media, these slides were also the latest. The Biorama Company boasted of 'thoroughly up to date film stock, some made just thirty days before the company left London for New Zealand'.[47] Later movies, like the travelogue series *Wonderful London*, with over twenty films, or *Seeing London*, which seemed to number over a hundred episodes, are little more than technologically advanced versions of these early actuality films.[48] They were often composed of simple static camera shots, framing the historic and picturesque, sometimes reusing exactly the same footage. With titles like *London Landmarks*, *Known London* (and its partner *Unknown London*), *London Sundays* and the desperate *Flowers of London*, travelogue filmmakers quite literally used every angle to bring the same London to the screen.

London on screen in 1898: Theatre Royal audiences for Fuller's Myriorama would be 'mentally transported to the scene of the tour' which took in sights like St Paul's, Piccadilly, Hyde Park and Whitechapel slum life. Eph-A-Cinema-Theatre Royal, Alexander Turnbull Library, Wellington, New Zealand.

The proliferation of travelogues, particularly those featuring landmarks, was the product of easy convention and rather more complicated legislation. Initially, it seemed that actuality films would fall outside new quota legislation introduced in Britain in 1927 to stimulate its film industry. Films 'consisting wholly or mainly of natural scenery, of industrial or manufacturing processes, or of commercial advertisement; those wholly or mainly for education purposes and scientific and natural history films' would not be counted towards a cinema's quota of British film.[49] But filmmakers quickly found a loophole, one that may have stimulated production of London travelogues, because they concentrated less on natural scenery than on buildings and people.[50] St Paul's was scenic, but it was not natural, so it could be counted towards the quota. Production of short features in Britain increased after 1933, when the system of registration, or perhaps how to get around it, became better known. A few producers emerged 'who knew how to put the very minimum of effort and expenditure into a film and yet exploit the regulations to secure quota registration. Strings of shots of buildings, even strings of shots of pictures of buildings were "travel pictures" which brought disrepute to the genre but provided renters and exhibitors with British footage for next to nothing.'[51] It may also have provided New Zealand audiences with yet another set of views of London.

British quota regulations for short features were eased in 1938, meaning that a greater range of shorts was now eligible, and this again boosted production levels. (It also led to more American feature films being made in Britain.) These British quota-registered shorts could enter New Zealand unexamined, making it easier to screen them. But besides this, there was no local incentive to do so. In New Zealand, quota levels for showing British films were measured per feature film, not by total footage, so running a British short would not help a theatre reach its required quota. Along with a general scarcity of shorts, reflecting their reduced use in other markets, the best explanation for the increased prevalence of British shorts seems to be a predilection for supporting British productions. After all, the New Zealand government relied on a 'gentleman's agreement' with exhibitors over quota enforcement. Some commercial moviemakers may have seen this tendency as an opportunity. *Dear Old London*, a scenic film, was 'made, quite clearly specifically for showing in Australia and, to only a lesser extent, in the other Dominions'.[52] There is no evidence that this particular movie was shown in New Zealand, but the British Film Institute's account indicates that the dominions were seen as a potential market for commercial short features on London, perhaps because of their willingness to continue to screen British films in general.[53]

Another example of government intervention in the film industry is the creation of propaganda films. Despite the British government's initial reluctance to engage in propaganda after World War I, the growing use of film as a propaganda medium by countries like Russia and Germany could not be ignored. It was argued that a film industry supported by a quota would keep the right kind of images of Britain on screen.[54] The British Council, which also commissioned movies, was officially formed in 1935 to spearhead British cultural propaganda. Its head, Australian Rex Leeper, argued that Britain's aloofness in matters of cultural, political and economic propaganda, its position that 'good wine needs no bush', was 'materially damaging'.[55] These concerns intersected neatly with twentieth-century 'constructive imperialism', which together created a powerful ideological platform for filmmaking. Under these conditions, it is not surprising that the pioneer of the British film propaganda movement was the Empire Marketing Board (EMB). Its secretary, Sir Stephen Tallents, termed this process 'the projection of Britain'. But even New Zealand's enthusiasm could not withstand the EMB's one attempt at a commercial feature. *One Family* reflected an ongoing EMB obsession with portraying imperial cohesiveness, this time through the medium of puddings, in 'a fable about the gathering of the ingredients for the royal Christmas pudding from all parts of the empire as viewed through the eyes of a small boy, with society ladies personifying the Empire's Colonies and Dominions'. Baroness Ravensdale featured as New Zealand, and the film made a grand total of £334.[56]

The Empire Marketing Board Film Unit was short-lived, but it made a contribution to filmmaking that surpassed the value of its actual output. It was headed by John Grierson, whose name is synonymous with the development of the British documentary film movement (and who coined the term 'documentary'). Staff from his unit spread out to its successors. Some moved to the General Post Office Film Unit, a rather more enterprising organisation than its name suggests. In a remarkable piece of bureaucratic sleight of hand, movies made by this film unit could be on any topic, including locomotives and Ceylon. (They also resisted classification by style: expatriate New Zealand artist and filmmaker Len Lye's *Colour Box* was a GPO commission.) Still others worked for the Travel and

Hybrid screenings: the Picturedrome, on Auckland's North Shore, ran a mix of British, 'British' and American movies through January and February 1942. Picturedrome Milford, MS 432, Records 1924–1964, Auckland Museum Library.

Industrial Development Association, an initiative of private businessmen that 'set out to develop through travel a greater knowledge of, and interest in, British culture and British goods, thus bringing about, we are confident, an increase in our export trade, visible as well as invisible'.[57] The role of the association was explicitly externally oriented, its work intended to 'exert what may be called a human tidal pull towards these shores'.[58] It was given some financial support by the Department of Overseas Trade, and was attached to the Empire Marketing Board Film Unit first, then the British Council, in a perfect example of the intersection of empire and British cultural propaganda. That London could comfortably accommodate this ideology, and was also a cheap and easy source of imagery, is evident in the multiple films made from footage shot in 1933. These included *London* (1933), *London Town* (with the EMB, 1933), *So This is London* (1933) and

London River (1939). With boundless enthusiasm for the topic, they also made *London on Parade, Heart of an Empire, For All Eternity* (and its silent version, *Cathedrals of Britain*) and *Lights o' London* during this period, and probably *London Wakes Up* as well. *City of Progress* (made by the Realist Film Unit in 1941) drew on these films for footage, and it is likely other films such as *St James Park* did so too.

Propaganda movies increased with the advent of World War II and the establishment of the wartime Ministry of Information. London's function as icon for all things British was again particularly useful in a series of movies such as *London Can Take It!, London 1942, Christmas Under Fire* and *War and Order*.[59] In *New Britain*, scenes of British progress were undercut by Graham Greene's ominous tones repeating, 'We forgot Germany'. Images of London stood for progress: 'London calling; we gave entertainment to the world for a few pence a week ... led the world in television ... children were taught only to be happy, not drilled in brown shirts for war.' *Morning Paper*, ostensibly about the production of *The Times*, connected London's historic role in newspaper production, and Londoners' 'ritual' reading of the news, with the wartime stoicism portrayed as being inherent in British people.[60] Air raids may come, but the 'presses thunder on'.[61] New Zealand audiences did not need much convincing that Britain was worth saving, but the Americans did: hence movies such as *London Scrapbook*, which cemented a chipper tone onto footage designed to show London battered but resolute. Actors Bessie Lowe and Basil Radford provided continuity for pictures of Big Ben surrounded by barbed wire and bombing around St Paul's. These were contrasted with British people humorously 'making do', using ration coupons to shop for clothing and sharing taxis.[62]

PICTURING LONDON

Propaganda movies increased the likelihood that London would continue to appear on New Zealand screens while reinforcing a set of cohesive tropes. Short films of London were subject to the same processes of ordering space that occur in travellers' version of London. Like that 'tourist view', London's monumental architecture could be easily reorganised on film to emphasise its symbolic qualities. London on film, like London in guidebooks, became the stronghold of history, heritage and British values. It reached both back and forward in time; modern London co-existed with historic London, and the tension between the two served only to emphasise the enduring nature of the metropolis itself and the timelessness of the British values it signified. Conventions in short filmmaking meant New Zealand audiences, in mainstream theatres and elsewhere, saw a repetitive series of images of buildings, pageantry and people that were imbued with particular values, inscribing the metropolis as icon. Familiar characteristics attributed to London, like 'heart of empire', 'commercial capital of the world' and 'home of democracy', were reassembled then replayed with the heightened sense of reality that film brings.

Filmmakers used this imaginative geography as an ordering device for short films, a practice that led to a tremendous amount of repetition. The 1933 Travel and Industrial Development Association film, *London*, functions in this icon-inscribing fashion by making London's various roles correspond to geographical positions and notable landmarks, an approach emphasised by beginning each new section with a map. The section titled 'The City' includes St Paul's and the Tower of London, but the rest of the section is characterised by commerce, with the Bank of England, surrounded by men in top hats, the Guildhall, the Inns of Court and stores selling legal paraphernalia. Similarly, the 'West End' section becomes synonymous with entertainment and street life, whilst 'Westminster' signifies imperial and parliamentary functions. Actual geography was subordinated to this values-based arrangement – St James's Palace, although featured in the Westminster map, emerges instead in the section 'Palaces'. This symbolic shorthand existed outside of propaganda: the *Wonderful London* series of commercial travelogues engaged in the same inscribing process. London guards the sacred centre of democracy in *Wonders of Westminster*, which features the 'Mother of Parliaments' along with notable surrounding buildings. Democracy's history and geography are specific: the film included the 'ancient rites of summoning' and the 'most sacred spot of all', the Coronation Chair.[63]

Monumental buildings were central to this imagery, creating a series of value-laden icons that defied time. 'Truly St Paul's dominates London', one travelogue noted, and it certainly dominated short films.[64] It was proxy for London itself, often used as an opening shot. It stood for history, as 'noble St Paul's, centre of the ancient city of London' and, less often, as a religious centre.[65] Its enduring qualities were paramount. The 1934 movie

For All Eternity, which may have given its audiences a good idea of what that felt like, featured British cathedrals including Westminster Abbey and St Paul's Cathedral, and its storyline emphasises their unchanging purpose in changing times: 'The cathedral stands firm, though factory workers kneel in the place of knights and peasants.'⁶⁶ The film also included footage of Liverpool cathedral being built. St Paul's featured in its own eponymous film made in 1943 after it had been bombed, when there was 'a new tale of wonder to tell about St Paul's'.⁶⁷ The film was specifically commissioned by the British Council for use outside Britain to suggest Britain's endurance under wartime conditions. While cathedrals make the connection between monuments and values obvious, these two films reflect more than the centrality of religious observance. The incorporation of factory workers in *For All Eternity* suggests the fundamentally democratic nature of British life; this is repeated in *St Paul's Cathedral*, where 'people bring their children to show them their church'. Travelogues likewise repetitively connected St Paul's and 'the people' in footage of visitors feeding the pigeons outside. With its wartime setting, *St Paul's Cathedral* also extends the unchanging nature of the monument to the British people themselves, for the church was 'saved by people who came of their own free will to risk their lives for their church. When the city was crashing around them, they did not fail.'⁶⁸ Should viewers be unaware of the essentially British nature of this courage, the young boy at the centre of the film visits Nelson's tomb, and 'conjures up a vision of the Battle of Trafalgar'.⁶⁹

Such enduring values were also constructed in the tension between the modern metropolis and its historic time. London's dual role as modern metropolis and home of the historic is evident in a 1920s era *Wonderful London* episode, *London – Old and New*.⁷⁰ The viewer is taken around London by a relic of the past, the horse-drawn cab, and the film is narrated by a stock character, the London cab driver. Intertitles, when not simply signposting the obvious, indulge in Cockney-flavoured contrasts of old and new: 'The Tower of London's still there I see. Wonder they ain't pulled it down and built a blinkin' picture pallis.' Ephemeral achievements of modern life serve only to highlight the enduring past. Staple Inn, a half-timbered Tudor building, is another frequent emblem of old London, which in this film is contrasted with the new dominion buildings: 'Orsetralia House may come and Bush 'ouses may go, but our Staple Inn seems to go on forever!' Indeed, time is transcended in another episode, *Dickens' London*, in which nineteenth-century London is recreated by simply transposing ghostly figures from his books over contemporary footage of buildings.[71]

Commercial propaganda movies, like those commissioned by the Travel Association, needed to stress that London was, for all its history, a vital commercial centre and part of the modern world. The usual solution was direct contrast, again relying on icons signifying age. From 'noble St Paul's', *London on Parade* explored the city's commercial life, having safely located this as an ancient function. A convenient device was the Thames, an icon of timelessness itself, in *Wonderful London* episodes such as *Along Old Father Thames to Shepperton*, *Barging Through London* or the Travel Association movie *London River*. Modernity in *London on Parade* and other films was represented by the underground, by commuting and suburbs, by the worker in 'the City, the richest square mile in the world'. Scenes of switchboard operators were intercut with pictures of the BBC building, stressing that 'every great city is in touch with modern London, and the BBC keeps London within the hearing of English-speaking people of the whole world'. Yet modernity was always neatly sandwiched within tradition. Scenes of historic buildings accompanied a voiceover which assured viewers that while 'demolition gangs are at work everywhere . . . much which is old and lovely is being preserved'. Indeed, this rush to modernise was immediately counterbalanced by scenes of pageantry, with the trooping of the colours, the state opening of Parliament and even that 'pageant of the people', the Lord Mayor's Show.

Yet 'modern' London remained an important theme in the imaging of London. Audiences would soon have become familiar with London's transport systems, as these were often used to signify progress. *City Bound* spends thirty-five minutes on the London transport system, filming trains, buses and the underground, to present the network as connective tissue between 'the ordinary people of London' and the great work of the city, carried out in 'offices which lie in the shadow of St Paul's cathedral, to the busy newspaper offices of Fleet Street . . . clerks hurry to their desks down the city's ancient alleys and byways . . . through the maze of warehouses, workers make their way to the docks'.[72] Similarly, communication systems symbolised modernity. The London to Aberdeen overnight postal services became the subject of John Grierson's widely screened documentary *Night Mail*.[73]

The consistency of this imagery, both civilised and civilising, grows stronger over time although, as travellers were aware, its doppelganger, the

'Improving film': in the early 1900s, moving pictures, including scenes of London, were brought to towns throughout New Zealand by the Salvation Army's touring Biorama Company. Salvation Army Heritage Centre and Archives.

metropolis as 'dark city', as 'abyss of moral despair', did exist.[74] Early films were often 'improving' in nature, and those great improvers the Salvation Army and their Biorama Company toured New Zealand extensively in 1905 and 1907. Although entertainment formed part of their programme, they also screened footage of the pathetic 'waifs and strays of the greatest city on earth manag[ing] to struggle through life, sleeping on benches in parks, despair; a mother leaving her baby on the doorstep; selling matches and finishing up with a typical Whitechapel brawl', all calculated to support the Army's lectures on 'self-denial'.[75]

Similarly, travelogues of the twenties made excursions into the 'dark city', but the subject matter had changed. 'Waifs and strays' were remade into picturesque characters, such as flower sellers, street hawkers and chimney sweeps. Migrants were the new strays: *Wonderful London*'s *Sidelights of London* featured immigrant areas in a crass exploitation of difference. Pictures of 'foreign' restaurants, 'lascars around the docks', children and street stalls came with the warning, 'one mustn't dub them peculiar just because they happen to be foreign. London immigrants are quite normal and content.'[76] *Cosmopolitan London* was an even more extensive treatment, featuring 'sinister Pennyfields, where the Chink either slinks away at the sight of the camera or bursts into volleys of hysterical laughter . . . . dim and mysterious is London's Chinatown, and in Limehouse causeway, one gets the tang of betel nut, of bhang and of – opium.' Italians and Irish joined the 'swarming hive of Jewish humanity' on this tour, which in an odd juxtaposition also took in Australia and New Zealand House along the Strand. Audiences may have found pictures of Sir James Allen shaking hands outside New Zealand House dissonant with the other images of 'cosmopolitan London' and it seems the filmmakers did too, for the images were prefaced as the 'houses of our colonial brethren'.[77] In this respect, as in others, the white dominions would be accorded a favoured place in the family of empire.

By the 1930s, exotic difference on film was located on the wharves, and no longer in lounging lascars but in trade items like bunches of bananas. Cosmopolitan people were replaced by cosmopolitan commerce, as images of London as the world's trading centre developed: 'all roads lead to London, the biggest city in the world'.[78] *London Town* epitomised its centripetal force, with 'goods and people . . . constantly passing to and from the ends of the earth', an intertitle supported by footage of smoking trains, buses, ocean liners and aeroplanes.[79] Those emblems of modernity, transport systems and communications were combined with the commonplace symbols of London's commercial geography: the Bank of England, the docks and the Thames, 'highway of trade since the days of the Romans'. Covent Garden, Billingsgate, Tooley Street and Smithfield were presented as part of the 'essential activities that make London an Imperial and a World City'.[80]

In this film, and others, London as 'World City' was also constructed by the presence of its rural hinterlands. *London on Parade* featured scenes of goods, including 'apples from some far off orchard in Canada or New Zealand', arriving in metropolitan markets.[81] This commercial relationship was naturalised by historicising: cargo ships were featured unloading on the Thames 'exactly where the Roman traders did'.[82]

New Zealand was incorporated further into the reciprocal construction of empire, with scenes of the *Rangitikei* emptying its holds of frozen carcasses at the New Zealand Steamship Company wharves, while *Heart of an Empire* featured New Zealand House as 'another unofficial embassy for visitors and trade', and showed 'New Zealand butter being unloaded at London docks'.[83] On cinema screens, as in books and billboards, New Zealand once again played farm to its metropolis.

LONDON AND EDUCATIONAL FILM

Hybrid British films, actual British films and the domination of the short feature market by Britain are likely to have kept London in front of New Zealand cinema audiences to a greater degree than the 'Americanisation' story of film assumes. In the educational film market, British influence was even greater, and was apparent from its beginnings.

In 1905 the Wanganui School Board invested in two stereoscopes and a series of geographical pictures, all to help with teaching the new subject of geography. The board also sought a lanternslide projector and accompanying slides, arguing that 'no better means can be found for enlarging our knowledge and vivifying our ideas of other people and other lands'.[84] Such innovations marked the beginning of the visual education movement and 'the possibility of a new kind of mastery – an access to a vast pictorial knowledge that could transcend physical limitations'.[85] This transcendence would be made possible by the space-conquering qualities of film, and would include the 12,000 miles between New Zealand and Home. In 1913, the same board was interested in exploring the use of moving pictures.[86]

In the meantime, however, the *School Journal* may have been a useful, universal alternative in stimulating the imaginative hinterland. The central text for schools after 1907, it took a strong role in promoting visual education, releasing picture sets to accompany the journal itself 'as aids to oral instruction on modern lines' for history, geography and nature study.[87] Increasingly, it appears these images were British. We can only speculate as to the exact content of them, as the picture series has never been analysed or noted before, and there are no extant examples. However, records indicate that the first set, released in 1908, had a local flavour, including native bird prints and eight prints of New Zealand geography.[88] By 1909,

New Zealand content, especially native flora, was joined by twenty-four British battle scenes, and sixteen covering geography of the British Isles.[89] A year later, there were twenty-eight pictures of the British Isles, twenty-four dealing with British history, twenty-four on New Zealand and, in a nod to the concept of empire, a set on South Africa.[90] Reports end in the next year with seventy-two cards on Britain.[91]

The growth of print-based visual education was the result of improved, inexpensive printing techniques. Yet even these were subject to attempts to improve their powers of realism. Various rudimentary projection techniques such as the balopticon were adopted in attempts to transcend the page and vivify those other lands. Until school projectors were cheap enough, film-based education was limited to experimental programmes in mainstream theatres and field trips.

For the educational market, social and cultural betterment was paramount, and the imaginative hinterland that developed would be dominated by the metropolis. But film was initially seen as a less than benign new entrant into New Zealand, particularly for the children it would later be used to educate. Whilst early anxiety centred on general detrimental effects on health and morals, after World War I films were commonly associated with a negative influence upon the young.[92] In 1916, a Censorship Act was passed that was intended, among other things, to protect children from 'the disastrous effects that would result from film pictures of a not necessarily immoral but highly suggestive character being placed before [them]'.[93]

Educationists were among the anxious. The Wellington School Board was concerned about the impact of film upon young minds, recording 'with regret the failure of the efforts to secure, in the interests of children, an adequate censorship of films', along with the posters on public hoardings.[94] Uneasiness about pernicious effects only increased as America came to dominate the screen after 1917. Schools were already concerned about the deleterious effects of American culture seeping into New Zealand in other forms. The early emergence of an alternative cultural capital was not welcome. In 1910 a Marlborough school inspector claimed 'American novel reading is becoming more and more prevalent in New Zealand and the result on the language is beginning to be visible in the frequent use of such Americanisms as "belong there", the use of "like" as a conjunction and even such expressions as "where did you used to see these?" which may be found in otherwise good writers.'[95] The school inspector must have had a particularly sensitive ear, as book imports from America were worth about £9,000 that year, fairly insignificant besides the £151,000 imported from Britain.[96]

However, by 1927, the Imperial Education Conference 'was alive to the enormous influences exerted on children by the public films, to the dominance of foreign ideals in these as presented in all parts of the Empire, but more especially overseas, and to the necessity of encouraging the use of films in the theatres which shall truly represent the past history of the British peoples, their economic resources, their own special culture and ideas and their industrial and artistic values'.[97] Quota legislation followed. By 1929, and the arrival of 'talkies', not the least part of this 'special culture' was speech. The *Education Gazette* was able to recommend *Skippy*, an American movie, but only with the proviso that 'the young folk do not, of course, speak as English children do, but the picture is of such high quality that this, which must be called a defect as far as English ears are concerned, does not detract from its general merit'.[98] Not only were children saying 'belong there', but the new media also meant they could do it in American accents.

School visual education programmes developed from these tensions over film's influence. It could have 'corrupting' effects, but it could also make subjects come alive, compensating for a lack of direct experience by supplying '"vicarious experiences" – a term extremely popular among visual educators'.[99] Here, London's economic importance and its cultural power became intertwined. Amongst the subjects best suited to visual education were history, geography and, later, social studies, subjects in which London and Britain more generally had a central role. For example, until the development of social studies in the 1940s, New Zealand's geography curriculum was split in two: physical geography, to be taught using the local landscape, and commercial geography, which emphasised the importance of Britain and London. A typical question from the Junior Civil Service examination asked students to describe the route a letter might take to London; and a scholarship examination asked students to explain which cargoes a ship might collect in London for discharge in New Zealand, and which might be taken there from New Zealand.[100] The 1929 syllabus required that 'Great Britain should be studied from the point of view of its being the heart of our Empire, the market for 80% of our exports, the source of most of our imports.'[101] Older classes were expected to understand 'that economic conditions there are quickly reflected in the prices obtained for our own primary produce [which] indicates how largely the prosperity of our country is interwoven with that of the Motherland. Next to our own, it should be the best-known of all countries under review.'[102]

Early schemes for cinema visits for schools were promoted by a stalwart of British cinema, theatre entrepreneur Henry Hayward.[103] In 1932, the *Education Gazette* recommended the feature film *Mighty London* to schools as 'a picture that will make strong appeal to every New Zealander because it presents to him the greatness and beauty of the Mother-city of Empire. The student of history will enjoy the views that are given of London's famous buildings, the Houses of Parliament, the palaces, the churches, the monuments and the Inns of Court . . . . The Department can confidently recommend *Mighty London* as a picture that children should be taken to see.'[104]

From 1941, with the establishment of an official school film library, visual education, courtesy of the movies, would become part of every New Zealand school child's education, and 'living' views of London's famous buildings would be brought into school halls and classrooms. The library's stock was drawn from the British High Commission, the Canadian High Commission, the Trade Commissioner, and the New Zealand Tourist and Publicity Department, even though specifically educational films were in short supply. Many of the films discussed earlier were included in the catalogue, including British propaganda movies. These could be found under the new category of social studies. For this subject, there were over 140 films that reflected an old dependency. Half of the films were about Britain, and remarkably, 10 per cent of them were devoted to London. London could even escape the confines of social studies: *London Pigeon*, a glimpse of bird life in the capital, was recommended as 'of interest not only for the pigeons but also for the scenes of London'.[105] New Zealand was also represented, but there were no short features devoted to its towns. Its essentially rural relation to the capital was explored in *From Meadow to Market*, a study of the meat export trade.[106] Even in the small world of school cinema, the reciprocal imaging of the two places would be maintained.

Further, it was soon evident that American influence was to be avoided. An early assessment of visual education was carried out in Wellington, using American YMCA films. The experiment was a qualified success, but the headmaster cautioned delay: 'the possibility of a New Zealand-made instrument, with New Zealand-made films of New Zealand, colonial, and Empire reference and interest is worth investigation before consideration

Film in the classroom: teachers in the 1950s being shown how to use a film projector. Negatives of the *Evening Post* newspaper. EP/1956/1798-F, Alexander Turnbull Library, Wellington, New Zealand.

is given to subsidizing or stocking the American-made or German-made machines'.[107] Film education programmes had begun as early as 1933 at Kowhai Intermediate School in Auckland, and then the school's chief sources were the Canadian Trade Commissioner, the New Zealand Government Tourist Bureau, the Auckland War Memorial Museum and Kodak Ltd. (Although American, Kodak titles included *Tides of the Moon* and *Wheat to Bread*, which posed no real threat to British culture. A later title, *Fish Cooking*, did, however, come with the warning that the methods demonstrated would be 'unfamiliar to New Zealanders but more common in the USA'.)[108] By 1939, the Visual Education Association had fifty member organisations and two hundred films, 116 of which it owned, and the rest borrowed. These films probably formed the basis of the Education Department's own library. If film was to be beneficial, it appears it needed to be British.

Demand for the films was high. Instructions for borrowing noted, 'It has been found in practice that one film a week is sufficient for most schools to use effectively. There are scarcely enough films to provide more than one a week for schools, but under special circumstances more than one may be sent.'[109] Not only was the small social studies selection dominated by films about London, but the manner of teaching suggested in the catalogue only increased the number of times this subject matter was shown. In ideal circumstances selected children might preview the chosen film. The class would then be given a short preparatory talk, followed by two screenings of the film. Then class work on the film would be completed, and the film could potentially be screened a third time.[110] There can be little doubt, then, that children could be regular, and thanks to the screening instruction, repeat viewers of London.

School halls joined public theatres as places repeatedly reinventing the heart of empire in the hinterland. The London of travelogues and documentaries, feature film evocations of empire and 'cultural' costume dramas together produced a surprisingly coherent set of images and a consistent set of values. Through the powerful new medium of film, these familiar images were reanimated and repeated, layered over imagery carried by other cultural channels such as literature, textbooks, radio broadcasts and the press, increasing volume and range. Film also brought with it competing imagery. But whilst there is no question that America harnessed the cultural power of film, the culture it chose to project was not always so foreign. Hollywood's hybrids made a paradoxical contribution to London's familiar presence in New Zealand.

It was not simply what was transferred that was significant, but how. Colonial forms, which emphasised New Zealand's separation both in time and space from London, were overlaid and outrun by media that instead placed emphasis on simultaneity and proximity. News would be read as it happened, not when it arrived: radio would bring the King for Christmas. As mass media came to be characterised by realism and immediacy, their cultural impact changed. Space-binding forms were augmented and superseded by space-conquering forms. Whilst they reanimated images of New Zealand's London, they were also reconfiguring the relationship between the two, drawing a distant periphery into close contact with the centre. The result was not the Victorians' shrinking world, or a postcolonial global village. It was instead an imaginative hinterland, constructed from within at the same time as it was imposed from without.

CHAPTER NINE

LONDON'S LEGACY

New Zealand on Television, 1960–1989

TELEVISION MADE its eagerly awaited official debut on a winter's evening in Auckland, in June 1960. It had been a long wait: various governments had managed to put off its introduction since 1949, when the Labour government formed the first committee to consider its introduction. In the meantime, small-scale entrepreneurial and experimental broadcasts fuelled public anticipation, although some of their content was as dull and worthy as the committee meetings must have been. An official experimental broadcast in 1959 for Auckland consisted of a film on hydatids, a Health Department film on eating establishments, a contribution from the Transport Department on road accidents and coverage of a court case, while TV pirate operator Al Bell's informal broadcasts were restricted to being educational in nature. When he became too entertaining, government technicians changed the broadcasting frequency on him.[1] Television's real magic was clear, though, in another experiment in May 1960. Traffic on Auckland's Queen Street came to a standstill as crowds gathered around shop windows to watch a broadcast of Princess Margaret's wedding and overflowed into the street.[2] Television's official debut in Auckland, and those that followed around the country, shared something of this excitement. Homes and businesses with television sets hosted viewing parties, and traffic stopped in Christchurch too as people again got their first glimpses of television through shop windows.[3]

June's first broadcast was reportedly a 'slick and thoroughly professional' introduction to the newest mass communications medium.[4] It was also thoroughly British. The evening opened with an episode of *The Adventures of Robin Hood*, followed by a local interview with visiting British ballerina Beryl Grey. The next item was an example of 'British' American television, a hybrid form like the 'British' American movie, with an episode of *The Halls of Ivy*.[5] This American-made sitcom, set in a midwestern college, starred British actors Ronald Colman and Benita Hume. Their Britishness was part of the story, with Colman as a slightly stuffy professor, and Hume playing his wife as 'a former reigning belle of British theatre'.[6] An Academy Award-winning actor, Colman would have been well-known to New Zealanders, having starred in silent movies like *Beau Geste*, as well as epics such as *Clive of India*, *The Prisoner of Zenda*, *Lost Horizon* and *Random Harvest*. Hume, his wife in real life, had a similarly long career, encompassing everything from Alfred Hitchcock's silent feature *Easy Virtue* to *Tarzan Escapes*. Their small-screen appearance was followed by the only fully local content of the night, a performance by the Howard Morrison Quartet. Then the Home-made theme continued with a public health film, 'Your Children's Eyes', made by the British Central Office of Information, and in the evening's final entertainment, *Four Just Men*.[7] Again, it was British/American TV. *Four Just Men*, like *The Adventures of Robin Hood*, was made by Sapphire Films, a British film company run by an American, Hannah Weinstein. Based on the best-selling British novel by Edgar Wallace, it featured a transatlantic cast, starring American Dan Dailey, known for his films with Betty Grable, along with British actors Jack Hawkins (*The Cruel Sea*, *Bridge Over the River Kwai*) and Honor Blackman.[8] The evening's odd collection of serials shared more than hybrid status though. They were all produced for British television entrepreneur Lew Grade's Independent Television Company.

The dominance of British content on opening night is surprising. Television in New Zealand has become part of the story of late twentieth-century cultural change rather than a story of continuity. Like film before it, television has largely been considered an American medium, powerful and popular enough to corrode the older British cultural influence.[9]

Television arrives in New Zealand, and it's British: Princess Margaret's wedding screened as a test broadcast a few weeks ahead of the official opening. *Auckland Star*/Fairfax Media, 10 May 1960, p.1.

Newer histories, more interested in the 'world's place in New Zealand' than in following a 'colony to nation' narrative, also equate new media with American influence.[10] Television's history in New Zealand has also been written as a struggle to articulate New Zealandness on screen.[11] All argue for diminishing British influence, and there is no question that the introduction of television was one of a number of changes in postwar New Zealand that would erode the long relationship between London and its distant hinterland. But, as the first evening's viewing suggests, its role in unravelling this long relationship was neither straightforward nor speedy. London's influence, a permanent feature of New Zealand's culture and identity from Cook's first voyage, declined more slowly than is suggested by the pace of other changes throughout the later twentieth century. Its role in creating New Zealand identity, surveyed in preceding chapters, lingered. The legacy of an imagined rural hinterland faded slowly, just as New Zealand's economic role as London's farm only gradually declined in the postwar period. This meant that for New Zealanders in the second half of the twentieth century, London continued to have a strong, but subtly shifting, cultural resonance.

Air travel, for example, opened New Zealand to the world, yet for all the choice of destinations the numbers of New Zealanders travelling to Britain doubled from 1955 to 1970, and then tripled again by 1975.[12] The big prize in the hugely popular 1970s New Zealand quiz show *It's in the Bag* was a trip to Britain, courtesy of New Zealand travel agency, London Shoppe Holidays. But the nature and strength of Home was changing. Sunny Carter, wife of the High Commissioner in London, commented in 1977, 'Our young people back in New Zealand often forget to refer to Britain as "home"', even though 'they still love to come here to live and to look up relatives'.[13] By this time, the older antipodean pilgrimage had taken on a new shape, as the 'Big OE' (overseas experience). In this guise, at the beginning of the twenty-first century London still functioned as the principal metropolitan destination, attracting around 12,000 New Zealanders a year. But whilst these travellers were still going to London, they were no longer going Home. New Zealand's London had changed.

This chapter explores the gradual and equivocal dismantling, and perhaps re-assembling, of New Zealand's long relationship with London by examining the role of television. Earlier chapters have outlined how new media, concentrated on London, shaped New Zealand as a hinterland, then worked like drawstrings to pull it closer to its metropolis. This relationship, often misunderstood as a sentimental legacy of colonial demography, was actively constructed by the most modern of media. Nostalgia had powerful friends. But London's centrality diminished in the postwar period, and the drawstrings loosened too. Television is just one example of the gentle loosening of these cultural bonds.

COLONIAL TELEVISION

The advent of television should have been yet another signifier of New Zealand's modernity, but its delayed arrival seemed to compromise that status. In the decade of debate leading up to the introduction of TV, press and politicians regularly invoked a familiar colonial discourse of backwardness to strengthen the case for television. In 1953, a year after Canada had introduced TV, *Truth* claimed that New Zealand was in danger of becoming a 'real cultural backwater'.[14] The heavier-weight *Listener* agreed, noting that even the Dominican Republic and the Philippines had television.[15] In 1957, in the wake of Australia's adoption of TV, and in a year when the Labour Party campaigned on introducing it, television was

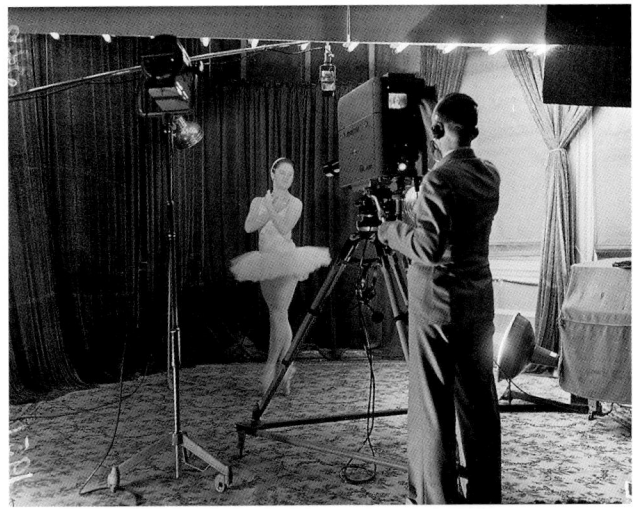

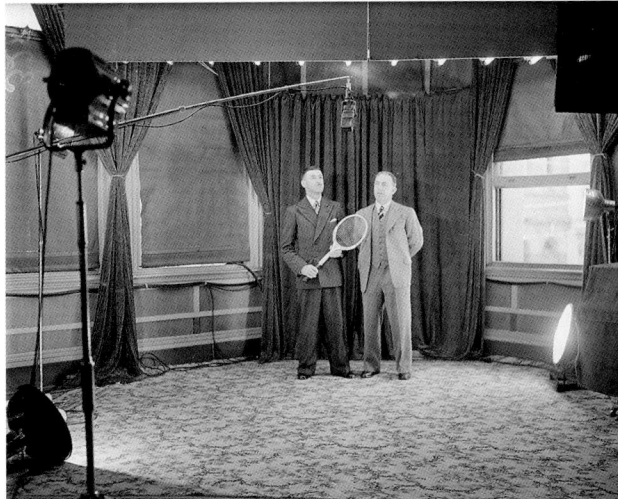

Better than a broadcast on hydatids? Other early experiments in television included a ballet dancer and two men with tennis rackets. Television experiments at the National Broadcasting Service, *Evening Post* collection, 114/269/05, 114/269/07, Alexander Turnbull Library, Wellington, New Zealand.

presented as a symbol of a 'young competent country'.[16] Its absence endangered New Zealand's first-world status: television could now be found in 'primitive if not also barbarous lands' but not yet in New Zealand.[17]

When television did eventually arrive, its potential for cultural change was constrained, and not only because the new medium remained heavily dependent on the old metropolis for content. Like the first newspapers or book imports, early television was 'colonial' in form, with infrequent broadcasts, a fragmented audience and a high percentage of outdated content. Viewer numbers were restricted in the first instance by limited regional coverage. Aucklanders might have seen a 'slick and professional' debut in June 1960, but Wellington and Christchurch waited another year, and Dunedin did not begin broadcasting until 1962. In the mid-1960s, coverage was still so poor that keen viewers formed their own not-for-profit groups that paid for translator equipment to relay coverage into their area ahead of the New Zealand Broadcasting Corporation's roll-out schedule. Some 90,000 of the 415,000 television licences held in 1965 were covered by these private translators (and they would be needed again after 1975 to extend coverage of the new second channel).[18] Low TV numbers were matched by scarce broadcasts: British viewers had fifty hours of television a week in 1955,[19] whereas Auckland began with two sessions a week, of just two hours each, one of which showed nothing but a test pattern.[20] By January 1961, Auckland had just eighteen hours of television a week, and by 1962, the three operating stations ran for a total of twenty-eight hours a week.

Eventually, enough infrastructure was developed to give TV access to the mass it was designed for. Numbers of viewers and broadcasts rose markedly over the decade, reaching sixty-five hours a week in 1970 and over 150 hours across two channels in 1975.[21] National coverage, immensely difficult and expensive because of New Zealand's extreme terrain and small population, was continually extended, radiating out from the urban centres to capture more than 90 per cent of the country by 1971.[22] Programmes, as discussed later, did give viewers the same sense of realism found in films. However, in terms of the medium, they were superannuated. On opening night, *Four Just Men* was only a year old, but the episodes of *Robin Hood* and *The Halls of Ivy* were five and six years old respectively, whilst the public health film dated back to 1945. This was to be an enduring characteristic. New Zealand bought its programme inventory cheaply by purchasing shows after they had run elsewhere. A shift to showing up-to-date imported programming was delayed until the 1980s: New Zealand viewers had immediate access to the latest BBC programmes only after 1986.[23]

New Zealand coverage was organised around four regional centres – Auckland, Wellington, Christchurch and Dunedin – and these were not networked to provide simultaneous national coverage until 1969. This gave television, otherwise a 'window on the world', something of a local

An *Auckland Star* photographer captures last-minute instructions for the Howard Morrison Quartet's live performance on television's opening night. (Howard Morrison second from right, Noel Kingi third from right). *Auckland Star* photographic collection, Auckland Museum Library.

appearance. All stations eventually broadcast the same imported shows, shuttling the alternative imaginative hinterlands offered by the American *Bonanza* or the British *Z Cars* between regions. These shows were no less effective as cultural vectors for this, but the system allowed another competitive hinterland to emerge. Early television led to the creation of four 'distinct local identities' based on locally produced programmes and locally based announcers, in particular continuity announcers, who appeared in between programmes to let viewers know what would be coming up next.[24] Even though these areas stretched the definition of local – Wellington's region included Kaikoura and Gisborne – shows like *Town and Around*, a nightly news magazine produced in each region with its own stories and presenters, became 'much-loved expressions of local identity'. Station announcers became 'constant companions' and local celebrities.[25] One reason for this is that regional television monopolised the potential for immediacy. Most of *Town and Around* was shot on film, then compiled live to tape, usually airing just an hour or so later and even going out live on some occasions.[26] Continuity announcers were live every night and, from 1962, each region had its own newsreader presenting a standardised five-minute bulletin. News formats would eventually become more sophisticated, but for almost a decade, this was the extent of immediate television. Howard Morrison's appearance on opening night symbolised both form and content. Live television in New Zealand was local.

Television news, as well as newsreading, began in colonial form. The first bulletins contained spoken, not visual, news, and little of that. Lacking its own journalists, and barred from the New Zealand Press Association as a potential competitor, New Zealand Broadcasting Corporation (NZBC) news was confined largely to government information and stories cribbed via shortwave from the BBC, Voice of America and Radio Australia. The bulletin was collated in Wellington and sent to the four regions where it would simply be read, first as it was dictated over the phone line and by 1962 as it came off the teleprinter (although on one occasion, the news became a little more lively when a studio hand set fire to the pile of teleprinter paper under the desk as announcer Lindsay Broburg was reading it).[27] Visual news had a separate format, played like a film newsreel after the verbal bulletin had ended. This too gave the new mass medium a colonial feel. Visual news came late and it came from London, a return of old news from the metropolitan centre in a new format. The first newsreels took a week to arrive, a delay which, given television's potential for immediacy, made New Zealand's distance from the centre reappear. After the first year's efforts, one critic judged, 'New Zealand is too far away to benefit from overseas topical news.'[28] By 1962, footage came three times a week, supplied by the British Commonwealth International Newsfilm Agency, later known as Visnews. Visnews itself was 'a colonial affair'. It was founded by the BBC, together with its film partner, the Rank Organisation, to counter American domination of the growing market for film images for television. Its key partners were the public broadcasting corporations in Canada and Australia (who requested 'Commonwealth' be added to the existing name). New Zealand joined in 1965, but interested parties like Ghana were discouraged, for fear they would reduce the organisation's credibility.[29]

In these early years, news from any external source remained dated, especially because the regional system meant news footage had to be cycled round the stations over two or three days. Once again, this made local news the most current, as each of the four regional stations shot their

London on the small screen: Majestic co-opts Big Ben to sell their televisions. *Auckland Star/* Fairfax Media, 3 May 1962, p.43.

own news footage to supplement the imported stock. This local footage was soon added to the Visnews film, which, although not exclusively British in images, remained metropolitan-sourced. Like the earlier history of overseas news and the press, the 'selection of items was made in London and was beyond New Zealand control'. As a result, 'We got what they thought we wanted which tended to be as they would see the Commonwealth through British eyes ... a lot of the Queen doing fairly minor things.'[30] Not all of British news came through British eyes, though. In the early 1960s, New Zealand television also featured a weekly news magazine, *This Week in Britain*. Another Central Office of Information production, this show, made between 1959 and 1980, was specifically designed to 'project Britain' to Latin America, the Middle East and the Commonwealth. However, different presenters were used for each region.[31] New Zealander Noeline Pritchard presented the Australasian version, and she was so popular with viewers that the show devoted an episode to her wedding.[32] Visnews film was also briefly supplemented by America's CBS, but this service ended in 1974. In the two-channel era, beginning in 1975, speed improved but the source remained the same. A new satellite service was added, but news was still selected in London. Nor was it fully immediate: for the first years, satellite news came only as far as Sydney, where it was compiled, then sent by air to New Zealand. Only with the impending arrival of a private competitor, TV3, in the late 1980s did Television New Zealand see the need to make its news really current. The old Visnews service ended, replaced by a permanent satellite link in 1988. At the same time, the first New Zealand journalists were appointed in Sydney and London to select and interpret news for New Zealand audiences.[33]

The sole aspect of television's introduction that was not gradual was popular acceptance. By 1969, there were over 620,000 licensed sets, tuned to one channel offering less than half a day's programming per day.[34] Viewers were so receptive that large numbers stayed up to watch a series of medical training films, specially screened at 11 pm after normal transmission closed, on such topics as epilepsy in childhood and atrial septal defects.[35] By the mid-1970s, though, what Patrick Day calls the 'pioneering' phase – here described as the 'colonial' period – of television had passed. By 1979, 95 per cent of homes had televisions, national television was networked, and colour, on two channels, arrived in 1975.[36] But the gradual nature of its introduction had slowed the arrival of a new and very competitive 'American' metropolis. Other factors, such as institutional structure and programming, would have the same effect.

BRITISH TELEVISION

With this background, it is not surprising to find a high degree of British influence on the running of New Zealand television. As with radio, the BBC was the key institutional model, and visiting BBC experts were common. As one senior television executive recalled, when it came to organisational culture, 'American influence was negligible'.[37] However, with only one channel, it was never possible in New Zealand to replicate the BBC's model of public service broadcasting. Instead, New Zealand television fused it with an American commercial model. Funding reflected both modes, coming, in diminishing quantities, from public licence fees and, in ever-increasing amounts, from advertising revenues. This model gradually decreased the BBC-inspired public service nature of broadcasting, exemplified by the gradual proliferation of advertising through the schedule. For almost all the first year, television was advertising-free.[38] Lacking a separate, non-commercial channel, the NZBC, when advertising was introduced, used time to create public service zones in the schedule, keeping certain days advertising-free. Initially, advertising, at seven minutes an hour, was restricted to half the broadcasting days. But gradually, the allowed number of minutes expanded, while the ratio of ad-free days contracted. By the mid-1970s, ads ran five days a week, with different commercial-free days on each channel, except Sunday, which was commercial-free for both. It remained sacred until 1989, when Sunday mornings until 12 noon became the only commercial-free zone left on the schedule.[39]

However, while this model may seem to have left the high-minded BBC ideal of public service broadcasting in tatters, it was hardly fully commercial. The nature of programming still broadly followed a public service ethos and was not driven by commercially competitive considerations until the late 1980s.[40] Similarly, the public service bureaucracy remained, as advertisers did not select programmes but were granted time slots. Changes to booked campaigns required special pleading to the Sales Department.[41] A shift to a more fully commercial model, with advertisers selecting slots in shows that were programmed and purchased according to research and ratings, would wait until the end of the 1980s and the preparation for private competition.

These institutional issues helped prolong metropolitan influence, first by simply continuing the old connection. The ongoing presence of British television also mediated the competing American version, while local or sub-national 'New Zealand' television, which was given a little extra power by its early monopoly on immediacy, had a similar, if lesser, effect. These issues impacted on viewers through their interaction with programmes. Yet we know much less about the crucial business of viewing than almost any other aspect of television. Most estimates of what New Zealanders were watching are based on a survey of listings – what programmes were on, rather than what programmes were watched. These point to fragmentation between American, British and New Zealand-sourced material, with imported material making up about 80 per cent of the schedule for the first fifteen years.[42] Programme purchasers could choose from a vast inventory of American and British programmes, and it was, as one programmer described it, 'like buying sausages'.[43] The split between American and British programming seems to have been relatively even: early television 'sought a balance' between them.[44] The first purchasing contracts were struck with the BBC but the American NBC matched their low hourly rate. Even-handed purchase may not have been matched by even audience preference. The first managers, wary of market research, conducted only minor surveys in the late 1960s, preferring blissful ignorance over things such as audience size and viewing choices.[45] Eventually, inhouse research and then finally independent research was commissioned. Some of these surviving records are used here to consider the hinterland that television created, and the metropolis's place within it.

By Saturday, 11 September 1976, someone living in Auckland could watch television for most of the day, and if they could afford a new television set, they might even be able to watch in colour. They could choose programmes from two channels. However, the majority would watch TV1 which, on its big viewing night, offered an almost unbroken schedule of local New Zealand shows and British programming. The afternoon began with *Sport On One*. Then at around 5.15, this compilation of sporting events ended, and in the run-up to the evening news at six, viewers were entertained by two distinctively British productions, first Bruce Forsyth's *Generation Game* and then an episode of *The Wombles*, a stop-motion animation series featuring imaginary furry creatures who lived on Wimbledon Common in London. This unlikely lead-in attracted between 22–30 per cent of viewers – older New Zealanders can still remember snatches of its theme song.[46] The news was followed by British comedy duo *Morecambe and Wise*, which drew 36 per cent of viewers, before the big event of the evening, *It's in the Bag*, a live local game show that took 48 per cent of the available audience. The Saturday night movie followed, which this week was an American movie, *The Comic*, starring Dick Van Dyke and Mickey Rooney. Given Hollywood's dominance this is not surprising, but British movies were also scheduled in this slot: the next week's feature was British war movie *The Last Grenade*, and a week or two later Michael Caine would appear in *The Ipcress Files*. Viewing declined over the length of the movie, falling from 41 per cent to 14 per cent at close. Some viewers might have switched over to TV2, but after a night of largely British entertainment with a local highlight, most probably just went to bed.[47]

We can assume this from TV2's viewing figures, which, for the whole Saturday schedule, ran from a low of 2 per cent to a peak viewing of only 18 per cent, reached with yet another British comedy, *The Two Ronnies*. As this suggests, TV2 still featured British shows, but there was stronger emphasis on American programming, although some of it was quite old. That same Saturday afternoon offered audiences a Marilyn Monroe movie from 1952, *Don't Bother to Knock*, an episode of the 1960s western *Big Valley* and popular American star Dinah Shore's talk show along with an episode of the British puppet series, *Thunderbirds*.[48] However, as the ratings indicate, American dominance in the schedule was not matched by dominance in viewing. The same pattern was repeated in primetime. Viewers showed some interest in the American pioneering series *Little House on the Prairie*, lifting ratings from 6 to 15 per cent, but they then stayed in front of their sets to travel out of the American West to the London suburb of Twickenham for the comedy *Love Thy Neighbour*, which led into *The Two Ronnies*. Just as on TV1, audience numbers dwindled after the big show of the night, fewer and fewer staying up to return to the wide open spaces of America featured in trucking show *Movin' On*, or to its urban settings in made-for-TV movie *The Face of Fear*.[49]

That an episode of *The Wombles* outrated every American show on both channels except a movie was not unusual. The new channel's coverage was limited to Auckland, reducing the numbers of viewers and, consequently, the reach of the alternative metropolis. On Monday night, *Mission Impossible* was outrated by TV1's legal drama set in Scotland, *Sutherland's Law*, 42 per cent to 17 per cent. Even the brand new American cop show *Starsky and Hutch* drew only around the same audience numbers as TV1's offering, which was yet another British comedy, *It Ain't Half Hot Mum*. Television's latest crime fighting duo might have drawn a few viewers away from the antics of a British army concert party stationed in India: ratings during *It Ain't Half Hot Mum* dropped from 33 per cent to 26 per cent, whilst *Starsky and Hutch* rose from 21 per cent to 28 per cent. But elsewhere that week, iconic American detective drama *Kojak* rated just 14 per cent, and *Batman* managed 6 per cent, whilst *Daniel Boone* and *The Beverley Hillbillies* were consigned to the new channel's pre-news ratings graveyard, capturing less than 10 per cent of viewers.[50]

The persistence of British TV: the *Listener*'s coverage of TV2's new lineup included British police drama *Softly Softly* and comedies like *The Goodies* and Sid James in *Bless this House*, along with American shows like police drama *Kojak*. Ben Murphy, star of western-styled comedy *Alias Smith and Jones*, was a popular telethon guest and star of a local Oak-brand jam commercial.
New Zealand Listener, TV2 Supplement, Vol. 79, No. 1856, 28 June 1975, p.8.

Obviously, these ratings attest to the continued popularity of British shows. Indeed, some internal NZBC audience research between 1966 and 1971 indicated a 'strong preference for British programmes'. Of the twenty-one highest-rating shows in that period, seventeen were British.[51] The top shows of 1966 and 1967 were British spy shows, *Dangerman* and *The Avengers*, while the only non-British show to take top place in the six years surveyed was *The Undersea World of Jacques Cousteau*, in 1970. By 1971, however, life in Weatherfield beat life on the ocean wave when *Coronation*

Street took top place.⁵² But in 1976, it was not simply viewer preference for British television that made these shows so popular. In part, the continued preference for British television was sustained by a continued preference for TV1.⁵³ This survey was taken just a year after the second channel had begun, and viewers' habits may be as strongly expressed here as their viewing preferences. For example, when the very British *Upstairs Downstairs*, a series set in an upper class town house in Edwardian London, played on the second channel, it garnered just 9–11 per cent of the audience. Forty per cent stayed on TV1 and watched an episode of *Good Times*, a comedy about an African-American family living in the Chicago projects. In the same way, British police drama *The Sweeney*, on TV1, outrated British police drama *Softly Softly*, played at the same time on the other channel. This meant, as with *Good Times*, that an American show on TV1 could do very well indeed. And they did: *M*A*S*H*, *Barney Miller* and Angie Dickinson's *Policewoman* all brought primetime ratings in the 30s and 40s. The same effect held true for local shows. New Zealand's first soap, *Close to Home*, played after the news, in this week holding more than 40 per cent of viewers on Monday 13 and Tuesday 14 September 1976.⁵⁴ SPTV's (TV2) soap *A Going Concern* failed to fire.⁵⁵

British presence on New Zealand television was structural as much as cultural. TV1's ability to deliver an audience to programmes (as much as the other way around) worked in its favour. But TV1's dominance also led to a change in broadcasting policy, which would reduce the British presence or, more accurately, strengthen the delivery of the American alternative. When the two channels were first established, they remained under one umbrella organisation, but were run as separate entities and given separate identities. They were supposed to be 'competitive yet complementary'. Yet, as these survey results show, competing channels did not serve viewers equally. For this reason, amongst others, after only a year of competition, the channels were directed to stop competing for viewers, and instead aimed to maximise total viewing by scheduling complementary shows, creating a 50:50 share of viewers.⁵⁶ This change was gradual, as 'agreement was easier than implementation', and broadcasters were reluctant to 'mute their competition'.⁵⁷ It took amalgamation under one Controller of Programmes, Des Monaghan, for viewing to be split evenly between the channels.

The complementary channels kept some separate characteristics: 'TV1 tended to be comparatively "serious", British and aimed at older viewers, whereas TV2's tended to be entertainment-oriented American, and appealed to younger viewers.'[58] This tendency hardened in the late eighties. At first, however, ratings research in 1980 suggests that British and American programmes were more evenly shared across the two channels under the new system, with consequent levelling effects on ratings.[59] Popular British shows could bring audiences across to the less watched TV2 – *Fawlty Towers* and ratings winner *To the Manor Born* were both screened on TV2 in this period, and outrated their opposite shows on TV1.[60] Meanwhile, TV1's primacy – the *Womble* effect – delivered strong audiences to popular American shows: *Dallas*, for example, held more than 20 per cent of viewers in a late-night Monday time slot on TV1. *Charlie's Angels*, screening in primetime the next night on TV2, rated about the same.[61] But American shows on TV2, like *CHiPs*, based around two officers of the Californian Highway Patrol, probably did better under the new rules than they might have done under the previous system. On a Saturday night in September 1980, *CHiPs* played on TV2 against a local variety show, *Radio Times*. This was unlikely to have happened under a competitive system where one ratings threat would have been countered by another (and in the case of local shows, rules were put in place to stop the previous practice of pitting locally made, and therefore, expensive shows, against each other). But as complementary programming, a local variety show and an American police drama had quite separate audiences. In this case, they also had quite separate ratings. Over a three-week survey, *CHiPS* drew between 35 per cent and 40 per cent of viewers, whilst *Radio Times* rated 10–17 per cent.[62]

Complementary programming had an equivocal role, maintaining a British presence while strengthening America's role as an alternative cultural centre. It also laid out the audience template for truly competitive channel identities from 1987. But fragmentation seems to be indicated in the shifting volumes of imported shows.[63] The balance established in early buying was still operating in 1975, when NZBC statistics showed imported programming shared almost evenly, with 52 per cent from America and 48 per cent sourced from Britain.[64] That year, TV1's Controller of Programmes responded to viewer criticism of 'too much American twaddle' over the two channels by insisting that 'there has been no increase in the balance of American and British shows. One night has *M*A*S*H* and *The Streets of San Francisco* but then another night has *Z Cars* and *The Likely Lads*.'[65] Indeed, given the fact that America's output of shows was

'The second channel's coming – how will it change your viewing?' asks the *New Zealand Listener*. But with very British serial *Upstairs Downstairs* as its flagship show, the answer seemed to be 'Not very much'. *New Zealand Listener*, Vol. 79, No. 1856, 28 June 1975, p.8.

far higher, this in itself indicates a mild pro-British bias. However, by the early 1980s, some twenty years after television's introduction, American programming seemed to have the upper hand, and complementary programming (along with better channel coverage) meant it had the ratings to match. Small surveys of programmes by origin in 1983 and 1985 show the British share of imported television programming dropped to 30 per cent, the difference being taken up by increased American programming and a small amount of Australian television.[66] At the same time, channel shares of viewers had shifted. TV1 held 70 per cent of the audience in 1976: by 1981, it hovered around 50 per cent.[67]

Both these changes suggest that British programmes would reach a decreasing number of New Zealand viewers. Yet they seemed to gain a new lease of life from 1987, when once again Television New Zealand gave its two channels separate identities and a competitive brief. This time, however, the competition was not internal, but with a private broadcaster, TV3. Although this new channel would not be on air until 1989, TVNZ reorganised well in advance. As part of its transition to commercial competition, it rebranded its channels, with Channel 2 as the 'entertainer', and Television One as the 'information channel', then went after separate viewing audiences to match.[68] The idea was to make it hard for TV3 to capture any particular audience segment (and although this was not the only pre-emptive move, TV3 did struggle for audiences). Under this system, British programming, along with a greater emphasis on current affairs – as seen in the late introduction of satellite and foreign correspondents – was a core part of the new TV One.

But the persisting British presence may have been changing its resonance. The long-standing association of the metropolis and cultural quality, part of the 'information' channel's competitive positioning, was also becoming associated with the age of viewers. Television One was skewed to an older, thirty-five years and over, audience. This was still a significant audience, as TVNZ was reminded in 1994 when a new programmer, fresh from Australia, attempted to reduce screenings of *Coronation Street* and caused strident public protests. Nevertheless, the 'channelling' of metropolitan culture and its association with an older audience represented a shift away from its former general significance. Channel changes once again accelerated the process of fragmentation. New Zealand's London, once pervasive in its culture, was now largely confined to TV One. For 'entertainment', younger viewers changed channels and changed cultures, watching Channel 2 scheduling that was dominated by American programming. A process that began as a tendency when programming was complementary hardened as it was used to market competitive channels. From the late 1980s, on television at least, New Zealand's long relationship as imaginative hinterland to the metropolitan centre not only fragmented but also atrophied.

Although competition diminished London's particular importance as cultural centre, it may actually have reinforced one of London's cultural legacies. Whether New Zealand audiences watched police chases in *The Streets of San Francisco* or *The Sweeney*'s Flying Squad in the streets of London, they remained a hinterland audience for a metropolis. Real city life remained elsewhere. Of course, not all imported shows were urban-based.

Television offered a multitude of imaginative settings. But some of these, like the Western, or historical dramas, or shows set in nostalgic rural English locations, such as veterinary drama *All Creatures Great and Small*, may have mirrored, in their various forms, the hinterland habit of borrowing history from London. Through *Bonanza*, or *The Virginian*, the American West joined dear old rural England as replacement for New Zealand's own colonial past.[69] Even in late twentieth-century New Zealand, it seems other cities and other pasts were sometimes still preferable to the local version. This legacy of the metropolitan relationship would fragment too. Its presence and dissolution is charted through the following history of New Zealand drama.

DRAMA IN THE HINTERLAND

The history of New Zealand television drama may seem an unlikely place to locate the continuing role of New Zealand's metropolitan-shaped identity as a rural hinterland and to discover signs of its dissolution. It usually forms a strand in the growing development of, and insistence on, a sense of New Zealand identity, part of the late twentieth-century impulse towards cultural nationalism. This, and the very real difficulties involved in screening local drama, has parallels with other attempts to articulate New Zealandness in high cultural forms. Like the writers and artists of the 1930s, for the first drama-makers, 'the ability to tell New Zealand stories, create recognizably local characters and hear genuine local accents on television were elements of a much larger cultural project that involved all of the arts and aimed to deliver New Zealand from the doldrums of a "colonial condition"'.[70] However difficult and compromised this process was, television drama did play its part in that larger cultural project, and continues, within the strictures of a highly competitive and commercial market, to bring New Zealanders their own stories on screen.

But for the first twenty years, and even beyond, the successes and failures of local drama reflected the continuing influence of London in New Zealand's habit of imagining itself as a rural hinterland. Drama's variable results were produced by other circumstances as well, but this aspect has remained undetected or, as discussed later, misdiagnosed. As we have seen, the tendency to see urban life and a proper past as belonging somewhere other than New Zealand itself was part of the close relationship that developed between New Zealand and London from around the end of the nineteenth century. Colonial aspirations of being a 'Greater Britain' moderated, and New Zealand began to treat London not simply as imperial centre in a colonial system but as part of its own landscape, an appropriated metropolis for an imagined hinterland. Underwritten by the economics of the pastoral export trade, energised by the concentration of new forms of cultural transfer and expressed in a combination of both – as butter advertising in London shops or in classrooms as educational films on London – the imagined rural hinterland had a pervasive presence. In television, it helped define which local shows would succeed, and which would not.

This process is clearly articulated in the audience response to drama series. For a considerable period of time, viewers found it difficult to believe in anything other than portrayals of New Zealand as a rural hinterland. The first local series, a thriller called *The Alpha Plan* that screened in 1969, conformed to this in its broad plot outline which made New Zealand a remote haven for overseas brains, knowledge and culture that was threatened by some future holocaust.[71] The series originator had some experience with the limits of the hinterland imaginary: when writing radio series, he had 'usually set them in overseas locations where New Zealand listeners would be more likely to accept the existence of large scale organised crime, espionage plots, smuggling rings and similar skullduggery'.[72] Although *Alpha Plan* seems to have been well received, the first continuing drama series, *Pukemanu*, was specifically given a more local setting.[73] Its subject was small-town New Zealand, portraying the lives of workers in a North Island forestry town. There are no ratings left to indicate its popularity, but it did well enough to run for two seasons. Its hinterland setting seems to have been a factor in its success. For one critic, it struck a chord because 'we are not yet an urban people'.[74] She meant this conceptually for, by 1973, 80 per cent of New Zealanders were living in urban, not rural, areas. Nor was this particularly new – close to 50 per cent of the population had been urban at the turn of the nineteenth century, although town sizes were small.[75] But for most of that time, the dominant metropolitan centre for New Zealand had been London. Imagining a metropolitan New Zealand in its place was new.

Trisha Dunleavy, in her authoritative history of New Zealand's television drama, notes this preference for imagining ourselves as rural, not urban, and suggests that this preference was played out in the fates of dramas.

Rural New Zealand life: the pub in *Pukemanu*. Stills collection, New Zealand Film Archive Ngā Kaitiaki O Ngā Taonga Whitiāhua. Courtesy of Chris Ghent and Television New Zealand.

Section Seven, an urban crime show, rated poorly, as 'New Zealand viewers preferred the "down-country" style of *Pukemanu*'.[76] They continued to prefer it into the 1980s with rurally flavoured shows like *Country GP*, *Jocko* and the successful country police series *Mortimer's Patch*. Even a suburban setting worked: *Close to Home*, a twice-weekly evening soap, ran for eight years. Interestingly, it was partnered with New Zealand's longest-running soap, *Coronation Street*, which was also its nearest model. *Close to Home* was 'designed as a family show, but instead of being about people who live in England, it will be about people who live here'.[77] It played on Monday and Tuesday, scheduling that helped it to succeed, first, because those nights tended to have larger audiences anyway, giving better exposure; and second, because those large audiences meant higher advertising revenues, which would help defray the greater costs involved in local productions.[78] Then soap fans could slide effortlessly from suburban life in Wellington to suburban life in Manchester, when *Coronation Street* took over the same time slot on Wednesday and Thursday.[79]

New Zealand's answer to *Coronation Street*: a wedding scene from a 1982 episode of local soap *Close to Home*. Stills collection, New Zealand Film Archive Ngā Kaitiaki O Ngā Taonga Whitiāhua. Courtesy of Television New Zealand.

Shows with urban, not suburban, settings, on the other hand, did not do so well. Despite an early success in 1976 with *Moynihan*, urban drama series struggled. *Radio Waves*, a 1978 soap about a commercial radio station, was unsuccessful 'perhaps because of its overt urbanism'. It was set in 'Auckland as a try-hard metropolis', which probably compounded the hinterland problem, replacing a genuine metropolis with a lightweight local version.[80] In part because of their patchy track record, other urban dramas are scarce. In 1984, another attempt was made to show that 'New Zealand was not *Country Calendar* any more' with *Inside Straight*, a series set in inner-city Wellington.[81] It fared poorly and was replaced by a trucking drama, *Roche*, set somewhere between the rural and the urban, which fared even worse. The urban success story of early 1980s drama was *Gliding On*, a sit-com set in a government department office in Wellington. However the comedy, written by an English expatriate and satirising the monochrome monotony

The return of New Zealand's history: a production still from local hit series *Hunter's Gold*, set in nineteenth-century New Zealand. Stills collection, New Zealand Film Archive Ngā Kaitiaki O Ngā Taonga Whitiāhua. Courtesy of Television New Zealand.

of the public service, was hardly a harbinger of a new and dynamic antipodean urbanism.

But there were indications that the influential metropolitan/hinterland relationship was receding. First amongst these, in television drama at least, was a growing interest in New Zealand's own colonial past. A key function of the metropolitan relationship was to provide an alternative past, one that allowed New Zealand to shuck off its 'colonial' status and appear 'new'. A sign that this might be changing came in 1971 with *The Killing of Kane*, a one-off docudrama based around two Europeans, Kimble Bent and Charles Kane, during Titokowaru's 1868 attack on Turuturu Mokai redoubt.[82] Another one-off historical drama and a short series were produced in 1973 and 1974.[83] But the past became hugely popular in the form of children's serial *Hunter's Gold*, set in the Otago goldrushes.[84] It was followed a year later by another very popular, but considerably more controversial, historical series, *The Governor*. A revisionist history of the colonial period centred on Governor George Grey, the series reflected and reinforced growing public disquiet about the process and outcome of colonisation. This, combined with a perceived budget blowout and antipathy between the Prime Minister at the time, Robert Muldoon, and television executives, made *The Governor* the centre of a political storm.[85] The fallout stalled interest in depicting New Zealand's past again until 1985, with the successful *Hanlon*, a series based around a lawyer defending capital cases in nineteenth-century Dunedin.[86] By the late 1980s, however, urban New Zealand had joined colonial New Zealand as an imaginative possibility. In the cult soap *Gloss* (1987), in the Wellington police drama *Shark in the Park* (1989) and, finally, in the nightly soap *Shortland Street* (1992), an urban New Zealand could exist alongside its rural counterpart.

COLONIAL CRINGE OR LONDON'S LEGACY?

Local drama's successes and failures help trace an aspect of the gradual dissolution of London's cultural influence on New Zealand identity. At the same time, drama's ups and downs revise one of the ways we think about identity in the postwar period. Negative reactions to New Zealand television drama have been ascribed in part to colonial or cultural cringe, kindly described as 'an insecure attitude to local culture expressed as either embarrassment or over-assertiveness', and explained as a legacy of 'New Zealand's lengthy period as a British colony'.[87] Cultural insecurities certainly existed: early broadcasters worried over whether New Zealand accents were BBC-ish enough, while later actors worried that obvious New Zealand accents would put viewers off.[88] At the same time, the late arrival of television in New Zealand put locally produced shows at a disadvantage, pitting them against productions that had years of experience behind them. *The Adventures of Robin Hood* may have been a few years old on opening night, but it was still a product of British television in the 1950s, and not a product of pioneering British television from the 1930s.[89] New Zealand's first dramas, given a less than generous reception as a result, were also produced under difficult circumstances, filmed in studios that had been used for broadcasting children's radio shows in the 1920s, and under technical limitations that meant whole scenes needed to be shot as one take.[90]

More of New Zealand on air: The Fellowmen, 'three twenty-two year old boys with banjos, and guitars whose specialty is folk singing', came second in the Wellington final of talent show *Have a Shot*. *New Zealand Listener*, Vol. 49, No. 1264, 13 December 1963, p.3.

As currently formulated, the idea of cultural cringe works as part of a broader, 'colony to nation' narrative, with cringing colonialism eventually giving way to a more self-confident, locally generated sense of identity. Yet New Zealand's shifting identities do not conform to this evolutionary pattern. As nineteenth-century aspirations for New Zealand as a 'Greater Britain' show, the 'colonial condition' did not mean that New Zealand always mapped its relationship to the centre deferentially. Nor did audience reaction to television. Whilst responses to local drama were mixed, local television was popular. New Zealanders liked seeing themselves on screen – indeed, regional shows were criticised for not being local enough, and viewers complained when the networking of news nationally led to the loss of local items. At the same time, light entertainment shows brought local talent to the screen. These must have included some cringe-worthy moments: in 1961, a television version of the radio show *Have a Shot*, an amateur talent quest, was trialled. Yet by 1963, a national version of the show was popular enough to generate 30,000 postal votes.[91] Shows like

C'mon, which relied on local musicians to cover international hits, could also have induced cringe but instead were very popular, whilst quiz programmes such as *It's in the Bag* became local institutions. Even cooking shows made local celebrities, turning Air Force officer Graham Kerr into *The Galloping Gourmet*, making Alison Holst an enduring icon of home-style cooking and, by 1977, introducing *Hudson and Halls*, whose show acquainted television audiences with gay couples as well as new recipes.[92]

Like drama, light entertainment had its misses as well as its hits. But popular local shows suggest that cultural cringe was, at best, highly selective. We have already observed its selective, not general, effects in drama, where programmes that closely conformed to the imagined rural hinterland succeeded faster, and more often, than shows in urban settings. Audiences cringed at *Radio Waves*, but they watched *Pukemanu*. They liked *Mortimer's Patch*, but they didn't like *Inside Straight*. There were, of course, other variables, notably quality, that determined a show's success or failure. But regardless, this selectivity is problematic for a generalised 'colonial condition'. So too is its pattern through time. Although nationalist histories follow a progressive path, responses to local drama varied over time. Almost fifteen years separated *Pukemanu* from *Inside Straight*, yet, if cringe is the guide, it seemed to increase not decrease over the period.

It may be more useful, then, to understand audience reactions to television drama, and, more broadly, public reaction to the wider cultural nationalist project, not as the product of a 'colonial condition' but as the product of the long-term cultural relationship between New Zealand and London. This was, of course, an outcome of colonialism, but it did not work in the same way. Colonialism and empire instead underwrite, and add texture to, a more prosaic metropolis and hinterland relationship. This relationship is easy to miss, for cities and their hinterland are usually contiguous. But, from around 1900, New Zealand was no longer separated from its metropolis by colonial time and space. New media, culminating in the arrival of television, overlaid and reconstituted older links to draw New Zealand closer to London. This relationship replaced its colonial forerunner, then gained intensity through the first part of the twentieth century, before slowly being dismantled towards that century's end. It was this partnership and not the older, colonial version that television first prolonged and then gradually and equivocally began to dissolve.

EPILOGUE

LONDON
REVISITED

THIS BOOK STARTED on London Bridge, with one of the oldest symbols of New Zealand's cultural relationship with the metropolis. It ends not too far away from there, with one of the newest. On Armistice Day in 2006, New Zealand honoured its war dead with a brand-new memorial, located not in New Zealand, but in Hyde Park, London. The 'Southern Stand' is a collection of sixteen bronze pillars, or 'standards', roughly gathered into two groups. Six of the standards are grouped to form the Southern Cross, while the second is arrayed, almost protectively, in front of them, with the standards tilted forward in 'a defiant pose "reminiscent of warriors during haka, the defensive bat in cricket, and the barrel of a shouldered gun"'.[1]

The experience of war has long been associated with the development of a distinct 'New Zealand' identity, and the 'Southern Stand' carries a full complement of the common symbols of this New Zealandness. Etched into its bronze standards are a silver fern, an ANZAC poppy and patterns based on Maori carving, while sculpted native birds rest on ledges in the pillars. Yet this conventional marker of national identity was designed as another sort of memorial too. It is intended to commemorate New Zealand's long relationship with Britain. On the memorial's sixteen uprights, the familiar iconography of war and nation is commingled with symbols of this other relationship. Sailing ships, bales of wool, a black-singleted farmer and snatches of text by writers such as William Pember Reeves, Katherine Mansfield and Robin Hyde evoke some of the cultural and economic ties that underwrote the 'enduring bonds between New Zealand and the United Kingdom' that the Stand commemorates.[2] We could add some other overlooked images to those already on the pillars: a tourist looking for his heritage in Westminster Abbey; another lost in London's traffic; a bored school girl watching an old school film on pigeons; a journalist knocking on doors in Fleet Street; a cut-out 'British New Zealand' sheep in a butcher's window; a kitchen radio broadcasting the sound of Big Ben; later, canned laughter from *The Two Ronnies* playing on the TV in the lounge. The soldiers themselves might have enjoyed some other reminders of London: its theatres, its bars, its women, its life.

These images too were part of those 'enduring bonds', although the purpose of this book has to been to examine rather than commemorate them. Indeed, I argue that 'enduring' is not really the right way to describe them. London's presence in New Zealand cultural landscape was not set in stone, or etched in bronze, but reflected the changing conditions of contemporary New Zealand life, not just its colonial past. When soldiers arrived on leave from the Western Front, they exchanged the unimaginable horror of war for the imagined home comforts of London, created for them by volunteer organisations like the YMCA. When writers arrived with their manuscripts and a few pounds, they expected to participate in London's literary life, one they already had something of an introduction to through their reading and their networks. When New Zealanders travelled Home, they arrived in a London they had imagined from movies as much as from memories. For all its air of nostalgia and sentiment, Home was a contemporary cultural project, and not just a cultural legacy.

That project got under way towards the end of the nineteenth century, and lasted well into the twentieth. In that period, new technologies changed the emphasis of New Zealand's London relationship. Colony and metropolis became city and hinterland. Refrigeration meant New Zealand could become a farm for the metropolis, whilst new supercharged forms of communication – the kinds usually associated with the growth of nationalism – reinforced London's imaginative presence. The heightened realism and immediacy of film, radio or cabled news made it seem closer. They drew the hinterland nearer to its city. New Zealand still lay 12,000 miles away, but it had been transformed. The old colony, once home to the New Zealander on the bridge, became an up-to-date, virtual and virtuous, rural hinterland. And it was connected to its metropolis by stronger bonds than settler sentiment and the hopeful imperial rhetoric of kith and kin.

Empire is now long gone, but echoes of this old relationship remain. Although no longer a 'Mecca' for colonial pilgrims, London still functions as a New Zealand city. It is the most popular staging point for New Zealanders on their big OE, and a key destination for expatriate working New Zealanders. A 2011 survey of expatriates found around 27 per cent were based in Britain: if that holds true for the same survey's total estimated expatriate population, there are well over 100,000 resident there.[3] For many of these – perhaps the majority – London is home, and their presence weaves a new set of linkages between the metropolis and its former hinterland. These new connections with the old centre were brought into sharp focus during the London Underground bombings of 2005. A 'blizzard of phone calls and e-mails between the nation's travellers, or expatriates, and the folk back home' made the extent of New Zealand's current metropolitan relationship clear.[4] At the same time, press reports suggested that an imagined London still existed in the old hinterland.[5] The Prime Minister expressed New Zealand's shock as a result of that imagined familiarity: 'Not only do most of us have family or friends in London, but many of us have been on those same streets or in the same Underground stations where the bombings took place.'[6] For a moment, just as in 1940, 'our' London was under attack. And once again New Zealand's London was not just the product of nostalgia and family ties. One report claimed, 'Television and familiarity have made London seem so close. After Sydney and Melbourne, this is our city of choice. The High Commission estimates about 250,000 New Zealanders are in London or her outskirts. How many of us have scuttled down those steps at Edgware Rd or bought a coffee at Prêt à Manger on the way to the Tube?'[7]

New Zealand's familiar metropolis can still conjure up its rural hinterland too. In 2007, Australasian brewery Lion Nathan launched an advertising campaign for beer brand Speight's. In 'The Great Beer Delivery', 'six guys took a pub to London for a mate'.[8] Using an elaborate campaign involving competitions for crew members, building and shipping the pub, video diaries and even a 'documentary', marketers used London's cultural role as expatriate metropolis to sell more beer in New Zealand. The campaign drew on the old hinterland/metropolis divide. Speight's brand image draws on rural imagery of an anachronistic type. Sponsor of the alpine multisport Coast to Coast event, it is the 'pride of the South', the preferred beer of those southern 'hard men', imagined to exist in the South Island high country, who are laconic, clever and the antithesis of city types. These values are generalised as 'New Zealand' characteristics by the story of the New Zealander in London missing his Speight's beer. Some southern 'mates' take a faux colonial-style pub (in a further stab at anachronism, the marketers called it an 'alehouse') to London for him. As New Zealand played country cousin to the urbane metropolis, this campaign used the old habit of reciprocity in new ways. At the same time, the old imagined London, full of familiar sights, was constructed anew. One 'mate' was 'completely disoriented' by the traffic; for another, it was 'old school, lots of landmarks, it's a Monopoly board, it's fantastic'.[9] Familiar London has deep roots. Promotional material featured a map which recreated the journey between New Zealand and London as a straight line, emphasising propinquity, while new media, such as web videos, television commercials that were trip updates, and the documentary, which ran every half-hour on pay television, kept New Zealand in touch with metropolitan time. Finally, it reified New Zealand's familiar London space. The 'alehouse' was shipped up the Thames to Essex Street, appropriating space just below the 'Dominion promenade', the Strand.

Beer is not the only product that relies on, and reconstructs, some of the old cultural outlines. Like audiences for local television dramas of the 1980s, it seems tourist marketers find it difficult to imagine a compelling version of urban New Zealand. The long-running '100% Pure New Zealand' tourism campaign has given the older pastoral paradise a touch of wilderness and a burst of adrenaline, but it continues to imagine New Zealand as haven from industry and urbanisation. Appropriately enough, Britain remains a key target of this campaign, as, after Australians, British tourists still form the second-largest group of visitors to New Zealand.[10] In an updated version of settler panoramas and Empire Marketing Board posters, scenes of empty New Zealand landscapes stretch across billboards in crowded tube stations, as tourism becomes only the latest in a series of commodity marketing exercises that have essentialised rural New Zealand for the metropolitan marketplace. In tourist fantasy, as in earlier versions, urban life hardly exists: 100% Pure's website suggests that the best way to enjoy a day in Auckland city is to kayak away from it to Browns Island.[11] Of course, one consequence of the changed relationship between New Zealand and London in the last part of the twentieth century is that we now have more than one metropolitan market. Yet the same rural idyll has been redeployed to draw tourists from America, and from the fastest-emerging market, China. Nor is this old essentialising of rural New Zealand limited to tourism markets. Although New Zealand may no longer be London's farm, in 2011 70 per cent of New Zealand's exports still came from the primary sector.[12] Hinterland habits are hard to break.

OTHER LONDONS

This book has explored New Zealand's London as a long-neglected historical phenomenon. But it may not be an isolated one. Threaded through this story of New Zealand's London have been traces of other settler versions of the same phenomenon. This suggests that there are other Londons to uncover – Australia's London, South Africa's London, Canada's London. And these other Londons may also have consequences for their particular histories of colonisation and national identity, although their individual versions may not look or function in exactly the same way as New Zealand's London did. Further, New Zealand itself may have other 'Londons', other sites of cultural influence that, because they fall outside New Zealand's geography, have also fallen outside New Zealand's history. Sydney's role in early colonial New Zealand settler culture or its later role as alternative and accessible (if less prestigious) outlet for high cultural ambitions are a couple of examples. New Zealand's Scottish connections, and indeed the direct evocation of a Scottish metropolis – Dunedin, or Edinburgh – in the local landscape could prompt similar questions. To what extent was New Zealand's Scottishness a collaboration with the old centre? More importantly, how might these differing influences have interacted upon each other?

The real London's lingering legacies continue to have consequences for the present. They are compelling reasons to take New Zealand's broader British past seriously. Historians have been reluctant to do so, first because it ran counter to the demands of a national history and now because revisiting a British past seems unfashionable and uncomfortable. But this reluctance has risks. By accepting New Zealand's relationship with London as simply nostalgia borne out of a settler past, we underestimate its colonising power. In this book London played an active role in creating New Zealand as a modern dominion. London's heritage and history replaced an indigenous version; in this newly cleared space, a 'new' New Zealand could emerge, one that was quick to disassociate itself from the colonial past. And there are also rewards in revisiting this part of our history. One of these is a new perspective on New Zealand's culture in this period.

Whether characterising cultural wasteland or a servile and docile 'dutiful Dominion', New Zealand's culture has been the subject of unforgiving historical assessments for most of the twentieth century. Reconnecting New Zealand with its metropolis, as Home and hinterland, not as a servile colony to an imperial centre, changes the story. It was not all cultural cringe and thwarted nationalism. New Zealand's relationship with London was also culturally productive. Expatriates used London as an extension of New Zealand. Travellers discovered their 'heritage' there, and promptly laid claim to it, transformed from colonials to proud co-owners of metropolitan cultural icons such as St Paul's, or Westminster Abbey. For those who never visited, London remained a central part of their world, woven into the daily round of morning newspapers, popular novels, radio programming, picture-going and school lessons. It was a part of New Zealand's culture. Indeed, New Zealand itself was reimagined in London. In the modern world of commodity advertising, New Zealand shed its old nineteenth-century image, with its Maori, myths and migrants, and its hopeful rhetoric of Greater Britishness, emerging instead as a modern 'British' farming hinterland. Looking back, we may not like the nature of London's influence, or its lingering effects. But, like it or not, we still need to understand them. For being dutiful had its costs – the Southern Stand is testimony to the greatest of them – but a continued misreading of the cultural past need not be one of them.

NOTES

INTRODUCTION

1. T. B. Macaulay, review of Leopold van Ranke's *The Ecclesiastical and Political History of the Popes during the Sixteenth and Seventeenth Centuries*, in the *Edinburgh Review*, Vol. 72, October 1840, p.228.
2. David Skilton, 'Contemplating the Ruins of London: Macaulay's New Zealander and Others', *Literary London Journal*, Vol. 2, No. 1, 2004, p.1. See also Michael Bright, 'Macaulay's New Zealander', *The Arnoldian*, No. 10, 1982, pp.8–27; and Felix Driver and David Gilbert, 'Heart of Empire? Landscape, Space and Performance in Imperial London', *Environment and Planning D: Society and Space*, Vol. 16, 1998, pp.24–26.
3. *Punch*, No. 48, 7 January 1865, p.9, quoted in Skilton, 'Contemplating the Ruins', p.1.
4. James Belich, *Making Peoples: A History of the New Zealanders from Polynesian Settlement to the End of the Nineteenth Century*, Auckland, 1996, p.297. For its use as a metaphor in a conventional narrative of national identity, see R. A. Palenski, 'The Making of New Zealanders: The Evolution of National Identity in the Nineteenth Century', PhD thesis, Otago Unversity, 2010, pp.1–3.
5. The contemporary distance is used throughout. The modern equivalent is 20,000 kilometres.
6. *Punch*, No. 48, 7 January 1865, p.9, quoted in Skilton, 'Contemplating the Ruins', p.1.
7. There are no official figures, and estimates vary widely. UK census figures in 2001 totalled 58,000 New Zealand-born residents in the United Kingdom, but this does not include those on working holidays. The British Home Office estimated there were about 250,000 New Zealand passport-holders in the United Kingdom in 2005: *New Zealand Herald* (*NZH*), 8 July 2005.
8. *NZH*, 23 February 2008, p.A1.
9. Ibid.
10. Keith Sinclair, 'Life in the Provinces', in Keith Sinclair (ed.), *Distance Looks our Way*, Auckland, 1961, p.41.
11. Cringe is discussed more fully in Chapter Nine.
12. Phillip A. Buckner and R. Douglas Francis (eds), *Canada and the British World: Culture, Migration and Identity*, Vancouver, 2006, p.5.
13. Linda Colley, 'Britishness and Otherness: An Argument', *Journal of British Studies*, Vol. 31, No. 4, 1992, p.311.
14. J. G. A. Pocock, 'British History: A Plea for a New Subject', *Journal of Modern History*, Vol. 4, No. 4, 1975, pp.601–24. He updates this discussion, and its relevance to New Zealand, in *The Discovery of Islands: Essays in British History*, Cambridge and New York, 2005.
15. For New Zealand, see James Belich, *Paradise Reforged: A History of the New Zealanders from the 1880s to the Year 2000*, Auckland, 2001. For Australia, see Stuart Ward, *Australia and the British Embrace: The Demise of the Imperial Ideal*, Melbourne, 2001, p.5; and Neville Meaney, 'Britishness and Australian Identity', *Australian Historical Studies*, Vol. 32, Issue 116, April 2001, pp.76–90. For a recent summary of the trajectory of Australian national histories, see Anne Curthoys, 'We've Just Started Making National Histories, and You Want Us to Stop Already?', in Antoinette Burton (ed.), *After the Imperial Turn: Thinking With and Through the Nation*, Durham and London, 2003, pp.70–89. For Canada, see Buckner and Francis (eds), *Canada and the British World*; and Philip A. Buckner (ed.), *Canada and the End of Empire*, Vancouver, 2005.
16. Belich, *Making Peoples*, p.319.
17. See Ian Baucom, *Out of Place: Englishness, Empire and the Location of Identity*, Princeton, 1999; Robert Colls and Philip Dodd, *Englishness: Politics and Culture 1880–1920*, London, 1986; Stephen Daniels, *Fields of Vision: Landscape Imagery and National Identity in England and the United States*, Oxford, 1994; Roger Ebbatson, *An Imaginary England: Nation, Landscape and Literature, 1840–1920*, Aldershot, 2005; Simon Gikandi, *Maps of Englishness: Writing Identity in the Culture of Colonialism*, New York, 1996; Elizabeth Helsinger, *Rural Scenes and National Representation: Britain, 1815–1850*, Princeton, 1997; C. J. Wan-ling Wee, *Culture, Empire, and the Question of Being Modern*, Lanham, 2003.

18 K. Pickles, 'Colonisation, Empire and Gender', in G. Byrnes (ed.), *The New Oxford History of New Zealand*, South Melbourne, 2009, p.223.
19 Peter Gibbons, 'Cultural Colonization and National Identity', *New Zealand Journal of History*, (*NZJH*), Vol. 36, No. 1, 2002, pp.5–17; for some of its conceptual limits, see C. Hilliard, 'Colonial Culture and the Province of Cultural History', *NZJH*, Vol. 36, No. 1, 2002, pp.82–97. There are some affinities here with an emerging 'settler colonialism' field of study, although it is yet to fully engage with settler culture. For examples, see Patrick Wolfe, *Settler Colonialism and the Transformation of Anthropology: The Politics and Poetics of an Ethnographic Event*, London, New York, 1999; Lorenzo Veracini, *Settler Colonialism: A Theoretical Overview*, Basingstoke, 2010.
20 His 'Studies in Empire' series now contains over sixty volumes. But see especially John MacKenzie, *Propaganda and Empire: The Manipulation of British Public Opinion, 1880–1960*, Manchester and New York, 1986; also John MacKenzie (ed.), *Imperialism and Popular Culture*, Manchester and New York, 1986.
21 For a recent discussion, see Simon J. Potter, 'Empire, Cultures and Identities in Nineteenth and Twentieth Century Britain', *History Compass*, Vol. 1, No. 5, 2007, pp.51–71. For studies considering the dominions, see John Darwin, 'A Third British Empire? The Dominion Idea in Imperial Politics', in Judith M. Brown and W. Roger Lewis (eds), *The Oxford History of the British Empire, Vol. IV, The Twentieth Century*, Oxford, New York, 1999, pp.64–87; and Simon J. Potter, *News and the British World: The Emergence of an Imperial Press System*, Oxford, 2003. See also Andrew Thompson, *Imperial Britain: The Empire in Politics, c. 1880–1932*, Harlow, 2000, and *The Empire Strikes Back? The Impact of Imperialism on Britain from the Mid-Nineteenth Century*, Harlow, 2005.
22 A. G. Hopkins, 'Rethinking Decolonization', *Past and Present*, No. 200, 2008, p.214.
23 Antoinette Burton, *At the Heart of Empire: Indians and the Colonial Encounter in Late-Victorian Britain*, California, 1998.
24 Antoinette Burton, 'On the Inadequacy and the Indispensability of the Nation', in Burton (ed.), *After the Imperial Turn*, p.6.
25 Paul Bairoch, *Cities and Economic Development: From the Dawn of History to the Present*, London, 1988, p.309.
26 James Belich, *Replenishing the Earth: The Settler Revolution and the Rise of the Anglo World 1783–1939*, Oxford, 2009, pp.437–8.
27 Ben Fine and Ellen Leopold, *The World of Consumption*, London, New York, 1993, p.159.
28 *The Times*, 27 May 1882, p.11.
29 Belich, *Paradise Reforged*, p.66.
30 Ibid., p.30.
31 The classic study of this cultural relationship is Raymond Williams, *The Country and the City*, London, 1973.
32 Alan Grey, *Aotearoa and New Zealand: A Historical Geography*, Christchurch, 1994, p.294.
33 Benedict Anderson, *Imagined Communities: Reflections on the Origins and Spread of Nationalism*, rev. edn, London, New York, 1991.
34 Keith Sinclair, *A Destiny Apart: New Zealand's Search for National Identity*, Wellington, 1986, p.61.
35 Ibid., pp.62–63.
36 See Stephen Kern, *The Culture of Time and Space, 1880–1918*, Cambridge, 1983; Duncan Bell, 'Dissolving Distance: Technology, Space and Empire in British Political Thought, 1770–1900', *Journal of Modern History*, Vol. 77, No. 3, 2005, pp.523–62.
37 An example of this tendency can be found in Jonathan Schneer, *London 1900: The Imperial Metropolis*, Michigan, 1999.
38 For example, Maxine Berg, *Luxury and Pleasure in Eighteenth-Century Britain*, Oxford, 2005; M. Berg and H. Clifford (eds), *Consumers and Luxury: Consumer Culture in Europe, 1650–1850*, Manchester, 1999; J. Brewer and R. Porter (eds), *Consumption and the World of Goods in the Eighteenth Century*, London, New York, 1993; Fine and Leopold, *The World of Consumption*; Julie E. Fromer, '"Deeply Indebted to the Tea Plant": Representations of English National Identity in Victorian Histories of Tea', *Victorian Literature and Culture*, Vol. 36, 2008, pp.531–47; Jan De Vries, *The Industrious Revolution: Consumer Behavior and the Household Economy, 1650 to the Present*, Cambridge, New York, 2008; Elizabeth Kowaleski-Wallace, *Consuming Subjects: Women, Shopping and Business in the Eighteenth Century*, New York, 1997; N. McKendrick, J. Brewer and J. H. Plumb, *The Birth of a Consumer Society: The Commercialisation of Eighteenth-Century*

England, London, 1982; Sidney W. Mintz, *Sweetness and Power: The Place of Sugar in Modern History*, New York, 1985; W. D. Smith, 'Complications of the Commonplace: Tea, Sugar and Imperialism', *Journal of Interdisciplinary History*, Vol. 23, No. 2, 1992, pp.259–78; F. Trentmann, *The Making of the Consumer: Knowledge, Power and Identity in the Modern World*, Oxford, 2006, pp.125–46; James Walvin, *Fruits of Empire: Exotic Produce and British Taste, 1660-1800*, New York, 1997.

39   Anne McClintock, *Imperial Leather: Race, Gender, and Sexuality in the Colonial Contest*, New York, London, 1995.

CHAPTER ONE **NEW ZEALAND'S LONDON**

1   I. Donnelly, *The Joyous Pilgrimage*, Hertfordshire, 1935, p.4.
2   Ibid.
3   For Australia, see Richard White, 'Bluebells and Fogtown: Australians' First Impressions of England, 1860-1940', *Australian Cultural History*, No. 5, 1986, pp.44–59.
4   Sinclair, *A Destiny Apart*, p.173.
5   E. W. Allison, *A New Zealander Sees the World*, Auckland, 1937; R. Carr, *Travel Diary of a Young New Zealand Girl*, London, 1927; Donnelly, *The Joyous Pilgrimage*; G. E. Hunter, *Round and About*, Wellington, c.1937; M. Johnson, *English Theme with Some Variations in Verse*, Dunedin, 1937; T. C. List, *The Briton at Home: Impressions of a Visit to Great Britain*, New Plymouth, 1930; A. Mulgan, *Home: A New Zealander's Adventure*, London, 1927, 1929, 1934; R. Noble Adams, *Let's Go Home: The Journal of a Jubilee Journey*, Blenheim, 1936; H. K. Sumpter, *Travelling Light: To Europe and Back on £200*, Invercargill, 1934; A. Wall, *A Run Off the Chain: Impressions of Travel in Ceylon, Italy, Great Britain and Norway*, Auckland, 1929. Other works outside that period but discussed here include T. Allen, *A New Zealander in Many Lands*, London, 1924; W. W. Jacobson, *Homeward Voyage*, Akaroa, 1948; Forrestina (Mrs Malcolm) Ross, *Round the World with a Fountain Pen*, Wellington, 1913; A. W. Rutherford, *The Impressions of a New Zealand Pastoralist on Tour*, Christchurch, 1912.
6   Mitchell to Mulgan, 17 June 1925, Mulgan Papers, NZMS 748, Box 7, Folder 1, Auckland Public Library (APL).
7   Roger Robinson and Nelson Wattie (eds), *The Oxford Companion to New Zealand Literature*, Auckland, 1998, p.385. Some later works, if not kinder to his writing, acknowledge his role in the broader New Zealand literary context. See Lawrence Jones, *Picking Up the Traces: The Making of a New Zealand Literary Culture, 1932–1945*, Wellington, 2003; and Chris Hilliard, *The Bookmen's Dominion: Cultural Life in New Zealand, 1920–1950*, Auckland, 2006.
8   Noble Adams, *Let's Go Home*, p.49.
9   List, *The Briton at Home*, p.9.
10 Sumpter, *Travelling Light*, p.35.
11 Edward W. Said, *Culture and Imperialism*, London, 1994, p.74.
12 Rutherford, *Impressions*, p.75.
13 Mulgan, *Home*, p.6.
14 Hirst to Mulgan, 22 December 1927, Mulgan Papers, NZMS 748, Box 6, Folder 1, APL.
15 Johnson, *English Theme with Some Variations*, p.8.
16 25 May 1934, 'Pilgrimage', Ian Donnelly Diary, Donnelly Family Papers, Private Collection, p.147.
17 Donnelly, *The Joyous Pilgrimage*, p.8.
18 Mrs Leo Myers, 'London – Initial Impressions', *Auckland Weekly News*, 3 December 1908, p.17.
19 Johnson, *English Theme*, p.1.
20 Donnelly, *The Joyous Pilgrimage*, p.2.
21 G. V. Luxford Papers, MS 94/6, Auckland Institute and Museum Library (AML).
22 Mulgan, *Home*, p.18.
23 Ibid.
24 Rutherford, *Impressions*, p.66.
25 Sumpter, *Travelling Light*, p.30.
26 Carr, *Travel Diary*, p.52.
27 Ross, *Round the World*, p.35.
28 White, 'Bluebells and Fogtown', p.50.

29 Erika Rappaport, 'Travelling in the Lady Guides' London: Consumption, Modernity, and the *Fin-de-Siècle* Metropolis', in Martin Daunton and Bernhard Rieger (eds), *Meanings of Modernity: Britain From the Late Victorian Era to World War Two*, Oxford, 2001, p.29; *Ward Locke and Co's London*, London, n.d, p.10.
30 George Knight, 16 July 1916, in Nancy Croad (ed.), *My Dear Home*, Auckland, 1995, p.92.
31 Noble Adams, *Let's Go Home*, p.49.
32 Russell Weir interview, in Nicholas Boyack and Jane Tolerton (eds), *In the Shadow of War: New Zealand Soldiers Talk about World War One and Their Lives*, Auckland, 1990, p.208.
33 Myers, *Auckland Weekly News*, p.17; Ross, *Round the World*, p.37. Australians also ignored the journey between disembarkation and arriving in London proper: see White, 'Bluebells and Fogtown', p.56.
34 Mulgan, *Home*, p.27.
35 Sumpter, *Travelling Light*, p.31.
36 Donnelly, *The Joyous Pilgrimage*, p.4.
37 Johnson, *English Theme*, p.1.
38 Ibid., p.3.
39 Donnelly, *The Joyous Pilgrimage*, p.18.
40 20 June 1918, H. C. Grierson Diary, H. C. Grierson Papers, MS 92/22, AML.
41 29 October 1916, F. S. Varnham Diary, F. S. Varnham Papers, MS 2002/62, AML.
42 31 October 1916, F. S. Varnham Diary, F. S. Varnham Papers, MS 2002/62, AML.
43 Hunter, *Round and About*, p.58.
44 Cooke to Charlie, 23 October 1914, Ella Cooke Papers, MS94/36, AML.
45 9 October 1918, '"The Great Adventure" – the Diaries and Correspondence of 48548 Private James McKenzie, 1917-19, Embellished with Historical Context by Alan W. Hughes, 1988', James McKenzie Papers, MS 1701, AML; 14 March 1918, Stan Chester, 'A Brief Diary of My Travels as a Member of the NZEF', Stan Chester Papers, MS 1046, AML; 27 April 1917, R. A. Stables Diary, Hugh R. Clark Papers, MS 1615, AML; 10 October 1918, James McKenzie Papers, MS 1701, AML.
46 For a study of soldiers' use of photography in World War I, see Sandra Callister, *The Face of War: New Zealand's Great War Photography*, Auckland, 2008.
47 24 June 1918, H. C. Grierson Diary, H. C. Grierson Papers, MS 92/22, AML; 16 January 1919, Martin G. Brown Diary, Martin G. Brown Papers, MS 1176, AML.
48 Leslie Carrick Hewson Correspondence, 21 October 1917, Leslie Carrick Hewson Papers, MS 89/158, AML.
49 King to Slodel, 13 November 1916, Daisy Slodel Papers, 2002/108, AML.
50 Cooke to Charlie, 23 October 1914, Ella Cooke Papers, MS 94/36, AML.
51 David Gilbert, 'London of the Future: The Metropolis Reimagined after the Great War', *Journal of British Studies*, Vol. 43, No. 1, 2004, p.111.
52 Williams to Jeffreys, 28 October 1917, P. G. Williams Papers, MS 89/210, AML.
53 These experiences support Driver and Gilbert's assertion that imperial London was not only to be found 'in its most public and ceremonial face': Driver and Gilbert, 'Heart of Empire?', p.12.
54 Mulgan, *Home*, p.28.
55 Johnson, *English Theme*, p.3.
56 Rutherford, *Impressions*, p.75
57 Johnson, *English Theme*, p.6.
58 London is the original 'big smoke', a British term for London adopted by New Zealanders during World War I. Subsequently it travelled with them and remains in use in New Zealand to describe any town or city from a provincial perspective.
59 Henry Herbert Gill to Sophia Gill, 10 February 1918, Henry Herbert Gill Papers, MS 1130, AML.
60 White, 'Bluebells and Fogtown', pp.52-53
61 A. Staines Manders, *The Colonials' Guide To London*, London, 1916, quoted in David Gilbert and Fiona Henderson, 'London and the Tourist Imagination', in Pamela K. Gilbert (ed.), *Imagined Londons*, New York, 2002, p.131.
62 W. S. Percy, *The Empire Comes Home*, London, 1937, p.13.
63 Mary Louise Pratt, *Imperial Eyes: Travel Writing and Transculturation*, London, New York, 1992, p.7. See also Gilbert, '"London in All Its Glory– or How to Enjoy London": Guidebook Representations of Imperial London', *Journal of Historical Geography*, Vol. 25, No.3, 1999, pp.279-97.

64 Johnson, *English Theme*, p.5.
65 List, *The Briton at Home*, p.9.
66 Ibid., p.15.
67 Sumpter, *Travelling Light*, p.34.
68 Donnelly, *The Joyous Pilgrimage*, p.61.
69 Mulgan, *Home*, p.37.
70 Ibid., pp.60–61.
71 Sumpter, *Travelling Light*, p.34.
72 Mulgan, *Home*, p.60.
73 Ibid., p.45.
74 Donnelly, *The Joyous Pilgrimage*, p.4.
75 Noble Adams, *Let's Go Home*, p.153.
76 See David Gilbert, '"London in All Its Glory"' p.286.
77 Donnelly, *The Joyous Pilgrimage*, p.91.
78 Ibid., pp.6–7.
79 Rutherford, *Impressions*, p.235.
80 Ross, *Round the World*, pp.113–14.
81 Johnson, *English Theme*, p.13.
82 Angela Woollacott, '"All This is Empire, I Told Myself": Australian Women's Voyages "Home" and the Articulation of Colonial Whiteness', *American Historical Review*, Vol. 102, No. 4, 1997, p.1004.
83 For a discussion of the normativity of whiteness in the metropolitan setting, see Angela Woollacott, 'The Colonial Flaneuse: Australian Women Negotiating Turn-of-the-Century London', *Signs*, Vol. 25, No. 3, 2000, p.762.
84 Cooke to Florrie, 23 July 1915, Ella Cooke Papers, 94/36, AML.
85 Diary, F. S. Varnham, 6 May 1917, F. S. Varnham Papers, MS 2002/62, AML.
86 Burton, *At the Heart of Empire*.
87 Gilbert, '"London in All Its Glory"', p.284.
88 Ibid.
89 Charles Spragg to Hetty, 24 August 1915, Spragg Family Papers, MSS and Archives A-264, University of Auckland (UOA).
90 'London Has a Hot Time', *Auckland Sun*, 28 August 1926, Mander Papers, NZMS 535, APL.
91 Donnelly, *The Joyous Pilgrimage*, pp.221–22.
92 Rutherford, *Impressions*, p.90.
93 William Malcolm in Barbara Harper, *Letters from Gunner 7/516 and Gunner 7/517*, Wellington, 1978, p.74.
94 Rutherford, *Impressions*, p.222.
95 Ross, *Round the World*, p.73.
96 Noble Adams, *Let's Go Home*, p.163.
97 Ibid., p.34.
98 Allison, *A New Zealander Sees the World*, p.212.
99 Rutherford, *Impressions*, pp.223–4.
100 Johnson, *English Theme*, p.256.
101 Ibid., p.11.

CHAPTER TWO AT HOME IN LONDON

1 By 1905 Meath claimed that Empire Day was celebrated in all self-governing colonies, in twenty-two Crown colonies and of course in Britain itself: MacKenzie, *Propaganda and Empire*, p.232.
2 Lord Meath, 'London as the Heart of Empire', in Sir Aston Webb (ed.), *London of the Future*, London, 1921, pp.257–8, quoted in Gilbert, 'London of the Future', p.109.
3 The High Commission succeeded the Agents-General Office in 1905. For the history of Agents-General in London, see R. M. Dalziel, *The Origins of New Zealand Diplomacy: The Agent General in London, 1870–1905*, Wellington, 1975.
4 For this idea in the context of literary cultures, see C. Hilliard, 'The Provincial Press and the Imperial Traffic in Fiction, 1870s–1930s', *Journal of British Studies*, Vol. 48, No. 3, p.655.

5   Driver and Gilbert, 'Heart of Empire?', p.20.
6   *Auckland Star (AS)*, 28 August 1926.
7   Percy, *The Empire Comes Home*, p.25. For his background, see *Evening Post (EP)*, 5 June 1945, p.8.
8   Olwen Pryke, 'Australia House: Representing Australia in Great Britain, 1901–1939', PhD thesis, University of Sydney, 2006, p.89.
9   Schneer, *London 1900*, p.28.
10 Jan Payne (ed.), *Australia House: 75 Years of Service*, London, 1993, p.23.
11 Driver and Gilbert, 'Heart of Empire?', p.21.
12 *EP*, 24 September 1913, p.6.
13 Alfred Deakin, *CPD*, Representative, 12 December 1911, p.4127, in Pryke, 'Australia House', p.94.
14 Nancy Gelber, *Canada in London: An Unofficial Glimpse of Canada's Sixteen High Commissioners, 1880–1980*, London, c.1980, p.36.
15 Miller to Forbes, 12 November 1932, Appreciation and Complaints, EA 1 61/201/18 Pt1a, Archives New Zealand, Wellington (ANZW); The 1930 Visitors' Book contained 3982 entries: High Commission Report, 1931, EA 1 62/201/37 Pt 1, ANZW.
16 Payne (ed.), *Australia House*, p.25.
17 Mackenzie to Bell, 12 March 1913, Sir Francis Bell Papers, MS Papers 5210-106, Alexander Turnbull Library (ATL).
18 Annual Report to Government, 1910, General, Sir William Hall-Jones Papers, MS Papers 5755-16, ATL; High Commission Report, 1931, EA 1 62/201/37/ Pt1, ANZW.
19 Parr to Bell, 23 July 1935, Sir Francis Bell Papers, MS 5210-120, ATL. Gordon Coates was then Minister of Finance; George Forbes was Prime Minister.
20 Said, *Culture and Imperialism*, p.100.
21 Schneer, *London 1990*, p.19
22 Ibid., pp.17–36.
23 *Handbook for New Zealand Visitors to London*, London, 1934.
24 Barltrop to Minister of Internal Affairs, 12 March 1928, Appreciation and Complaints, EA 1/201/18 Pt1a, ANZW.
25 *Auckland Weekly News*, 22 October 1908, p.16.
26 Notes of interview between J. A. Young and Rev. Whitley, 17 September 1928, Appreciation and Complaints, EA 1/201/18/Pt1a, ANZW.
27 Ibid.
28 1912 Report, *Appendices to the Journals of the House of Representatives (AJHR)* 1913, H-28, p.3.
29 1916 Report, *AJHR*, H-28, 1918, p.18.
30 Mackenzie to Bell, 12 March 1913, Sir Francis Bell Papers, MS Papers 5210-106, ATL. The Wards were former Prime Minster, Sir Joseph Ward, and his wife; the Allens were Sir James Allen and his wife.
31 Wilford to Jones, 25 September 1930, Appreciation and Complaints, EA 1 61/201/18/Pt 1a, ANZW.
32 Allen to Bell, 1 August 1925, Sir Francis Bell Papers, MS Papers 5210-055, ATL.
33 Jordan to Savage, 21 October 1936, PM 16/1, ANZW.
34 *Notes For Visitors from New Zealand*, London, 1953, p.13.
35 Jordan to Savage, 25 April 1938, PM 16/1, ANZW.
36 H. T. B. Drew, *The War Effort of New Zealand: A Popular History of A) Minor Campaigns in which New Zealanders Took Part B) Services Not Fully Dealt With in the Campaign Volumes C) The Work at the Bases*, Auckland, 1923, p.274.
37 Ibid., p.189.
38 For a Canadian example, see Katie Pickles, *Female Imperialism and National Identity: The Imperial Order Daughters of Empire*, New York, 2002; for British women, see Angela Woollacott, 'From Moral to Professional Authority: Secularism, Social Work, and Middle-Class Women's Self-construction in World War I Britain', *Journal of Women's History*, Vol. 10, No. 2, 1998, pp.85–112.
39 Alison Forrest, 'Milling Around Outside the Town Hall: Motivation for Enlistment of the First AIF', *Melbourne Historical Journal*, Vol. 18, 1987, p.107.
40 Despite conscription, the vast majority (91,941 out of 124,211) of New Zealand's recruits were volunteers, although there may have been considerable variation in their enthusiasm: see Nicholas Boyack, *Behind the Lines: The Lives of New Zealand Soldiers in the First World War*, Wellington, 1989, p.6.

41 Paul Baker, *When King and Country Call: New Zealanders, Conscription and the Great War*, Auckland, 1988, p.17.
42 Guy Berry to Geoffrey Berry, 6 February 1917, La Trobe, MS 10025, quoted in B. Ziino, '"A Kind of Round Trip": Australian Soldiers and the Tourist Analogy, 1914–1918' , *War and Society*, Vol. 25, No. 2, 2006, p.49.
43 Richard White, 'The Soldier as Tourist: The Australian Experience of the Great War', *War and Society*, Vol. 5, No. 1, 1987, p.67.
44 Harper, *Letters*, p.8.
45 Richard White, 'Sun, Sand and Syphilis', *Australian Cultural History*, No. 9, 1990, p.64.
46 Dorothy McKenzie and Lindsay Malcolm (eds), *Boots, Belt, Rifle and Pack*, Dunedin, 1992, p.77.
47 White, 'The Soldier as Tourist', p.71.
48 King to Slodel, 30 October 1916, Daisy Slodel Papers, MS 2002/108, AML.
49 Drew, *The War Effort of New Zealand*, p.249.
50 King to Slodel, 13 November 1916, Daisy Slodel Papers, MS 2002/108, AML.
51 Owen Clark correspondence, 9 August 1918, Hugh R. Clark Papers, MS 1615, AML.
52 28 December 1918, Stan Chester Diary, Stan Chester Papers, MS 1046, AML.
53 E. Nicklin to Olive Nicklin, 6 July 1918, E. Nicklin Papers, MS 1173, AML.
54 Philippa Levine, 'Battle Colours: Race, Sex and Colonial Soldiery in World War I', *Journal of Women's History*, Vol. 9, No. 4, 2003, p.115.
55 N. M. Ingram, *ANZAC Diary: A Nonentity in Khaki*, Sydney, n.d., p.73. The Eccentric Club is a London gentlemen's club formed in 1890.
56 Christopher Pugsley, *On the Fringe of Hell: New Zealanders and Military Discipline in the First World War*, Auckland, 1991, p.151.
57 Ibid., p.108.
58 Ibid., p.107.
59 Levine, 'Battle Colours', p.108.
60 Jock Phillips, *A Man's Country: The Image of the Pakeha Male – A History*, Auckland, 1987, p.161.
61 Ingram, *ANZAC Diary*, p.82.
62 Tommy to Sophia Gill, 9 January 1918, Henry Herbert Gill Papers, MS 1130, AML.
63 Levine, 'Battle Colours', p.111.
64 Antje Kampf, 'Controlling Male Sexuality: Combating Venereal Disease in the New Zealand Military During Two World Wars', *Journal of the History of Sexuality*, Vol. 17, No. 2, May 2008, pp.235–58.
65 'Buckshee', *A Pictorial Record of the Work of the NZ YMCA on Active Service*, London, 1919, p.9.
66 This was the subheading of the New Zealand YMCA newsletter, *The Triangle Trail*.
67 I. W. Raymond, *New Zealanders in Mufti, 1914–1918*, London, 1924, p.5.
68 Drew, *The War Effort of New Zealand*, p.185.
69 Raymond, *New Zealanders in Mufti*, p.16.
70 Ibid., p.18.
71 3 July 1916, 'Life of a Hospital Orderly in Cairo and England 1915–16', C. M. Gordon, 13 August 1984, C. M. Gordon Papers, MS 90/77, AML. The NZ Soldier's Club was not open until 1 August 1916, which explains why he did not stay there. See also Gordon's interview in Boyack and Tolerton (eds), *In the Shadow of War*.
72 See Woollacott, 'From Moral to Professional Authority'; Katie Pickles, 'A Link in "The Great Chain of Empire Friendship": The Victoria League in New Zealand', *Journal of Imperial and Commonwealth History*, Vol. 33, No. 1, 2005, pp.29–50; Melanie Oppenheimer, '"The Best P.M. for the Empire in War"?: Lady Helen Munro Ferguson and the Australian Red Cross Society, 1914–1920', *Australian Historical Studies*, Vol. 119, 2002, pp.108–24.
73 *Chronicles of the N.Z.E.F.*, 27 March 1918, p.88.
74 *The Triangle Trail*, 16 February 1918, p.5; Drew, *The War Effort of New Zealand*, p.188.
75 Letter, *Blighty: With the Compliments of NZ YMCA*, London, 1916.
76 See Angela Woollacott, '"Khaki fever" and its Control: Gender, Class, Age and Morality on the British Homefront in the First World War', *Journal of Contemporary History*, Vol. 29, No. 2, 1994, pp.325–47.
77 Levine, 'Battle Colours', p.114.
78 *The Times*, 20 December 1917, p.2.
79 Richardson, quoted in Pugsley, *On the Fringe of Hell*, in Kampf, 'Controlling Male Sexuality', p.252.

80 *The Triangle Trail*, 16 February 1918, p.5.
81 Drew, *The War Effort of New Zealand*, p.189.
82 Phillips, *A Man's Country*, p.191.
83 'Pilgrimage', Ian Donnelly Diary, Donnelly Family Papers, Private Collection, p.119.
84 Gunner Hassall, quoted in Boyack, *Behind the Lines*, p.137. There are few studies comparing London and Egypt, but a number on both New Zealand and Egypt. Examples include Bronwyn Dalley, '"Come Back With Honour": Prostitution and the New Zealand Soldier, at Home and Abroad', in John Crawford and Ian McGibbon (eds), *New Zealand's Great War: New Zealand, the Allies and the First World War*, Auckland, 2007, pp.364–77; Bronwyn Dalley, '"Lolly Shops of the Red Light Kind" and "Soldiers of the King": Suppressing One-Woman Brothels in New Zealand, 1908–1916', *NZJH*, Vol. 30, No. 1, 1996, pp.3–23; Philip Fleming, 'Fighting the "Red Plague": Observations on the Response to Venereal Disease in New Zealand, 1910–1945', *NZJH*, Vol. 22, No. 1, 1988, pp.56–64; Jane Tolerton, *Ettie: A Life of Ettie Rout*, Auckland, 1992. For Australia, see White, 'Sun, Sand and Syphilis', pp.49–64.
85 Woollacott, '"Khaki fever"', pp.326–7.
86 Boyack, *Behind the Lines*, pp.137–8.
87 Boyack and Tolerton (eds), *In the Shadow of War*, p.41.
88 'Buckshee', *A Pictorial Record*, p.66; *Chronicles of the NZEF*, 27 March 1918, p.79.
89 *The Triangle Trail*, 16 February 1918, p.4.
90 'Buckshee', *A Pictorial Record*, p.66.
91 *Chronicles of the NZEF*, 27 March 1918, p.79.
92 Harper, *Letters*, p.29.
93 Raymond, *New Zealanders in Mufti*, p.23.
94 'Buckshee', *A Pictorial Record*, p.66. For patrols in the context of women's policing, see Philippa Levine, '"Walking the Streets in a Way No Decent Woman Should": Women Police in World War I', *Journal of Modern History*, Vol. 66, No. 1, March 1994, pp. 34–78; for gender roles in World War I, see Woollacott, '"Khaki fever"'.
95 *The New Zealand Soldier's Guide to the British Isles: With the Compliments of the NZ YMCA*, London, c.1917, p.2.
96 *Blighty: With the Compliments of the NZ YMCA*, London, 1916, p.1.
97 'Buckshee', *A Pictorial Record*, p.61.
98 Ibid., p.66.
99 4 June 1917, Owen Le Gallais Diary, Le Gallais Papers, MS 95/11, AML.
100 E. W. Newton to Father, Mother, Brother, 13 May 1916, A. J. and E. W. Newton Papers, MS 921, AML.
101 Harper, *Letters*, p.79.
102 White, 'Bluebells and Fogtown', p.50.
103 Boyack and Tolerton (eds), *In the Shadow of War*, p.232.

CHAPTER THREE A 'NEW' NEW ZEALAND

1 Mulgan, *Home*, p.18.
2 Donnelly, *The Joyous Pilgrimage*, pp.2–3.
3 Charles Spragg Correspondence, 2 September 1915, Spragg Family Papers, MS A264, UOA.
4 Myers, *Auckland Weekly News*, p.17.
5 See, for example, McClintock, *Imperial Leather*, pp.30–31; Anthony Pagden, *European Encounters with the New World: From Renaissance to Romanticism*, New Haven and London, 1993, p.117.
6 McClintock, *Imperial Leather*, p.30.
7 Myers, *Auckland Weekly News*, p.17.
8 Belich, *Paradise Reforged*, p.76.
9 *EP*, 28 June 1907, p.8.
10 For an analysis of the cultural uses of dominion status, see Felicity Barnes, '"Thinking From a Place Called London": The Metropolis and Colonial Culture, 1837–1907', *Journal of New Zealand Studies*, Special Issue, No. 12, 2011, pp.107–24.
11 This draws from Anne McClintock's idea of colonies as 'anachronistic space': McClintock, *Imperial Leather*, p.30

12 Peter Gibbons, 'Non-Fiction', in Terry Sturm (ed.), *The Oxford History of New Zealand Literature in English*, 2nd edn, Auckland, 1998, pp.35, 53. See also the discussion of separate Maori and 'New Zealand history' in Chris Hilliard, 'Stories of Becoming: The Centennial Surveys and the Colonisation of New Zealand', *NZJH*, Vol. 33, No. 1, pp.3–20.
13 Belich, *Paradise Reforged*, pp.338–41.
14 Jane Stafford and Mark Williams, *Maoriland: New Zealand Literature, 1872–1914*, Wellington, 2006, p.13. See also Keith Sinclair, 'The Empty Land: Literary Nationalism', in Sinclair, *A Destiny Apart*, pp.46–60.
15 John Mulgan, *Report on Experience*, rev. edn, London, 2010, p.37.
16 Angela Woollacott, 'The Metropole as Antipodes: Australian Women in London and Constructing National Identity', in Gilbert (ed.), *Imagined Londons*, pp.85–100.
17 See Ebbatson, *An Imaginary England*; Baucom, *Out of Place*; Colls and Dodd, *Englishness*; Wee, *Culture, Empire, and the Question of Being Modern*.
18 Mulgan, *Home*, p.19.
19 McClintock, *Imperial Leather*, pp.40–42.
20 Pierre Nora, 'Between Memory and History: Les Lieux des Memoire', *Representations*, Vol. 26, 1989, p.19.
21 Charles Brasch, *Indirections*, Wellington, 1980, p.141.
22 For a discussion of the appropriation of time and space to historicise the English rural landscape, see Catherine Brace, 'Looking Back: The Cotswolds and English National Identity, c.1890–1950', *Journal of Historical Geography*, Vol. 25, No. 4, 1999, pp.502–16. See also Ebbatson, *An Imaginary England*; Baucom, *Out of Place*; Wee, *Culture, Empire, and the Question of Being Modern*; Helsinger, *Rural Scenes and National Representation*. See also Daniels, *Fields of Vision*; Alun Howkins, 'The Discovery of Rural England', in Colls and Dodd (eds), *Englishness*, pp.62–88.
23 Helsinger, *Rural Scenes*, p.7.
24 C. Lewis Hind, *Constable*, London, 1909, p.18, 52, quoted in Daniels, *Fields of Vision*, p.211.
25 Helsinger, *Rural Scenes*, p.42.
26 Daniels, *Fields of Vision*, p.214.
27 For a discussion of the gendering of landscape art and the relationship between the picturesque and the sublime, see Jacqueline M. Labbe, *Romantic Visualities: Landscape, Gender and Romanticism*, London and New York, 1998, pp.36–65; Howkins, 'The Discovery of Rural England', p.64.
28 Daniels, *Fields of Vision*, p.214.
29 See Barry Reay, *Rural Englands*, Basingstoke, 2004, pp.172–203.
30 Daniels, *Fields of Vision*, p.214; Hind, *Constable*, p.52, quoted in Daniels, *Fields of Vision*, p.211.
31 Helsinger, *Rural Scenes*, p.7.
32 John Waring Saxton, 'The Town and Part of the Harbour of Nelson in 1842, About a Year after its First Foundation', in E. J. Wakefield, *Illustrations to "Adventure in New Zealand", Lithographed from original drawings taken on the spot by Mrs Wickstead, Miss King, Mrs Fox, Mr John Saxton, Mr Charles Heaphy, Mr C. Brees and Captain W. Mein Smith, R.A.*, London, 1845.
33 Belich, *Paradise Reforged*, p.78.
34 McKenzie and Malcolm (eds), *Boots, Belts, Rifle and Pack*, p.63.
35 H. C. Grierson Diary, 5 June 1918, H. C. Grierson Papers, MS 92/22, AML.
36 R. A. Stables Diary, 16 May 1917, Hugh R. Clark Papers, MS 1615, AML.
37 White, 'Bluebells and Fogtown', p.46, and in this case he means countryside, although he also suggests that the 'ideal landscape' of poverty was English too: see p.54.
38 Johnson, *English Theme*, p.37.
39 Allison, *A New Zealander Sees the World*, pp.193, 192, 194.
40 Ross, *Round the World*, Wellington, 1913, p.38.
41 Sinclair, *A Destiny Apart*, p.207. See also Phillips, *A Man's Country*, for a discussion of New Zealand's masculine cultural characteristics.
42 McClintock, *Imperial Leather*, pp.358–9. The idea of the frontier as a masculine place is a commonplace; likewise, the imaging of 'new' lands as virgin territory.
43 Mulgan, *Home*, p.87.
44 Johnston, *English Theme*, p.76.
45 Ngaio Marsh, *Black Beech and Honeydew*, Auckland, 1981, p.175.
46 Rutherford, *Impressions*, p.74.

47 List, *The Briton At Home*, p.5.
48 Gilbert, '"London in All Its Glory"', p.286.
49 Mulgan, *Home*, p.46.
50 Bill Luckin, 'Revisiting the Idea of Degeneration in Urban Britain, 1830–1900', *Urban Studies*, Vol. 32, No. 2, 2006, p.245.
51 This argument is made about Australia in Woollacott, 'Metropole as Antipodes', pp.85–100.
52 Jones, *Picking Up the Traces*, pp.173–4.
53 Ross, *Round the World*, p.119.
54 Ibid., p.168.
55 Allison, *A New Zealander Sees the World*, p.211.
56 Woollacott, 'Metropole as Antipodes', p.87.
57 White, 'Bluebells and Fogtown', p.55.
58 T. Allen, *A New Zealander in Many Lands*, London, 1924, p.7.
59 Woollacott, 'Metropole as Antipodes', p.86.
60 Rutherford, *Impressions*, p.76.
61 Donnelly, *The Joyous Pilgrimage*, p.59.
62 Sumpter, *Travelling Light*, p.41.
63 Mulgan, *Home*, p.84.
64 Ibid., p.85.
65 Ibid., p.218.
66 Mackenzie to Bell, 4 July 1913, Sir Francis Bell Papers, MS Papers 5210-106, ATL.
67 Sumpter, *Travelling Light*, p.38.
68 Rutherford, *Impressions*, pp.68, 86–87.
69 Mulgan, *Home*, pp.108–9.
70 Ibid., p.32.
71 White, 'Bluebells and Fogtown', p.53.
72 Myers, *Auckland Weekly News*, p.17.
73 Sumpter, *Travelling Light*, p.32.
74 Noble Adams, *Let's Go Home*, p.48.
75 List, *The Briton at Home*, p.45.
76 Allison, *A New Zealander Sees the World*, p.201.
77 Myers, *Auckland Weekly News*, p.17.
78 Ross, *Round the World*, p.55.
79 Sumpter, *Travelling Light*, p.33.
80 Allison, *A New Zealander Sees the World*, p.221.
81 E. H. McCormick, *Letters and Art in New Zealand*, Wellington, 1940, p.125.
82 Sinclair, *A Destiny Apart*, p.46.
83 Ashcroft, Griffiths and Tiffin note that 'the task of compiling a national literary history has usually been an important element of the establishment of an independent cultural identity', adding that 'by the values implicit in their selection, [they have] been important sites for recording and even initiating shifts in critical taste and cultural stance': see Bill Ashcroft, Gareth Griffiths and Helen Tiffin, *The Empire Writes Back: Theory and Practice in Post-Colonial Literatures*, London, 1989, p.133.
84 New Zealand Authors' Week Speech, Mander Papers, NZMS 535, APL.
85 See Stafford and Williams, *Maoriland*; Belich, *Paradise Reforged*, pp.339–41.
86 See also Keith Sinclair, 'The Empty Land: Literary Nationalism', in Sinclair, *A Destiny Apart*, pp.46–60.
87 This literature has been the subject of little critical study, but Stafford and Williams' *Maoriland* offers a thorough recent analysis. Writers of the thirties have garnered considerably more interest: here I have focused upon the critical work of Lawrence Jones in *Picking Up the Traces*, and 'The Novel', in Sturm (ed.), *The Oxford History of New Zealand Literature in English*; and Stuart Murray, *Never A Soul At Home: New Zealand Literary Nationalism and the 1930s*, Wellington, 1998.
88 Edith Searle Grossman, *The Heart of the Bush*, London, 1910, p.1.
89 Ibid., p.163.
90 Ibid., p.32.
91 Ibid., p.176.

92   Ibid., p.332.
93   Ibid., p.10.
94   Stafford and Williams, *Maoriland*, p.273.
95   Jones, *Picking Up the Traces*, p.174.
96   Ibid., p.184.
97   John Mulgan, *Man Alone*, rev. edn, Kent, 1949, p.25.
98   Ibid., p.76.
99   Ibid., pp.94–95.
100 Ibid., p.174.
101 Ibid., p.141.
102 Ibid., p.8.
103 Ibid., p.12.
104 Stafford and Williams, *Maoriland*, p.16.
105 Isobel Andrews, Letter to the Editor, *New Zealand Listener*, 24 January 1941, p.4, quoted in Jones, *Picking Up the Traces*, p.222.
106 Hilliard, *The Bookmen's Dominion*, p.102.
107 See also Hilliard, 'Stories of Becoming', p.3.
108 Jones, *Picking Up the Traces*, pp.209, 208: Roderick Finlayson, and to a lesser extent Robin Hyde are exceptions. For a full discussion, see pp.208–14.
109 Ibid., p.187.
110 Ibid., p.24.

CHAPTER FOUR LONDON LITERATE

1   Hilliard, 'The Provincial Press and the Imperial Traffic in Fiction', p.663. For the role of news, see Chapter Seven.
2   *Auckland Sun* (*ASN*), n.d.; *ASN*, 24 October 1925; *ASN*, 27 August 1927; *ASN*, 26 February 1927; Mander Papers, NZMS 535, APL.
3   *Daily Chronicle*, 3 November 1928, Mander Papers, NZMS 535, APL.
4   Many of the titles will still be familiar. However, Mrs Hemans was a popular and prolific Victorian poet, best known for 'Casabianca' ('The boy stood on the burning deck'); *Peep of the Day* and *Line by Line*, by F. L. Mortimer, were well-known, but by this time outdated, Victorian children's bible primers; Cruden's was a bible concordance.
5   Helen Bones, 'A Dual Exile?: New Zealand and the Colonial Writing World, 1890–1945', PhD thesis, University of Canterbury, 2011, p.81.
6   McCormick, *Letters and Art*, p.129.
7   Ibid., p.141. See H. Guthrie-Smith, *Tutira: The Story of a New Zealand Sheep Station*, London, 1926.
8   McCormick, *Letters and Art*, pp.141–2.
9   Ibid., p.32.
10 Ibid. See also Hilliard, 'Stories of Becoming', which considers McCormick's adaptation thesis.
11 Charlotte Brontë, *Villette*, London, reprinted 1983. I am grateful to Professor Carolyn Steedman for this reference.
12 Mansfield to [?Marion Tweed], 16 April 1903, in Vincent O'Sullivan and Margaret Scott (eds), *The Collected Letters of Katherine Mansfield, Volume One, 1903–1917*, Oxford, 1984, pp.4–5.
13 J. Middleton Murry (ed.), *Journal of Katherine Mansfield*, London, 1954, p.21, quoted in Sydney Janet Kaplan, '"A Gigantic Mother": Katherine Mansfield's London', in Susan Merrill Squier (ed.), *Women Writers and the City: Essays in Feminist Literary Criticism*, Knoxville, 1984, p.161.
14 Fairburn to Mason, 13 October 1930, quoted in Denys Trussell, *Fairburn*, Auckland, 1984, p.88; but not in Lauris Edmond (ed.), *The Letters of A. R. D. Fairburn*, Auckland, 1981. Edmond's collection does not include letters from the early London period.
15 Brasch, *Indirections*, pp.129–30.
16 Quoted in Michael King, *Frank Sargeson: A Life*, Auckland, 1995, p.67.
17 Marsh, *Black Beech and Honeydew*, pp.176–7.
18 Ibid., p.176.
19 Brasch, *Indirections*, p.129.

20 'A Few Interesting Things About London', IYA Radio Talks, 1932, Mander Papers, NZMS 535, APL.
21 Ibid.
22 Ibid. A similar talk survives among writer Isabel Peacocke's papers: see I. M. Peacocke Papers, MSS and Archives 94/5, UOA.
23 *Christchurch Sun* (*CS*), 1 December 1928; *CS*, 15 December 1928; *ASN*, 21 March 1931; *ASN*, 28 March 1931; *ASN*, 5 December 1931.
24 McCormick, *Letters and Art*, pp.130–1.
25 Frank Sargeson, 'Writing a Novel', in *Conversation in a Train*, Oxford, 1983, p.60, originally radio broadcasts in 1950, quoted in Jones, *Picking Up the Traces*, p.223; but see also pp.223–56.
26 'London has a "Hot Time"', *ASN*, 28 August 1926, n.p., Mander Papers, NZMS 535, APL.
27 *ASN*, 4 December 1924.
28 Fairburn to Mason, 22 March 1931, in Edmond (ed.), *The Letters of A. R. D. Fairburn*, p.46.
29 Fairburn to Mason, 3 December 1930; Fairburn to Mason, 22 December 1931, in ibid., pp.43 and 58.
30 Trussell, *Fairburn*, p.88.
31 Fairburn to Firth, 21 October 1930, quoted in James and Helen McNeish, *Walking On My Feet: A. R. D. Fairburn, a Kind of Biography*, Auckland, 1983, p.36.
32 King, *Frank Sargeson: A Life*, p.67.
33 Eric McCormick, *An Absurd Ambition*, Auckland, 1996, p.120.
34 Fairburn to Firth, 8 January 1931, in Edmond (ed.), *The Letters of A. R. D. Fairburn*, p.45.
35 Kaplan, '"A Gigantic Mother"', p.167. For a discussion of the relationship of the metropolis and sexual freedom for Australian women writers, see Angela Woollacott, 'White Colonialism and Sexual Modernity: Australian Women in the Early 20th-Century Metropolis', in Antoinette Burton (ed.), *Gender, Sexuality and Colonial Modernities*, London, 1999, pp.49–63.
36 Bridget Griffen-Foley, '"The Crumbs are Better than a Feast Elsewhere": Australian Journalists on Fleet Street', *Journalism History*, Vol. 28, Issue 1, 2002, p.29.
37 See Rae McGregor, *Jane Mander: The Story of a New Zealand Writer*, Dunedin, 1998, p.102.
38 Mander was 35 when she left New Zealand for America, and 46 on moving to London. Marsh was 33, Nelle Scanlan 41 and Edith Lyttleton 36. On the other hand, Bolitho was 25, Brasch 17, Fairburn 26 and Sargeson 23.
39 Fairburn was invited to tea with Walter de la Mare after the publication of *He Shall Not Rise*. He also met with Epstein to write an article for the *Auckland Star*. Mander lived near him in Chelsea. Finally, Hector Bolitho was an accomplished nose pianist.
40 Frank Sargeson, *Sargeson*, 2nd edn, Auckland, 1981, p.409.
41 Hector Bolitho, *My Restless Years*, London, 1962, pp.89–90.
42 Brasch, *Indirections*, p.130.
43 Fairburn to Mason, 24 June 1932, in Edmond (ed.), *The Letters of A. R. D. Fairburn*, p.79. His letters contain a number of criticisms about the English landscape, which reflect in part his interest in, and growing involvement with, art.
44 Fairburn to Mason, 22 March 1931, ibid., p.46.
45 Bones, 'A Dual Exile?', pp.82–98.
46 'My Life in Two Worlds', *Daily Chronicle*, 3 November 1928, Mander Papers, NZMS 535, APL.
47 McGregor, *Jane Mander*, p.92. As further proof that colonials can make it, she is referring to Henry Handel Richardson, an Australian author.
48 Bolitho, *My Restless Years*, p.160.
49 Graeme Johnson, '"Cultural Cringe" or Colonial Fringe?', *Melbourne Historical Journal*, Vol. 17, 1985, p.81.
50 Ibid., p.80.
51 Terry Sturm, 'Attila of the Antipodes; or, The Mad Hatter's Tea Party: The Publishing History of Edith Lyttleton (G. B. Lancaster) in the 1930s', in Penny Griffith, Peter Hughes and Alan Loney (eds), *A Book in the Hand: Essays on the History of the Book in New Zealand*, Auckland, 2000, p.87.
52 McNeish, and McNeish, *Walking On My Feet*, p.32; Bolitho, *My Restless Years*, p.88; King, *Frank Sargeson*, p.63. Sargeson himself was somewhat amazed by what he accomplished on that £200: see Sargeson, *Sargeson*, pp.364–5.
53 McGregor, *Jane Mander*, p.88.
54 Margaret Lewis, *Ngaio Marsh: A Life*, Wellington, 1991, p.39.

55 Derek Challis and Gloria Rawlinson, *The Book of Iris: A Life of Robin Hyde*, Auckland, 2002, p.738.
56 *CS*, 4 December 1924.
57 McGregor, *Jane Mander*, p.92.
58 Hilliard, 'The Provincial Press', pp.655–7.
59 J. E. Traue, 'The Public Library Explosion in Colonial New Zealand', *Libraries & the Cultural Record*, Vol. 42, No. 2, 2007, p.152. These ranged widely in size: see G. Northey, 'Merely Boxes of Books? The Management and Administration of Auckland's Nineteenth Century Libraries', *New Zealand Libraries*, Vol. 49, No. 1, 1999, pp.18–32.
60 For colonial editions, see Chapter Eight.
61 L. Wevers, *Reading on the Farm: Victorian Fiction in the Colonial World*, Wellington, 2010, p.198.
62 E. P. Williams, *A New Zealander's Diary, Gallipoli and France, 1915–1917*, 1924, reprinted Christchurch, 1998, p.180. See McCormick's *Letters and Art*, for the most well known of this kind of criticism. See also Wevers, *Reading on the Farm*, and Dulcie Gillespie Needham, 'The Colonial and His Books: A Study of Reading in Nineteenth Century New Zealand', PhD thesis, Victoria University, 1971.
63 *Gordon and Gotch London: The Story of the G. and G. Century 1853–1953*, London, 1953, p.79, quoted in Johnson, '"Cultural Cringe" or Colonial Fringe?', p.78.
64 Auckland Public Library Non-Fiction Lending Records, 1916–17, APL.
65 Marsh, *Black Beech and Honeydew*, p.8.
66 C. Hilliard, 'The Literary Underground of 1920s London', *Social History*, Vol. 33, No. 2, p.168.
67 Dennis McEldowney, 'Publishing, Patronage, Literary Magazines', in Sturm (ed.), *The Oxford History of New Zealand Literature*, p.567.
68 This type of interconnectedness would later be exemplified in the relationship between New Zealand and Oxford University Press, which developed slightly later.
69 Bolitho, *My Restless Years*, p.91.
70 Ibid.
71 Ibid., p.90.
72 Joyce Fairgray, *From Windsor Castle to Windsor Reserve*, Devonport, 2009, p.19.
73 Bolitho's experiences offer more insights. He had sent a short story to the *Adelphi*, run by John Middleton Murry, and 'only because [Bolitho] came from the same country as his wife', he was asked to dinner. Once again we can assume the connection was as much high cultural as national, particularly as Murry took him to visit D. H. Lawrence. Lawrence gave him advice on being a writer that, in the event, he would not follow: 'you must be willing to leave London and all the people you have met. You must go away and be content to live on only three pounds a week': ibid., pp.94–95. Instead, perhaps sensing early in which direction he would be pulled in the struggle between writing as art and as business, Bolitho moved to Mayfair.
74 Trussell, *Fairburn*, p.93. L. Wertheim, *Adventure in Art*, London, 1947.
75 Lyceum Club Talk, 8 June 1933, Mander Papers, NZMS 535, APL.
76 Invitation, Mander Papers, NZMS 535, APL.
77 Robinson and Wattie (eds), *The Oxford Companion to New Zealand Literature*, p.434.
78 BBC interview, 1960, quoted in Lewis, *Ngaio Marsh*, p.68.
79 Kaplan, '"A Gigantic Mother"', p.173.
80 'The Making of An Authoress', in *The Lady's World*, Mander Papers, NZMS 535, APL.
81 *ASN*, 4 December 1924, Mander Papers, NZMS 535, APL. For a study of New Zealand journalists in London, see H. Benbow, '"I Like New Zealand Best": London Correspondents for New Zealand Newspapers, 1884–1942', MA thesis, University of Canterbury, 2009.
82 'Let's Go to A Party', IYA Radio talks, 1932, Mander Papers, NZMS 535, APL.
83 'On Making Good – Colonials in London', *CS*, 4 December 1924, Mander Papers, NZMS 535, APL.
84 Bolitho, *My Restless Years*, pp.239–40.
85 *ASN*, 16 June 1928, pp.16–17.
86 Fairburn to Mason, 9 January 1932, in Edmond (ed.), *The Letters of A. R. D. Fairburn*, p.63.
87 Mander to Holcroft, 9 November 1931, quoted in McGregor, *Jane Mander*, p.91.
88 *ASN*, n.d., Mander Papers, NZ 535, APL.
89 Writing about the Australian experience, Stephen Alomes notes ambiguously that 'for many Australians, the overseas odyssey was central to their own coming of age. At the same time, the continued absence of so many talented young people would frustrate the nation's social, cultural, and political development, or as some observers call it, Australia's "Coming of Age"':

Stephen Alomes, *When London Calls: The Expatriation of Australian Creative Artists to Britain*, Cambridge, 1999, p.7.
90 Sinclair, *A Destiny Apart*, p.51.
91 Robinson and Wattie (eds), *The Oxford Companion to New Zealand Literature*.
92 For a revisionist approach to exile, see Bones, 'A Dual Exile?'.
93 Jones, 'The Novel', p.123.
94 Fairburn to Mason, 11 November 1930, in ibid., p.42.
95 Alomes, *When London Calls*, pp.262–3.
96 Fairburn to Mason, 15 August 1931, in Edmond (ed.), *The Letters of A. R. D. Fairburn*, p.51.
97 Marsh, *Black Beech and Honeydew*, p.183.
98 Sargeson, *Sargeson*, p.113.
99 Ibid.
100 Trussell, *Fairburn*, p.94.
101 Ibid., p.96.
102 Fairburn to Mason, 22 March 1931, in Edmond (ed.), *The Letters of A. R. D. Fairburn*, p.46.
103 Pamela Williamson, letter, *Writer*, October 1923, p.21, in C. Hilliard, *To Exercise our Talents: The Democratisation of Writing in Britain*, Cambridge, MA, 2006, p.34.
104 Mimicry is associated with the work of Homi Bhabha: see 'Of Mimicry and Man', in H. Bhabha, *The Location of Culture*, London, 1994, pp.85–92. For mimicry in New Zealand, see K. Pickles, 'The Obvious and the Awkward: Postcolonialism and the British World', *NZJH*, Vol. 45, No. 1, 2011, p.87.
105 For Britain, see ibid, p.3. For an example of participation, see the colonial role in British feminism, in Angela Woollacott, *To Try Her Fortune in London: Australian Women, Colonialism, and Modernity*, New York, 2001.
106 Ibid., p.5.
107 Bones, 'A Dual Exile?', p.129.
108 McGregor, *Jane Mander*, pp. 92, 90.
109 Fairburn to Mason, 6 January 1932, in Edmond (ed.), *The Letters of A. R. D. Fairburn*, pp.62–63.
110 Trussell, *Fairburn*, p.125; McNeish and McNeish, *Walking on My Feet*, p.71; they quote James Boswell on this issue: 'I remember thinking to myself, *I cannot understand* why he wants to go back. I said, "You'll come back, Rex?" And he said, "Yes, of course I'll come back".'
111 Rachel Barrowman, *A Popular Vision: The Arts and the Left In New Zealand, 1930–1950*, Wellington, 1991, p.2.
112 'My Life in Two Worlds', *Daily Chronicle*, 3 November 1928, n.p., Mander Papers, NZ 535, APL.

CHAPTER FIVE LONDON'S FARM

1 J. T. Critchell and J. Raymond, *A History of the Frozen Meat Trade*, London, 1912, pp.279–80.
2 Examples include P. Mein Smith, 'New Zealand Milk for "Building Britons"', in Mary Sutphen and Bridie Andrews (eds), *Medicine and Colonial Identity*, London, 2003, pp.79–102; and Frances Steele, '"New Zealand *is* Butterland": Interpreting the Historical Significance of Daily Spread', *NZJH*, Vol. 39, No. 2, 2005, pp.179–94. For colonising effects, see T. Brooking, '"Busting up" the Greatest Estate of All: Liberal Maori Land Policy, 1891–1911', *NZJH*, Vol. 26, No. 1, April 1992.
3 For London's role, see J. Darwin, *The Empire Project: The Rise and Fall of the British World System 1830–1970*, Cambridge, 2009, pp.279–82.
4 William Cronon, *Nature's Metropolis: Chicago and the Great West*, New York, 1991, p.56.
5 M. Fairburn, 'The Rural Myth and the New Urban Frontier: An Approach to New Zealand Social History, 1870–1940', *NZJH*, Vol. 9, No. 1, 1975, pp.3–21.
6 McClintock, *Imperial Leather*, p.210.
7 Ewan Johnston, 'Representing the Pacific at International Exhibitions, 1851–1940', PhD thesis, University of Auckland, 1999, p.208.
8 *The Times*, 26 December 1849, p.5.
9 Ibid.
10 Ibid.
11 Leonard Bell, *Colonial Constructs: European Images of Maori, 1840–1914*, Auckland, 1992, p.29. The handbill is reproduced on p.31. See also Johnston, 'Representing the Pacific', pp.207–9.

12 'A Pioneer's Story', *Star*, 13 June 1903, p.4.
13 McClintock, *Imperial Leather*, 1995.
14 'A Pioneer's Story', *Star*, 13 June 1903, p.4.
15 Robert Grant, *Representations of British Emigration, Colonisation and Settlement: Imagining Empire, 1800–1860*, New York, 2005, p.194.
16 Thomas Richards, *The Commodity Culture of Victorian England: Advertising and Spectacle, 1851–1914*, Stanford, 1990, pp.59–66.
17 Grant, *Representations*, p.7.
18 Ibid., pp.195–6.
19 Jonathon Easthope, 'Imaging Ourselves: The Projection of Pakeha Culture Overseas 1870–1925', MA thesis, Victoria University of Wellington, 1995, pp.14–16.
20 W. D. Borrie, *Immigration to New Zealand 1854–1938*, Canberra, 1991, p.149.
21 These figures are from the most detailed study of New Zealand and exhibitions: Johnston, 'Representing the Pacific', p.324.
22 Belich, *Replenishing the Earth*, pp.447–51.
23 Britain imported 60 per cent of its grain from 1870, mostly from North America: W. H. Fraser, *The Coming of the Mass Market, 1850–1914*, London, 1981, p.150.
24 Ibid., p.16.
25 Ibid., p.29.
26 James B. Jefferys, *Retail Trading in Britain, 1850–1950*, Cambridge, 1954, p.182. This figure does not include pork products and live animals.
27 Fraser, *Mass Market*, p.108.
28 See Table 11.6, 'Estimated weekly per capita consumption, selected foods, 1860–1913', in Mary McKinnon, 'Living Standards, 1870–1914', in Roderick Floud and Donald McCloskey (eds), *The Economic History of Britain Since 1700, Volume 2, 1860–1939*, 2nd edn, Cambridge, 1994, p. 279.
29 Liquid milk production rose from 25 per cent of total British dairy production in 1860 to more than 70 per cent by World War I, with corresponding declines in local cheese and butter production: see David Taylor, 'The English Dairy Industry, 1860–1939', *Economic History Review*, New Series, Vol. 29, No. 4, 1976, pp.585–601.
30 John Burnett, *Plenty and Want: A Social History of the Diet in England from 1815 to the Present Day*, London, 1966, p.146.
31 J. Blackman, 'The Development of the Retail Grocery Trade in the Nineteenth Century', in John Benson and Gareth Shaw (eds), *The Retailing Industry: Volume Two, The Coming of the Mass Market, 1800–1945*, London, 1999, p.62.
32 Fraser, *Mass Market*, p.111.
33 Jefferys, *Retail Trading*, p.139.
34 Ibid., p.140.
35 The Midlands and parts of Lancashire were also important areas of consumption: Jefferys, *Retail Trading*, p.190–1.
36 Ibid., p.165. The figures for this are based on a comparison of customer registration for butter following World War I in 1919. Important exceptions are Danish butter and Argentinian meat, but these were consumed largely outside London.
37 For example, in Joanna De Groot, 'Metropolitan Desires and Colonial Connections', in Catherine Hall and Sonya O. Rose (eds), *At Home with the Empire: Metropolitan Culture and the Imperial World*, Cambridge, 2006, p.177. For pastoralism in imperial history generally, see T. Brooking and E. Pawson, 'Silences of Grass: Retrieving the Role of Pasture Plants in the Development of New Zealand and the British Empire', *Journal of Imperial and Commonwealth History*, Vol. 35, No. 3, 2007, pp.417–35.
38 Richards, *Commodity Culture*, pp.1 and 53.
39 The wholesale price of meat and dairy rose by around 40 per cent between 1850 and 1867, last duties on sugar were removed in 1874 and tea duty reduced in 1875: see Fraser, *Mass Market*, pp.149–74.
40 Imported wheat may have been causal in this process too. From an initial start in 1862, the Aerated Bread Company expanded rapidly from the mid-1870s with the development of ABC tea stores. Although technological changes were important, by 1870, 60 per cent of wheat imports were coming from North America: see Fraser, *Mass Market*, pp.150–1; also Gareth Shaw, Louise Hill Curth and Andrew Alexander, 'Creating New Spaces of Food Consumption: The Rise of

Mass Catering and the Activities of the Aerated Bread Company', in John Benson and Laura Ugolini (eds), *Cultures of Selling: Perspectives of Consumption and Society Since 1700*, Aldershot, 2006, pp.81–102.
41 Jefferys, *Retail Trading*, p.129.
42 Ibid., p.146.
43 Ibid., p.37.
44 William Leiss, Stephen Kline and Sut Jhally, *Social Communication in Advertising: Persons, Products and Images of Wellbeing*, Toronto, New York, 1986, p.279.
45 See MacKenzie, *Propaganda and Empire*, esp. pp.15–38.
46 Richards, *Commodity Culture*, p.33.
47 MacKenzie, *Propaganda and Empire*, p.97.
48 Frank Goldberg, *My Life in Advertising*, n.p., n.d., p.1.
49 *The Times*, 27 May 1882, p.11.
50 Between 1910 and 1912, when it was separated, then amalgamated again in 1930: see 'Tourism: The Invisible Export', *The New Zealand Official Year Book*, Wellington, 1976, pp.1032–45.
51 G. T. Bloomfield, *New Zealand: A Handbook of Historical Statistics*, Boston, 1984, p.320.
52 Sir A. F. Roberts, 'Report of the New Zealand Exhibition Commissioner', in Johnston, 'Representing the Pacific', p.289.
53 *NZH*, 14 February 1940, p.12.
54 Joubert had considerable experience in running exhibitions both locally and internationally, including exhibitions in Adelaide (1881), Calcutta (1883–84) and Christchurch (1882): see Peter H. Hoffenberg, *An Empire on Display: English, Indian and Australian Exhibitions from the Crystal Palace to the Great War*, Berkeley and Los Angeles, 2001, Appendix B, p.283.
55 Jules Joubert, *The Proposed New Zealand Exhibition in London*, Dunedin, 1890, pp.1–6.
56 Hoffenberg, *An Empire on Display*, p.10; see also Appendix A, p.279. Allwood lists seventy-four exhibitions between 1851 and 1940, and this number does not include colonial-only exhibitions: see John Allwood, *The Great Exhibitions*, London, 1977, pp.179–85.
57 Ibid.; Jeffrey A. Auerbach and Peter H. Hoffenberg, *Britain, the Empire, and the World at the Great Exhibition of 1851*, Abingdon, 2008; Paul Greenhalgh, *Ephemeral Vistas: The Expositions Universelles, Great Exhibitions and World's Fairs, 1851–1939*, Manchester, 1988; N. Gywnn and Robert W. Rydell (eds), *Fair Representations: World's Fairs and the Modern World*, Amsterdam, 1994; MacKenzie, *Propaganda and Empire*; Louise Purbrick (ed.), *The Great Exhibition of 1851: New Interdisciplinary Essays*, New York, 2001; Robert W. Rydell, *World of Fairs: The Century of Progress Expositions*, Chicago and London, 1993; Paul Young, *Globalization and the Great Exhibition: The Victorian New World Order*, Basingstoke; James Buzard, Joseph W. Childers and Eileen Gillooly (eds), *Victorian Prism: Refractions of the Crystal Palace*, Charlottesville, 2007.
58 For New Zealand, the most comprehensive source is Johnston, 'Representing the Pacific'; see also John Mansfield Thomson (ed.), *Farewell Colonialism: The New Zealand International Exhibition Christchurch, 1906–7*, Palmerston North, 1998.
59 For example, see Johnston, 'Representing the Pacific', p.208. For high culture and identity, see Christopher Tait, 'Brushes, Budgets, and Butter: Canadian Culture and Identity at the British Empire Exhibition, 1924–5', in Buckner and Francis (eds), *Canada and the British World*, p.239.
60 Thomas Richards, *The Imperial Archive: Knowledge and the Fantasy of Empire*, New York, London, 1993.
61 Greenhalgh, *Ephemeral Vistas*, p.54.
62 MacKenzie, *Propaganda and Empire*, p.118.
63 Easthope, 'Imaging Ourselves', p.19.
64 E. Johnston, '"A Valuable and Tolerably Extensive Collection of Native and Other Products": New Zealand at the Crystal Palace', in Auerbach and Hoffenberg, *Britain, the Empire, and the World*, p.80.
65 Ibid.
66 'Our London Letter', *EP*, 30 July 1884, p.3.
67 Ibid.
68 *Colonial and Indian Exhibition – Guide to New Zealand Exhibits*, London, 1886.
69 See Hoffenberg, *An Empire on Display*, p.106 and Fig. 4; also Easthope, 'Imaging Ourselves', p.23.
70 *Colonial and Indian Exhibition, London, Catalogue of New Zealand Exhibits*.
71 *Colonial and Indian Exhibition, London 1886, Official Catalogue*, p.45.

72 *The Times*, 8 May 1908, p.20.
73 Report of the Department of Tourism and Publicity, 1909, in *AJHR* 1909, H-2, p.7.
74 *The Times*, 1 July 1908, p.7.
75 'High Commissioner of New Zealand's Report for the Year Ending 31 March 1912', *AJHR*, 1912, H-28, p.4.
76 *The Times*, 24 January 1911, p.10.
77 *The Times*, 12 January 1911, p.6.
78 'Report of the Exhibition Commissioner to the British Empire Exhibition, held at Wembley, England 1924–1925', 22 June 1926, p.6, Sir A. F. Roberts Collection, MS-Papers 1693, ATL.
79 *Daily Telegraph*, 6 February 1924, in *New Zealand's Contribution to the British Empire Exhibition*, Wembley, London, 1924.
80 *Souvenir of the New Zealand Pavilion at the British Empire Exhibition*, Wembley, London, 1924, p.1.
81 *Daily Telegraph*, 6 February 1924, in *New Zealand's Contribution to the British Empire Exhibition*.
82 'Report of the Exhibition Commissioner to the British Empire Exhibition, held at Wembley, England 1924–1925', 22 June 1926, p.2, Sir A. F. Roberts Collection, MS-Papers 1693, ATL.
83 *The Times*, 17 April 1924, p.9.
84 The *Empire Mail*, May 1926, p.16, in *New Zealand's Contribution to the British Empire Exhibition*.
85 *The Times*, 23 May 1925, p.ix.
86 'The Prince as Indian Chief', *Montreal Herald*, 15 July 1925, p.4, quoted in Anne Clendinning, 'Exhibiting a Nation: Canada at the British Empire Exhibition, 1924–1925', *Social History/Histoire Social*, Vol. 39, No. 77, 2006, p.103.
87 'Report of the Exhibition Commissioner to the British Empire Exhibition, held at Wembley, England 1924–1925', 22 June 1926, p.11, Sir A. F. Roberts Collection, MS-Papers 1693, ATL.
88 Ibid., p.11.
89 Ibid., p.11.
90 Ibid., p.13.
91 *The Times*, 2 July 1925.
92 John E. Martin, 'The "Social Laboratory" Writ Large? The Department of Labour's Court', in Thomson (ed.), *Farewell Colonialism*, p.135.
93 James Cowan, *Official Record*, p.6, quoted in Jock Phillips, 'Exhibiting Ourselves: The Exhibition and National Identity', in Thomson (ed.), *Farewell Colonialism*, pp.19–20.
94 *The Times*, 12 January 1911, p.6.
95 *The Times*, 24 January 1911, p.10.
96 S. Britton, '"Come and See the Empire by the All Red Route!": Anti-imperialism and Exhibitions', *History Workshop Journal*, No. 69, 2010, pp.68–89; Deborah Hughes, 'Contesting Whiteness: Race, Nationalism and British Empire Exhibitions Between the Wars', PhD thesis, University of Illinois at Urbana-Champaign, 2008.
97 Greenhalgh, *Ephemeral Vistas*, p.63.
98 Hoffenberg, *An Empire on Display*, p.131.
99 *Graphic*, 8 May 1886, p.495, quoted in ibid., p.25.
100 MacKenzie links the dominance of dominion pavilions at exhibitions and their habit of building the 'most impressive High Commissions on the choicest sites in Trafalgar Square and the Strand': MacKenzie, *Propaganda and Empire*, p.100.
101 Even geysers were to be subject to human control in Rotorua. McClure discusses the work of Camille Malfroy, a French hydraulics engineer who 'boasted he could organize a geyser for eminent visitors at a few hours' notice': see Margaret McClure, *The Wonder Country: Making New Zealand Tourism*, Auckland, 2004, p.21.
102 For a recent study of Maori and exhibitions, see Conal McCarthy, *Exhibiting Maori: A History of Colonial Cultures on Display*, Wellington, 2007.
103 *Colonial and Indian Exhibition, London, Catalogue of New Zealand Exhibits*, p.xv.
104 Minutes of the Meeting of New Zealand Commissioners held at the Colonial and Indian Exhibition, Monday, 12 July 1886, p.3, Haast Family Papers, MS Papers 0037-001, ATL, quoted in Johnston, 'Representing the Pacific', p.262.
105 'The Colonial and Indian Exhibition: New Zealand', *The Times*, 24 July 1886, quoted in Johnston, 'Representing the Pacific', p.262.

106 John Bradshaw, *New Zealand of Today (1884–1887)*, London, 1888, pp.88–89, quoted in Easthope, 'Imaging Ourselves', p.24.
107 'Maoris Quit Festival Village', *Otautau Standard and Wallace Country Chronicle*, 11 July 1911, p.2.
108 Sophie C. Lomas (ed.), *Book of the Pageant: Festival of Empire*, London, 1911, pp.139–40.
109 F. Brangwyn, E. V. Lucas and S. Pryse, *Pageant of Empire*, London, 1924, pp.7–8.
110 *New Zealand's Contribution to the British Empire Exhibition*, p.7.
111 It is important to emphasise that these representations could be subverted to carry quite different meanings for the people whose culture was on display: see B. Kernot, 'Maoriland Metaphors and the Model Pa', in Thomson (ed.), *Farewell Colonialism*, pp.61–78; and C. McCarthy, 'Objects of Empire? Displaying Maori at International Exhibitions, 1873–1924', *Journal of New Zealand Literature*, No. 23, 2005, pp.52–70.
112 Dunedin *Evening Star*, 24 January, 1890, cited in Joubert, *Proposed New Zealand Exhibition*, p.7.
113 *Tuapeka Times*, 28 December 1889, in Joubert, *Proposed New Zealand Exhibition*, p.7.
114 James Allen, 'British Empire Exhibition Progress Report No. 3', 18 May 1923, Te Papa Archives Wembley Exhibition files, 1922–33 MU 1 26/15, quoted in McCarthy, 'Objects of Empire?', p.62.
115 *New Zealand's Contribution to the British Empire Exhibition, Wembley*, 1924, p.3.
116 Ibid., p.4.
117 *Souvenir of the New Zealand Pavilion at the British Empire Exhibition*, p.1.

CHAPTER SIX 'PRODUCED BY BRITONS FOR BRITISH HOMES'

1 New Zealand appeared at the 1939 New York World's Fair, with its exhibit rather ambiguously 'included in that of the entire part of the British group but . . . distinctly on its own': R 3 W2476 1922/2177/1, British Empire Exhibition 1929 and others overseas, ANZW.
2 Annual Reports of the Empire Marketing Board, 1927–28, 1928–29, 1929–30, cited in Anandi Ramamurthy, *Imperial Persuaders: Images of Africa and Asia in British Advertising*, Manchester, 2003, p.133.
3 Leiss, Kline and Jhally, *Social Communication in Advertising*, pp.279–84.
4 For a recent exception, see Ian Hunter, *Age of Enterprise: Rediscovering the New Zealand Entrepreneur, 1880–1910*, Auckland, 2007, pp.165–99.
5 Invoice to the NZ Meat Producers Board, 8 March 1934, A5 144 23/59 2, ANZW.
6 Some preferences already existed: Canada introduced the first for UK exports in 1897. See A. S. Thompson, 'Tariff Reform: An Imperial Strategy, 1903–1913', *The Historical Journal*, Vol. 40, No. 4, 1997, pp.1033–54; L. L. Witherill, 'Sir Henry Page Croft and the Conservative Backbench Campaigns for Empire, 1903–1932', *Parliamentary History*, Vol. 25, Pt 3, 2006, pp.357–81.
7 These have been co-opted into narratives of dominion economic nationalism, especially in Australia. For a summary, see Bernard Attard, 'The Limits of Influence: The Political Economy of Australian Commercial Policy After the Ottawa Conference', *Australian Historical Studies*, Vol. 29, No. 111, 1998, pp.325–43.
8 Belich, *Replenishing the Earth*, p.470.
9 Darwin, *The Empire Project*, p.443.
10 Disputes were sharpest where these roles were to be curbed; in the case of the dominions, protecting their fledgling secondary industries against established British manufacturing; in Britain's case, to protect the remainder of their agriculture against dominion output.
11 *The Times*, 27 May 1882, p.11.
12 New Zealand Meat Producers Board, *Annual Report and Statement of Accounts, 1922–23*, Wellington, 1923, p.8.
13 NZ Meat Producers Board, *Annual Report and Statement of Accounts, 1931*, Wellington, 1931, n.p.; Critchell and Raymond, *A History of the Frozen Meat Trade*, p.209.
14 NZ Meat Producers Board, *Annual Report and Statement of Accounts, 1930*, Wellington, 1930, p.12.
15 Michael French and Jim Phillips, 'Sophisticates or Dupes? Attitudes towards Food Consumers in Edwardian Britain', *Enterprise and Society*, Vol. 4, No. 3, 2003, p.467. Adulteration issues in Victorian advertising are discussed in Lori Anne Loeb, *Consuming Angels: Advertising and Victorian Women*, New York, 1994, pp.111–15.
16 French and Phillips, 'Sophisticates or Dupes?', p.461.

17 Ibid., p.465.
18 NZ Meat Producers Board, *Annual Report and Statement of Accounts, 1938*, Wellington, 1938, p.10.
19 NZ Meat Producers Board, *Annual Report and Statement of Accounts, 1930*, p.12.
20 For a discussion of Sunlight Leagues, and the association of sunshine and health, see Caroline Daley, *Leisure and Pleasure: Reshaping and Revealing the New Zealand Body, 1900–1960*, Auckland, 2003, pp.126–43.
21 French and Phillips, 'Sophisticates or Dupes?', p.444.
22 Notes from the Imperial Conference, 1930, and Annual Report of the Empire Marketing Board, p.5, EA 1 154/4/15 part I, ANZW.
23 'Message to the Shopping Public', *The Times*, 20 October 1926, p.9.
24 NZ Meat Producers Board, *Annual Report and Statement of Accounts, 1931*, p.8.
25 NZ Meat Producers Board, *Annual Report and Statement of Accounts, 1935*, Wellington, 1935, p.8. Newspaper advertisements also stressed that Canterbury lamb was branded New Zealand.
26 NZ Meat Producers Board, *Annual Report and Statement of Accounts, 1932*, Wellington, 1932, p.8.
27 Cross promotion was not uncommon: the New Zealand stand at the Royal Agricultural Show was devoted to tourism and sport: *NZH*, 29 February 1931, p.5. In order to give those figures some sense of scale, total advertising expenditure in Britain in 1928 was £57 million, almost double that spent in 1920: Stephen Constantine, *Buy and Build: The Advertising Posters of the Empire Marketing Board*, London, 1986, p.4.
28 Ibid., p.9.
29 Ibid., p.9.
30 NZ Meat Producers Board, *Annual Report and Statement of Accounts, 1935*, p.9.
31 NZ Meat Producers Board, *Annual Report and Statement of Accounts, 1937*, p.8. From 1931, point of sale material was only made available to retailers who obtained certification as a genuine New Zealand lamb stockist: see NZ Meat Producers Board, *Annual Report and Statement of Accounts 1932*, p.10.
32 NZ Meat Producers Board, *Annual Report and Statement of Accounts, 1932*, p.10.
33 NZ Meat Producers Board, *Annual Report and Statement of Accounts, 1934*, Wellington, 1934, p.7.
34 Ibid., p.7; NZ Meat Producers Board, *Annual Report and Statement of Accounts 1939*, Wellington, 1939, p.10.
35 NZ Meat Producers Board, *Annual Report and Statement of Accounts 1934*, p.7. Arthur Marwick provides circulation figures for the estimates of the eight national dailies at 10,280,000: see Arthur Marwick, 'Print, Pictures and Sound: The Second World War and the British Experience', *Daedalus*, Vol. 3, No. 4, 1982, p.136.
36 Leiss, Kline and Jhally, *Social Communication in Advertising*, p.284.
37 The most detailed overview is Arthur Ward, *A Command of Cooperatives: The Development of Leadership, Marketing and Price Control in the Cooperative Dairy Industry of New Zealand*, Wellington, 1975.
38 Hunter, *Age of Enterprise*, p.195; pp.184–5.
39 David M. Higgins and Mads Mordhorst, 'Reputation and Export Performance: Danish Butter Exports and the British Market, c.1880–c.1914', *Business History*, Vol. 50, No. 2, 2008, p.185.
40 Belich, *Replenishing the Earth*, p.447.
41 Ward, *A Command of Cooperatives*, p.56.
42 NZ Dairy Produce Control Board, *Second Annual Report and Statement of Accounts, 1926*, Wellington, 1926, p.9.
43 NZ Dairy Produce Control Board, *Third Annual Report and Statement of Accounts, 1927*, Wellington, 1927, p.9.
44 Ibid. There were 1913 such cartons.
45 New Zealand Dairy Industry Commission, *1934 New Zealand Dairy Industry Commission presented to both Houses of the General Assembly by command of His Excellency*, New Zealand, 1934, p.34.
46 NZ Dairy Produce Control Board, *Third Annual Report and Statement of Accounts, 1927*, p.10.
47 *NZ Dairy Exporter*, 19 December 1931, p.13.
48 *The Times*, 17 December 1930, p.6.
49 *NZ Dairy Exporter*, 30 January 1932, p.12.
50 *NZ Dairy Exporter*, 11 November 1931, p.9.

51 New Zealand Dairy Industry Commission, *1934 New Zealand Dairy Industry Commission*, New Zealand, 1934, p.34.
52 *NZ Dairy Exporter*, 30 January 1932, p.18.
53 *NZ Dairy Exporter*, 29 May 1930, p.40.
54 *NZ Dairy Exporter*, 30 January 1932, p.18.
55 *NZ Dairy Exporter*, 27 March 1930, p.8.
56 Richard Wolfe, *Well Made New Zealand*, Auckland, 1987, p.8, p.45.
57 For a discussion of the development of the sailor, patriotism and imperialism in melodrama and music hall, see Penny Summerfield, 'Patriotism and Empire: Music Hall Entertainment 1870–1914', in MacKenzie (ed.), *Imperialism and Popular Culture*, pp.17–48.
58 See Stephen Constantine, '"Bringing the Empire Alive": The Empire Marketing Board and Imperial Propaganda, 1926–33', in MacKenzie (ed.), *Imperialism and Popular Culture*, pp.192–231.
59 *The New Zealand Farmer Stock and Station Journal*, 1 March 1930, p.311.
60 Belich, *Replenishing the Earth*, p.451.
61 'Message to the Shopping Public', *The Times*, 20 October 1926, p.9.
62 The Board spent £426,879 on posters: Constantine, *Buy and Build*, p.5. Another £277,771 was spent on shopping weeks and exhibitions and a further £326,280 on press advertising, amongst other activities: Constantine, '"Bringing the Empire Alive"', pp.205–7. Crawford was the managing director of one of the two largest advertising agencies in Britain, and Pick was responsible for the marketing and publicity of the London Underground.
63 I. M. Drummond, *British Economic Policy and the Empire, 1919–1939*, London, 1972, p.67.
64 *The Times*, 2 June 1930, p.15. Constantine suggests prices and prevailing trends may have been more important explanations for the change. To this we might add the work of organisations such as the NZ Meat Producers Board that, as we have seen, linked their sales-oriented approaches to the more general publicity provided by the EMB: see Constantine, *Buy and Build*, pp.15–17.
65 Empire Marketing Board Report, 17 October 1930, Economic Affairs, Imperial trade, Empire Marketing Board 1930–31, EA1 154/4/15 part 1, ANZW.
66 Minutes of Poster Sub-committee, 28 August 1930, p.2, CO 760/26, Public Records Office (PRO), National Archives, Britain.
67 Ibid.
68 Constantine, *Buy and Build*, p.17.
69 Ibid., pp.15–17.
70 For a comparative study of dominion and dependent empire images, see F. Barnes, 'Bringing Another Empire Alive? The Empire Marketing Board and the Construction of Dominion Identity, 1926–33', *NZJH*, forthcoming, 2012.
71 This EMB campaign was intended to promote New Zealand honey sales.
72 *The Times*, 10 January 1927, p.18.
73 Ibid., 15 July 1927, p.13.
74 'Map of New Zealand', MacDonald Gill, CO 956/302, PRO.
75 I will exempt at this point the 'kiwi' poster, which is discussed later.
76 CO 956/348, PRO.
77 *The Times*, 8 November 1926, p.11.
78 *The Times*, 8 June 1927, p.11.
79 Minutes of Poster Sub-committee, 30 June 1927, p.1, CO 760/26, PRO.
80 Ibid.; Ramaurthy, *Imperial Persuaders*, pp.134–5; Constantine, '"Bringing the Empire Alive"', p. 211.
81 Constantine, *Buy and Build*, p.6.
82 *NZ Dairy Exporter*, 26 July 1930, p.8; CO 956/148, PRO.
83 'New Zealand Serves Our Tables', H. S. Williamson, CO 956/147, PRO.
84 'British Cloth in New Zealand', H. S. Williamson, CO 956/145, PRO.
85 New Zealand Dairy Industry Commission, *1934 New Zealand Dairy Industry Commission*, p.69.
86 '1928 Export of Frozen Mutton and Lamb From NZ to UK', CO 956/146, PRO.
87 'Empire Buying Makes Busy Factories', Keith Henderson, CO 956/181–186, PRO.
88 Two New Zealand artists were considered: E. Heber Thompson and R. Wallwork, but neither was commissioned. Carlton Studios might possibly have had 'dominion' artists working there, but other works are completed by named artists: see *NZH*, 14 January 1932, p.11.

89 Mike Cronin, 'Selling Irish Bacon: The Empire Marketing Board and Artists of the Free State', Éire-Ireland, No. 39, Vol. 3 and 4, Fall/Winter, 2004, p.136. Some Irish posters were designed by Irish artists, and Cronin suggests they attempted to subvert what he describes as some of 'the basic tenets of an EMB art of racial stereotyping': see p.138.
90 *The Times*, 20 October 1926, p.9.
91 CO 956/2, PRO.
92 *The Times*, 13 December 1926, p.21.
93 *The Times*, 1 May 1930, p.8.
94 *The Times*, 14 February 1927, p.18.
95 *The Times*, 22 December 1926, p.9.
96 Constantine, *Buy and Build*, p.13.
97 *The Times*, 7 February 1927, p.13.
98 David Meredith, 'Imperial Images: The Empire Marketing Board 1926–32', *History Today*, January 1986, p.33. The most detailed discussion of orientalism in EMB poster art is in Ramamurthy, *Imperial Persuaders*, pp.131–72.
99 Marilyn Lake shows the Australian frontier as a disorderly masculine arena that feminists sought to domesticate and civilise. Whilst women were important in creating the shift, the farm was still imaged as a masculine domain: see Marilyn Lake, 'Australian Frontier Feminism and the Marauding White Man', in Clare Midgley (ed.), *Gender and Imperialism*, Manchester and New York, 1998, pp.123–36.
100 Meredith, 'Imperial Images', p.33. For the creation of a 'dominion discourse' in empire marketing: see Barnes, 'Bringing another Empire Alive?'.
101 Inspectors' Report on Retail Display Material, Retail Grocers Sub-committee, EMB, 8 November 1928, p.1, CO 760/26, PRO.
102 'Buy South African Dried Fruit, Buy New Zealand Lamb', F. C. Herrick, CO 956/61, PRO.
103 *The New Zealand Farmer Weekly*, 17 August 1939, p.23.
104 *NZ Dairy Exporter*, 25 July 1931, p.25.
105 *NZH*, 28 December 1931, p.4; it was also reported on 24 December 1931, p.6.
106 *NZH*, 14 November 1932, p.11; also 15 January 1932, p.11; 16 January 1932, p.7.
107 *NZ Dairy Exporter*, 1 August 1932, n.p.
108 His initiative became New Zealand's first national broadcaster, the Radio Broadcasting Company of New Zealand.

CHAPTER SEVEN LONDON'S IMAGINATIVE HINTERLAND

1 The first official broadcast took place at 9.30 pm, 19 December 1932, and was available via shortwave. Shortwave receivers were not readily available in New Zealand at this time, hence the rebroadcasting.
2 K. Inglis, *This is the ABC: The Australian Broadcasting Commission, 1932–1983*, Melbourne, 1983, p.33.
3 *The Times*, 14 March 1935, p.17.
4 Simon J. Potter, 'Who Listened When London Called? Reactions to the BBC Empire Service in Canada, Australia and New Zealand, 1932–1939', *Historical Journal of Film, Radio and Television*, Vol. 28, No. 4, 2008, pp.475–6.
5 There is some literature reviewing the BBC and its links to empire, although these works largely address the impact of empire upon the metropole. See Thomas Hajowski, 'The BBC, the Empire, and the Second World War, 1939–45', *Historical Journal of Film, Radio and Television*, Vol. 22, No. 2, 2002, pp.135–55; John MacKenzie, 'In Touch With the Infinite: The BBC and the Empire, 1923–53', in MacKenzie (ed.), *Imperialism and Popular Culture*, pp.165–91; Sián Nicholas, 'Brushing Up Your Empire', in Bridge and Fedorowich, *The British World*, pp.207–30.
6 Peter Hall, *Cities in Civilization: Culture, Innovation and Urban Order*, London, 1998, p.514; see Harold Innis, *Empire and Communication*, Oxford, 1950; also Harold Innis, *The Bias of Communication*, Toronto, 1951.
7 Sinclair, *A Destiny Apart*, p.61.
8 The idea of an imperial press system comes from Potter's detailed analysis, *News and the British World*, p.33.

9 *EP*, 28 May 1937, p.11.
10 Quoted in Asa Briggs, *The BBC: The First Fifty Years*, Oxford, New York, 1985, p.140.
11 For London's earlier central role, see Zoë Laidlaw, *Colonial Connections, 1815–1845: Patronage, the Information Revolution and Colonial Government*, Manchester and New York, 2005.
12 Graeme Johanson, *Colonial Editions in Australia, 1843–1972*, Wellington, 2000, p.58. Most of the information about colonial editions used here is sourced from Graeme Johanson's work. There is no comparable study for New Zealand, so the present study assumes a certain amount of similarity across the two markets. This, while not ideal, is not unreasonable, particularly as, in the early years of the trade, British publishers considered this an Australasian market.
13 Ibid., p.227.
14 *Statistics for the Colony of New Zealand, 1860*, Table 28. There are no general circulation or readership figures available for this period. However, postal records enumerate the quantities of newspapers posted and received. These are not the same thing, but provide a compromised, indicative proxy.
15 Johanson, *Colonial Editions*, p.1, p.287.
16 Ibid., p.104.
17 *The Colonial Librarians' Handbook*, London 1912, advertisement inserted between pages 76 and 77, quoted in ibid., p.13.
18 Johanson, *Colonial Editions*, p.74.
19 Belich, *Paradise Reforged*, p. 86.
20 *Statistics of the Colony of New Zealand, 1886*, Import Table; *New Zealand Official Year Book*, 1931, p.313.
21 Patrick Day, *Radio Years: A History of Broadcasting in New Zealand*, Vol. 1, Auckland, 1994, p.21.
22 H. Mark Glancy, *When Hollywood Loved Britain: The Hollywood 'British' Film*, Manchester, 1999, p.9.
23 Cronon, *Nature's Metropolis*, p.333.
24 Bell, 'Dissolving Distance', p.531.
25 Ibid., p.554, p.528.
26 Chandrika Kaul (ed.), *Media and the British Empire*, Houndmills, 2006, pp.3–5. See also Potter, *News and the British World*.
27 G. O'Hara, 'New Histories of British Imperial Communication and the "Networked World" of the 19th and Early 20th Centuries', *History Compass*, Vol. 8, No. 7, 2010, pp.614–15.
28 Denis Cryle, 'The Empire Press Union and Antipodean Communications: Australian-New Zealand Involvement 1909–1950', *Media History*, Vol. 8, No. 1, 2002, p.60, p.187; and Ross Harvey, 'Bringing the News to New Zealand: The Supply and Control of Overseas News in the Nineteenth Century', *Media History*, Vol. 8, No. 1, 2002, pp.21–34.
29 Miles Fairburn, 'Is There a Good Case for New Zealand Exceptionalism?', in Tony Ballantyne and Brian Moloughey (eds), *Disputed Histories: Imagining New Zealand's Pasts*, Otago, 2006, fn.54, p.262.
30 *New Zealand Official Year Book, 1938*, p.260.
31 Gordon and Gotch, *Gordon and Gotch (Australasia Ltd) Centenary, 1853–1953*, Melbourne, 1953, n.p. Of the remaining volumes, 562 came from the United Kingdom and Europe and 352 were Australasian titles. The thirty-two American titles were distributed only in New Zealand, as bulk importation into Australia was banned due to postwar currency issues.
32 Ibid.
33 Johanson, '"Cultural Cringe" or Cultural Fringe', pp.78–79.
34 Chris Bourke, *Blue Smoke: The Lost Dawn of New Zealand Popular Music, 1918–1964*, Auckland, 2010, pp.155–7.
35 Griffen-Foley, '"The Crumbs are Better than a Feast Elsewhere"', p.30. Griffen-Foley's quotation refers to Australians, but as Potter has shown, is equally applicable to the other white dominions: see Potter, *News and the British World*, pp.16–27.
36 Patricia L. Garside, 'Representing the Metropolis: The Changing Relationship between London and the Press, 1870–1939', *The London Journal*, Vol. 16, No. 21, 1991, p.157.
37 Inglis, *This is the ABC*, p.26.
38 Belich, *Paradise Reforged*, p.253.
39 Paddy Scannel and David Cardiff, *A Social History of Broadcasting: Vol. 1, 1922–1939, Serving the Nation*, Oxford, Cambridge, 1991, p.16.

40 *The Times*, 18 January 1933, p.8. See also Asa Briggs, *The History of Broadcasting in the United Kingdom: Vol. 2, The Golden Age of Wireless*, Oxford, 1965, p.384.
41 Day, *The Radio Years*, p.164.
42 *New Zealand Spectator and Cook's Straits Guardian*, 7 December, 1844, quoted in Patrick Day, *The Making of the New Zealand Press, 1840-1880: A Study of the Organisational and Political Concerns of New Zealand Newspaper Controllers*, Wellington, 1990, p.61.
43 Harvey, 'Bringing the News to New Zealand', p.22.
44 Ibid., p.30.
45 *Statistics for the Colony of New Zealand, 1878*; Table of Newspapers Posted, p.161.
46 Harvey, 'Bringing the News to New Zealand', p.25.
47 G. H. Scholefield, *Newspapers in New Zealand*, Wellington, 1958, p.8. This figure includes the sizeable run of the *Otago Daily Times*.
48 See Day, *The Making of the New Zealand Press*.
49 Jeb Byrne, 'The Comparative Development of Newspapers in New Zealand and the United States in the Nineteenth Century', *American Studies International*, Vol. 37, No. 1, 1999, p.57. Day puts its circulation as high as 7000, but notes that it also suffered when goldfield populations declined.
50 Figures drawn from *Statistics for the Colony of New Zealand*, the *New Zealand Official Year Book* and G. T. Bloomfield, *New Zealand: A Handbook of Historical Statistics*, Boston, 1984. Formats for collation change. These per capita statistics cannot be related to Scholefield's earlier figure of twenty-nine per head: see Scholefield, *Newspapers in New Zealand*, Wellington, 1958. The relevant postal-based figure would be around nine papers per head.
51 Scholefield, *Newspapers in New Zealand*, p.6.
52 Day, *The Making of the New Zealand Press*, p.159.
53 Ibid., p.173.
54 Ibid., p.201.
55 Ibid., p.6.
56 Figures drawn from *Statistics for the Colony of New Zealand*, the *New Zealand Official Year Book* and Bloomfield, *New Zealand: A Handbook of Historical Statistics*.
57 Scholefield, *Newspapers in New Zealand*, p.23.
58 Ibid., p.22.
59 Ibid.
60 Harvey, 'Bringing the News to New Zealand', p.21.
61 Lucy Brown, *Victorian News and Newspapers*, Oxford, 1985, p.124, quoted in ibid.
62 Brown, *Victorian News and Newspapers*, p.96.
63 R. B. O'Neill, *The Press 1861-1961: The Story of a Newspaper*, Christchurch, 1963, p.97.
64 Potter, *News and the British World*, p.28. See also John Lambert, 'South Africa's English Language Press and Imperialism', in Kaul (ed.), *Media and the British Empire*, pp.37–54.
65 Harvey, 'Bringing the News to New Zealand', p.31.
66 Garside, 'Representing the Metropolis', p.160, p.170.
67 Ibid., pp.160–1.
68 Ibid., pp.161–9.
69 Potter, *News and the British World*, p.29.
70 O'Neill, *The Press*, pp.147–9.
71 Press agency rules allowed newspapers to continue to receive their own mailed, not cabled news.
72 The NZPA replaced the older press association: James Sanders, *Dateline NZPA: The New Zealand Press Association, 1880–1980*, Auckland, 1979, pp.129–30. An Australian correspondent was required after the Reuters service was discontinued in 1887: ibid., p.24. A San Francisco agent was paid on a per letter basis till 1908, when the steamer service ended. 'It does not appear to have been missed greatly': ibid., p.40. Australian press correspondents were in Washington from 1941: see Griffen-Foley, '"The Crumbs are Better than a Feast Elsewhere"', p.33.
73 *New Zealand Parliamentary Debates*, Vol. 42, 1882, pp. 108, quoted in Byrne, 'The Comparative Development of Newspapers in New Zealand', p.66.
74 Cryle, 'The Empire Press Union and Antipodean Communications', pp.50–51. This cheaper access to overseas news may have contributed to the peak of daily papers noted in 1910.
75 Potter, *News and the British World*, p.156.
76 For a discussion of the importance of cable news access to even relatively minor papers, see Ross

Harvey, 'A "Sense of Common Citizenship?" Mrs Potts of Reefton, New Zealand, Communicates with the Empire', in Kaul (ed.), *Media and the British Empire*, pp.190–204.
77 NZPA Archive, box 70, 'United Press Association of New Zealand Ltd, Annual Meeting of shareholders at Rotorua, 23 February 1910', quoted in Potter, *News and the British World*, p.33.
78 Potter, *News and the British World*, p.91. Reuters returned in 1916: see Sanders, *Dateline NZPA*, p.51.
79 Potter, *News and the British World*, p.33.
80 Ibid., p.156.
81 A Canadian news service was founded by the *Argus* in 1910, but it is unclear how much news was sourced from it: see Potter, *News and the British World*, p.157. In 1930 it was described as 'scanty and irregular': see Cryle, 'The Empire Press Union and Antipodean Communications', p.52.
82 Sanders, *Dateline NZPA*, p.45.
83 H. Benbow, '"I Like New Zealand Best"', p.67.
84 Cryle, 'The Empire Press Union and Antipodean Communications', p.51.
85 Empire Press Union, New Zealand section, *Annual Meetings*, Auckland, 1931, p.13, quoted in ibid.
86 Brown, *Victorian News and Newspapers*, p.99.
87 Cryle, 'The Empire Press Union and Antipodean Communications', p.52.
88 H. L. Verry, 'Onboard the SS Tairoa', p.29, Horace Leslie Verry Papers, MS-Papers-6811, ATL, quoted in Benbow, '"I Like New Zealand Best"', p.34.
89 Griffen-Foley, '"The Crumbs are Better than a Feast Elsewhere"', p.26. Her study includes some New Zealand journalists.
90 Potter, *News and the British World*, p.21.
91 O'Neill, *The Press*, p.147.
92 The same phenomenon has been noted in the case of radio after World War II: see Simon J. Potter, 'Strengthening the Bonds of the Commonwealth: The Imperial Relations Trust and Australian, New Zealand and Canadian Broadcasting Personnel in Britain, 1946–52', *Media History*, Vol. 11, No. 3, 2005, pp.193–205.
93 *AS*, 16 August 1940, p.6.
94 Malcolm Smith, *Britain and 1940: History, Myth and Popular Memory*, London, 2000, p.68.
95 Michael King, *The Penguin History of New Zealand*, Auckland, 2003, p.402. See also Belich, *Paradise Reforged*, p.273: 'New Zealanders in the RAF were 90% aircrew ... they made up about 5% of the British aircrew total.'
96 *AS*, 20 September 1940, p.3.
97 *AS*, 19 August 1940, p.7; 16 August 1940, p.7; 20 August 1940.
98 *NZH*, 11 September 1940, p.9; 27 September 1940, p.7.
99 *AS*, 18 September 1940, p.7.
100 *AS*, 10 September 1940, p.7.
101 Smith, *Britain and 1940*, p.84.
102 O'Neill, *The Press*, p.218. Its competitor, the *Sun*, had been publishing them daily since 1914.
103 *AS*, 16 September, p.5.
104 *The Weekly News* (*WN*), 18 September 1940, pp.38–39.
105 *The Press*, 31 October 1940, p.10.
106 *AS*, 21 September 1939, pp.6–7.
107 Ibid., p.7.
108 *WN*, 25 September 1940, p.29.
109 *AS*, 20 September 1940, p.6.
110 *NZH*, 12 October 1940, p.12.
111 *AS*, *Enzed Junior*, Vol. VII, No. 6, 26 October 1940, p.1.
112 *NZH*, 23 October 1940, p.9.
113 *NZH*, 20 September 1940, p.7.
114 *AS Weekend Pictorial*, 18 October 1940, p.3.
115 *NZH*, 21 August 1940, p.11.
116 *AS*, 2 August 1940, p.8.
117 *NZH*, 4 September 1940, p.6.
118 *AS*, 26 September 1940, p.20.
119 *AS*, 16 October 1940, p.8.
120 *NZH*, 18 September 1940, p.6.

121 *The Press*, 20 September 1940, p.3.
122 *AS*, 17 September 1940, p.8.
123 *NZH*, 19 September 1940, p.8.
124 *NZH*, 18 September 1940, p.6.
125 *AS*, 16 September 1940, p.7; *The Press*, 20 September 1940, p.3.
126 *Woman's Weekly* (*WW*), 19 September 1940, p.1.
127 *NZH*, 23 September 1940, p.6.
128 *AS*, 26 September 1940, p.16.
129 *NZH*, 26 September 1940, p.16.
130 Nancy Taylor, *The Home Front*, Vol. 1, *Official History of New Zealand in the Second World War, 1939–1945*, Wellington, 1986, p.150.
131 Ibid., p.153.
132 *AS*, 11 May 1940, p.6.
133 An advertisement for the appeal listed the following purposes: 'Grants to hospitals for mobilisation camps – fortress troops and air force stations – seamen of the Royal Navy, Auxiliaries and Mercantile Marine – troopships – ambulance transport – hospital ships – hospital and convalescent stores – aftercare of sick and disabled etc – Grants overseas to British and Allied Red Cross': *AS*, 16 May 1940, p.22.
134 *NZH*, 15 January 1941, p.12.
135 The *AS* ran a photo on 2 February 1940, p.5, captioned 'From a Stove to a Spitfire', showing British donations of aluminium pots and pans.
136 *EP*, 5 December 1940, p.14.
137 *EP*, 12 July 1940, p.5.
138 *EP*, 5 December 1940, p.14.
139 *NZH*, 9 September 1940, p.6.
140 *NZH*, 14 September 1940, p.6.
141 *AS*, 17 September 1940, p.7.
142 *AS*, 20 September 1940, p.3.
143 *AS*, 18 September 1940, p.7.
144 *AS*, 16 September 1940, p.7.
145 Taylor, *The Home Front*, p.162. Her figure of £30,000 for the Auckland province does not tally with the totals from the two newspaper appeals.
146 *AS*, 24 October 1940, p.11; *NZH*, 12 October 1940, p.12.
147 *NZH*, 1 October 1940, p.8.
148 *NZH*, 27 September 1940, p.6.
149 *AS*, 5 October 1940, p.10; *NZH*, 27 September 1940, p.6; *AS*, 23 September 1940, p.9.
150 *AS*, 27 September 1940, p.8.
151 Ibid.
152 *AS*, 12 October 1940, p.6.

CHAPTER EIGHT HOME MOVIES

1 Jonathan Dennis, *Aotearoa and the Sentimental Strine: Films in Australia and New Zealand in the Silent Period*, Wellington, 1993, p.6.
2 *National Education* (*NE*), 1 September 1941, p.281.
3 Dennis, *Aotearoa and the Sentimental Strine*, p.6. In my research, contemporary newspapers refer to street scenes in Leeds, but the programme did vary from screening to screening.
4 Kern, *The Culture of Time and Space*, p.88.
5 Hall, *Cities in Civilization*, p.504.
6 Voice of America did not begin until 1942.
7 Glancy, *When Hollywood Loved Britain*. His study of the feature film market forms the base for these comments.
8 Foreign in this case is dominated by English-speaking countries. Britain and the dominions had over 8000 cinemas in 1938. Russia, by contrast, had 30,000, but did not import American films; and Germany, which had 6500 cinemas, only imported 1,548,689 feet of film compared with Britain's 13,620,160 feet in 1933: Glancy, *When Hollywood Loved Britain*, p.69, pp.8–9.

9 Ibid., pp.8–9, p.20.
10 Ibid., p.28.
11 Nerida J. Elliot, 'Anzac, Hollywood and Home: Film-going in Auckland, 1909–1939', MA thesis, University of Auckland, 1989, p.99. One source makes Mrs Louise Hayward the driving force behind the change: see B. W. and S. P. Hayward, *Cinemas of Auckland, 1896–1976*, Auckland, 1979, p.10.
12 Wayne Brittenden, *The Celluloid Circus: The Heyday of the New Zealand Picture Theatre, 1925–1970*, Auckland, 2008, p.124.
13 See John Sedgewick, 'Cinema-going Preferences in Britain in the 1930s', in Jeffrey Richards (ed.), *The Unknown 1930s: An Alternative History of the British Cinema, 1929–1939*, London, 1998, pp.1–36.
14 *AJHR*, 1934, H-44A, p.17.
15 St James Scrapbook, n.d., AML.
16 Figures from *AJHR*, 1949, Vol. IV, 1–17, p.7, quoted in Elliot, 'Anzac, Hollywood and Home', p.175. A similar rise occurs in Australian screenings: see Mike Walsh, 'Tackling the Big Boy of Empire: British Film in Australia, 1918–1931', in Andrew Higson (ed.), *Young and Innocent: The Cinema in Britain 1896–1930*, Exeter, 2002, p.280.
17 Les Cleveland, 'What They Liked: Movies and Modernity Downunder', *Journal of Popular Culture*, Vol. 36, No. 4, 2003, pp.764–5. A number were made by Herbert Wilcox's British and Dominion Films, so the concentration here may reflect distribution patterns. These too often had a hybrid, British/American character, and are worthy of further study: see R. Low, *The History of British Film, Vol. VII: The History of British Film 1929–1939*, rev. edn, London, 1997, pp.143–50.
18 James Chapman and Nicholas J. Cull, *Projecting Empire: Imperialism and Popular Cinema*, London, 2009, p.7.
19 Glancy, *When Hollywood Loved Britain*, p.96, pp.70–71.
20 Ibid., p.3.
21 Ibid., p.75.
22 Ibid., p.3.
23 Colin McArthur, 'Chinese Boxes and Russian Dolls: Tracking the Elusive Cinematic City', in David B. Clarke (ed.), *The Cinematic City*, London, 1997, p. 34.
24 Ibid., pp.34–35. Author P. L. Travers eventually entrusted to Disney the work of recreating her stories on film, the result of which she was at best ambivalent about. Travers was the quintessential colonial expatriate, starting her writing career as a journalist, writing for the Christchurch *Sun* and the *Triad*, before moving to London.
25 Jeffry Richards, 'Boy's Own Empire: Feature Films and Imperialism in the 1930s', in MacKenzie (ed.), *Imperialism and Popular Culture*, p.162. For imperial films generally, see Chapman and Cull, *Projecting Empire*.
26 Glancy, *When Hollywood Loved Britain*, p.131.
27 Gordon Mirams, *Speaking Candidly: Film and People in New Zealand*, Hamilton, 1945, p.91.
28 Ibid., p.96.
29 Kathryn H. Fuller, *At the Picture Show: Small-town Audiences and the Creation of a Movie Fan Culture*, Washington, London, 1996, p.77.
30 Initially suggested at 50 per cent: it was set at 20 per cent.
31 Paul Swann, *The British Documentary Film Movement, 1926–1946*, Cambridge, 1989, p.125.
32 *AJHR*, 1934, H-44A, p.17.
33 *AJHR*, 1934, H-44A, p.3.
34 Mirams, *Speaking Candidly*, p.131.
35 Figures from *AJHR*, 1949, Vol. IV, 1–17, p.7, quoted in Elliot, 'ANZAC, Hollywood, and Home', p.175.
36 Rachael Low, *The History of British Film, 1929–1939: Films of Comment and Persuasion of the 1930s*, London, 1979, p.6.
37 *AJHR*, 1934, H-44A, p.25.
38 St James Scrapbook, AML.
39 *AJHR*, 1934, H-44A, p.3.
40 Swann, *The British Documentary Film Movement*, p.72.
41 Mirams, *Speaking Candidly*, p.195.
42 *AS*, 9 January 1941, p.24.

43 The films considered in detail were either held by the New Zealand Film Archive, or listed in New Zealand National Film Library, *Catalogue of Sound and Silent 16mm Cinematograph Films*.
44 Low, *The History of British Film*, p.76.
45 *London's Free Shows*, Wonderful London series, Graham Wilcox Productions, 1924, BFI NFTVA Non-fiction Collection.
46 'Rambler', *Biorama Ramblings*, n.p., n.d., p.10, New Zealand Film Archive (NZFA). See also Chris Pugsley, 'The Magic of Moving Pictures: Filmmaking 1895–1918', in Dianne Pivac, Frank Stark and Lawrence McDonald (eds), *New Zealand Film: An Illustrated History*, Wellington, 2011, pp.35–38.
47 Pugsley, 'The Magic of Moving Pictures', p.14.
48 'London Types' is numbered 103 in the *Seeing London* series.
49 Low, *The History of British Film*, p.3.
50 Ibid.
51 Ibid., p.6.
52 British Film Institute, *Monthly Film Bulletin*, Vol. 2, No. 14, March 1935, p.17.
53 Swann, *The British Documentary Film Movement*, pp.34–35.
54 James Chapman, *The British at War: Cinema, State and Propaganda, 1939–1945*, London and New York, 1998, p.2.
55 Rex Leeper, 'British Culture Abroad', *The Contemporary Review*, No, 148, 1935, pp.201–7.
56 Ibid.
57 Speech by Lord Derby, 20 December 1929, Board of Trade, BT 61/54/2 (*Department of Overseas Trade*) DOT E14888, quoted in Philip Taylor, *British Propaganda in the Twentieth Century*, Edinburgh, 1999, p.75.
58 Enclosed memorandum in L. A. de L. Meredith to R. Kenney, 1/8/29, FO 395/435, P1140/178/150, quoted in Taylor, *British Propaganda in the Twentieth Century*, p.75.
59 *London Can Take It! War and Order* and *Christmas under Fire* had general exhibition in New Zealand: *EP*, 12 November 1049, p.9; *EP*, 14 April 1941, p.2; *EP*, 7 February 1941, p.2.
60 *Morning Paper*, Gaumont British Instructional, 1942.
61 Ibid.
62 *London Scrapbook*, Spectator Short Films, 1942.
63 An 8-minute film, *The Mother of Parliaments*, 1934, was available in New Zealand but no copies remain in either the BFI NFTVA Non-fiction Collection, or the New Zealand Film Archive.
64 *London off the Track*, Wonderful London series, 1924, BFI NFTVA Non-fiction Collection.
65 *London on Parade*, Tourist and Industrial Development Association (TIDA), 1937, BFI NFTVA Non-fiction Collection.
66 *For All Eternity*, TIDA, 1933, BFI NFTVA Non-fiction Collection.
67 *St Paul's Cathedral*, 1943, Merton Park Productions, NZFA.
68 Ibid.
69 Ibid.
70 *Wonderful London, London – Old and New*, Graham Wilcox Productions, 1924, BFI NFTVA Non-fiction Collection.
71 *Wonderful London, Dickens' London*, Graham Wilcox Productions, 1924, BFI NFTVA Non-fiction Collection.
72 *City Bound*, Spectator Short Films, 1941, BFI NFTVA Non-fiction Collection.
73 *Night Mail*, General Post Office/Grierson group, 1936, BFI NFTVA Non-fiction Collection.
74 Cronon, *Nature's Metropolis*, p.364.
75 'Rambler', *Biorama Ramblings*, p.10.
76 *Wonderful London, Sidelights of London*, Graham Wilcox Productions, 1924, BFI NFTVA Non-fiction Collection.
77 *Wonderful London, Cosmopolitan London*, Graham Wilcox Productions, 1924, BFI NFTVA Non-fiction Collection.
78 *So This Is London*, TIDA, 1933, BFI NFTVA Non-fiction Collection.
79 *London Town*, Dir. Marion Grierson, TIDA, 1933, BFI NFTVA Non-fiction Collection.
80 British Film Institute, *Monthly Film Bulletin*, Vol. 1, No. 1, February, 1934, p.2.
81 This footage was used in *London*, TIDA, 1933; *London Town*, TIDA, 1932; *So This is London*, TIDA, 1933; *City of Progress*, Realist Film Unit, 1941; and *London River*, TIDA, 1939: all BFI NFTVA Non-fiction Collection.

82 *London On Parade*, TIDA.
83 *Heart of an Empire*, TIDA, 1935, BFI NFTVA Non-fiction Collection.
84 *AJHR*, 1905, E1-B, p.11.
85 Wiatr, 'Between Word, Image and the Machine', p.336.
86 Correspondence, Wanganui Board of Education, E2/1945/24e 29/16, Miscellaneous, Visual Instruction in Schools, Lantern Slides and Proposed Schemes, ANZW.
87 *AJHR*, 1911, E-1, p.13.
88 *AJHR*, 1908, E-1, pp.xxii–xxiii.
89 *AJHR*, 1909, E-1, p.9.
90 *AJHR*, 1911, E-1, p.13.
91 *AJHR*, 1912, E-1, p.14. Other related topics included cards of Cook and Nelson, and twenty of HMS *New Zealand*, while nature study topics used New Zealand flora. See also E. P. Malone, 'The New Zealand School Journal and the Imperial Ideology', *NZJH*, Vol. 7, No. 1, April 1973, pp.12–27; R. Openshaw, 'Patriotism and the New Zealand Primary School: The Decisive Years of the Twenties', DPhil thesis, University of Waikato, 1978; and Colin McGeorge, 'Learning About God's Own Country', *New Zealand Journal of Educational Studies*, Vol. 18, No. 1, 1983, pp.3–12.
92 For a discussion of moral anxiety about children and films, see Roy Shuker and Roger Openshaw, 'New Zealand Youth and Silent Movies', *New Zealand Journal of Educational Studies*, Vol. 22, No. 1, 1987, pp.87–99; see also Elliot, 'Anzac, Hollywood, and Home', pp.126–9.
93 *AJHR*, 1918, E-1, p.x.
94 Ibid.
95 *AJHR*, 1911, E-2, p.xxxi.
96 *Statistics of New Zealand*, 1910.
97 *New Zealand Education Gazette (NZEG)*, Vol. 7, No. 6, 1 June 1928, p.95.
98 *NZEG*, Vol. X, No. 10, 1 October 1931, p.171. Concerns about speech in children were long-standing, galvanising efforts to preserve 'English' characteristics in New Zealand speech: see Colin McGeorge, 'Hear Our Voices We Entreat: Schools and the "Colonial Twang", 1880–1930', *NZJH*, Vol. 18, No. 1, April 1984, pp.3–18.
99 Elizabeth Wiatr, 'Between Word, Image and the Machine: Visual Education and Films of the Industrial Process', *Historical Journal of Film, Radio and Television*, Vol. 22, No. 3, 2002, p.334.
100 *AJHR*, 1905, E1-A, p.44; *New Zealand Journal of Education (NZJE)*, 15 June 1908, p.119.
101 Education Department, *Syllabus of Instruction for Public Schools*, Wellington, 1929, p.156.
102 Ibid., p.159.
103 The *Education Gazette* also records a 'private scheme, but now up and running in Auckland, directed by Mr. D. D. McDonald. In conjunction with his enterprise, Mr. McDonald has issued free to Auckland schools a little magazine entitled "Our Journal". This magazine contains suitable lessons on the pictures he is providing. Some lessons of this kind have already appeared in the School Journal': see Vol. 2, No. 4, 1923, pp.37–38.
104 *NZEG*, Vol. XI, no. 5, 2 May 1932, p.67.
105 New Zealand National Film Library, *Catalogue of Sound and Silent 16mm Cinematograph Films*, Wellington, 1945, p.61.
106 Ibid., p.53.
107 Correspondence, Thorndon Normal School, 12 August 1926, E2/1945/24e 29/16, Miscellaneous, Visual Instruction in Schools, Lantern Slides and Proposed Schemes.
108 New Zealand National Film Library, *Catalogue of Sound and Silent 16mm Cinematograph Films*, p.46.
109 Ibid., p.6.
110 Ibid., p.8.

CHAPTER NINE LONDON'S LEGACY

1 R. Boyd Bell, *New Zealand Television: The First Twenty-Five Years*, Auckland, 1985 p.71.
2 Ashley Gorringe, 'Consol[ing] Vision? Aspects of Early New Zealand Television Audiences, 1960–1975', MA thesis, University of Auckland, 2002, p.3.
3 Ibid.
4 Boyd Bell, *New Zealand Television*, p.75.

5   The title 'Malls of Ivy' is given in ibid., but this seems to be an error: see L. Simmons, 'Television Then', in R. Horrocks and N. Perry (eds), *Television in New Zealand: Programming the Nation*, South Melbourne, 2004, p.44. For hybrid television, see Michele Hilmes, 'The North Atlantic Triangle', *Media History*, Vol. 16, No. 1, 2010, p.42.
6   *TV Radio Mirror*, August 1955, at http://ronaldcolmanarchives.net, accessed 19 September 2011. See also www.imdb.com/title/tt0046606/.
7   COI films were used by the BBC's television service: see Tom Wildy, 'British Television and Official Film, 1946-1951', *Historical Journal of Film, Radio and Television*, Vol. 8, No. 2, pp.195-202. Details of this film are held at the British Film Archive, COI/6DB, accessed at http://www.bfi.cambridgeimaging.co.uk/, 19 September 2011.
8   Hannah Weinstein joined other Americans in England to escape the McCarthy era's blacklists: Rebecca Prime, '"The Old Bogey": The Hollywood Blacklist in Europe', *Film History: An International Journal*, Vol. 20, No. 4, 2008, p.475; Steve Neale, 'Pseudonyms, Sapphire and Salt: "Un-American" Contributions to Television Costume Adventure Series in the 1950s', *Historical Journal of Film, Radio and Television*, Vol. 23, No. 3, 2003, p.247.
9   See Geoff Lealand, *A Foreign Egg in Our Nest? American Popular Culture in New Zealand*, Wellington, 1988.
10 See Miles Fairburn, 'Is There a Good Case for New Zealand Exceptionalism', pp.143-67; Peter Gibbons, 'The Far Side of the Search for Identity: Reconsidering New Zealand History', *NZJH*, Vol. 37, No. 1, 2003, p.38-49.
11 Trisha Dunleavy, *Ourselves in Primetime: A History of New Zealand Television*, Auckland, 2005.
12 Jonathan Easthope, 'Home Away from Home: The Recent History of Overseas Travel by New Zealanders to Britain, c.1960-1975', History Honours Research Paper, 1993, Victoria University of Wellington, p.10.
13 *WW*, 27 June 1977, p.28.
14 *Truth*, 23 September 1953, p.20, in Gorringe, 'Consol[ing] Vision?', p.17.
15 *NZ Listener*, 27 November 1953, p.24, in ibid., p.16.
16 New Zealand Parliamentary Debates (NZPD), 1957, 312, p.1116, in ibid., p.17.
17 NZPD, 1957, 311, p.116, in ibid., p.16.
18 Patrick Day, *Voice and Vision: A History of Broadcasting in New Zealand*, Vol. II, Auckland, 2000, p.53. The NZBC eventually subsidised costs.
19 B. Paulu, *Television and Radio in the United Kingdom*, Minnesota, 1981, p.170.
20 Day, *Voice and Vision*, p.30.
21 Boyd Bell, *New Zealand Television*, p.40.
22 Day, *Voice and Vision*, p.54.
23 Ibid., p.359.
24 Simmons, 'Television Then', p.54.
25 Day, *Voice and Vision*, p.115.
26 Personal communication with Tom Finlayson, 1 October 2011.
27 Personal communication with Tom Finlayson, 21 September 2011.
28 Gabriella MacLeod, 'Television in Auckland', *Comment*, Vol. 2, No. 3, pp.14-15, in Simmons, 'Television Then', p.58.
29 John Tebbutt, 'News From Asia', *Media History*, Vol. 17, No. 3, p.293. Reuters was added in 1967.
30 Edmunds TX1448, Radio New Zealand Sound Archives, quoted in Day, *Voice and Vision*, p.73.
31 Linda Kaye, 'Reconciling Policy and Propaganda: The British Overseas Television Service, 1954-64', *Historical Journal of Film, Radio and Television*, Vol. 27, No. 2, p.216.
32 Obituary, *NZH*, 10 January 2004, http://www.nzherald.co.nz/nz/news/article.cfm?c_id=1&objectid=3542786, accessed 14 October 2011.
33 The decision to send them was made in 1986: see Day, *Voice and Vision*, p.359.
34 Boyd Bell, *New Zealand Television*, p.28.
35 Day, *Voice and Vision*, p.118.
36 Boyd Bell, *New Zealand Television*, p.48.
37 Interview, Des Monaghan, 4 August 2011.
38 Boyd Bell, *New Zealand Television*, pp.81-82.
39 R. Horrocks, 'The History of New Zealand Television', in Horrocks and Perry, *Television in New Zealand*, p.28.

40 Roger Horrocks identifies the period 1989–95 as one of commercial broadcasting counterbalanced by NZ On Air, then 1995–99 as a period of dominant commercialism: see ibid., p.26.
41 Correspondence, Masius to Television New Zealand, September 1979–March 1980: Beecham NZ Limited AAANJ W2598 979 1, ANZW.
42 Dunleavy, *Ourselves in Primetime*, p.6.
43 Interview, Des Monaghan, 4 August 2011.
44 Day, *Voice and Vision*, p.57.
45 It also reflects a concern that the non-commercial radio station ratings would be too low compared with commercial stations: ibid., pp.146–7.
46 Figures are percentage share of available viewers.
47 DDAV D57, Box 1b, Audience Research, All New Zealand Television, September–October 1976, ANZ (Dunedin).
48 Ibid.
49 Ibid. In any case the government was shutting TV down early because of a winter power crisis: ibid., p.6.
50 Ibid. Afternoon slots are generally lower rating: the point here is not that they underperformed in a time slot, but that overall, their impact was diluted.
51 The only Western included was *High Chaparral*. *New Zealand Heritage*, Vol. 7, No. 104, p.2888.
52 Ibid.
53 It is important to note that SPTV had only main centre coverage this point. TV1 was the only option for those outside these areas. This underlines the lower penetration of American shows, but not necessarily their potential popularity.
54 DAAV D57, Box 1 b.
55 Dunleavy, *Ourselves in Primetime*, p.77.
56 Day, *Voice and Vision*, p.249.
57 Ibid., p.246.
58 Dunleavy, *Ourselves in Primetime*, p.128.
59 DAAV D57, Box 1 ak, Audience Research, All New Zealand Television, September 1980, ANZ (Dunedin.)
60 Ibid.; DAAV D57, Box 1 al, Audience Research, All New Zealand Television, October 1980, ANZ (Dunedin).
61 DAAV D57, Box 1 ak, Audience Research, All New Zealand Television, September 1980, ANZ (Dunedin).
62 Ibid.
63 There is some conflict between sources, though. Day (*Voice and Vision*, p.359) gives British shows a slight advantage in 1986, while Lealand's analysis differs.
64 Patrick Day, 'Cultural Imperialism in New Zealand', *Journal of Sociology*, Vol. 11, No. 43, 1975, p.43.
65 *NZ Listener*, May 3, 1975, p.10.
66 Lealand, *A Foreign Egg in Our Nest?*, pp.40–41. Australian programming remained marginal on New Zealand screens for the first twenty years as it was too expensive.
67 DAAV D57, Box 1 b, Audience Research, All New Zealand Television, September–October 1976; DAAV D57, Box 2 f, Audience Research, All New Zealand Television, September 1981, ANZ (Dunedin).
68 Interview, John Macready, August 2011.
69 For the borrowing of American culture in Australia, see Ann McGrath, 'Playing Colonial: Cowgirls, Cowboys and Indians in Australia and North America', *Journal of Colonialism and Colonial History*, Vol. 2, No. 1, 2001, pp.1–24.
70 T. Dunleavy, 'The Genre of Television Drama', in Horrocks and Perry, *Television in New Zealand*, p.205.
71 Dunleavy, *Ourselves in Primetime*, p.27.
72 *NZ Listener*, 5 September 1969 p.3, quoted in Dunleavy, *Ourselves in Primetime*, p.31.
73 Boyd Bell, *New Zealand Television*, p.124; Dunleavy, *Ourselves in Primetime*, p.42.
74 Christine Cole Catley, 'TV Drama in New Zealand', *Landfall*, Vol. 27, No. 1, 1973, pp.43–44, quoted in Dunleavy, *Ourselves in Primetime*, p.42.
75 Proportion of People Living in Urban and Rural Areas 1886–2001 Censuses of Population and Dwellings, http://www.stats.govt.nz/browse_for_stats /people_and_communities/ geographic-areas/urban-rural-profile/historical-context.aspx, accessed 27 September 2010.

76 Dunleavy, *Ourselves in Primetime*, p.51.
77 *NZ Listener*, 10 May 1975, p.16.
78 Interview, Des Monaghan, 4 August 2011.
79 DAAV D57, Box 1 ak, Audience Research, All New Zealand Television, September 1980, ANZ (Dunedin).
80 Dunleavy, *Ourselves in Primetime*, p. 114.
81 Graham Ford, 'Willis Street Blues', *NZ Listener*, 25 August 1984, pp.81–82, in Dunleavy, *Ourselves in Primetime*, p.162.
82 Dunleavy, *Ourselves in Primetime*, p.34.
83 Day, *Voice and Vision*, p.237.
84 Dunleavy *Ourselves in Primetime*, p.77.
85 Ibid., pp.104–8.
86 Ibid., p.166.
87 Horrocks, 'Construction Site: Local Content on Television', in Horrocks and Perry, *Television in New Zealand*, p.280; Dunleavy, *Ourselves in Primetime*, p.5.
88 Day, *Voice and Vision*, p.109; Horrocks, 'Construction Site', p.281.
89 British televised drama benefited from a long experimental phase; a small, elite audience; the best West End actors; and massive volumes – some 326 plays over two and a half years: see Neil Robson, 'Living Pictures Out of Space: The Forlorn Hopes for Television in Pre-1939 London', *Historical Journal of Film, Radio and Television*, Vol. 24, No. 2, 2004, pp.224–7.
90 Dunleavy, *Ourselves in Primetime*, p.18.
91 Boyd Bell, *New Zealand Television*, p.108.
92 Day, *Voice and Vision*, p.64.

EPILOGUE **LONDON REVISITED**

1 Ministry of Culture and Heritage, *The New Zealand Memorial*, Wellington, 2006, p.18.
2 Ibid., p.3.
3 KEA New Zealand, *Every Kiwi Counts 2011: Research on New Zealanders Living Offshore*, 2011, http://www.keanewzealand.com/sites/default/files/Every_Kiwi_Counts_2011_Kea_NZ_final.pdf, accessed 7 December 2011.
4 *Southland Times*, 9 July 2005, p.6.
5 For a full discussion, see Felicity Barnes, 'War "Zones": The Metropolis and New Zealand, 1940 and 2005', *History Compass*, Vol. 3, 2005, pp.1–8.
6 *Herald on Sunday*, 10 July 2005, p.A28.
7 *NZH*, 9 July 2005, p.A2
8 www.greatbeerdelivery.co.nz
9 www.greatbeerdelivery.co.nz, video, accessed 23 October 2007.
10 Ministry of Economic Development Key Tourism Statistics, 22 November 2011, http://www.tourismresearch.govt.nz/Data--Analysis/Key-Statistics/, accessed 5 December 2011.
11 http://www.newzealand.com/int/article/best-day-out-in-auckland/, accessed 7 December 2011.
12 Only 53 per cent of these were processed: Statistics New Zealand, *Global New Zealand – International Trade, Investment and Travel Profile*, Year Ended June 2011, Wellington, 2011, p.2.

SELECT BIBLIOGRAPHY

ARCHIVAL AND UNPUBLISHED SOURCES

Archives New Zealand (ANZ)
AAANJ W2598 979 1, Correspondence, Masius to Television New Zealand, September 1979–March 1980.
DAAV D57 Box 1 ak, Audience Research All New Zealand Television, September 1980.
DAAV D57 Box 1 al, Audience Research All New Zealand Television, October 1980.
DAAV D57 Box 1 b, Audience Research, All New Zealand Television, September–October 1976.
EA 1 3/2/2 Pt 2, Accounts – Estimates and Financial Statements.
EA 1 55/3/12 Pt 1a, Handbook for New Zealand Visitors to London.
EA 1 61/201/18 Pt 1a, Appreciation and Complaints.
EA 1 62/201/37 Pt 1, Reports on Inspection of the High Commission.
EA 1 62/201/44, Regulations Relating to High Commission.
EA 1 151/1/13, Commonwealth Affairs.
EA 1 152/1/4, British Empire.
EA 1 154/4/16 Pt 1, Importation of Books.
EA 1 154/4/15 Pt 1, Economic Affairs – Imperial Trade – Empire Marketing Board 1930–31.
E2/1945/24e 29/16, Miscellaneous, Visual Instruction in Schools, Lantern Slides and Proposed Schemes.
G 13 Box 6, 39, 16/8/1886, Letter Indian and Colonial Exhibition.
IA 10/1/1, New Zealand Section, British Empire Exhibition Wembley, London, 1924.
IA 25 Box 6, Colonial and Indian Exhibition, 1886.
IA 25 Box 29, Papers of the British and Intercolonial Exhibition, 1923–24.
IC 10/2/2, Photographs of New Zealand Pavilion, Stands and Exhibits, 1925.
IC 10/3/3, Photographs of New Zealand Pavilion, Photographs of Exhibits, 1925–1926.
PM 16/1, Jordan/Savage, Jordan/Fraser.
R 3 W2476 1922/2177/1, British Empire Exhibition 1929 and Others Overseas.

Alexander Turnbull Library (ATL)
Bell, Sir Francis, Papers, MS Papers 5210.
Campbell, R. M., Papers, MS Papers 1900.
Chief Cashier's Records Policy Files, Bank of England Archive Report, Micro-MS-Coll-20-2925.
Corpus, L., Collection, MS Papers 1628.
Ford, Harold M., Papers, Micro-Ms-Coll-20-2995-3032.
Hall Jones, Sir William, MS Papers 5755.
Heenan, Sir J. W. A., Collection, MS Papers 1132.
Mackenzie, Sir Clutha, MS Papers 3532.
Mackenzie, Sir Thomas, MS Papers 3922.
McIntosh, Sir A. D., Papers, MS Papers 6759.
New Zealand's Contribution to the British Empire Exhibition, 1924.
New Zealand's Contribution to the British Empire Exhibition, 1925.
Pageant of Empire, Wembley, 1924, MS Papers 2977.
Penrose-Fitzgerald, Isabel, MS Papers 6882-4.
Roberts, Sir A. F. Collection, MS Papers 1693.
Seddon Family Collection, MS Papers 1619-213.

Auckland Museum Library (AML)
Brown, M. G., Papers, MS 1176.
Campbell, David Henry, Papers, MS 2003/110.
Cherry, Clara Edwards, Papers, MS 823.
Chester, Stan, Papers, MS 1046.
Clark, Frank, Papers, MS 98/8.

SELECT BIBLIOGRAPHY

Cook, Ella, Papers, MS 94/36.
Cranwell, B. E., Papers, MS 91/15.
Davison, Fred, Papers, MS 2002/43.
Dredge, E. V., Papers, MS 99/22.
Gill, H., Papers, MS 1130.
Gordon, C. M., Papers, MS 90/77.
Grierson, H. C., Papers, MS 92/22.
Hewson, L. C., Papers, MS 89/158.
Johns, W. H., Papers, MS 1392.
Keesing, H. W., Papers, MS 2003/124.
Kerridge Odeon Archive, MS 98/39.
Larnach, M. J., Papers, MS 1355.
Law, J. O., Papers, MS 90/20.
Le Gallais Family, Papers, MS 95/11.
Luxford, G. V., Papers, MS 94/6.
Martin, M., Papers, MS 92/24.
McKenzie, James, Papers, MS 1701.
McNeish, A. W., Papers, MS 696.
Nicklin, E., Papers, MS 1173.
Picturedrome Theatre Milford Records, MS 432.
Richardson, George S. Album 413.
Scott, R., Papers, MS 1671.
Spedding, E. C., Papers, MS 960.
Spencer, F. A., Papers, MS 91/31.
St James Theatre Scrapbook, MS 91/20.
Varnham, F. S., Papers, MS 2002/62.
Williams, P. G., Papers, MS 89/210.

Auckland Public Library (APL)
Jordan, Sir William, Unfinished Notes, NZMS 1027.
Mander, Jane, Papers, NZMS 535.
Mulgan, Alan, Papers, NZMS 748.
Non-Fiction Lending Records, 1916–1917.

New Zealand Film Archive (NZFA)
Diamond Jubilee, 1897.
Firefighters, Pathescope, 1941.
From England to New Zealand, 1920.
London Streets for Edward VII, 1902.
Movietone News – New Zealanders Overseas, 1936.
News Parade of the Year, 1939.
Night Mail, GPO Film Unit/Grierson Group, 1936.
Parade of Guardsmen, 1898.
'Rambler', *Biorama Ramblings*, n.p., n.d.
Seeing London, No. 103, (Types) (probably Burton Holmes), n.d.
Seeing London No. 11, Burton Holmes, 1931.
Sir Robert J. Kerridge Theatre Album, MA 216070.
Sir Robert Kerridge Album, 0520.
St Paul's Cathedral, Merton Park Productions, 1943.

British Film Institute National Film and Television Archive, Non-fiction Collection (BFINFTVA, Non-fiction Collection)
Christmas Under Fire, Crown Film Unit, 1941.
City Bound, Spectator Short Films, 1941.
City of Progress, Realist Film Unit, 1941.
Come Again, Crown Film Unit, 1943.
England Awake, British Instructional Films, 1932.

SELECT BIBLIOGRAPHY

Farmers' Day, Selwyn Films, 1940.
Farm Factory, Gaumont British Instructional, 1935.
For All Eternity, TIDA, 1934.
Island People, Realist Film Unit, 1940.
New Britain, Strand Film Company, 1940.
Heart of an Empire, TIDA, 1935.
Heart of Britain, Crown Film Unit, 1941.
Lights o' London, TIDA, 1938.
London, TIDA, 1933.
London, 1942, Greenpark Productions, 1943.
London Can Take It! General Post Office, 1940.
London on Parade, TIDA, 1937.
London River, British Films, 1939.
London Scrapbook, Spectator Short Films, 1942.
London Town, Empire Marketing Board Film Unit, 1933.
Lowland Village, Gaumont British Instructional, 1942.
Market Town, Gaumont British Instructional, 1942.
Morning Paper Gaumont British Instructional, 1942.
Royal and Ancient City of Canterbury, Religious Films, 1936.
So This is London, TIDA, 1933.
The Londoners, Realist Film Unit, 1939.
They Met In London, Paul Rotha Productions, 1941.
War and Order, General Post Office Film Unit, 1940.
Wonderful London, Graham Wilcox Productions, c.1920
    Along Father Thames to Shepperton
    Barging through London
    Cosmopolitan London (1924)
    Derby Day
    Dickens' London
    Flowers Of London
    Known London
    London's Contrasts
    London Off the Track
    London Old and New
    London's Free Shows
    London's Outer Ring
    London's Sunday
    Snapshots of London
    Unknown London
    Wonders of Westminster
World Garden, Spectator Short Films, 1941.

National Archives, United Kingdom (NA)
CO 760/26 Dominions Office: Empire Marketing Board Minutes and Papers, 1926–33.
CO 956, Empire Marketing Board Poster Series, 1926–39.
CO 956/2 'The Dairies of New Zealand', Dora Batty.
CO 956/3 'Dairy Factory New Zealand', F. C. Herrick.
CO 956/61 'Buy South African Dried Fruits, Buy New Zealand Lamb', F. C. Herrick.
CO 956/112 'Buy New Zealand Lamb, Buy British West Indian Arrowroot', F. C. Herrick.
CO 956/145 'British Cloth in New Zealand', H. S. Williamson.
CO 956/146 '1928 Exports of Frozen Mutton and Lamb from NZ to UK'.
CO 956/147 'New Zealand Serves Our Tables', H. S Williamson.
CO 956/229 'Empire Marketing Board to NZ Meat Producer Board', Carlton Studio.
CO 956/230 'Empire Marketing Board to NZ Honey Producer Board', Carlton Studio.
CO 956/231 'Empire Marketing Board to NZ Dairy Producer Board', Carlton Studio.
CO 956/232 'Empire Marketing Board to NZ Fruit Board', Carlton Studio.
CO 956/233 'Empire Marketing Board to NZ Dairy Producer Board', Carlton Studio.

SELECT BIBLIOGRAPHY

CO 956/234 'Ask for the Produce of New Zealand'.
CO 956/279 'Apples from New Zealand', V. Polunin.
CO 956/290 'Always Empire Butter', Frank Newbould.
CO 956/302 'Map of New Zealand', MacDonald Gill.
CO 956/303 'Wool', Frank Newbould.
CO 956/304 'Mutton Lamb Apples', Frank Newbould.
CO 956/305 'Honey', Frank Newbould.
CO 956/306 'Butter and Cheese', Frank Newbould.
CO 956/307 'Buy New Zealand Produce'.
CO 956/322 'Buy New Zealand Produce'.
CO 956/328 'Buy New Zealand Produce'.
CO 956/348 'A Contract For New Zealand'.
CO 956/349 'Orders For New Zealand'.
CO 956/477 'Lamb and Mutton'.
CO 956/479 'Imported Meat'.
CO 956/525 'A Map of NZ.', MacDonald Gill.
CO 956/528 'Sheep Raising', G. Brown.
CO 956/592 'Buy NZ Products', F. C. Herrick.
CO 956/669 'Buy NZ Apples'.
CO 956/712 'Canadian Tobacco, Australian Vines, NZ Milking Machines, South African Maize'.

University of Auckland (UOA)
Cocker, W. H., Papers, MSS and Archives A-7.
Fairburn, A. R. D., Letters 1932–41, MSS and Archives A-123.
Franklin, Miles, MSS and Archives 89/3, 89/5.
Jordan, William, Papers, MSS and Archives A-178.
Lyttleton, Edith, MSS and Archives 89/2, 89/3.
Peacocke, I. M., MSS and Archives 94/5.
Spragg Family Papers, MSS and Archives A-264.

Private collection
Donnelly Family Papers.
Journal of Adolph Feist, 1926.
Journal of Murray Feist, 1926.

Newspapers, Periodicals and Official Publications
Appendices to the Journals of the House of Representatives
Auckland Star
The British Australasian
Bulletin of the Imperial Institute, 1900–1945
Chronicles of the N.Z.E.F.
Monthly Film Bulletin (British Film Institute)
National Education
New Zealand Dairy Exporter
New Zealand Education Gazette
New Zealand Farmer Stock and Station Journal
The New Zealand Farmer Weekly
New Zealand Herald
New Zealand Journal of Agriculture
New Zealand Journal of Education
New Zealand Official Yearbook
The New Zealand Woman's Weekly
The Press
Statistics for the Colony of New Zealand
The Times
The Triangle Trail: Troopship-Training Camp-Trench: The New Zealand YMCA on Active Service.
The Weekly News

SELECT BIBLIOGRAPHY

BOOKS, CHAPTERS, ARTICLES AND THESES

Alessio, Dominic David, 'Domesticating "the Heart of the Wild": Female Personifications of the Colonies, 1886–1940', *Women's History Review*, Vol. 6, No. 2, 1997, pp.239–70.

Allison, Ewen William, *A New Zealander Sees the World*, Auckland, 1937.

Allwood, John, *The Great Exhibitions*, London, 1977.

Alomes, Stephen, *When London Calls: The Expatriation of Australian Creative Artists to Britain*, Cambridge, New York, 1999.

Anderson, Benedict, *Imagined Communities: Reflections on the Origins and Spread of Nationalism*, rev. edn, London, New York, 1991.

Armstrong, Meg, '"A Jumble of Foreignness": The Sublime Musayums of Nineteenth Century Fairs and Expositions', *Cultural Critique*, No. 23, (Winter 1992–1993), pp.199–250.

Arnold, Dana, ed., *Cultural Identities and the Aesthetics of Britishness*, Manchester, 2004.

Arthur, Paul, 'Antipodean Myths Transformed: The Evolution of Australian Identity', *History Compass*, Vol. 5, No. 6, 2007, pp.862–78.

Ashcroft, Bill, Gareth Griffiths, and Helen Tiffin, eds, *The Empire Writes Back: Theory and Practice in Post-Colonial Literatures*, London 1989.

Attard, Bernard, 'The Limits of Influence: the Political Economy of Australian Commercial Policy After the Ottawa Conference', *Australian Historical Studies*, Vol. 29, No. 111, 1998, pp.325–43.

August, Thomas G., *The Selling of Empire: British and French Imperialist Propaganda, 1890–1940*, Westport, 1985.

August, Tom, 'Art and Empire: Wembley, 1924', *History Today*, Vol. 43, October, 1993, pp.38–45.

Baedeker, Karl, *London and its Environs: Handbook for Travellers*, 1908.

Baker, Paul, *When King and Country Call: New Zealanders, Conscription and the Great War*, Auckland, 1988.

Ballantyne, Tony, and Brian Moloughney, *Disputed Histories: Imagining New Zealand's Pasts*, Dunedin, 2006.

Barker, Francis, Peter Hulme, and Margaret Iversen, eds, *Colonial Discourse, Post-colonial Theory*, Manchester 1994.

Barrowman, Rachel, *Mason: The Life of R. A. K. Mason*, Wellington, 2003.

Barrowman, Rachel, *A Popular Vision: The Arts and the Left in New Zealand, 1930–1950*, Wellington, 1991.

Bassett, Judith, 'A Thousand Miles of Loyalty: The Royal Tour of 1901', *NZJH*, Vol. 21, No. 2, 1987, pp.125–38.

Bassett, Michael, *Coates of Kaipara*, Auckland, 1995.

Bassett, Michael, *Sir Joseph Ward: A Political Biography*, Auckland, 1993.

Bassett, Michael, *Three Party Politics in New Zealand, 1911–1931*, Auckland, 1982.

Bassett, Michael, and Michael King, *Tomorrow Comes the Song: A Life of Peter Fraser*, Auckland, 2000.

Bateman, W., *The Colonist: A Work on the Past And Present Position of the Colony of New Zealand*, Christchurch, 1881, facsimile edn,1998.

Baucom, Ian, *Out Of Place: Englishness, Empire, and the Locations of Identity*, Princeton, 1999.

Baumgarten, Murray, 'Imperial London: Dickens, Nationalism and Urban Possibility', *History of European Ideas*, Vol. 16, No. 1–3, 1993, pp.13–22.

Bayley, C. A., *The Birth of the Modern World, 1780–1914: Global Connections and Comparisons*, Oxford, 2003.

Bean, C. E. W., *The ANZAC Book*, London, 1916.

Belich, James, *Making Peoples: A History of the New Zealanders from Polynesian Settlement to the End of the Nineteenth Century*, Auckland, 1996.

Belich, James, *Paradise Reforged: A History of the New Zealanders from the 1880s to the Year 2000*, Auckland, 2001.

Belich, James, *Replenishing the Earth: The Settler Revolution and the Rise of the Anglo-World, 1783–1939*, Oxford, 2009.

Bell, Duncan, 'Dissolving Distance: Technology, Space and Empire in British Political Thought, 1770–1900', *Journal of Modern History*, Vol. 77, No. 3, 2005, pp.523–62.

Bell, Leonard, *Colonial Constructs: European Images of Maori, 1840–1914*, Auckland, 1992.

Benbow, Hannah-Lee, '"I Like New Zealand Best": London Correspondents for New Zealand Newspapers, 1884–1942', MA Thesis, University of Canterbury, 2009.

SELECT BIBLIOGRAPHY

Benedict, Burton, 'International Exhibitions and National Identity', *Anthropology Today*, Vol. 7, No. 3, 1991, pp.5–9.
Benson, John, and Gareth Shaw, *The Retailing Industry: Volume Two, The Coming of the Mass Market 1800–1945*, London, New York, 1999.
Bertram, James, *Flight of the Phoenix: Critical Notes on New Zealand Writers*, Wellington, 1985.
Blackman, J., 'The Development of the Retail Grocery Trade in the Nineteenth Century', in Benson, John and Gareth Shaw, eds, *The Retailing Industry: Volume Two, The Coming of the Mass Market, 1800–1945*, London, 1999, pp.61–67.
Bolitho, Hector, *My Restless Years*, London, 1962.
Bolitho, Hector, *Thirty Years*, Auckland, 1947.
Bolitho, Hector, *War in the Strand*, London, 1942.
Bones, Helen, 'A Dual Exile? New Zealand and the Colonial Writing World, 1890–1945', PhD thesis, University of Canterbury, 2011.
Bornholdt, Jenny, Gregory O'Brien, and Mark Williams, eds, *An Anthology of New Zealand Poetry in English*, Auckland, 1997.
Borrie, W. D., *Immigration to New Zealand, 1854–1938*, Canberra, 1991.
Bourke, Chris, *Blue Smoke: The Lost Dawn of New Zealand Popular Music 1918–1964*, Auckland, 2010.
Boyack, Nicholas, *Behind the Lines: The Lives of New Zealand Soldiers in the First World War*, Wellington, 1989.
Boyack, Nicholas, and Jane Tolerton, *In the Shadow of War: New Zealand Soldiers Talk about World War One and Their Lives*, Auckland, 1990.
Brace, Catherine, 'Looking Back: The Cotswolds and English National Identity, c.1890–1950', *Journal of Historical Geography*, Vol. 25, No. 4, 1999, pp.502–16.
Brangwyn, F., E. V. Lucas, and S. Pryse, *Pageant of Empire*, London, 1924.
Brasch, Charles, *Indirections*, Wellington, 1980.
Brewer, John and Roy Porter, eds, *Consumption and the World of Goods*, London, New York, 1993.
Brewer, N. H. (Joe), *The Soldier Tourist: A Personal Account of World War II*, Auckland, 1999.
Bridge, Carl, and Kent Fedorowich, *The British World: Diaspora, Culture and Identity*, London, 2003.
Bridge, Carl, and Kent Fedorowich, 'Mapping the British World', *Journal of Imperial and Commonwealth Studies*, Vol. 31, No. 2, 2003, pp.1–15.
Bright, Michael, 'Macaulay's New Zealander,' *The Arnoldian*, No. 10, Winter, 1982, pp.8–27.
Briggs, Asa, *The BBC: The First Fifty Years*, Oxford, 1985.
Briggs, Asa, *The History of Broadcasting in the United Kingdom: Vol. 2, The Golden Age of Wireless*, Oxford, 1965.
Britton, S., '"Come and See the Empire by the All Red Route!": Anti-imperialism and Exhibitions', *History Workshop Journal*, No. 69, 2010, pp.68–89.
Brown, Lucy, *Victorian News and Newspapers*, Oxford, 1985.
'Buckshee', *A Pictorial Record of the Work of the NZ YMCA On Active Service*, London, 1919.
Buckner, Phillip A., ed., *Canada and the End of Empire*, Vancouver, 2005.
Buckner, Phillip A., and R. Douglas Francis, *Canada and the British World: Culture, Migration and Identity*, Vancouver, 2006.
Burdon, R. M., *The New Dominion: A Social and Political History of New Zealand, 1918–1939*, Wellington, 1965.
Burton, Antoinette, ed., *After the Imperial Turn: Thinking With and Through the Nation*, Durham and London, 2003.
Burton, Antoinette, *At the Heart of Empire: Indians and the Colonial Encounter in Late-Victorian Britain*, Berkeley, 1998.
Burton, Antoinette, ed., *Gender, Sexuality and Colonial Modernities*, London and New York, 1999.
Burton, Antoinette 'Making a Spectacle of Empire: Indian Travellers in Fin-de-siècle London', *History Workshop Journal*, No. 42, 1996, pp.126–46.
Burton, O. E., *The Silent Division: New Zealanders at the Front, 1914–1919*, Sydney, 1935.
Butterworth, Susan, *The Department of Education, 1877–1989: A Guide to its Development*, Wellington, 1993.
Byrne, Jeb, 'The Comparative Development of Newspapers in New Zealand and the United States in the Nineteenth Century', *American Studies International*, Vol. 37, No. 1, 1999, pp.55–70.
Byrnes, Giselle, 'A Dead Sheet Covered With Meaningless Words? Place Names and the Cultural Colonization of Tauranga', *NZJH, Vol.* 36, No.1, 2002, pp.18–35.

SELECT BIBLIOGRAPHY

Byrnes, Giselle, ed., *The New Oxford History of New Zealand*, South Melbourne, 2009.
Callister, Sandra, *The Face of War: New Zealand's Great War Photography*, Auckland, 2008.
Campbell, W. S., *The Overseas Soldier's Guide to London*, London, c.1916.
Carr, Russell, *Travel Diary of a Young New Zealand Girl*, London, 1927.
Challis, Derek, and Gloria Rawlinson, *The Book of Iris: A Life of Robin Hyde*, Auckland, 2002.
Chapman, James, *The British at War: Cinema, State and Propaganda, 1939–1945*, London and New York, 1998.
Chapman, James, 'Cinemas of Empire', *History Compass*, Vol. 4, No. 5, 2006, pp.814–19.
Cholmondeley, Thomas, *Ultima Thule, or Thoughts Suggested by a Residence in New Zealand*, London, 1854, facsimile edn, Christchurch, 2000.
Clark, Steve, ed., *Travel Writing and Empire: Post-colonial Theory in Transit*, London, 1999.
Clendinning, Anne, 'Exhibiting a Nation: Canada at the British Empire Exhibition, 1924–1925', *Social History*, May, 2006, pp.79–107.
Codell, Julie F., ed. *Imperial Co-Histories: National Identities and the British and Colonial Press*, Madison, 2003.
Colley, Linda, 'Britishness and Otherness: An Argument', *Journal of British Studies*, Vol. 31, No. 4, 1992, pp.309–29.
Colls, Robert, *Identity of England*, Oxford, 2002.
Colls, Robert, and Philip Dodd, *Englishness: Politics and Culture 1880–1920*, London, 1986.
Colonial and Indian Exhibition – Guide to New Zealand Exhibits, London, 1886.
Colonial and Indian Exhibition, Official Catalogue, London, 1886.
Colonial Office, Visual Instruction Committee, *Seven Lectures on the United Kingdom for Use in India, reissued for use in the United Kingdom*, London, 1909.
Condliffe, J. B., *New Zealand in the Making: A Study of Economic and Social Developments*, London, 2nd edn, 1959.
Constantine, Stephen, *Buy and Build: The Advertising Posters of the Empire Marketing Board*, London, 1986.
Cooper, Frederick, *Colonialism in Question: Theory, Knowledge, History*, London and Los Angeles, 2005.
Cox, Geoffrey, *Eyewitness: A Memoir of Europe in the 1930s*, Dunedin, 1999.
Crawford, John, and Ian McGibbon, eds, *New Zealand's Great War: New Zealand, the Allies, and the First World War*, Auckland, 2007.
Critchell, J. T., and J. Raymond, *A History of the Frozen Meat Trade*, London, 1912.
Croad, Nancy, ed., *My Dear Home*, Auckland, 1995.
Cronin, Mike, 'Selling Irish Bacon: The Empire Marketing Board and Artists of the Free State', *Eire Ireland*, Vol. 39, Fall 2004, pp.132–43.
Cronon, William, *Nature's Metropolis: Chicago and the Great West*, New York, London, 1991.
Cryle, Denis, 'The Empire Press Union and Antipodean Communications; Australian-New Zealand Involvement 1909–1950', *Media History*, Vol. 8, No. 1, 2002, pp.49–62.
Daley, Caroline, *Leisure and Pleasure: Reshaping and Revealing the New Zealand Body, 1900–1960*, Auckland, 2003.
Daley, Caroline, and Deborah Montgomerie, *The Gendered Kiwi*, Auckland, 1999.
Dalley, Bronwyn, '"Lolly Shops of the Red Light Kind" and "Soldiers of the King": Suppressing One-Woman Brothels in New Zealand, 1908–1916', *NZJH*, Vol. 30, No. 1, 1996, pp.3–23.
Dalziel, R. M., *The Origins of New Zealand Diplomacy: The Agent General in London, 1870–1905*, Wellington, 1975.
Daniels, Stephen, *Fields of Vision: Landscape Imagery and National Identity in England and the United States*, Oxford, 1994.
Darwin, John, *The Empire Project: The Rise and Fall of the British World System, 1830–1970*, Cambridge, New York, 2009.
Darwin, John, 'A Third British Empire? The Dominion Idea in Imperial Politics' in W. Roger Lewis, ed., *The Oxford History of the British Empire: Vol. IV, The Twentieth Century*, Oxford, New York, 1999, pp.64–87.
Davin, Anna, 'Imperialism and Motherhood', *History Workshop Journal*, Vol. 5, 1968, pp.9–65.
Davis, Donald F., 'The "Metropolitan Thesis" and the Writing of Canadian Urban History', *Urban History Review*, Vol. XIV, No. 2, October, 1985, pp.95–113.
Davis, John K., *The Great Exhibition*, Gloucestershire, 1999.

Day, Patrick, *The Making of the New Zealand Press, 1840–1880: A Study of the Organisational and Political Concerns of New Zealand Newspaper Controllers*, Wellington, 1990.
Day, Patrick, *The Radio Years: A History of Broadcasting in New Zealand*, Vol. 1, Auckland, 1994.
Day, Patrick, *Voice and Vision: A History of Broadcasting in New Zealand*, Vol. 2, Auckland, 2000.
De Groot, Joanna, 'Metropolitan Desires and Colonial Connections: Reflections on Consumption and Empire', in Hall, Catherine, and Sonya O. Rose, eds, *At Home with the Empire: Metropolitan Culture and the Imperial World*, Cambridge, 2006, pp.166–90.
Dennis, Jonathon, *Aotearoa and the Sentimental Strine: Making Films in Australia and New Zealand in the Silent Period*, Wellington, 1993.
Donnelly, Ian, *The Joyous Pilgrimage*, Hertfordshire, 1935.
Drew, H. T. B., *The War Effort of New Zealand: A Popular History of A) Minor Campaigns in which New Zealanders Took Part B) Services Not Fully Dealt With in the Campaign Volumes C) the Work at the Bases*, Auckland, 1923.
Driver, Felix, and David Gilbert, *Imperial Cities: Landscape, Display and Identity*, Manchester, New York, 1999.
Driver, Felix, and David Gilbert, 'Heart of Empire? Landscape, Space and Performance in Imperial London', *Environment and Planning D: Society and Space*, Vol. 16, 1998, pp.11–28.
Duncan, G. A., *The New Zealand Dairy Industry*, Palmerston North, 1933.
Eade, John, *Placing London: From Imperial Capital to Global City*, New York, 2000.
His Excellency the Earl of Liverpool, ed., *The Voyages of His Majesty's New Zealand Hospital Ships 'Marama' and 'Maheno'*, 3rd Volume, Christchurch, 1919.
Easthope, Anthony, *Englishness and National Culture*, London, New York, 1999.
Easthope, Jonathon, 'Home Away from Home: the Recent History of Overseas Travel by New Zealanders to Britain, c.1960–1975', History Honours Research Paper, Victoria University of Wellington, 1993.
Easthope, Jonathon, 'Imaging Ourselves: The Projection of Pakeha Culture Overseas 1870–1925', MA Thesis, Victoria University of Wellington, 1995.
Ebbatson, Roger, *An Imaginary England: Nation, Landscape and Literature, 1840–1920*, Aldershot, 2005.
Eddy, John, and Deryck Schreuder, ed., *The Rise of Colonial Nationalism*, Sydney, 1988.
Edmond, Lauris, ed., *The Letters of A. R. D. Fairburn*, Auckland, 1981.
Education Department, *Geography of the British Isles*, Wellington, 1910–14.
Education Department, *British History in Picture*, Wellington, 1911–12.
Education Department, *Syllabus of Instruction for Public Schools*, Wellington, 1929.
Eggert, Paul, 'Robbery Under Arms: The Colonial Market, Imperial Publishers and the Demise of the Three-Decker Novel, *Book History*, No. 6, 2003, pp.127–46.
Elliot, Nerida J., 'Anzac, Hollywood, and Home: Film-going in Auckland, 1909–1939', MA Thesis, University of Auckland, 1989.
Ellis, Gavin, *Word War: How 125 Years of Newspaper Co-operation was Consigned to History*, Saarbrucken, 2009.
The Empire's Dairy Farm: Covering the Organisation and Activities of the New Zealand Co-operative Dairy Company Limited, the Largest Individual Dairy Company of the British Empire and of the World, 1923–24, Hamilton, 1924.
Empire Marketing Board, *Empire Marketing Board, May 1927–28*, London, 1928.
Empire Marketing Board, *Empire Marketing Board, May 1929–30*, London, 1930.
Empire Marketing Board, *Empire Marketing Board, May 1930–31*, London, 1931.
Empire Marketing Board, *Empire Marketing Board, May 1931–32*, London 1932.
Empire Marketing Board, *Changes in the Demand for Butter: November 1928 and November 1930, Report of an Investigation by the Economic Section of the Empire Marketing Board into the Retail Marketing of Butter in Four Midland Towns*, London, 1931.
Empire Marketing Board, *The Demand for Empire Butter: Report of an Investigation by the Economic Section of the Empire Marketing Board in to the Retail Marketing of Butter in the United Kingdom*, London, 1930.
Evans, B. L., *History of Agricultural Production and Marketing in New Zealand*, Palmerston North, 1969.
Fanning, Leo, *Progressive New Zealand*, Wellington, 1924.
Fanning, Leo, *New Zealand Today*, Dunedin and Wellington, 1925.
Fifty Years Anniversary, 1969: The New Zealand Co-operative Dairy Company Limited, Auckland, 1969.

SELECT BIBLIOGRAPHY

Fine, Ben, and Ellen Leopold, *The World of Consumption*, London, 1993.
Fleming, Philip, 'Fighting the "Red Plague": Observations on the Response to Venereal Disease in New Zealand, 1910-1945', *NZJH*, Vol. 22, No.1, 1988, pp.56-64.
Floud, Roderick, *The People and the British Economy, 1830-1914*, Oxford, 1997.
Floud, Roderick, and Donald McCloskey, eds, *The Economic History of Britain Since 1700: Vol. 2, 1860-1939*, 2nd edn, Cambridge, 1994.
Forrest, Alison, 'Milling Around Outside the Town Hall: Motivation for Enlistment of the First AIF, *Melbourne Historical Journal*, Vol. 18, 1987, pp.97-111.
Fraser, W. H., *The Coming of the Mass Market, 1850-1914*, London, 1981.
French, Michael, and Jim Phillips, 'Sophisticates or Dupes? Attitudes Toward Food Consumers in Edwardian Britain', *Enterprise and Society*, Vol. 4, No. 3, 2003, pp.442-70.
Fuller, Kathryn H., *At the Picture Show: Small-town Audiences and the Creation of a Movie Fan Culture*, Washington, London, 1996.
Galbraith, P. J., 'Colonials in Wonderland: The Colonial Construction of Rotorua as Fantasy Space', MA Thesis, University of Auckland, 1992.
Gare, Deborah, 'Dating Australia's Independence: National Sovereignty and the 1986 Australia Acts', *Australian Historical Studies*, Vol. 113, 1999, pp.251-66.
Garside, Patricia, 'Representing the Metropolis – The Changing Relationship between London and the Press, 1870-1939', *The London Journal*, Vol. 16, No. 2., 1991, pp.156-73.
Gascoigne, John, 'The Expanding Historiography of British Imperialism', *The Historical Journal*, Vol. 49, No. 2, 2006, pp.577-92.
Gelber, Nancy, *Canada in London: An Unofficial Glimpse of Canada's Sixteen High Commissioners, 1880-1980*, London, c.1980.
Geraets, John, 'Literary Biography in New Zealand', *Journal of New Zealand Literature*, No.7, 1989, pp.87-105.
Gibbons, Peter, 'The Far Side of the Search for Identity: Reconsidering New Zealand's History', *NZJH*, Vol. 37, No. 1, 2003, pp.38-49.
Gikandi, Simon, *Maps of Englishness: Writing Identity in the Culture of Colonialism*, New York, 1996.
Gilbert, David, '"London in All Its Glory – or How to Enjoy London": Guidebook Representations of Imperial London', *Journal of Historical Geography*, Vol. 25, No. 3, 1999, pp.279-97.
Gilbert, David, '*London of the Future*: the Metropolis Reimagined after the Great War', *Journal of British Studies*, Vol. 43, No. 1, 2004, pp.91-120.
Gilbert, David, and Fiona Henderson 'London and the Tourist Imagination', in Pamela K. Gilbert, ed., *Imagined Londons*, New York, 2002, pp.121-36.
Gilbert, Pamela K., ed., *Imagined Londons*, New York, 2002.
Gillespie-Needham, Dulcie, 'The Colonial and His Books: A Study of Reading In Nineteenth Century New Zealand', PhD Thesis, Victoria University, 1971.
Glancy, H. Mark, *When Hollywood Loved Britain: The Hollywood "British" Film, 1939-1945*, Manchester, 1999.
Glover, F. Graham, *London: A Pictorial Record of Legal London and Other Places of Interest to Lawyers*, Chichester, 1955.
Goldberg, Frank, *My Life in Advertising*, n.p., n.d.
Gordon and Gotch, *Gordon and Gotch (Australasia Ltd) Centenary, 1853-1953*, Melbourne, 1953.
Gorringe, Ashley, 'Consol[ing] Vision?: Aspects of Early New Zealand Television Audiences, 1960-75', MA Thesis, University of Auckland, 2002.
Grant, Robert D., *Representations of British Emigration, Colonisation, and Settlement: Imagining Empire, 1800-1860*, Houndmills, 2005.
Greenhalgh, Paul, *Ephemeral Vistas: The Expositions Universelles, Great Exhibitions and World's Fairs, 1851-1939*, Manchester, 1988.
Grenier, Katherine Haldane, '"Scottishness", "Britishness" and Scottish Tourism, 1770-1914', *History Compass*, Vol. 4, No. 6, 2006, pp.1000-21.
Griffen-Foley, Bridget, '"The Crumbs are Better than a Feast Elsewhere": Australian Journalists on Fleet Street,' *Journalism History*, Vol. 28, No. 1, 2002, pp.26-37.
Griffith, Penny, Ross Harvey, and Keith Maslen, *Book and Print in New Zealand: A Guide to Print Culture in Aotearoa*, Wellington, 1997.
Grossman, Edith Searle, *The Heart of the Bush*, London, 1910.

SELECT BIBLIOGRAPHY

Gurr, Andrew, *Writers in Exile*, Sussex, 1981.
Guthrie-Smith, H., *Tutira: The Story of a New Zealand Sheep Station*, London, 1926.
Gywnn, N., and R. W. Rydell, eds, *Fair Representations: World's Fairs and the Modern World*, Amsterdam, 1994.
Hajowski, Thomas, 'The BBC, the Empire, and the Second World War, 1939–45', *Historical Journal of Film, Radio and Television*, Vol. 22, No. 2, 2002, pp.135–55.
Hall, Peter, *Cities in Civilisation: Culture, Innovation and Urban Order*, London, 1998.
Hall-Jones, F. G., *Sir William Hall-Jones: The Last of the Old Liberals*, Invercargill, 1969.
Hamer, David, *New Towns in the New World: Images and Perceptions of the Nineteenth Century Urban Frontier*, New York, 1990.
Handbook for New ZealandVisitors to London, London, 1934.
Handbook for New Zealand Visitors to London, London, 1937.
Harper, Barbara, *Letters from Gunner 7/516 and Gunner 7/517*, Wellington, 1978.
Harper, Marjory, '"Personal Contact is Worth a Ton of Text Books": Education Tours of the Empire, 1926–39', *Journal of Imperial and Commonwealth History*, Vol. 32, No. 3, pp.48–76.
Harrison, P. A., 'The Motion Picture Industry in New Zealand, 1896–1930', MA Thesis, University of Auckland, 1974.
Harvey, Ross, 'Bringing the News to New Zealand: the Supply and Control of Overseas News in the Nineteenth Century', *Media History*, Vol. 8, No. 1, 2002, pp.21–34.
Haseler, Stephen, *The English Tribe: Identity, Nation and Europe*, Houndmills, 1996.
Hassam, Andrew '"As I Write": Narrative Occasions and the Quest for Self-Presence in the Travel Diary', *Ariel*, Vol. 21, No. 4, October 1990, pp.33–47.
Hawke, G. R., *The Making of New Zealand: An Economic History*, Cambridge, 1985.
Hayward, Bruce W., and Selwyn P. Hayward, *Cinemas in Auckland 1896 to 1979*, Auckland, 1979.
Headrick, Daniel R., *The Tools of Empire: Technology and European Imperialism in the Nineteenth Century*, New York, Oxford, 1981.
Headrick, Daniel R., *When Information Came of Age: Technologies of Knowledge in the Age of Reason and Revolution*, New York, 2000.
Heighway, Arthur J., *My Inky Way Through Life*, Bramley, 1979.
Helsinger, Elizabeth, *Rural Scenes and National Representation: Britain, 1815–1850*, Princeton, 1997.
Hereford, Phillip S. E., *The New Zealand Frozen Meat Trade*, Wellington, 1932.
Hill, R. J. M., 'The Quest for Control: The New Zealand Dairy Industry and the Guaranteed Price, 1921–36', MA Thesis, University of Auckland, 1974.
Hilliard, Christopher, *The Bookmen's Dominion: Cultural Life in New Zealand, 1920–1950*, Auckland, 2006.
Hilliard, Christopher, *To Exercise Our Talents: The Democratization of Writing in Britain*, Cambridge, MA, 2006.
Hilliard, Christopher, 'The Literary Underground of 1920s London', *Social History*, Vol. 33, No. 2, 2008, pp.164–82.
Hilliard, Christopher, 'The Provincial Press and the Imperial Traffic in Fiction', *Journal of British Studies*, Vol. 48, No. 3, 2009, pp.653–73.
Hilliard, Christopher, 'Stories of Becoming: The Centennial Surveys and the Colonisation of New Zealand', *NZJH*, Vol. 33, No. 1, pp.3–20.
Hobsbawm, E. J., *Industry and Empire: An Economic History of Britain Since 1750*, London, 1968.
Hobsbawm, E. J., and T. Ranger, eds, *The Invention of Tradition*, Cambridge, 1983.
Hoffenberg, Peter H., *An Empire on Display: English, Indian and Australian Exhibitions from the Crystal Palace to the Great War*, Berkeley and Los Angeles, 2001.
Holcroft, M. H., *Mary Ursula Bethell*, Wellington, 1975.
Hooper, Glenn, ed., *Landscape and Empire*, Aldershot and Burlington, 2005.
Horrocks, Roger and Nick Perry, eds, *Television in New Zealand: Programming the Nation*, South Melbourne, 2004.
Howkins, Alun, 'The Discovery of Rural England', in Robert Colls and Philip Dodd, eds. *Englishness: Politics and Culture 1880–1920*, London, 1986, pp.62–88.
Hughes, Deborah, 'Contesting Whiteness: Race, Nationalism and British Empire Exhibitions Between the Wars', PhD Thesis, University of Illinois at Urbana-Champaign, 2008.
Hulme, Peter and Tim Youngs, eds, *The Cambridge Companion to Travel Writing*, Cambridge, 2002.
Hunter, G.E., *Round and About*, Wellington, c.1937.

Hunter, Ian, 'Commodity Chains and Networks in Emerging Markets: New Zealand, 1880–1910', *Business History Review*, Vol. 75, No. 2, 2005, pp.275–304.
Hursthouse, Charles, *New Zealand: The "Britain of the South"*, London, 1861, facsimile edn, Christchurch, 1997.
Hutchinson, Marian Frances, 'Flagships of Maritime Modernity: A Study in the Pursuit of Technological Change in the New Zealand Shipping Industry, 1870–1939', PhD Thesis, University of Auckland, 2001.
Ilott, Jack, *Creating Customers: Ilott Advertising New Zealand, 1892–1982*, Auckland, 1985.
Imperial Institute, *Central Film Library: Catalogue of Empire Films, 1941*, London, 1941.
Ingham, Gordon, *Everyone's Gone to the Movies: The Sixty Cinemas of Auckland and Some Others*, Auckland, 1973.
Inglis, K. S., *This is the ABC: The Australian Broadcasting Commission, 1932–1983*, Melbourne, 1983.
Ingram, N. M., *ANZAC Diary: A Nonentity in Khaki*, Sydney, n.d.
Innis, Harold, *Empire and Communication*, Oxford, 1950.
Innis, Harold, *The Bias of Communication*, Toronto, 1951.
Iversen, Maxine A., 'Inextricable Links: Pakeha Perceptions of Identity and their Relationships with Britain at the Time of the Statute of Westminster', M.Litt Thesis, University of Auckland, 1996.
Jackson, Peter, 'Commodity Culture: The Traffic in Things', *Transactions of the British Institute of Geographers*, New Series, Vol. 24, No. 1, 99, pp.99–108.
Jacobson, W. W., *Homeward Voyage*, Akaroa, 1948.
Jefferys, James B., *Retail Trading in Britain, 1850–1950*, Cambridge, 1954.
Jhally, Sut, *The Codes of Advertising: Fetishism and the Political Economy of Meaning in the Consumer Society*, New York, 1987.
Johanson, Graeme, *Colonial Editions in Australia, 1843–1972*, Wellington, 2000.
Johanson, Graeme, '"Cultural Cringe" or Colonial Fringe?', *Melbourne Historical Journal*, Vol. 17, 1985, pp.79–85.
Johnson, Margaret, *English Theme with Some Variations in Verse*, Dunedin, 1937.
Johnson, Simon, 'The Home Front: Aspects of Civilian Patriotism In New Zealand during the First World War', MA Thesis, Massey University, 1976.
Johnston, Ewan, 'Representing the Pacific at International Exhibitions, 1851–1949', PhD Thesis, University of Auckland, 1999.
Jones, David, *Empire Marketing with Special Reference to the Work of the New Zealand Meat Board*, London, 1930.
Jones, Lawrence, *Picking Up the Traces: The Making of a New Zealand Literary Culture, 1932–1945*, Wellington, 2003.
Joubert, Jules, *The Proposed New Zealand Exhibition in London*, Dunedin, 1890.
Kampf, Antje, 'Controlling Male Sexuality: Combating Venereal Disease in the New Zealand Military During Two World Wars', *Journal of the History of Sexuality*, Vol. 17, No. 2, May 2008, pp.235–58.
Kaplan, Sydney Janet, '"A Gigantic Mother": Katherine Mansfield's London', in Susan Merrill Squier ed., *Women Writers and the City: Essays in Feminist Literary Criticism*, Knoxville, 1984, pp.161–75.
Kaul, Chandrika, ed., *Media and the British Empire*, Houndmills, 2006.
Kemper, Steven, *Buying and Believing: Sri Lankan Advertising and Consumers in a Transnational World*, Chicago, 2001.
Kennedy, Dane, *Britain and Empire, 1880–1945*, Harlow, 2002.
Kern, Stephen, *The Culture of Time and Space, 1880–1918*, Cambridge, 1983.
King, Michael, *Frank Sargeson: A Life*, Auckland, 1995.
King, Michael, *New Zealanders At War*, Auckland, 1981.
King, Michael, *The Penguin History of New Zealand*, Auckland, 2003.
King, Michael, *Wrestling with the Angel: A Life of Janet Frame*, Auckland, 2002.
Labbe, Jacqueline M., *Romantic Visualities: Landscape, Gender, and Romanticism*, London and New York, 1998.
Leeper, Rex, 'British Culture Abroad', *The Contemporary Review*, No. 14b, 1935, pp.201–7.
Leiss, William, Stephen Kline, and Sut Jhally, *Social Communication in Advertising: Persons, Products and Images of Wellbeing*, Toronto, New York, 1986.
Leiss, William, and Jackie Bottrill, *Social Communication in Advertising: Consumption in the Mediated Marketplace*, 3rd edn, New York, 2005.

Lester, Alan, 'British Settler Discourse and the Circuits of Empire', *History Workshop Journal*, Vol. 54, 2002, pp.25–48.
Lester, Alan, *Imperial Networks: Creating Identities in Nineteenth Century South Africa and Britain*, London, 2001.
Levine, Philippa, '"Walking the Streets in a Way No Decent Woman Should": Women Police in World War I', *Journal of Modern History*, Vol. 66, No. 1, March, 1994, pp.34–78.
Levine, Philippa, 'Battle Colours: Race, Sex and Colonial Soldiery in World War I', *Journal of Women's History*, Vol. 9, No. 4, 2003, pp.104–30.
Lewis, Margaret, *Ngaio Marsh: A Life*, Wellington, 1991.
Liell, Pam, *Messages From the War: Postcards from World War I*, Strathfield North, 1999.
List, T. C., *The Briton at Home: Impressions of a Visit to Great Britain*, New Plymouth, 1930.
Loach, Cyril, *A History Of the New Zealand Refrigerating Company*, Christchurch, 1970.
Lomas, Sophie C., ed., *Book of the Pageant: Festival of Empire*, 1911, London.
Lorenzkowski, Barbara, and Steven High, 'Culture, Canada, and the Nation', *Social History*, May 2006, pp.1–10.
Low, Rachael, *The History of the British Film*, Vols. 1–4, London, 1971.
Low, Rachael, *The History of the British Film: Films of Comment and Persuasion 1929–39*, London, 1979.
Low, Rachael, *The History of the British Film: Documentary and Educational Films of the 1930s*, London, 1979.
Luckin, Bill, 'Revisiting the Idea of Degeneration in Urban Britain, 1830–1900', *Urban Studies*, Vol. 32, No. 2, 2006, pp.234–52.
Lynn, Martin, ed., *The British Empire in The 1950s: Retreat or Revival?*, Houndmills, 2006.
Mainwaring, J., *New Zealand: Its History, Institutions and Industries: A Narrative with Statistics*, London, 1884.
Macaulay, T. B., review of Leopold von Ranke's *The Ecclesiastical and Political History of the Popes during the Sixteenth and Seventeenth Centuries*, in the *Edinburgh Review*, Vol. 72, October, 1840, pp.227–58.
MacKenzie, John M., ed., *Imperialism and Popular Culture*, Manchester, 1986.
MacKenzie, John M., *Orientalism: History, Theory, and the Arts*, Manchester, 1995.
MacKenzie, John M., *Propaganda and Empire: The Manipulation of British Public Opinion, 1880–1960*, Manchester, 1984.
Macky, Michael, 'New Zealand and the Decline of British Power, 1939–1956', MA Thesis, University of Auckland, 1999.
Maddrell, Avril M. C., 'Empire, Emigration, and School Geography: Changing Discourses of Imperial Citizenship, 1880–1925', *Journal of Historical Geography*, Vol. 22, No. 4, 1996, pp.373–87.
Malone, E. P., 'The New Zealand School Journal and the Imperial Ideology', *NZJH*, Vol. 7, No. 1, April 1973, pp.2–27.
Mansell, Gerard, *Let Truth Be Told: Fifty Years of BBC External Broadcasting*, London, 1982.
Marsh, Ngaio, *Black Beech and Honeydew*, London and Glasgow, 1966.
McArthur, Colin, 'Chinese Boxes and Russian Dolls: Tracking the Elusive Cinematic City', in Clarke, David B., ed., *The Cinematic City*, London, 1997, pp.19–45.
McCarthy, Conal, *Exhibiting Maori: A History of Colonial Cultures on Display*, Wellington, 2007.
McClean, Rosalind, '"How We Prepare Them in India": British Diasporic Imaginings and Migration to New Zealand', *NZJH*, Vol. 37, No. 2, 2003, pp.131–51.
McClintock, Anne, *Imperial Leather: Race, Gender and Sexuality in the Colonial Contest*, New York, London, 1995.
McClure, Margaret, *The Wonder Country: Making New Zealand Tourism*, Auckland, 2004.
McCormick, E. H., *An Absurd Ambition*, Auckland, 1996.
McCormick, E. H., *Letters and Art in New Zealand*, Wellington, 1940.
McGeorge, Colin, 'Hear Our Voices We Entreat: Schools and the "Colonial Twang", 1880–1930', *NZJH*, Vol. 18, No. 1, April 1984, pp.3–18.
McGeorge, Colin, 'Learning About God's Own Country', *New Zealand Journal of Educational Studies*, Vol. 18, No. 1, 1983, pp.3–12.
McGregor, Rae, *Jane Mander: The Story of a New Zealand Writer*, Dunedin, 1998.
McKenzie, Dorothy and Lindsay Malcolm, eds, *Boots, Belts, Rifle and Pack*, Dunedin, 1992.
McKinnon, Malcolm, *Independence and Foreign Policy: New Zealand in the World Since 1935*, Auckland, 1993.

SELECT BIBLIOGRAPHY

McNeish, James, *Dance of the Peacocks*, Auckland, 2003.
McNeish, James, and Helen McNeish, *Walking On My Feet: A.R.D. Fairburn, a Kind of Biography*, Auckland, 1983.
Meaney, Neville, 'Britishness and Australian Identity', *Australian Historical Studies*, Vol. 32, No. 116, 2001, pp.76–90.
Meredith, David, 'Imperial Images: the Empire Marketing Board, 1926–1932', *History Today*, Vol. 37, No. 1, 1987, pp.30–37.
Midgley, Clare, ed., *Gender and Imperialism*, Manchester and New York, 1998.
Milner, Ian, 'Thoughts in England', *Tomorrow*, 28 October 1936, pp.10–14.
Mintz, Sidney W., *Sweetness and Power: The Place of Sugar in Modern History*, New York, 1985.
Mirams, Gordon, *Speaking Candidly: Films and People in New Zealand*, Hamilton, 1945.
Montgomery, Deborah, 'Reconnaissance: Twentieth Century New Zealand War History at Century's Turn', *NZJH*, Vol. 37, No. 1, 2003, pp.62–79.
Morgan, Cecilia, '"A Choke of Emotion, a Great Heart Leap": English Canadian Tourists in Britain, 1880s–1914', *Social History*, Vol. 39, No. 77, pp.11–43.
Mulgan, Alan, *Home: A New Zealander's Adventure*, London, 1927. (Reprinted in 1929 as *Home: A Colonial's Adventure*.)
Mulgan, Alan, *Literature and Authorship in New Zealand*, reprinted London, 1971.
Mulgan, John, *Man Alone*, rev. edn, Kent, 1949.
Mumford, Lewis, *The City in History*, Harmondsworth, 1961.
Murray, Stuart, *Never a Soul At Home: New Zealand Literary Nationalism and the 1930s*, Wellington, 1998.
Myers, Fred, *The Empire of Things: Regimes of Value and Material Culture*, Oxford, 2001.
Nava, Mica, and Alan O'Shea, ed., *Modern Times: Reflections on a Century of English Modernity*, London, 1996.
Newport, J. N. W., *Sovereign Butter: Seventy-five Years of Production*, Blenheim, 1977.
New Zealand Dairy Board, *Annual Reports and Statement of Accounts*, Wellington, 1925, 1926, 1927, 1930, 1938.
New Zealand Dairy Industry Commission, *Report on the 1934 New Zealand Dairy Industry Commission, Presented to Both Houses of the General Assembly by Command of His Excellency*, New Zealand, 1934.
New Zealand Meat Producers Board, *Annual Reports and Statements of Accounts, Wellington, 1922–1942*.
New Zealand National Film Library, *Catalogue of Sound and Silent 16mm Cinematograph Films*, Wellington, 1945.
New Zealand National Film Library, *Catalogue of Sound and Silent 16mm Cinematograph Films*, Wellington, 1953.
The New Zealand Shipping Company's Pocket Book, London, 1908.
The New Zealand Soldier's Guide to the British Isles, With the Compliments of the NZ YMCA, London, c.1917.
Nevett, T. R., *Advertising in Britain: A History*, London, 1982.
Nicholas, Sian, *The Echo of War: Home Front Propaganda and the Wartime BBC, 1939–45*, Manchester, 1996.
Noble Adams, R., *Let's Go Home: The Journal of a Jubilee Journey*, Blenheim, 1936.
Nora, Pierre, 'Between Memory and History: Les Lieux des Memoire', *Representations*, Vol. 26, Spring, 1989, pp.7–24.
Notes for Visitors from New Zealand, London, 1950.
Notes for Visitors from New Zealand, London, 1953.
Notes for Visitors from New Zealand, London, 1956.
O'Neill, R. B., *The Press 1861–1961: The Story of a Newspaper*, Christchurch, 1963.
O'Sullivan, Vincent, *Long Journey to the Border: A Life of John Mulgan*, Auckland, 2003.
O'Sullivan, Vincent, and Margaret Scott, eds., *The Collected Letters of Katherine Mansfield, Volume One, 1903–1917*, Oxford, 1984.
One Hundred Anchor Years, Hamilton, 1986.
Orsman, H., ed., *The Oxford Dictionary of New Zealand English*, Auckland, 1997.
Owen, Sir David J., *The Ports of the United Kingdom*, London, 1939, rev. edn 1948.
Payne, Jan, *Australia House: 75 Years of Service*, London, c.1993.

Peacocke, Isabel, *London Called Them*, London, 1946.
Pember Reeves, William, *The Long White Cloud: Ao Tea Roa*, 4th edn, London, 1956.
Percy, W. S., *The Empire Comes Home*, London, 1937.
Perfect, Thomas Charles, *Hornchurch During the Great War*, Colchester, 1920.
Pesman, Ros, David Walker, and Richard White, eds, *The Oxford Book of Australian Travel Writing*, Oxford, 1996.
Phillips, Jock, *A Man's Country? The Image of the Pakeha Male – A History*, rev. edn, Auckland, 1996.
Phillips, Jock, Nicholas Boyack, and E. P. Malone, *The Great Adventure: New Zealand Soldiers Describe the First World War*, Wellington, 1988.
Pickles, Katie, *Female Imperialism and National Identity: The Imperial Order Daughters of Empire*, New York, 2002.
Pirtle, T. R., *History of the Dairy Industry*, Chicago, 1926.
Pivac, Diane, Frank Stark and Lawrence McDonald, eds, *New Zealand Film: An Illustrated History*, Wellington, 2011.
Playne, Somerset, *New Zealand: Aotearoa*, London, 1912–13.
Pocock, J. G. A., 'British History: A Plea for a New Subject', *Journal of Modern History*, Vol. 47, No. 4, 1975, pp.601–24.
Pocock, J. G. A., *The Discovery of Islands: Essays in British History*, Cambridge, New York, 2005.
Pollock, Jacob, 'From Colony to Culture: Historiographical Discourse and Historical Identity in Aotearoa/New Zealand, 1883–2003', MA Thesis, University of Auckland, 2005.
Potter, Simon J., 'Empire, Cultures, and Identities in Nineteenth- and Twentieth-Century Britain', *History Compass*, Vol. 5, No. 1, 2007, pp.51–71.
Potter, Simon J., 'Strengthening the Bonds of the Commonwealth: The Imperial Relations Trust and Australian, New Zealand, and Canadian Broadcasting Personnel in Britain, 1946–1952', *Media History*, Vol. 11, No. 3, 2005, pp.193–205.
Potter, Simon J., *News and the British World: The Emergence of an Imperial Press System*, Oxford, 2003.
Potter, Simon J., 'Webs, Networks, and Systems: Globalization and the Mass Media in the Nineteenth- and Twentieth-Century British Empire', *Journal of British Studies*, Vol. 46, 2007, pp.621–46.
Potter, Simon J., 'Who Listened when London Called? Reactions to the BBC Empire Service in Canada, Australia and New Zealand, 1932–1939', *Historical Journal of Film, Radio and Television*, Vol. 28, No. 4, pp.475–87.
Port, M. H., *Imperial London: Civil Government Building in London 1851–1915*, New Haven and London, 1995.
Porter, Bernard, *The Absent-minded Imperialists: Empire, Society, and Culture in Britain*, Oxford, 2004.
Pratt, Mary Louise, *Imperial Eyes: Travel Writing and Transculturation*, 3rd edn, New York, 1994.
Price, Richard, 'One Big Thing: Britain, Its Empire and their Imperial Culture', *Journal of British Studies*, Vol. 45, 2006, pp.602–27.
Prichard, M. J., *An Economic History of New Zealand to 1939*, Auckland, 1970.
Pryke, Olwen, 'Australia House: Representing Australia in Great Britain, 1901–1939', PhD Thesis, University of Sydney, 2006.
Pugsley, Christopher, *The ANZAC Experience: New Zealand, Australia, and Empire in the First World War*, Auckland, 2004.
Pugsley, Christopher, *On the Fringe of Hell: New Zealanders and Military Discipline in the First World War*, Auckland, 1991.
Rahn, B. J., ed., *Ngaio Marsh: The Woman and Her Work*, London, 1995.
Ramamurthy, Anandi, *Imperial Persuaders: Images of Africa and Asia in British Advertising*, Manchester, 2003.
Rappaport, Erika D., 'Travelling in the Lady Guides' London: Consumption, Modernity, and the Fin-de-siècle Metropolis', in Daunton, Martin, and Bernhard Rieger, eds, *Meanings of Modernity: Britain From the Late-Victorian Era to World War Two*, Oxford, 2001, pp.25–44.
Raymond, I. W., *New Zealanders in Mufti, 1914–1918*, London, 1924.
Reay, Barry, *Rural Englands*, Houndmills, 2004.
Richards, Jeffrey, *The Unknown 1930s: An Alternative History of the British Cinema*, London, 1998.
Richards, Thomas, *The Commodity Culture of Victorian England: Advertising and Spectacle, 1851–1914*, Stanford, 1990.

Richards, Thomas, *The Imperial Archive: Knowledge and the Fantasy of Empire*, New York, London, 1993.
Riddet, W., and E. Marsden, *Problems of the Dairy Industry*, Wellington, 1933.
Robinson, Roger, and Nelson Wattie, *The Oxford Companion to New Zealand Literature*, Auckland, 1998.
Rogers, Anna, ed., *The War Years: New Zealanders Remember, 1939–1945*, Wellington, 1989.
Ross, Forrestina (Mrs Malcolm), *Round the World with a Fountain Pen*, Wellington, 1913.
Rutherford, A. W., *The Impressions of a New Zealand Pastoralist on Tour*, Christchurch, 1912.
Ryan, James R., *Picturing Empire: Photography and the Visualization of the British Empire*, London, 1997.
Rydell, Robert W., *World of Fairs: The Century of Progress Expositions*, Chicago and London, 1993.
Said, Edward, *Culture and Imperialism*, New York, 1993.
Said, Edward, *Orientalism*, New York, 1978.
Sanders, James, *Dateline NZPA: The New Zealand Press Association, 1880–1980*, Auckland, 1979.
Sargeson, Frank, *Sargeson*, 2nd edn, Auckland, 1981.
Scanlan, Nelle, *The Road to Pencarrow*, London, 1963.
Scannell, Paddy, and David Cardiff, *A Social History of Broadcasting: Vol. 1, 1922–1939, Serving the Nation*, Oxford, Cambridge, 1991.
Schneer, Jonathan, *London 1900: The Imperial Metropolis*, Michigan, 1999.
Scholefield, G. H., *Newspapers in New Zealand*, Wellington, 1958.
Scholefield, G. H., *New Zealand in Evolution*, London, 1909.
Shaw, Gareth, Louise Hill Curth, and Andrew Alexander, 'Creating New Spaces of Food Consumption: The Rise of Mass Catering and the Activities of the Aerated Bread Company', in John Benson and Laura Ugolini, eds, *Cultures of Selling: Perspectives of Consumption and Society Since 1700*, Aldershot, 2006, pp.81–102.
Shaw, Helen, ed., *The Letters of D'Arcy Cresswell*, Christchurch, 1971.
Schwarz, Bill, *The Expansion of England: Race, Ethnicity, and Cultural History*, London, 1996.
Shepard, Francis, *London: A History*, Oxford, 1998.
Shuker, Roy, and Roger Openshaw, 'New Zealand Youth and Silent Movies', *New Zealand Journal of Educational Studies*, Vol. 22, No. 1, 1987, pp.87–99.
Sinclair, Keith, *A Destiny Apart: New Zealand's Search for National Identity*, Wellington, 1986.
Sinclair, Keith, *A History of New Zealand*, 6th edn, Auckland, 1980.
Sinclair, Keith, *Walter Nash*, Dunedin, 1976.
Sinclair, Keith, *William Pember Reeves: New Zealand Fabian*, Oxford, 1965.
Skilton, David, 'Contemplating the Ruins of London: Macaulay's New Zealander and Others', *Literary London Journal*, Vol. 2, No. 1, 2004, pp.1–7.
Skinner, Robin, 'Home Away: A State House in London', in Brookes, Barbara, ed., *At Home in New Zealand: Houses, History, People*, Wellington, 2000, pp.155–64.
Skinner, S. R., *My Life with the Kiwis*, London, 1962.
Smith, Miriam E., 'The History of New Zealand Exhibitions, with particular reference to the New Zealand and South Seas International Exhibition, Dunedin, 1925–6', MA Research Essay, University of Auckland, 1976.
Souvenir of the New Zealand Pavilion at the British Empire Exhibition, Wembley, London, 1924.
Stafford, Jane, and Mark Williams, *Maoriland: New Zealand Literature 1872–1914*, Wellington, 2006.
Stead, C. K., *Kin of Place: Essays on Twenty New Zealand Writers*, Auckland, 2002.
Steel, Frances, '"New Zealand *is* Butterland": Interpreting the Historical Significance of Daily Spread', *New Zealand Journal of History*, Vol. 39, No. 2, 2005, pp.179–94.
Stewart, Col. H., *The New Zealand Division 1916–1919, A Popular History Based on Official Records*, Auckland, 1921.
Studholme, Lt Col. John, *Some Records of the New Zealand Expeditionary Force*, Wellington, 1928.
Sturm, Terry, 'Attila of the Antipodes; or, The Mad Hatter's Tea Party: The Publishing History of Edith Lyttleton (G.B. Lancaster) in the 1930's', in Griffith, Penny, Peter Hughes, and Alan Loney eds, *A Book in the Hand: Essays on the History of the Book in New Zealand*, Auckland, 2000, pp.95–117.
Sturm, Terry, ed., *The Oxford History of New Zealand Literature in English*, 1991, Auckland. Sullivan, Jim, *A History of Broadcasting News, 1921–1962*, Timaru, 1987.
Sullivan, Jim, ed., *Doing Our Bit: New Zealand Women Tell Their Stories of World War Two*, Auckland, 2002.

Sumpter, H. K., *Travelling Light: To Europe and Back on £200*, Invercargill, 1934.
Swann, Paul, *The British Documentary Film Movement, 1926-1946*, Cambridge, 1989.
Taylor, John Patrick, 'Consuming Identity: Modernity and Tourism in New Zealand', MA Thesis, University of Auckland, 1996.
Taylor, Nancy, *The Home Front*, Vol. 1, *The Official History of New Zealand in the Second World War 1939-1945*, Wellington, 1986.
Taylor, Philip M., *British Propaganda in the Twentieth Century: Selling Democracy*, Edinburgh, 1999.
Taylor, Philip M., *The Projection of Britain: British Overseas Publicity and Propaganda 1919-1939*, Cambridge, 1981.
Templeton, M., ed., *An Eye, an Ear, and a Voice: 50 years in New Zealand's External Relations, 1943-1993*, Wellington, 1993.
Thieme, John, *Postcolonial Con-texts: Writing Back to the Canon*, London, 2001.
Thompson, Andrew, *The Empire Strikes Back? The Impact of Imperialism on Britain from the mid-Nineteenth Century*, Harlow, 2005.
Thompson, Andrew, *Imperial Britain: The Empire in British Politics, 1880-1932*, Harlow, 2000.
Thompson, Andrew, 'The Language of Imperialism and the Meanings of Empire: Imperial Discourse in British Politics, 1895-1914', *The Journal of British Studies*, Vol. 36, No. 2, 1977, pp.147-77.
Thomson, John Mansfield, ed., *Farewell Colonialism: The New Zealand International Exhibition Christchurch, 1906-7*, Palmerston North, 1998.
Tolerton, Jane, *Ettie: A Life of Ettie Rout*, Auckland, 1992.
Toogood, Selwyn, *Out of the Bag*, Auckland, 1979.
Traue, J. E., 'The Public Library Explosion in Colonial New Zealand', *Libraries & the Cultural Record*, Vol. 42, No. 2, 2007, pp.151-64.
Trussell, Denys, *Fairburn*, Auckland, 1984.
Urry, John, *The Tourist Gaze*, 2nd edn, London, 2002.
Von Sturmer, Denham, *New Zealand – Down, Denmark – Up! Or A Modern Market Place*, Auckland, 1933.
Wall, Arnold, *A Run Off the Chain: Impressions of Travel in Ceylon, Italy, Great Britain and Norway*, Auckland, 1929.
Waller, Gregory A., *Main Street Amusements: Movies and Commercial Entertainment in a Southern City, 1896-1930*, Washington, 1995.
Walsh, Mike, 'Tackling the Big Boy of Empire: British Film in Australia, 1918-1931', in Higson, Andrew, eds, *Young and Innocent: The Cinema in Britain 1896-1930*, Exeter, 2002, pp.271-87.
Walthew, Kenneth, 'The British Empire Exhibition of 1924', *History Today*, August, 1981, pp.34-39.
Ward, Arthur H., *A Command of Cooperatives: The Development of Leadership, Marketing and Price Control in the Cooperative Dairy Industry of New Zealand*, Wellington, 1975.
Ward, Locke & Co., *London*, London, n.d.
Ward, Stuart, *Australia and the British Embrace: The Demise of the Imperial Ideal*, Melbourne, 2001.
Ward, Stuart, ed., *British Culture and the End of Empire*, Manchester, 2001.
Ward, Stuart, 'Sentiment and Self-interest: The Imperial Ideal in Anglo-Australian Commercial Culture', *Australian Historical Studies*, Vol. 32, No. 116, pp.91-109.
Wee, C. J. Wan-ling, *Culture, Empire, and the Question of Being Modern*, Lanham, 2003.
Wevers, Lydia, *Country of Writing*, Auckland, 2002.
Wevers, Lydia, *Reading on the Farm: Victorian Fiction and the Colonial World*, Wellington, 2010.
White, Richard, 'Bluebells and Fogtown: Australians' First Impressions of England, 1860-1940,' *Australian Cultural History*, No. 5, 1986, pp.44-59.
White, Richard, 'Cooees Across the Strand: Australian Travellers in London and the Performance of National Identity', *Australian Historical Studies*, Vol. 32, No. 116, 2001, pp.109-38.
White, Richard, 'The Soldier as Tourist: The Australian Experience of the Great War', *War and Society*, Vol. 5, No. 1, 1987, pp.63-77.
White, Richard, 'Sun, Sand, and Syphilis: Australian Soldiers and the Orient, Egypt', *Australian Cultural History*, No. 9, 1990, pp.49-64.
Wiatr, Elizabeth, 'Between Word, Image, and the Machine: Visual Education and Films of Industrial Process', *Historical Journal of Film, Radio, and Television*, Vol. 22, No. 3, 2002, pp.333-51.
Williams, E. P., *A New Zealander's Diary, Gallipoli, and France, 1915-1917*, 1924, reprinted Christchurch, 1998.
Williams, Raymond, *The Country and the City*, London, 1973.

Wilson, Kathleen, *The Island Race: Englishness, Empire and Gender in The Eighteenth Century*, London, New York, 2001.
Wilson, Kathleen, ed., *A New Imperial History: Culture, Identity, and Modernity in Britain and the Empire, 1660–1840*, Cambridge, 2004.
Wilson, Philippa Janet, 'We Are Still English at Heart', MA Thesis, University of Auckland, 1998.
Wolfe, Patrick, *Settler Colonialism and the Transformation of Anthropology: The Politics and Poetics of an Ethnographic Event*, London, 1999.
Wolfe, Richard, *Well Made New Zealand: A Century of Trademarks*, Auckland, 1987.
Woollacott, Angela, '"All This is Empire, I Told Myself": Australian Women's Voyages "Home" and the Articulation of Colonial Whiteness', *American Historical Review*, Vol. 102, No. 4, 1997, pp.1003–29.
Woollacott, Angela, 'The Colonial Flaneuse: Australian Women Negotiating Turn of the Century London,' *Signs*, Vol. 25, Issue 3, 2000, pp.761–87.
Woollacott, Angela, 'From Moral to Professional Authority: Secularism, Social Work, and Middle-Class Women's Self-construction in World War I Britain', *Journal of Women's History*, Vol. 10, No. 2, 1998, pp.85–112.
Woollacott, Angela, '"Khaki fever" and its Control: Gender, Class, Age and Morality on the British Homefront in the First World War', *Journal of Contemporary History*, Vol. 29, No. 2, 1994, pp.325–47.
Woollacott, Angela, *To Try Her Fortune in London: Australian Women, Colonialism, and Modernity*, New York, 2001.
Yarwood, Vaughan, 'Shibboleth of Empire: Attitudes to Empire in New Zealand Writing 1890–1930', MA Thesis, University of Auckland, 1982.
Yerex, David, *Empire of the Dairy Farmers*, Petone, 1989.
YMCA, *Blighty: With the Compliments of the NZ YMCA*, London, 1916.
Ziino, Bart, 'A Kind of Round Trip: Australian Soldiers and the Tourist Analogy, 1914–1918', *War and Society*, Vol. 25, No. 2, October 2006, pp.39–52.

INDEX

Page numbers in **bold** refer to images/captions.

A Destiny Apart (Keith Sinclair), 9, 80
A Going Concern (TV series), 261
A Handbook for Visitors to London (New Zealand High Commission), 47–49, **48**, 50
Adventures of Robin Hood, The (TV series), 227, 248, 252, 270
advertising, 11, 124, 125, 131, 155–7, 170, 185–6, 188, 278; beer, 275–6; butter, 136, **174**, **175**, 182, 266; dairy, 132, 161, **161**, 169–76, 181–2; farming, 139, 165; immigration, 124–8, 134, 139, 178; lamb, 158–64, 166–68, **167**, 175, 182, 186, **187**; meat, 123, **144**, 144–5, 157–61, **158**, **159**, 161, 164–8, **165**, **167**, **168**, **179**; primary produce, 12, 134, 140, 152, 153, 154–5, 164, 182, 186; tourist, 50, **133**, 134, 139; wool, 136, 144–5, **145**; *see also* butter sculptures; photographs: and advertising; window displays, office and shop
advertising devices and media: agencies, 131, 156, 177, 182; competitions, 166–7, **167**; magazine, 167; mass consumer, 154, 166–7; newspaper, 125, 131, 154, 160, 167–8, 171, 176–7, 178–9, 180, 183–4; postcards, 165; television, 257, 267; *see also* billboards; posters; marketing strategies; symbolism: in advertising; photographs: and advertising; S. L. A. Mastin (SLAM!); window displays, office and shop
After Office Hours (movie), 229
Alias Smith and Jones (TV series), **260**
Alice in Wonderland (movie), 225
All Blacks, 139
All Creatures Great and Small (TV series), 265
Allen, Sir James, 51, 240
Allen & Unwin, 110, 112
Allison, Ewen, 40, 78–79, 83, 87, 88
Alomes, Stephen, 119
Along Old Father Thames to Shepperton (film), 238
Alpha Plan, The (TV series), 266
Anderson, Benedict, 9, 190, 197
apples: Australian, 179; British dependence on, 10; Canadian, 240; New Zealand, 139, 178, 179–80, 182, 240
Argus press agency, 196, 203
Athenaeum magazine, 112
Auckland, **94**, 117, 198; and London, 106; rail connections with, 9; television broadcasts to, 247–8, 252, 258–9
Auckland Harbour Board, 219
Auckland Public Library, 112
Auckland Savings Bank, 219
Auckland Star, 17, 115, **207**, 208, 209, 212, 216–17, **217**, 219–20, **253**
Auckland Sun, 115, 116–17
Auckland Transport Board, 219
Auckland War Memorial Museum, 245

Auckland Weekly News, **87**, 200, **209**, 210–12, **211**, 213
Australia: and book trade, 192–3, 195–6; and exhibitions, 135, 138, 148; and London, 31, 43, 45, 74, 78, 83–84, 86, 119, 213, 214, 277; and mass media, 195; and New Zealand, 13, 164, 195, 196, 276; and television, 250, 254, 256; and World War I enlistment, 54–55; as modern, 74–75; historians from, 5; journalists from, 107, 205; migration to, 5; New Zealand population of, 3; *see also* apples: Australian; butter: Australian; cheese: Australian; guidebooks, Australian; soldiers, Australian in London; television, Australian programmes; wheat, Australian; writers: Australian in London
Australia House, London, 43, 45, **46**, 47, 240; *see also* libraries: at Australia House
Australian High Commission, 43, 45
Avengers, The (TV series), 260

Baker, Louisa, 107
Bank of New Zealand, London, 214, 215
Barging Through London (film), 238
Barney Miller (TV series), 261
Batman (TV series), 259
Battle of Britain, 206, 218, 229
BBC: Empire Service, 189–90, 191–2, 196–7, 221, 222; radio, 193, **194**, 196–7, 222, 238, 254, 256, 270; television, 252, 254, 256, 257–8
Beau Geste (movie), 248
Beaverbrook, Lord, 218
Belgium, Nazi invasion of, 216–18
Belich, James, 8, 105
Bell, Al, 247
Belloc, Hilaire, 108
Bent, Kimble, 269
'Better Britons', 71, 127; *see also* 'Greater Britain'
Beverley Hillbillies, The (TV series), 259
Big Ben, London, 189, 191, 193, 226, 235, **255**, 274
Big OE, 3, 250; *see also* 'Bill Massey's tourists'; soldier-tourists; working holidays and trips to Britain
Big Valley (movie on TV), 259
Bilborough, Ernest, 151
'Bill Massey's tourists', 11, 16, 53–54
billboards, 124, 154, 241, 276
Billingsgate, London, 240
Biorama Company, 231, 239, **239**
Blackfriars Bridge, London, 36
Blackman, Honor, 248
Blackwoods magazine, 112
Blake, William, 119
Bleak House (Charles Dickens), 227
Bledisloe, Lord, 187

327

INDEX

Bless this House (TV series), **260**
Blighty (YMCA booklet) 62, 66–67
Blue Moon Press, 112
Bodley Head, 112
Boer War, 39, 82
Bolitho, Hector, 108, 109, 110, 113, 115, 116, 121
Bonanza (TV series), 265
books, imports of to New Zealand, 192–3, 195, 196, 222, 243, 251, 278; *see also* colonial editions
Boyack, Nicholas, 64
Boy's Own, The, 18, 20
Bradshaw, John, 150
brands and food marketing, 130–1, 155, 164–5, 168, 169, 171, 172–5, 178, 276; *see also* marketing strategies
Brasch, Charles, 76, 101, 102–3, 108–9
Brees, Samuel, **125**, 125–6
Bridge Over the River Kwai (movie), 248
'Britain of the South', 5, 78, 132, 137; *see also* 'Better Britons'; 'British New Zealand'; 'Britishness'; 'Greater Britain'; New Zealand and London
British Commonwealth International Newsfilm Agency (Visnews), 254
British Council, 233, 234, 237
British Empire, 4, 5–7, 8, 31–32, 35, 39, 40, 43, 45, 116, 147; as trading unit, 176–8, 186–8; 'family' of, 13, 38, 50, 76, 178, 183–4, 194, 240, 275; New Zealand as part of, 1, 5, 15, 35–40, 71–72, 78, 141, 178; unity of, 45, 151, 156, 194, 233, 234
British Empire Academy Tea Party, 51
'British Empire Dairy Factory', 180, **181**, 183
British Empire Exhibition, Wembley, London, 1924–5, 134, 139–46, **140**, **141**, **142**, **144**, **145**, 148, **149**, 151–3, **152**, **153**, 154, 188
British Film Institute, 232–3
British High Commission, 244
British Museum, London, 100; *see also* libraries: British Museum
'British New Zealand', 5–7, 152–3, 162–4, 168, 172–3, 175, 176–7, 182–3, 274; *see also* 'Better Britons'; 'Britain of the South'; 'Britishness'; 'Greater Britain'; New Zealand and London
'Britishness', 5–7, 10, 39, 126, 127–8, 142, 152, 159, 161, 163, 175, 184–5, 215–16, 248, 278; *see also* 'Better Britons'; 'British New Zealand'; 'Greater Britain'
Briton at Home, The (T. C. List), 31–32
Broburg, Lindsay, 254
Brockenhurst hospital, 55, 64
Buckingham Palace, London, 23, 39, 68, 102; reports of bombing of, 210–12
Burton, Antoinette, 6
butter: Australian, 171; British dependence on, 10, 129; Danish, 170; New Zealand, 2, 7, 8–9, 10, 123, 128, 154, 155, 170, 171, 173, 177, 178, 182, 266
butter sculptures, 11, 136, 141, 142, **142**, **143**, 149, 154–5

cabled news, 9, 12, 191, 193, 195, 197, 200–3, 205, 207, 208, 274
Caine, Michael, 258
Cambridge, 21
Canada: and exhibitions, 142, 149; and London, 31, 40, 43, 45, 277; and television, 250, 254; as modern, 142; historians from, 5; migration to, 5; *see also* apples: Canadian; cheese: Canadian; newspapers, Canadian; soldiers, Canadian in London
Canada House, 45–46
Canadian High Commission, London, 43, 244, 245
Canadian Trade Commissioner, 245
Captain magazine, 19
Carr, Russell, 21
Carter, Sunny, 250
Cathedrals of Britain (film), 235
CBS, 256
Central Office of Information, 248, 255
Century Company, 110
Century theatre, Auckland, 229
chain stores, 2, 128, 129–31, 132
Channel 2, 264
Charlie's Angels (TV series), 262
cheese: Australian, 172; British dependence on, 10, 129; Canadian, 10, 170; New Zealand, 2, 7, 8, 123, 128, 155, 170, 171–3, 178, 182
Cheshire Cheese, London, 14, 22, 35
Chester, Stan, 24
Chesterton, G. K., 108, 113
Chesterton, Mrs G. K., 114
Chicago, and its hinterland, 8, 193
childhood ideas of London, 3, 18, 22, 32, 99–100, 102, 105, 212; *see also* nursery rhymes
Children of the Bush (Henry Lawson), 110
CHiPs (TV series), 262
Christchurch: film in, 231; images of, **90**, 126, 127, 128; newspapers in, 200–1; television broadcasts to, 248, 252; *see also* New Zealand International Exhibition
Christian Science Monitor, 17
Christmas Under Fire (film), 235
City Bound (film), 238
City of Progress (film), 235
Clark, Owen, 55
class structure, 7, 35, 79, 83, 121, 130, 131
Clive of India (movie), 227, 248
Close to Home (TV series), 261, 267, **268**
clubs, London, 46–47, 53, 55–56, 60–62, 66, 67, 106, 121; *see also* New Zealand Forces Club; New Zealand Soldiers' Club; Overseas Club Map and Guide; Shakespeare Hut; YMCA Club
C'mon (TV series), 272
Colman, Ronald, 248
Colonial and Indian Exhibition, London, 1886, 138, 148, 149–50
Colonial and Indian guidebook, 149
colonial brashness, 30, 74
'colonial cringe', *see* cultural cringe
colonial editions, 110, 111, 192–3
colonial superiority, 36, 38–39, 79, 83–84, 85–86
colonialism, 2, 4, 79, 251, 271–2
Colonials' Guide to London, The (A. Staines Manders), 31, 38
colonies: dependent, 6–7, 36, 38, 55–57, 71, 132, 147, 146, 148, 164, 178, 183–4, **184**, 185, 186; white and settler, 4, 6–7, 10, 18, 31, 36, 38–39, 42–43, 55–57, 62, 66, 77, 78, 121, 128–9, 130, 135, 145–6, 147–9, 164, 176, 178, 184–5, **185**, 223, 240

INDEX

colonisation, 5, 39, 75, 127, 151, 270, 277–8; *see also* recolonisation
Colour Box (film), 233
Comic, The (movie on TV), 258
Committee of Inquiry into the Motion Picture Industry, 1934, 229
Conley, Maurice, **170**
Constable, John, 76–77, 83
Constantine, Stephen, 178, 184
Cooke, Ella, 24, 26, 36
Cooper, Gary, 224
co-operative societies, 129
Coronation Street (TV series), 260–1, 264, 267
Cosmopolitan London (film), 240
Country Calendar (TV series), 268
Country GP (TV series), 267
Covent Garden, London, 240
Cowan, James, 146–7
Crawford, William, 177–8
Cresswell, D'Arcy, 112
Cronon, William, 8, 193
Cruel Sea, The (movie), 248
cultural cringe, 4, 39, 108, 163, 270–2, 278

Dailey, Dan, 248
Daily Telegraph, 139, 201
dairy factories, 132, 146, 169, 171, 180
Dallas (TV series), 262
Dangerman (TV series), 260
Daniel Boone (TV series), 259
'darkest London', 57, 69, 82–86, 95, 239–40
Darwin, John, 156
David Copperfield (movie), 226, **226**
Day, Patrick, 198, 199, 256
de la Mare, Walter, 102, 108
de Montalk, Geoffrey, 106, 112
Deakin, Alfred, 45
Dear Old London (film), 232
Dent publishers, 16, 112
Department of Agriculture, Commerce, and Tourists, 134, 146; *see also* New Zealand Tourist and Publicity Department
Department of Education, 245
Department of Health, 247
Department of Overseas Trade (GB), 234
Department of Transport, 247
department stores, 131, 159
diaries, as source of impressions of London, 11, 16, 19
Dickens, Charles, 26, 27, 74, 227
Dickens' London (film), 237–8
Dickinson, Angie, 261
Donnelly, Ian, 14–15, 19, 21, 23–24, 35–36, 39, 84–85
Don't Bother to Knock (movie on TV), 259
Doré, Gustave, **viii**, 1
Dover, impressions and sightings of, 19, 20, 226, **226**
Downing Street, London, 228
Doyle, Sir Arthur Conan, 227
Dunedin, 198, 270, 277; newspapers in, 198; television broadcasts to, 252; *see also* New Zealand and South Seas Exhibition
Dunleavy, Trisha, 266–7

East End, London, 35–36, **37**, 82, 102, 103
Easy Virtue (movie), 248
education, *see* film and films, educational; film and films, influences of on children
Education Gazette, 243–4
Edward, King: coronation of, **52**; funeral of, 88
Egypt, New Zealand soldiers in, 53, 54, 59, 63–64
Elgar, Edward, 108
Eliot, T. S., 120
emigration literature, *see* immigration, books and handbooks on
Empire Comes Home, The (W. S. Percy), 31, 38
Empire Dairies, 171
Empire Day, 41
Empire Marketing Board, 153, 155, 162, 170, 173, 175, 176–82, **182**, 183, 184, 185–8, 233, 276; *see also* 'British Empire Dairy Factory'
Empire Marketing Board Film Unit, 233, 234
Empire Service, *see* BBC
Epstein, Jacob, 108, 113
Europe: and trade with Britain, 8, 129; and World War I, 16, 53–54; and World War II, 210; New Zealand experiences of, 119–20, 122; *see also* film and films, European; France; Spain; Switzerland
Evening Herald (Wanganui), **199**
Evening Post (Wellington), 115, **245**
Evening Star (Dunedin), 17
exhibitions, international, 12, 124, 128, 131, 134–9, 145, 147, 157, 158–9, 180, 184, 194; and New Zealand, 128, 134–5, 136–9, 142, 145–53, 154; *see also* Australia: and exhibitions; British Empire Exhibition; Canada: and exhibitions; Colonial and Indian Exhibition; Festival of Empire; Franco-British Exhibition; Great Exhibition; India, and exhibitions; International Health Exhibition; London International Exhibition; Maori: in exhibitions; New Zealand and South Seas Exhibition; New Zealand International Exhibition
expatriation, 99, 117–22, 275

Face of Fear, The (TV movie), 259
Fairburn, A. R. D., 94, 100–1, 105, 106, 108, 109, 110, 112, 113–14, 115–16, 117, 119, 120, 121–2, 122
Fawlty Towers (TV series), 262
Festival of Empire, London, 1911, 139, 147, 148, 150
film and films, 3, 9, 12, 13, 15, 18, 190, 191, 195, 221–46, 274, 278; advertising of, 242; American, 196, 223–8, 232, 243, 244, 246; British, 196, 197, 222–38, 241, 245; Canadian, 245; cartoons, 229; censorship, 227, 242; documentary, 233; educational, 11, 222, 232, 241–6, **245**, 247, 266, 274; European, 223; feature, 222–8, 246; hybrid, 223–8, **234**, 241, 246; influences of on children, 243, 244–5; meat industry, 166; newsreel, 229; presence of London in, 221–2, 228–41, 244, 246; propaganda, 233–5, 236, 237, 238, 244; quotas, 223–4, 227–8, 232–3; scenic, 134, 232; short, 11, 13, 222, 228–36, 241; travel, 229, 231–2, 236, 237, 238, 239–40, 246; *see also* libraries: film; *names of individual films*
Firth, Clifton, 106
Fish Cooking (film), 245

329

INDEX

Flag Lieutenant, The (film), 225
Fleet Street, London, 2, 4, 14, 15, 22, 24, 196, 201, **204**, 205, 220, 238, 274
Flowers of London (film), 231
food, *see* brands and food marketing; London: food requirements of
For All Eternity (film), 235, 237
Forsyth, Bruce, 258
Forsyth, R. S., 177–8
Four Just Men (TV series), 248
France, 20, 22, 25, 36, 54, 55, 57, 62, 64, 120, 216, 218
Franco-British Exhibition, London, 1908, 50, **138**, 138–9, 148
Fraser, Peter, 214, 218
freezing works, 91–92, 132, 146, 160; *see also* Tokomaru Sheepfarmers' Freezing Company Limited
From Meadow to Market (film), 244
Fuller, John, **230**
fundraising campaigns, World War II, *see* newspapers, fund-raising campaigns organised by

Gable, Clark, 229
Galloping Gourmet, The (TV series), 272
garden parties, 2–3, 51–52; *see also* British Empire Academy Tea Party
Garnett, Edward, 112
General Post Office Film Unit, 233
Generation Game (TV series), 258
George V, King: coronation of, 40; first Christmas broadcast of, 189–90
Gibbons, Peter, 5, 72
Gibson, Bill, 216
Gilfillan, J. A., **137**
Gill, Private Herbert, 29–31
Glasgow, 36
Gliding On (TV series), 268–9
Globe (Christchurch newspaper), 200–1
Gloss (TV series), 270
Good Times (TV series), 261
Goodfellow, William, 188
Goodies, The (TV series), **260**
Gordon and Gotch, 111–12, 192, 195
Governor, The (TV series), 269–70
Grable, Betty, 248
Grade, Lew, 248
Graphic magazine, 18
Great Exhibition, Crystal Palace, London, 1851, 125, 127, 130, 131, 135, 136, **137**
'Greater Britain', 5, 127, 128, 136, 266, 271, 278; *see also* 'Better Britons'
Green, Herbert, **101**
Greene, Graham, 235
Grey, Beryl, 248
Grey, Governor George, 270
Grey, Lord, 45
Grierson, Hugh, 24
Grierson, John, 233, 238
Griffen-Foley, Bridget, 107
grocery stores, 130–1
Grossman, Edith Searle, 90–91, 93, 94, 107, **107**
guidebooks, 21, 31, 38, 57, 66–67, 82, 127, 212, 235; Australian, 43; exhibition, 127, 138–9, 149, 152;

Indian, 38; New Zealand High Commission, 47–49, 50, 51–52; *see also A Handbook for Visitors to London*; *Blighty*; *Colonial and Indian* guidebook; *Colonials' Guide to London*; *Empire Comes Home*; *Soldier's Guide to the British Isles*; Ward Lock, guidebooks
Guildhall, London, 67, 236
Gunga Din (movie), 227
Guthrie-Smith, H., 98

Hall-Jones, Sir William, 47
Halls of Ivy, The (TV series), 248
Hammond, Mr J., 158–9
Hampstead Heath, London, 100, **101**
Hanlon (TV series), 270
Harper, Gordon, 65
Harpers magazine, 112
Have a Shot (TV series), 271, **271**
Hawkins, Jack, 248
Hayes Code, 227
Hay's Wharf, London, 50
Haywain, The (John Constable), 76
Hayward, Henry, 223, 244
Heaphy, Charles, 136–7
Heart of an Empire (film), 235
Heart of the Bush (Edith Searle Grossman), 90–92
Helsinger, Elisabeth, 77
Hendon Airshow, 88
Hewson, Leslie, 25–26
historiography, nationalist, 4
Hitchcock, Alfred, 248
HMV, 196
Hobson, Governor William, 150
Hodgkins, Frances, 113–14
Holland House, Kensington, London, 212
Hollywood, 222, 223, 224, 225, **225**, 226, **226**, 227–8, 246, 258
Holst, Alison, 272
Home: A New Zealander's Adventure (Alan Mulgan), 16–17, **17**, 18–20, 75–76
Home and Colonial Tea Stores, London, **159**, 159–60, 162
Home Life in England (book), 77
homosexuality, and London, 106
hospitals, in England, 25, 53, 55, 56, 58–59, 64
House of Commons, London, 18, 51
Houses of Parliament, London, 22, 26, 31–32, **33**, 68, 103, 244
Howard Morrison Quartet, 248, **253**, 254
Howkins, Alun, 76
Hudson and Halls (TV series), 272
Hume, Benita, 248
Hunter's Gold (TV series), 269, **269**
Huntly and Palmers, 160
Hyde, Robin, 110, 274
Hyde Park, London, 26, **84**, 100, 273
hygiene and purity, promotion of, 159–60, 162–4, 168, 276–7; *see also* sunlight, attitudes towards

identity: construction of, 7, 74–75, 83, 84, 135–6, 277; emergence of New Zealand, 4–5, 6–7, 9, 12, 21, 71–72, 80–81, 88–89, 100, 119–20, 122, 155, 156, 185, 200, 249, 253, 265, 270–2, 273, 277

330

INDEX

Illustrated London News, The, 18, 108, 112
immigration: books and handbooks on, 72, 78, 127, 132, 144, 164; propaganda, 78, 128; *see also* advertising, immigration; New Zealand, migration to; *Pictorial Illustrations of New Zealand*
Imperial Conference, 1930, 177
Imperial Economic Conference, Ottawa, 1932, 156–7, 187
Imperial Education Conference, 1927, 243
Imperial Naval Conference, 203
Imperial Press Conference, 1925, 203, 205; 1930, 18
imperialism, 6–7, 16, 18, 45, 75, 76, 206, 233
Independent (Wellington), 199
Independent Television Company, 248
India, 6, 38, 40, 41, 77, 182, 184; and exhibitions, 135, 136, 148; *see also* Colonial and Indian Exhibition
Indians, in London, 6–7, 38; *see also* soldiers, Indian in London
industrialisation, 10, 73, 76, 82, 85–86, 131, 132, 146
Innis, Harold, 190
Inns of Court, London, 236, 244
Inside Straight (TV series), 268, 272
International Health Exhibition, London, 1884, 128, 137–8
International Hospitality League, 64–66, **66**, 67
Ipcress Files, The (movie on TV), 258–9
Ireland, 66; and exhibitions, 150, 186; and London, 240; and trade with Britain, 8, 129, 182–3
It Ain't Half Hot Mum (TV series), 259
It's in the Bag (TV series), 250, 258, 272

Jack the Ripper, 227
James, Sid, **260**
Jocko (TV series), 267
John, Augustus, 108, 113
John Burns and Co., 214–15
John O'Groats, 214
Johnson, Margaret, 19, 21, 29, 31, 36, 40, 78
Johnson, Samuel, 14, 26, 35
Johnson and Nephew, 187
Jones, Lawrence, 83, 92–93, 105–6, 118–19
Jonson, Ben, 32
Jordan, Sir William, 51, 52, 110
Joubert, Jules, 134–5, 150, 151
journalism and journalists, 14, 19, 70, 83, 84, 107, 109, 114, 115, 121, 196, 203, 205, 208, 254, 256, 274
Joyce, James, 106
Joyous Pilgrimage, The (Ian Donnelly), 17, 35–36, 84–85
Jubilee celebrations: New Zealanders' attendance at, 39–40, 47; screenings of, 221, 222, 229

Kane, Charles, 269
Kensington Gardens, London, 48, 105
Kerr, Graham, 272
Killing of Kane, The (TV series), 269
King, Captain Herbert, 26, 55
Kingi, Noel, **253**
King's Stables, London, 27, 68
Knight, George, 22
Known London (film), 231

Kodak Ltd, 245
Kojak (TV series), 259, **260**
Kowhai Intermediate School, Auckland, 245

Ladies' Home Journal, 167
Lady Guide Association, London, 21
Lahr, Charles, 112, 114
Lamb, Charles, 26, 27, 35
lamb, New Zealand, 8, 10, 88, 132, 140, 157–64, **158**, **159**, **161**, **162**, **163**, 166, 168, 175, 182; *see also* advertising, lamb; window displays, office and shop
Lancaster, G. B., 89; *see also* Lyttleton, Edith
Land's End, 19, 214
Lane, John, 112, 114
Lassie Come Home (movie), 226
Last Grenade, The (movie on TV), 258
Lawrence, D. H., 108, 113
Lawson, Henry, 110
Leeper, Rex, 233
Leighton, Clare, **17**
Let's Go Home (R. Noble Adams), 17
letters, as source of impressions of London, 11, 16, 19, 24–27, 29–31, 38, 69
Levine, Philippa, 62
libraries: at Australia House, 47; at New Zealand House, 46; British Museum, 120; film, 244–5; private, 96–97; public, 111–12
Lights o' London (film), 235
Likely Lads, The (TV series), 262
Lion Nathan, 275–6
Lipton's stores, 130
List, T. C., 18, 21, 31–32; *see also Briton at Home, The*
Lister Company, 186
literary connections between New Zealand and London, 2, 10–11, 35, 110–21
literary nationalism, 17, 72–73, 88–89, 92–93, 94, 98, 100, 116, 117–18, 119, 156
literature: British, 97, 98–99, 110–11, 112, 227; British provincial, 120–1; colonial, 94; Maoriland, 72–73, 88–95, **90**; New Zealand, 2, 10–11, 12, 72–73, 76, 88–89, 95, 100, 109, 112, 118; non-fiction, 72, 97–98; pan-British, 72, 89; Provincial, 92–93, 94–95; travel writing, 11, 12, 16–19, 36, 47, 93; *see also* immigration: books and handbooks on; colonial editions; literary nationalism; modern art and literature; writers: New Zealand in London
Little House on the Prairie (TV series), 259
Liverpool, 21, 161, **161**, 237
Liverpool Journal of Commerce, 45
Lives of a Bengal Lancer, The (movie), 224, **225**
London: as Home, 6, 7, 13, 15, 16–19, 21–22, 31–35, 36, 38, 40, 42, 47, 53–54, 57–58, 68–69, 75, 274, 278; as imagined hinterland, 3–4, 11–12, 13, 14–17, **17**, 18–22, **20**, 22–31, 39, 40, 42, 48, 50, 55, 68–69, 78, 80, 82, 97, 101, 188, 190–2, 194, 205, 206, 210, 217–18, 220, 222, 226–7, 236, 241, 242, 246, 253, 266, 274, 275, 276, 278; as imperial metropolis, 1, 2–3, 6–7, 9–10, 12, 14–15, 18, 24, 32, 35, 41, 46, 48, **49**, 52, 55–56, **56**, 62, 68–69, 70–71, 97–99, 105–6, 116–17, 121, 147, 184, 214, 228, 240, 266, 275–6, 278; as modern city, 9, 12, 29–30, 74–75, 83,

331

INDEX

London: as modern city (cont.), 86–88, 95, 100, 102, 106, 146, 147, 158, 163, 186, 188, 236–8; as 'mother city', 75–76, 147, 244; as synecdoche for England, 21–22, 196–7; familiar, 3–4, 5, 15, 18–22, 23–26, 27, 30, 35, 40, 42–43, 49–50, 66–69, 98–99, 100, 103, 111, 120, 189, 197, 205, **207**, 207–8, 210, 212, **213**, 222, 228, 246, 275–6; food requirements of, 7–8, 10, 124, 129–30; monumental architecture of, 4, 14–15, 18, 22–24, 26, 29, 31–35, 48, 68, 78, 99–100, 122, 206, 208–12, 226, 235–8, 244; New Zealand population of, 3, 275; performative, 15, 27, 29, 39–40, 47, 48, 51–52, **52**, **56**, 123–4, 221–2, 236, 238; suburban, 103, 105, 159, 238; see also World War II, images of
London (film), 234, 236
London 1942 (film), 235
London: A Pilgrimage (Gustave Doré and Blanchard Jerrold), 1
London Bridge, 23, 25
London Can Take It! (film), 235
London Day by Day (film/myriorama), **230**
London International Exhibition, 1862, 136
London Landmarks (film), 231
London of the Future (Aston Webb), 41
London – Old and New (film), 237
London on Parade (film), 235, 238, 240
London River (film), 235, 238
London Scrapbook (film), 235
London Theatre, Auckland, 223
London Times magazine, 112
London Town (film), 234, 240
London Wakes Up (film), 235
London Zoo, 68
Longmans publishers, 16
Lord Mayor's Show, 51, **56**, 123, 128, 157, 172, 238
Lost Horizon (movie), 248
Love Thy Neighbour (TV series), 259
Low, David, 114
Ludgate Circus, London, 14, 15, 102, **211**
Luxford, Gladys, 19
Lye, Len, 233
Lyttleton, Edith, 110, 116; see also Lancaster, G. B.

Macaulay, Thomas, 1–2, 6, 9
Mack, Louise, 107
MacKenzie, John, 6, 136
Mackenzie, Sir Thomas, 47, 51, 58, 62
Madame Tussaud's waxworks, London, 27, 68
magazines, 16, 18, 19, 112, 192, 195; see also advertising devices and media, magazine; *Athenaeum* magazine; *Blackwoods* magazine; *Captain* magazine; *Harpers* magazine; *Illustrated London News*; *Ladies' Home Journal*; *London Times* magazine; *Phoenix* magazine; *Punch* magazine; *Spectator*; *Strand* magazine; *Times Literary Supplement*; *Windsor* magazine; *Woman's Weekly*
Majestic theatre, Auckland, 223, **224**
Malcolm, William, 54, 78
Man Alone (John Mulgan), 93–94, **94**
Manawatu Times, 115
Marlborough Express, 198
Manchester, 21, 121, 267

Mander, Jane, 38, 43, 89, 96–98, 99, 103, 105, 106, 107, 109, 110–11, 112, 114, 115, 116, 117, **118**, 118–19, 121–2; see also *Story of a New Zealand River, The*
Mansfield, Katherine, 98, 99–100, 102, 107, 115, 274; see also 'Philistea'
Maori: and assimilation, 180; art, culture and motifs of, 136, 149, 151–2, 172, 185, 273; as anachronisms, 2, 72, 79, 81, 95, 132, 135, 138, 141, 149–50, 278; as dying race, 72, 150; as peripheral, 96, 141, **141**, 149–50, 165, 185–6; as romantic images, 126, 151, 165, 278; in exhibitions, 135–6, 138–9, 142, 149–52, 164–5; see also literature, Maoriland; soldiers, Maori in London
Maoriland and Maorilanders, 2, 72–73, 81, 89–90, **90**, 95, 142, 221; see also literature, Maoriland
marketing strategies, 11, 12, 132, 134, 154–5, 192, 275–6; dairy, 169–75; meat, 123, 157–8, **167**, 175; tourism, 73, 132, **133**, 134; see also advertising; advertising devices and media; brands and food marketing; Empire Marketing Board; producer boards
Marsh, Ngaio, 81–82, 101–2, 105, 109, 110, **111**, 112–13, 115, 116, 119, 126
Martin, John E., 146
Mary Poppins (movie), 227
*M*A*S*H* (TV series), 261, 262
Mason, R. A. K., 101, 112, 120
mass media, 12, 19, 189–93, 195–7, 200, 201, 246, 248, 254, 272
Mataatua meeting house, 150, 151–2, **152**, **153**
Maypole Stores, 130, 132
McClintock, Anne, 11, 71, 80–81
McCormick, Eric, 94–95, 97–99, 106
McEldowney, Dennis, 112
meat: British dependence on, 10, 129; frozen, 123–4, 128, 129, 130, 132, 138, 157, 160, 169, 242; New Zealand, 2, 7–8, 88, 123, 128, 144, 155, 157–8, 164–5, 178; see also lamb; mutton
Meat Marking Order, 164–5
Meath, Lord, 41, 42, 45, 52, 55
Meredith, David, 184, 185
metropolitan-ness, 38–39, 145–6
MGM, 223, 226, **226**
Mighty London (film), 244
Military High Commission, New Zealand's, 60
Milne and Choyce Ltd, 214
Ministry of Information (GB), 235
Mission Impossible (TV series), 259
Mitcheson, Naomi, 114
modern art and literature, 109, 113–14, 120, 122
modernism, 46, 94
modernity, 39, 74–75, 81, 82, 91, 92, 95, 132, 145, 146, 147, 160, 163–4, 172, 180–1, 197, 238, 240, 250
Monaghan, Des, 261
Monopoly, 3, 276
Monroe, Marilyn, 259
Morecambe and Wise (TV series), 258
Morning Paper (film), 235
Morrison, Howard, **253**; see also Howard Morrison Quartet
Mortimer's Patch (TV series), 267, 272
Mother Country, 45, 62, 66, 75, 132, 187, 244; see also London: as 'mother city'

332

INDEX

Moult, Harry, **23**, **29**, **33**, **34**, 80, 81, 85, **103**, **104**, 120, **204**
movies, *see* film and films
Movin' On (TV series), 259
Moynihan (TV series), 268
Mrs Miniver (movie), 226
Muldoon, Robert, 270
Mulgan, Alan, 16–17, 18, 19–20, 21, 27, 32–33, 70, 75–76, 85–86, 89; *see also Home: A New Zealander's Adventure*
Mulgan, John, 93–94, 95; *see also Man Alone*
multiples, *see* chain stores
Murphy, Ben, **260**
Mutiny on the Bounty (movie), 226
mutton, New Zealand, 8, 88, 123–4, 138, 139, 140, 157–8, 161–2, 182, 185
Myers, Mrs Leo, 70–71, 75, 76, 86–88, **87**
Myriorama, *see* Fuller, John; London Day by Day

Nash, Walter, 218
National Patriotic Fund, 218
National Training School of Cookery, 138
National Velvet (movie), 226
nationalism, 4–5, 9, 24, 39, 46, 80–81, 83, 89, 117–18, 190, 265, 272, 278; *see also* historiography, nationalist; literary nationalism
NBC, 258
Nelson, images of, **77**, 78
Nelson, Admiral Horatio, 32–33; *see also* St Paul's Cathedral, London, Nelson's tomb in
Nelson's Column, London, 22, 26, 48, 209
Netherlands, Nazi invasion of, 216, 217–18
New Britain (film), 235
New York, 8, 9, 13, 221
New Zealand, 43, 45, 72; as commodity producer, 11, 125, 128, 130–2, 134, 137–8, 139–40, 154–5; as dominion, 72; as modern, 6, 9, 11, 12–13, 71, 74–75, 79, 86–88, 95, 142, 186, 188, 197, 250, 278; as new, 74, 78–82, 83, 86–88, 91–93, 95, 98–99, 100, 122, 124–5, 132, 188; as social laboratory, 75; migration to, 5, 32, 78, 125–8, 134, 203; urban and rural dichotomy in, 9–10, 74–75, 80, 88, 124, 146, 172, 179–80, 185–6, 244, 266–7, 268, 270, 276–7; *see also* rural New Zealand, myths of
New Zealand and London: as British farming hinterland, 2, 8, 9–10, 11, 12, 124–5, 128, 131–2, 141, 144, 148, 153, 155, 156–7, 162, 164, 171, 175, 176, 178, 179–80, 181, **182**, 188, 192, 226, 228, 249, 265–6, 272, 275, 277, 278; as imaginative hinterland of London, 8–9, 12–13, 188, 189, 192–4, 200–16, 222, 246, 264; as London's 'other', 2, 124; as metropolitan hinterland, 13, 75, 144–6, 150, 264–5, 272; *see also* 'British New Zealand'; 'Greater Britain'
New Zealand and South Seas Exhibition, Dunedin, 134
New Zealand Associated Press agency, 202
New Zealand Authors' Week, 89
New Zealand Broadcasting Corporation, 252, 254, 257, 260, 262
New Zealand Company, 78, 126
New Zealand Co-operative Dairy Company, 156, 169, 170–1, 173–4, 188

New Zealand Dairy Export Produce Control Board, 161, 169, 171–3, 182, 188
New Zealand Dairy Exporter, 49–50, 188
New Zealand Forces Club, 214
New Zealand Herald (Auckland newspaper), 115, 198, 202, 208, 209, 212, 215–16, 218–19
New Zealand Farmer Stock and Station Journal, 188
New Zealand Forces Club, London, 214
New Zealand Fruit Sales Division, 214
New Zealand Government Tourist Bureau, 245
New Zealand High Commission and Commissioners, 11, 42, 46–47, 50–52, 58, 62–63, 69, 110, 148, 161, 163, **163**, 165, **165**, 166, 176, 186–7, 214, 250, 275; *see also* New Zealand House
New Zealand House, London, 2–3, 11, 15, 40, 42–43, **44**, 46–47, 49, 50–53, 60, 67, 69, 148, 161, 163–5, 240, 241; bomb damage to, 214, **215**; *see also* libraries: at New Zealand House
New Zealand International Exhibition, Christchurch, 1906–7, 146
New Zealand Journal of Agriculture, **170**
New Zealand Listener, **194**, 250, **260**, 263
New Zealand Loan and Mercantile Agency Company Limited, 123
New Zealand Meat Producers Board, 157–8, 160–1, 165–8, 169, 171, 172, 182, 218
New Zealand Press Association, 202, 205, 254
New Zealand Red Cross, 59
New Zealand Soldiers' Club, London, 53, 60, 61
New Zealand Spectator, 198
New Zealand Tourist and Publicity Department, 244
New Zealand Union Steamship Company, 241
New Zealand War Contingent Association, 58–61, **63**, 64, 65–67
'New Zealander on the bridge', 1–2, 6–7, 9, 13, 71, 92, 135, 273, 275
Newbould, Frank, 185, **185**
newspapers, 3, 9, 12, 15, 16, 18, 190, 192, 193, 195, 197, 206–7, 208, 227, 246, 250, 251, 255, 278; American influence on, 222; British, 196–7, 201, 202, 203, 205, 207, 218, 235, 238; Canadian, 142; censorship of, 208; fund-raising campaigns organised by, 216–20; 'London letters' in, 96, 202, 275; New Zealand, 112, 122, 192–7, 197–205, 208, 275; news and gossip columns in, 96, 110, 115, 117, 202; provincial, 96; serials in, 16–17, 111; World War II reporting, 206–16, 217–19, 235; *see also* advertising devices and media: newspaper; *Argus* press agency; journalism and journalists; New Zealand Associated Press agency; New Zealand Press Association; photographs, use of in newspapers; United Press Association
Newton, Albert, 68
Night Mail (film), 238
Noble Adams, Robert, 18, 35, 39–40; *see also Let's Go Home*
Northern Advocate, The (Whangarei newspaper), 115
nostalgia, 6, 13, 18, 71, 206, 250, 274, 275, 278
nursery rhymes, 18, 102
nurses, New Zealand, in London, 19, 24, 26, 36

333

OE, *see* Big OE
Oliver, W. H., 4
On Approval (film), 225
One Family (film), 233
Overseas Club Map and Guide, 60
Otago Daily Times (Dunedin newspaper), 198
Oxford, 21
Oxford Companion to New Zealand Literature, The (Robinson and Wattie), 118
Oxford Street, London, 48, 208

Papakura, Maggie, 150
Paris, 48, 120, 221
Paris Exhibition, 1866, 7
Park, Air Vice Marshall Keith, 206
Park Lane, London, 3, 208
parks, London, 84, **84**, 85, 100, 105; *see also* Hyde Park, London; St James's Park, London
Parr, Sir James, 47, 176, 187, 227–8
Peacocke, Isobel, 114
P.E.N. Club, 114
Percy, W. S., 31, 43; *see also Strolling Through Cottage England*; *Empire Comes Home, The*
Petticoat Lane, London, **37**
'Philistea', 100, 105
Phillips, Dr G., 52
Phillips, Jock, 146–7
Phoenix magazine, 95, 122
photographs: and advertising, 171; at exhibitions, 138–9, 141, 188; importance of in creation of New Zealand's London, 18, 19, **20**, 103; scenic, **20**, 136, 141; taking of in London, **23**, 24, **28**, **33**, **34**, **37**, **49**, **56**, 69, **79**, **80**, **81**, **84**, 85, 101, **104**; use of in newspapers, 208–12, **209**, **211**, **213**; *see also* Moult, Harry; postcards; Scales, Thomas Frederick
Piccadilly Circus, London, 23, **30**, 94, **94**, 95, 102, 105, 108, 208, 209
Pick, Frank, 177
Pictorial Illustrations of New Zealand (Samuel Brees), **125**
Picturedrome, Milford, Auckland, **234**
Pocock, J. G. A., 5
Policewoman (TV series), 261
Port Said, 36, 64
postcards, 16, 24–26, **25**, 69, **90**, 100, 131, **191**; *see also* advertising devices and media advertising, postcards
postcolonialism, 5, 121, 246
posters, 131, 134, 177–8, 180–1, 182, 194, 185, 186–7, **199**, 276; dairy, 161, 171, 172, **174**, 175, 180, 181, **181**, 183, 188; immigration, 125, 126; lamb, **133**; meat, 11, 158, 161, 163, **179**, 181, **187**; tourism, **73**, **133**, 134, 276; trade, **182**; wool, 181
Potter, Simon, 205
poverty, 74, 82–86, 105; *see also* 'darkest London'
Press, The (Christchurch newspaper), 17, 202, 205, 208, 209
press, *see* newspapers
Princess Margaret's wedding, television broadcasts of, 247–8, **249**
Prisoner of Zenda, The (movie), 248
Pritchard, Noeline, 256

producer boards, 153, 155–6, 182–3; *see also* New Zealand Dairy Export Produce Control Board; New Zealand Meat Producers Board
Progressive Bookshop, London, 112
propaganda, *see* film and films, propaganda; immigration, propaganda
public service broadcasting, 256–7
Pukemanu (TV series), 266, **267**, 272
Punch magazine, 1, 2, 112
puritanism, New Zealand, 106–7, 108

Radford, Basil, 235
radio, 9, 12, 18, 103, 105, 188, 189–91, 193, 195, 196, 197, 222, 246, 256, 274, 278; 1YA, 103, 189; 2ZB, **194**; National Programme, 196–7; *see also* BBC; Voice of America
Radio Australia, 254
Radio Times (TV series), 262
Radio Waves (TV series), 268, 272
Random Harvest (movie), 248
Ranfurly, Lord, 59
Rangitikei, SS, 241
Rank Organisation, 196, 254
Ravensdale, Baronness, 233
Realist Film Unit, 235
recolonisation, 8, 75, 89, 92, 95, 117, 132, 188, 192
Reed publishers, 16
Reeves, William Pember, 274
refrigeration, 8, 12, 123–4, 129, 131, 132, 140, 155, 274
retailing, *see* chain stores; co-operative societies; department stores; grocery stores; Home and Colonial Tea Stores; Lipton's stores; Maypole Stores
Reuters, 203
Rhodes family, 110, **111**, 113
Richards, Thomas, 127, 130
Roberts, Colonel, 139
Roche (TV series), 268
Rooney, Mickey, 258
Ross, Forrestina, 21, 36, 83
Rotorua, as tourist destination, 73, 149, 152
Royal Academy, London, 68
Royal Agricultural Show, 51
Royal Commission into the Dairy Industry, 1934, 172, 173, 181
Royal Mews, London, 51
rural England, myths of, 10, 70, 74–82, **80**, **81**, 83, **85**, 85–86, 95, 132, 147, 182, 186, 226, 265
rural New Zealand, myths of, 73–74, **77**, 124, 132, **133**, 138–9, 147, 165, 179–80, 182, 186, 249, 276–7
Russell, Bertrand, 108
Rutherford, A. W., 18, 20, 21, 29, 36, 39, 84, 86

Sackville West, Vita, 114
Said, Edward, 18, 47
Salvation Army, 231, 239; *see also* Biorama Company
Sapphire Films, 248
Sargeson, Frank, 101, 106, 108, 109, 110, 112, 115–16, 119–20, 121
Savage, Michael Joseph, 52
Scales, Thomas Frederick, **49**, **56**

INDEX

Scanlan, Nelle, 114, 115
Schneer, Jonathan, 48
Scholefield, Guy, 205
School Journal, 241–2
Scotland, 38, 277
Scotland Yard, London, 228
Seager, Edward, 126
Seeing London (film series), 231
Serpentine, London, 26
sexual freedom, London vs. New Zealand, 35, 106–7; *see also* homosexuality, and London; puritanism, New Zealand; soldiers, sexual behaviour of
Shakespeare Hut, London, 60, 61, **61**, 63
Shakespeare Quarterly, 113
Shark in the Park (TV series), 270
Shaw, George Bernard, 108, 113
Shore, Dinah, 259
Shortland Street (TV series), 270
Sinclair, Keith, 4, 9, 16, 18, 80, 89, 190; *see also A Destiny Apart*
Skippy (movie), 243
S. L. A. Mastin (SLAM!), 156
Sling, 25, 27, 53, 54, 55, 78, **79**
Smithfield, London, 49, 157–8, 159, 160, 240
So This is London (film), 234
social Darwinism, 72
Softly Softly (TV series), **260**, 261
Soldier's Guide to the British Isles, The (YMCA booklet), 66–67
soldier-tourists, 17, 24, **30**, 30–31, 42, 54–56, 78; *see also* 'Bill Massey's tourists'
soldiers, Australian in London, 30, 54–55
soldiers, Canadian in London, 60
soldiers, Indian in London, 56–57
soldiers, Maori in London, 213–14
soldiers, New Zealand in London: World War I, 4, 11, 16, 22, 24, 26, 27, 29, **37**, 39, 40, 42, 47, **49**, 53–69, **56**, **58**, **59**, **61**, 70, 78–79, **79**, 106, 111, 274; World War II, 4, 212–13, **213**; *see also* 'Bill Massey's tourists'; soldier-tourists
soldiers, sexual behaviour of, 57, 62–64, 68
sound recordings, 9, 15, 190
South Africa, 77; and London, 31, 43, 45, 277
South Africa House, London, 43
'Southern Stand', 273, 278
Spain, 120
Spectator, The, 112, 113
Sport On One (TV sports programme), 258
Spragg, Charles, 38, 70
St James Park (film), 235
St James Theatre, Auckland, 224, **225**, **226**, 229
St James's Palace, London, 23, 236
St James's Park, London, 103, **104**
St Paul's Cathedral, London, **23**, 23–24, 26, 27, 31, 32–33, 55, 67, 99–100, 102, 190, **211**, 226, 228, 232, 236–7, 238, 278; Nelson's tomb in, 32, 237; reports and images of bombing of, 207, 209–10, 212, 235, 237
St Paul's Cathedral (film), 237
Stafford, Jane, 92
Staines Manders, A., 31; *see also Colonials' Guide to London*

standards of living, comparisons between Britain and New Zealand, 74, 75, 83, 86, 105, 183
Stanfield, Stan, 64
Story of a New Zealand River, The (Jane Mander), 112
Strand, London, 15, 19, 22, 29, 42–43, 45, **52**, **59**, 60, 148, 161, **163**, 164, **165**, 214, **215**, 223, 240, 276
Strand magazine, 19, 112
Strand theatre, Auckland, 223
Starsky and Hutch (TV series), 259
Streets of San Francisco, The (TV series), 262, 264
Strolling Through Cottage England (W. S. Percy), 43
Sumpter, H. K., 18, 20, 32–33
sunlight, attitudes towards, 83, 84, 160–1, **161**, 163–4, 168, 171–2, 179
Sunlight Leagues, 161
Sutherland's Law (TV series), 259
Sweeney, The (TV series), 261, 264
Switzerland, 120
symbolism: in advertising, 131, 132, 173–5, 186; in art, 273–4

Tahiwi, Kingi, **194**
Tallents, Sir Stephen, 233
Tarata Boiling Springs, Roto Mahana, New Zealand, The (Charles Heaphy), 136–7
Tarzan and the Ape Man (movie), 226
Tarzan Escapes (movie), 248
Taylor, Elizabeth, 226
Taylor, Nancy, 216
telegraph, 15, 190, **191**, 194, 199, 200–2, 203
telephones, 9
television, 3, 13, **255**; American programmes, 248, 253, 254, 256–7, 258, 259, 261–3, 264–5; Australian programmes, 263; British programmes, 248–9, 253, 256–65, **260**, **263**; commercial, 256–7; introduction and uptake of, 247–56, **249**, 270, 272; live programmes, **253**, 254–5, 258; local programmes, 248, 251, **251**, 252–5, 257, 258, 259, 261, 262, 265–72, **267**, **268**, **269**, **271**, 275, 276; news, 254–6, 258; regional programmes, 253–4, 256, 271; *see also* advertising devices and media: television; Channel 2; Independent Television Company; Princess Margaret's wedding, television broadcasts of; TV1; TV2; TV3
Television New Zealand, 256, 264
Television One, 264
Thames, 22, 29, 36, 105, 231, 238, 240, 276
Thames Embankment, London, 209
The Times, 8, 126, 132, 177, 201, 203, 235
Theatre Royal, Christchurch, **230**
This Week in Britain (TV news magazine), 255
Thunderbirds (TV series), 259
Tides of the Moon (film), 245
Timaru Herald, 199
Times Literary Supplement, The, 112
To the Manor Born (TV series), 262
Tokomaru Sheepfarmers' Freezing Company Limited, **91**
Tooley Street, London, 49–50, 169, 240
tourism, New Zealand, 12, 73, **73**, 132, 149, 276–7; *see also* advertising, tourist; posters, tourism

335

INDEX

Tower Bridge, London, 48, 226
Tower of London, 26, 27, 31, 51, 67, 79, 119, **120**, 236, 237
Trafalgar Day, 40
Trafalgar Square, 228
travel, as pilgrimage, 14–15, 16–17, 19–22, 23, 115, 205, 249–50, 275; *see also Joyous Pilgrimage, The*; *London: A Pilgrimage*; working holidays and trips to Britain
Travel and Industrial Development Association, 233–5, 236, 238
Treaty of Waitangi, 150
Triangle Trail, The (YMCA booklet), 64–65
Trussell, Denys, 122
Truth tabloid, 250
Tutira (H. Guthrie-Smith), 98
TV1, 258, 259, 261–2, 263; *see also* Television One
TV2, 259, **260**, 262; *see also* Channel 2
TV3, 256, 264
Two Ronnies, The (TV series), 259, 274

Undersea World of Jacques Cousteau, The (TV series), 260
United Empire Circle Dinner for Artists from the Different Dominions, 114, **114**
United Press Association, 202–3, 207
United States of America: and new media, 13, 195–6; and New Zealand, 13, 195; and trade with Britain, 8, 129, 176; *see also* CBS; NBC; newspapers, American; television, American programmes; Voice of America
Unknown London (film), 231
Upstairs Downstairs (TV series), 261, **263**
urban decay, 73–74, 75, 82–83, 201
urbanisation, 10, 39, 75, 76, 160, 164, 179–80, 276
Unwin, Sir Stanley, 112

Valley Farm, The (John Constable), 76
Van Dyke, Dick, 258
Varnham, Captain F. S., 24, 36, 38
Verry, Leslie, 205
Victoria, Queen, *see* Jubilee celebrations: screenings of
Virginian, The (TV series), 265
Visnews, 254–6
Visual Education Association, 245
Voice of America, 254
volunteer organisations, 42, 54, 57–61, 63, 64–67, 274
Von Haast, Julius, 137

Waikato Times, 116
Wakefield, Edward Gibbon, 136
Wallace, Edgar, 248
Walton-on-Thames hospital, 59
Wanganui School Board, 241
Ward, Sir Joseph, 72, 203
Ward Lock, 114; guidebooks, 21
Waring, John Saxton, **77**
Warner Brothers, 227
Warsaw, Nazi bombing of, 210, 216
Weinstein, Hannah, 248

Wellington, **125**, 199, 244; compared with London, 29, 30, 100; images of, **125**; newspapers in, 199; rail connections with, 9; television in, 252, 253, 254, 267, 268, 270, **271**; *see also* 'Philistea'
Wertheim, Lucy, 113–14
West End, London, 87, 102, 105, 236
Westminster Abbey, London, 18, 22, 26, 27, 29, 30, 31, 32, **34**, 42, 47, 48, 60, 67, 68, 78–79, 86, 99, 100, 101, 103, **103**, 119, 122, 213–14, 236, 237, 274, 278; Poet's Corner at, 32, 79, 122; Unknown Warrior's Tomb at, 32, 213
wheat, 135, 146, 149, 178; Australian, 10; British dependence on, 10; imports of to Britain, 129
Wheat to Bread (film), 245
Whitley, Reverend Dr, 50
Whitcombe & Tombs publishers, 16
White, Richard, 68
Whitehall, London, 22, 27, 103
Wilford, Sir Thomas, 51, 186
Wilkie, Alan, 113
Wilkinson, Iris, *see* Hyde, Robin
Williams, Mark, 92
Williams, Patricia, 121
Williams, Private P. G., 27
Wilson, Alfred, 193
Wilson, Angus, 113
window displays, office and shop, 2, 124, 128, 131, 132, 158–66, **158**, **159**, **161**, **162**, **163**, **165**, 168, **168**, 169, 171, 172, 179, **199**, 274
Windsor, The, magazine, 112
Woman's Weekly, 167, 215
Wombles, The (TV series), 258, 259, 262
Women Writers Dinner, 114
women's suffrage, 6
Wonderful London (film series), 231, 236, 237, 238
Wonderful London's Sidelights of London (film), 240
Wonders of Westminster (film), 236
wool, New Zealand, 7, 86, 88, 124, 128, 134, 137, 138, 139, **140**, 140–1, 144–5, **145**, 181, 274; *see also* advertising, wool
Woollacott, Angela, 36, 74
working holidays and trips to Britain, 3, 249–50, 275; *see also* Big OE; travel, as pilgrimage
World War I, 42, 43, 53, 57, 72, 77, 86, 156, 213, 217, 218, 233, 242; *see* 'Bill Massey's tourists'; nurses, New Zealand, in London; soldier-tourists; soldiers, New Zealand in London: World War I
World War II, 206–220, 235; images of, **207**, **209**, **211**, **213**, **215**; *see also* newspapers, World War II reporting
Wren, Sir Christopher, 26, 197, 212
writers: Australian in London, 110; New Zealand in London, 97–122

YMCA, 27, 57–58, **59**, 60, 61–62, 64–67, **67**, 68, 244, 274; *see also Blighty*; International Hospitality League; New Zealand Soldiers' Club; Shakespeare Hut; *Soldier's Guide to the British Isles, The*; *Triangle Trail, The*
YMCA Club, London, **59**

Z Cars (TV series), 262

336